Russian Drama
from Its Beginnings
to the Age of Pushkin

Russian Drama
from Its Beginnings to the Age of Pushkin

SIMON KARLINSKY

University of California Press

Berkeley, Los Angeles, London

University of California Press
Berkeley and Los Angeles, California

University of California Press, Ltd.
London, England

© 1985 by
The Regents of the University of California

First Paperback Printing 1986
ISBN 0–520–05882–8

Library of Congress Cataloging in Publication Data

Karlinsky, Simon.
Russian drama from its beginnings
to the age of Pushkin.
Includes index.
1. Russian drama—17th century—History.
2. Russian drama—18th century—History.
3. Russian drama—19th century—History. I. Title.
PG3076.K35 1985   891.72′009   84–8442

Printed in the United States of America

1   2   3   4   5   6   7   8   9

Contents

Curtain Raiser

"You want to write about Russian plays *before* Pushkin?" An old friend with whom I went to high school in Los Angeles wrinkled his nose. "But aren't they all taken from the French? Aren't they musty and . . . and dusty?" A Berkeley specialist in Scandinavian literatures, told that neoclassical comedies were written in eighteenth-century Russia, laughed. "Oh, those Russians! I suppose they enjoyed putting on jabots and powdered wigs and felt this made them civilized." An Oxford colleague, who took me to task for pointing out in my book on Gogol the connection between Gogol's plays and those of his predecessors Vasily Kapnist and Alexander Shakhovskoy, advised me to stop wasting my time on such nonentities. Asked whether he had ever read any plays by Kapnist or Shakhovskoy, he replied: "Of course not. Why should I?"

The English colleague knew who Vissarion Belinsky (1811–48) was and realized that he was the most influential critic in the history of Russian literature. The old friend and the Scandinavian gentleman had never heard of Belinsky. But all three were echoing the attitude stated in Belinsky's 1840 essay on Alexander Griboedov, where he decreed that, apart from two satirical eighteenth-century comedies by Denis Fonvizin, Russian drama worth mentioning consisted of a total of three plays: Griboedov's comedy *The Misfortune of Being Clever* (*Gore ot uma*), Alexander Pushkin's *Boris Godunov*, and Gogol's *The Inspector General* (*Revizor*). All other Russian dramas, comedies, and tragedies, Belinsky ruled, did not merit wasting anyone's breath and should be forgotten for good.

This was, of course, a belated Russian echo of the romantic reaction against the neoclassicism of the seventeenth and eighteenth centuries, the same reaction that had earlier caused Wordsworth to attack and dismiss Alexander Pope and, in France, moved Stendhal to renounce Racine in the name of Shakespeare. Belinsky made it quite explicit in his 1840 essay why he wanted to do away with Russian drama that antedated Pushkin and Gogol. It was all descended from "misshapen poetic monstrosities, which is what Corneille, Racine, Boileau, Molière, Crébillon, Voltaire, Ducis, Addison, Pope, Alfieri and their likes were."[1] Tossing into the same pot the names of Molière and Crébillon, of Jean-François Ducis (the adapter of Shakespeare to French eighteenth-century tastes) and Alexander Pope (whose name Belinsky spelled as if it were a German one and had two syllables), shows that it was not the question of literary quality or lack of it that concerned Belinsky. The entire poetics of the past two centuries of Western literature and of the past century of Russian literature was what he wanted to jettison.

Belinsky possessed tremendous powers of persuasion. In the name of social progress and of bringing about a more humanitarian literature, he prevailed on his countrymen to give up a large portion of their literary heritage and to expel from literature some of the most attractive poets, playwrights, and prose writers of the eighteenth and the first half of the nineteenth century. Belinsky's derogatory label "pseudoclassical" was pasted on all French plays written in the period between Corneille's *Le Cid* and Victor Hugo's *Hernani* and on all Russian drama written between about 1750 and 1825. For the rest of the nineteenth century, except for a few hardy academics, educated Russians shunned anything "pseudoclassical" (the concept encompassed what is today meant by baroque, rococo, and neoclassical) as repellent and vaguely immoral.

During the second half of the nineteenth century, the realist mode came to be seen as the only valid form of dramatic portrayal

1. V. G. Belinsky, *Sobranie sochinenii v trekh tomakh* (St. Petersburg, 1911) vol. 1, p. 599.

of life on the stage. Henceforth, romantic drama could be admired only in a qualified and grudging manner. Russian plays that antedated the now despised "pseudoclassicism" were regarded as an embarrassment that one would do best to forget. Peter Morozov, whose pioneering *Essays in the History of Russian Drama of the 17th and 18th Centuries (Ocherki po istorii russkoi dramy XVII i XVIII stoletii,* 1888) tried to make his countrymen aware of the existence of earlier plays and playwrights, felt obliged to chide the dramatists he described for their lack of realism and of a progressive nineteenth-century consciousness. Boris Warnecke (or Varneke), in his once popular *History of Russian Theater (Istoriia russkogo teatra,* 1914), available in English translation, set up Gogol as the supreme photographic realist in drama, who supposedly transcribed his plays from scenes he had observed in real life. Warnecke sneered at Russian playwrights of the eighteenth and early twentieth century (including Chekhov) for failing to live up to the high standard of realism supposedly set by Gogol. Echoes of such typical nineteenth-century attitudes are discernible in some of the twentieth-century studies of Russian theater published in Western countries.

Rediscovery of Russian neoclassicism was initiated at the very beginning of the twentieth century. A primary impetus for the rehabilitation of that age came from Sergei Diaghilev's journal *The World of Art (Mir iskusstva)* and his epochal exhibition of Russian eighteenth-century portraits in 1905. By the second decade of the twentieth century a number of major literary figures, including Andrei Bely, Mikhail Kuzmin, Marina Tsvetaeva, and Osip Mandelshtam were studying and imitating the poets and playwrights of that age. Since the 1920s, there has been an ever-growing body of scholarly studies devoted to it. Yet, the prejudice against the literary culture of the eighteenth century (which in its Russian context usually includes the first two decades of the nineteenth) lingers on among Russian writers and scholars and among foreign specialists in Russian literature.

One striking instance of this prejudice is Vladimir Mayakovsky's screen play *Comrade Antiquary's Love Affair (Liubov'*

Shkafoliubova, 1927), in which the heroine is cured of her reactionary fascination with eighteenth-century culture and costume by her encounter with an idiotic museum keeper who imagines he is living in the age of powdered wigs and crinolines.[2] Vladimir Nabokov provides another instance, especially in his annotated edition of Pushkin's *Eugene Onegin*. In his novel *The Gift (Dar)*, Nabokov devotes an entire chapter to demonstrating how naive and unreliable the judgments of Belinsky ("an appealing ignoramus") and of the critical school he engendered were. Nevertheless, the moment Nabokov mentions Racine or Molière or any of the Russian poets and playwrights of neoclassical or sentimentalist persuasion, he exposes his typically nineteenth-century hostility and contempt for the neoclassical heathen.

As one studies the evolution of Russian drama, one comes to realize that the Belinskian excommunication of the neoclassicists was neither the first nor the last such episode in its history. Consigning the preceding cultural period to the dustbin was a custom practiced by the Russians long before Trotsky came up with this memorable formula during the October Revolution. New forms of written drama came to Russia in discrete waves, always from some other culture. Each new wave usually meant a whole new beginning and a discarding of the previous dramatic mode. The arrival of religious drama patterned after the school drama of the Jesuits at the end of the seventeenth century coincided, probably fortuitously, with the banning of earlier forms of religious and secular theatrical entertainment. The inauguration of neoclassical tragedy and comedy in the mid-eighteenth century led to the almost instant abandonment of both the religious school drama and the secular chivalric romance plays that were

2. The script was never filmed. But it was published in a Soviet film journal and is included in the thirteen-volume edition of Mayakovsky's complete collected writings (*Polnoe sobranie sochinenii*, vol. 11 [Moscow, 1958]). It is indeed paradoxical that Mayakovsky, whose metaphorical and baroque poetic manner owed so much to eighteenth-century poets such as Lomonosov, who revived the eighteenth-century genres of the panegyric ode and the Juvenalian satire and gave the characters of his plays typical eighteenth-century *noms parlants*, should have loathed that century and its culture.

dominant in the first half of that century. With the ascent of realistic melodrama around 1850, the dramatic genres inherited from romanticism were not only discarded, but were virtually anathematized.

And so it went, right up to the October Revolution, which caused one of the most brilliant epochs in Russian dramatic literature, the Symbolist age, to be consigned to oblivion. To some extent, this phenomenon has its parallels in other cultures. The advent of a new literary movement usually tends to discredit the preceding dramatic genres. But in the West, with the passage of time, the abandoned dramatic forms usually take their rightful place in cultural history and come to be seen as historical phenomena that are of interest because of the prominence they once enjoyed. In Russia, until very recently, the defeated literary or dramatic trends were likely to be forgotten for good.

The Origins of This Book

I first became dissatisfied with the earlier surveys of Russian drama a few years after I began teaching a course on it at Berkeley in the early 1960s. In looking back now and comparing the syllabus of my first Berkeley course with the one I prepared when invited to offer the same course at Harvard in the spring of 1966, I note a new section incorporated to cover the period between the plays at the end of the eighteenth century and the plays of Griboedov and Pushkin. The reason for this addition was that in the early 1960s the *Biblioteka poèta* (*The Poet's Library*) series, published in Moscow and Leningrad, made available for the first time in more than a century collections of plays by the early nineteenth-century authors Vladislav Ozerov, Pavel Katenin, Alexander Shakhovskoy, Nikolai Khmelnitsky, and a few others. These are names that even a Russian-literature specialist is likely to know only as footnotes to *Eugene Onegin* and to Pushkin's letters. The texts of their plays, accompanied by knowledgeable introductions by the noted Soviet scholars Irina Medvedeva, Abram Gozenpud, and Moisei Iankovsky, quickly convinced me that they were neither the nonentities Belinsky thought them to be nor mediocrities and "bibliographical burdens," as Nabokov would have it, but highly interesting playwrights, who deserved a place in any history of Russian drama.

Further inquiries led me to another significant area. This was the earliest form of written, literary drama in Russian, the school drama of the late seventeenth and early eighteenth centuries. Specimens of this genre were published by Nikolai Tikhonravov and other scholars in various nineteenth-century journals and collections. But there were no scholarly editions, and the scope of the corpus was hard to establish. The appearance of Nina Koroleva's two-volume set of the collected poetry and plays of Wilhelm Küchelbecker in the *Biblioteka poèta* series revealed this supposedly minor figure as a major romantic dramatist, whose plays are a key to understanding the transition of Russian drama from neoclassical to romantic poets. By 1969, I felt ready to tackle writing a history of Russian drama as literature. With the aid of a Guggenheim grant, I departed for Helsinki and Zagreb in search of materials for establishing the repertoire of plays, whether performed or not, that existed before the appearance of the first Russian neoclassical tragedy in 1747.

On the basis of what I found, I began writing a book early in 1970. Then the campus and the department in which I work were plunged into the turmoil of that period. Students and colleagues had a more immediate claim on my time than did my research, so I postponed things for a year. This delay turned out to have been fortunate, because when I got back to the project, the publication in the Soviet Union of a five-volume collection of Russian plays for the period from the 1670s to the 1740s had been announced. Prepared by a team of specialists headed by Olga Derzhavina and Andrei Robinson and lavishly annotated, the collection included everything I had found during my Guggenheim year and a great deal more—most important, a whole corpus of dramatizations of chivalric romances. This was a genre in which Russian playwrights specialized in the period between the heyday of school drama and the introduction of neoclassical tragedy (i.e., ca. 1715–50). Yet scholars had heretofore largely ignored these plays. The completion of the five-volume set in

1976 gave me the basic material for Chapters 1 and 2. This is the first of the many debts I gratefully acknowledge.[3]

As I proceeded with my study of plays and of criticism, I came to realize that I was not entirely alone in my desire to compile a history of Russian drama that would preserve its full continuity and not arbitrarily ignore or minimize certain periods because they were once thought to be derivative or antiquated or reactionary. Bertha Malnick, an English historian of Russian drama, in her essays published during the 1950s in the London *Slavonic and East European Review*, and the Polish scholar Tadeusz Kołakowski in the 1960s have both argued for the kind of dovetailing between the eighteenth-century Russian drama and the age of Pushkin and Gogol that Russian commentators have tended to ignore. The publication in 1978 of *Russian Minstrels* by the American historian Russell Zguta, who collected and presented much of the available information about the pre-literate forms of Russian theater, was a heartening occasion. That book and Professor Zguta's essays on tangential cultural topics that appeared in *Slavic Review* served to confirm and enlarge my concepts of the earliest forms of Russian drama.

A shock of recognition occurred when I discovered at the New York Public Library a rare copy of Sergei Danilov's *Essays in the History of Russian Dramatic Theater (Ocherki po istorii russkogo dramaticheskogo teatra)* sometime in the early 1970s. Published in a very small printing in 1948, at the height of the Stalinist repression of culture and falsification of history, here at last was a survey of the kind that I had dreamed of writing: equally fair to all periods, devoid of prejudice in favor of one particular dramatic mode to the detriment of all others, aware of the importance of lesser phenomena for the emergence of great works. For a few months, I mulled over the possibility of abandoning my own project and translating Danilov's book instead.

I decided against this move for two reasons. First, Danilov's book is a history of Russian theater, rather than of drama, with extensive sections about acting techniques, audiences, and ad-

3. *Ranniaia russkaia dramaturgiia (XVII—pervaia polovina XVIII v.)*, ed. A. N. Robinson et al., 5 vols. (Moscow 1972–76).

ministrative arrangements—fascinating matters all of them, but ones I intended to treat only marginally. Second, the Marxist-Leninist jargon and the conventionally official portraits of major figures, such as Fonvizin, Griboedov, and Gogol, do not clarify Danilov's meaning or reflect the depth of his understanding, but were clearly added to protect the author and the book from extermination. My book was fully planned and about one-third written by the time I discovered Danilov's. I absorbed whatever I could learn from him, but any possible resemblances of my book to his have resulted from an affinity of overall view rather than from a desire to imitate him.[4]

Because three fourths of my sources were published in the Soviet Union after the revolution, the question of ideological distortions has to be faced. Russian literary criticism and scholarship have been politicized since the 1840s in a way that has become more and more familiar in the West in the last two decades or so. But an author's ideological commitment does not necessarily prevent him or her from writing valid and valuable history. Peter Morozov's previously cited 1888 book on early Russian drama was written from the position of the radical utilitarians who dominated the criticism of his time. Vsevolod Vsevolodsky-Gerngross's two-volume *History of the Russian Theater (Istoriia russkogo teatra*, 1929), thoroughly and systematically Marxist, is one of the best sources we have on its subject. These books are good and honest because, whatever the ideology, their authors supply the readers with all the factual information they need and do not try to conceal or distort the historical record.

Since the 1930s, however, Soviet literary historians have been subjected to several powerful and conflicting imperatives, of which adherence to Marxism-Leninism is only one. Because of the Soviet system's compulsory need for continuous self-congrat-

4. *Istoriia russkoi dramaturgii XVII—pervaia polovina XIX veka (History of Russian Drama from the Seventeenth to the First Half of the Nineteenth Century)* (Leningrad, 1982), written by a collective of Soviet scholars under the editorship of Lydia Lotman and others, became available after the manuscript of the present book had been completed. In its comprehensiveness, it follows the example of Sergei Danilov's 1948 study, but the critical and scholarly level of individual contributions is uneven and the volume lacks Danilov's unified view of the surveyed period.

ulation and self-justification, a chauvinistic nationalism (associated before the revolution with tsarist imperialism rather than with revolutionary thought) and a search for precursors of Bolshevism in all past ages were made mandatory for cultural historians. They are required to assume automatically that in all periods in the past, good Russians were always progressive, were opposed to the tsars and the church, were immune from foreign influences, and favored realistic forms in the arts over symbolic or stylized ones.

But the historical record often shows the reality to have been the opposite of these compulsory assumptions. Therefore Marxist analysis and historic facts are frequently sacrificed to satisfy the nationalistic and self-legitimizing imperatives. Vsevolodsky-Gerngross, by applying scrupulously Marxist-Leninist categories, demonstrated in his 1929 book that the fashion for neoclassical tragedy in eighteenth-century Russia was created by aristocratic audiences who saw in this form a reflection of their own elitist values and that the rise of realism in Russian drama was due to the emergence of nineteenth-century bourgeois values in the society at large. By the early 1930s, such ideas were no longer acceptable. The book was denounced and withdrawn from circulation. For the rest of his long career, this once fine historian of the theater kept apologizing in print for having written his best book. He went on falsifying the cultural and political attitudes of the past in his numerous later publications.

In every decade since the October Revolution, there have been historians of Russian drama who have managed to bring out honest studies that have kept the required distortions and falsifications to a minimum. But they are a distinguished minority. The majority are the scholars whose books are used as texts in Soviet schools and universities and who get appointed to positions of power and authority at literary institutes and institutions of higher learning. They are the ones who manufacture accounts of censorship of eighteenth-century plays that actually never had any trouble passing the censor; who reinterpret innocuous adaptations of plays by Corneille or Favart or Metastasio—adaptations that caused hardly a ripple in their day—as powerful revolutionary statements that made the tsars blanch; and who attribute to moderately liberal or even to out-and-out reactionary playwrights of the eighteenth and nineteenth centuries radical convictions they either wouldn't have dreamed of entertaining or couldn't have entertained in any case because the ideas attributed to them didn't yet exist.

For half a century now, distortion of cultural history has been practiced in the Soviet Union on a scale that is unimaginable to anyone who has not had a chance to compare pre- and postrevolutionary sources. Few people in the West have had that chance. This lack of comparison leads to uncritical acceptance by Western commentators, at times rather knowledgeable ones, of events unknown to history and manufactured in recent decades by career-minded Soviet scholars. To establish the actual circumstances, I therefore found it necessary to go back to contemporary accounts of the writing and the first production of any play that was said to have had a history of being banned or censored. In this book I share with the readers some of my findings in the cases of two famous eighteenth-century plays with such histories, Fonvizin's *The Minor* (*Nedorosl'*) and Kniazhnin's *Vadim of Novgorod* (*Vadim Novgorodskii*).

After a comparison of the accounts of governmental interference with productions of dramas left by prerevolutionary historians (there is a wealth of such studies in the *Yearbooks of the Imperial Theaters* [*Ezhegodnik imperatorskikh teatrov*], published at the end of the nineteenth century) with recent Soviet writings on the same subject, an inescapable conclusion emerges. Liberal Russian scholars of the prerevolutionary decades who described the censorship abuses in the reigns of Catherine the Great or Nicholas I regarded them as outrages of the benighted past, to which they never expected to return. Soviet historians of drama, on the other hand, who today exaggerate the same incidents beyond all proportion, who forget to mention that many socially critical plays of those times had no censorship problems, or who invent cases of censorship for which there is no historical evidence, do so to justify current controls over literature by convincing their readers that the past must have been worse.

But it is not of the falsifications of history that I primarily think when I reflect on the Soviet critics and scholars who helped shape this book. As I look back on the years lived with a gradually growing manuscript, I am reminded of discovering the fine editions mentioned earlier in this introduction, of such splendid contributions to our knowledge of Russian drama as Kirill Pigarev's study of Fonvizin, Irina Medvedeva's biography of the great actress Semyonova, Boris Reizov's essay on the foreign parallels to *The Minor*, and many, many other contributions by excellent Soviet scholars that are mentioned in the text and in the notes. I remember colleagues who discussed my research with me and offered valuable advice, among them Olga and Robert Hughes, Michael Green, Hugh McLean, Francis J. Whitfield, Russell Zguta, Mark Altshuller, and Jurij Striedter, as well as several Soviet scholars, whose names I'd better not mention, though their kindness I will not forget.

Through the years, I was fortunate to have colleagues at other departments at Berkeley share special knowledge of their fields with me. Among them, I would like to mention Dunbar Ogden of the Department of Dramatic Art, Maria Kotzamanidou of the Department of Comparative Literature, Marie-Hélène Huet of the Department of French, Blake Lee Spahr and Hinrich Seeba of the Department of German, and Daniel Heartz of the Department of Music. Among the numerous librarians I consulted, the late Dr. Maria Vidnas of the Helsinki University Library, David Howells of the Taylorian Institution at Oxford, and Edward Kasinec of Berkeley were particularly helpful. Research assistants Barry Jordan and Kevin O'Brien deserve my gratitude for their patient help.

Most appreciated of all is the invaluable support of Peter Carleton, who conscientiously read all the chapters and clarified many previously awkward passages (he is in no way responsible for any such that may remain). And speaking of support, there were those two Guggenheim fellowships, one in 1969–70 and the other in 1977–78, the latter awarded even though I did not live up to my rash promise (made in 1969) to complete within two years a history of Russian drama from its beginnings *to the pres-*

ent (clearly, I had no idea then what this involved!). I salute the John Simon Guggenheim Memorial Foundation and thank it for its confidence in me and its generosity.

Aims and Audience

What I offer in this book is not a general historical overview of Russian drama but rather a detailed survey of prerealistic Russian literary (i.e., written) drama. The oral, preliterate dramatic genres, of which there is a brief account at the beginning of Chapter 1, belong to folklore rather than to the area of literary studies. The decision to concentrate on written drama meant that I had to begin with the three kinds of plays that antedated the arrival of neoclassical genres in Russia: the religious and school drama; the court drama of the 1670s (whose inclusion in the canon of Russian drama is somewhat problematic); and the chivalric romance plays of the early eighteenth century. From then on and for the rest of the book, I concentrate on that traditional stepchild of literary and dramatic studies, the neoclassical drama, which was the dominant form of Russian drama from around 1750 to the early 1820s.

The arrival of Russian neoclassical drama can be easily dated. It originated with the appearance of Alexander Sumarokov's French-style tragedies and comedies at the end of the 1740s. But the time of termination of this form of drama is almost impossible to pinpoint. Worthwhile works in the neoclassical mode went on being written in Russia after the arrival of sentimentalism, romanticism, and even realism. Some of the most successful plays of the early nineteenth century, including works by Ozerov, Pushkin, and Gogol, mingle neoclassical features with romantic or realistic ones in uneven and often hard-to-measure proportions. In an earlier draft, I had intended to end the book with the plays of Lermontov and Gogol. But even though Mikhail Lermontov's best-known play, *Masquerade*, drew for its style and diction on the plays of his senior neoclassicist contemporaries, Griboedov and Küchelbecker, Lermontov's plays are quintessentially romantic and thus ought to be outside the boundaries of this study. As for Gogol, his plays, especially *The Inspector General*, are a unique instance of neoclassical themes and structures shading off into nineteenth-century realism and then, beyond it, into twentieth-century surrealism. But I had already written an extensive section on Gogol's plays and their neoclassical roots a few years ago and did not want to restate the same points.[5]

Pushkin, then, was left as the only logical cutoff point. The title of my final chapter is not "Pushkin the Playwright" but rather "Pushkin and Neoclassical Drama." Innumerable studies have been written on Pushkin the dramatist, as there have been on every other aspect of his life and work. Rather than paraphrase or summarize this vast literature, I restricted myself to demonstrating the central importance of neoclassical drama for Pushkin's artistic formation and the pervasiveness of his neoclassical heritage in his later writings, including his romantic narrative poems and his ostensibly realistic prose fiction. Examination of this aspect of Pushkin in its entirety necessitated going beyond the limits of neoclassicism. This was also the case with the plays of Pushkin's school friend Küchelbecker, who began within the neoclassical fold, but whose best dramatic work, *Izhorsky*, is also one of the finest achievements of Russian romantic drama. Similarly, the section on vaudeville comedy had to take this genre from its neoclassical origins to the realistic specimens of the 1840s, partly because there was no convenient cutoff point and partly because it seemed fitting to show how the development of this genre leads in a continuous line from the vaudevilles of the early nineteenth century all the way to the one-act plays of Turgenev and Chekhov.

The great profusion of plays, playwrights, and dramatic genres during the century and a half that is the primary focus of this book made a uniform critical approach neither possible nor, indeed, desirable. Certain topics called for generic explanations or theoretical background, while others could be better conveyed through providing historical, sociological, or biographical information. A guided tour through Russian drama of the

5. See Simon Karlinsky, *The Sexual Labyrinth of Nikolai Gogol* (Cambridge, Mass., 1976), pp. 144–85.

period in question was what I hoped to offer. Subtler forms of literary analysis would have been an impediment on such a tour. Plot summary, which, I would be the first to admit, is one of the crudest tools in the critical arsenal, had to be wielded again and again for the sake of those readers who would have no other access to many of the plays I discuss because those works are available only in the original Russian. My aim was to demonstate the richness and variety of Russian prerealist drama and its crucial importance for the whole of Russian culture and for the intellectual and stylistic formation of the literary giants of the first half of the nineteenth century.

What was that question? To what sort of reader is this book addressed? Ah, yes. Actually, to anyone interested in drama, Russian or otherwise. To anyone who may want to learn about what kinds of plays were written in the first century and a half of the dramatic tradition that eventually gave the world the great masterpieces of Gogol and Chekhov and Alexander Blok. The book is also addressed to Western Slavicists and college students who tend to take for granted the literary importance of such playwrights as Alexander Sumarokov or Mikhail Kheraskov because they are always mentioned in literary histories and who may have never bothered to look at the genuinely attractive plays of St. Dimitry of Rostov, Pavel Potemkin, or Nikolai Khmelnitsky.

I would also like to show to the childhood friend, the Scandinavian specialist, and the Oxford colleague who were mentioned in the beginning that among the dozens and dozens of Russian plays written from who knows when to about 1840 and discussed in this book, many are indeed as derivative, stilted, and musty as popularly charged. But many are far better than that and are historically interesting to boot, while some ten to twenty are attractive or amusing or moving enough to be worth knowing about apart from any scholarly or historical considerations.

Another intended audience is a group of skeptical Russian ghosts, headed by Vladimir Nabokov, whom I would like to try to convince that in a cultural world that can appreciate a concerto by Pergolesi or a nocturne by John Field, a painting by Watteau or Canaletto or a poem by Robert Burns, André Chénier, or Konstantin Batiushkov, there should be room for

enjoying a play by, say, Bogdan Elchaninov or Alexander Shakhovskoy.[6] These plays will never imperil the laurels of Griboedov or Gogol, just as the enjoyment of Pergolesi or Field can in
no way dim the radiance of Mozart's glory. But appreciating them
might expand our understanding of art and of humanity just
a bit, and what is the harm in that?

6. When this introduction was drafted, the names of Elchaninov and Shakhovskoy were cited at random. Since then, however, my student Cassandra Politzer chose to stage, as her senior thesis, Elchaninov's *The Giddypate Undone* and
Shakhovskoy's *The New Sterne* on a triple bill with the Soviet absurdist comedy
Elizaveta Bam by Daniel Harms. After translating the three plays into English
in collaboration with several other students, Ms. Politzer drew on her connections
with the theater and film community of San Francisco to assemble a dedicated
group of directors, designers, and actors. The resultant production played on the
Berkeley campus for three evenings in May 1983. The modern audience, it turned
out, reacted quite favorably to an imaginative presentation of two Russian neoclassical comedies that had not been produced in their native country since the
1770s (*The Giddypate Undone*) and the first decade of the 19th century (*The New
Sterne*).

❋ I ❋

Religious Drama

In A.D. 957, Grand Princess Olga of Kiev, the grandmother of St. Vladimir, paid a state visit to the Emperor Constantine Porphyrogenitos of Byzantium in Constantinople. During that visit, she was entertained with an elaborate theatrical pageant, a choral performance and a troupe of dancers, acrobats, and musicians.[1] Olga's Kiev was one of the more culturally advanced cities in medieval Europe; for example, one of Olga's descendants, Anna Iaroslavna, who as Anne de Russie became queen of France, was able to read and write at least three languages, whereas King Henry I of France, whom Anna married in 1044, was illiterate. It would therefore have seemed natural for Olga to bring back to Kiev some of the theatrical marvels she saw in Constantinople. But this apparently did not occur to her. So her countrymen had to wait another 800 years before they could see theatrical performances as we understand them today. The dramatized hymnology and the mystery and miracle plays of the medieval religious theater, as it existed in Byzantium and later in Western Europe, did not take root in Russia.

The first recorded performance of a literary play (as opposed to a liturgical, instructional, or orally transmitted folk play) in Russia took place in 1672. In France, it was the time of Racine and Molière; in England, Shakespeare had been dead for more than half a century. The earliest successful production of a sec-

---

1. Nikolai Findeizen, *Ocherki po istorii muzyki v Rossii* (Moscow, 1928), vol. 1, pp. 47 ff.

1

ular play written in Russian by a reputable Russian playwright did not take place until 1749. The timetable of Russian drama is late not only in comparison with the advanced and mature dramatic literatures of seventeenth-century England, France, and Spain, but even in comparison with the rich theater traditions that had by then developed in other Slavic countries, notably Poland and Croatia.

There are numerous historical, social, and even purely literary reasons for the time lag. The enlightened Kievan period of Russian history (from the end of the ninth to the beginning of the twelfth century), during which Russians enjoyed full cultural contacts with the Western world, was followed by 250 years of invasions and domination by nomadic Mongol tribes, resulting in the near extinction of all cultural life. While the rest of Europe was living through the stimulating experiences of the Renaissance, the Reformation, the Counter-Reformation, and the development of the baroque in the arts, Russia went through the conservative Muscovite period, which culminated in the reign of terror and civil massacres under Ivan the Terrible. The flowering of Elizabethan drama in England occurred simultaneously with the near disintegration of the Russian state at the outset of the seventeenth century, during the Time of Troubles. Consequently, at the beginning of the eighteenth century, when Peter the Great forcibly brought Russia back into the contemporary Western world (from which it had been absent since the end of the Kievan period), Russian society and culture, including drama, had to take a giant step from the early Middle Ages into the Age of Enlightenment.

Although there was no professional theater or literary drama in Russia during the Kievan and Muscovite periods, various forms of preliterate theatrical activity are recorded from those times, many of which survived among the less literate strata of the population till the twentieth century. There were rituals of welcoming the solar deities at the onset of spring and of expelling the mischievous river nymphs (*rusalki*), with the villagers impersonating these supernatural beings. These dramatized ceremonies were of great antiquity. They initially had agrarian significance, and they survived into modern times by often being

2

disguised as celebrations of Christian holidays.[2] There were the ceremonies of village weddings in which the statements and the responses of the participants during the betrothal and the post-nuptial celebrations amounted to a prerehearsed script of an oral folk play.[3] And there were, from pre-Christian times, the itinerant minstrel-buffoons, the *skomorokhi*, who provided humor, satire, and musical entertainment in the villages and at the princely courts of Kievan and Muscovite Russia.[4] The *skomorokhi* ceased to exist as a social class when they were outlawed by a series of edicts promulgated in the mid-seventeenth century. But they were remembered for centuries in Russian folk songs, and in the nineteenth and twentieth centuries they appeared in numerous plays, operas, and ballets, extending all the way to Sergei Prokofiev's *The Buffoon* and Igor Stravinsky's *Renard*.[5] During both the Kievan and the Muscovite periods, the Russian Orthodox Church regarded all forms of theatrical expression as sinful and, except for the wedding rituals, tried to suppress various forms of preliterate theater whenever it had the power to do so.

Still, by the sixteenth century, with the ebb of the Mongol occupation and the resumption of closer contacts with their Orthodox co-religionists in Greece, Russians saw their way to

2. See Vladimir Propp, *Russkie agrarnye prazdniki* (Leningrad, 1963), on the origins and significance of such rituals; and Russell Zguta, "Origins of the Russian Puppet Theater: An Alternative Hypothesis," *Slavic Review* 33 (December 1974): 711–12, for a list of correspondences between the pagan-originated rituals and official Russian Orthodox holidays. Vsevolod Vsevolodsky-Gerngross's *Istoriia russkogo teatra*, (Leningrad, 1929), vol. 1, pp. 99–191, and Elizabeth A. Warner's *The Russian Folk Theatre* (The Hague, 1977) contain detailed accounts of dramatically enacted pagan rituals that existed in Russian culture well into modern times.

3. A thorough anthropological study of this entire phenomenon is Elsa Mahler's *Die russischen dörflichen Hochzeitsbräuche*, Berlin Free University Slavic Seminar Publications, vol. 40 (Berlin, 1960). See also Vsevolodsky-Gerngross, *Istoriia russkogo teatra*, pp. 81 ff.

4. The most valuable Russian studies of the *skomorokhi* are Findeizen, *Ocherki po istorii muzyki*, pp. 145–70, and Anatoly Belkin, *Russkie skomorokhi* (Moscow, 1975). In English, there is Russell Zguta's *Russian Minstrels* (Philadelphia, 1978).

5. On the significance of preliterary dramatized folklore in Stravinsky's works for the stage, see my article "Stravinsky and Russian Pre-literate Theater," *19th Century Music* 6 (Spring 1983): 232–40.

incorporating into their religious practices several dramatized ceremonies that scholars of a later age could interpret as rudimentary theater. At Easter time, for instance, two such ceremonies were the reenactment of Christ's entrance into Jerusalem, known as "The Donkey Procession" (*Shestvie na osliati*), in which an archbishop riding on a donkey impersonated Christ; and the ceremony of Christ washing the feet of his disciples, with dialogue loosely based on appropriate passages in the Gospels and with the archbishop taking the role of Christ and twelve priests playing the disciples.

The Furnace Play

The most elaborate of these dramatized ceremonies, *The Furnace Play* (*Peshchnoe deistvo*, literally *The Furnace Action*), performed in some churches annually on December 17 during the sixteenth and seventeenth centuries, amounted to a full-fledged liturgical drama with music. Liturgical plays about the three youths Hananiah, Azariah, and Mishael—who, according to the Old Testament (Book of Daniel), were cast into a burning furnace by the Chaldean servants of Nebuchadnezzar for refusing to worship idols and then rescued from the flames by an angel—were widespread in both Eastern and Western Christianity as part of pre-Christmas celebrations. Romanus the Melodist, a sixth-century Byzantine religious poet much honored in the Russian Orthodox tradition, composed an elaborate antiphonal hymn on this subject,[6] intended to be performed on the feast day of the three youths, December 17, just as was done in Russia a millennium later.

At the very end of the fourteenth century, Russian pilgrims to Constantinople reported seeing a performance in the Hagia Sophia cathedral of a dramatized ritual quite similar to *The Furnace Play*.[7] This presentation must have been the source

6. Romanos le Mélode, *Hymnes*, ed. Jose Grosdidier de Matons (Paris, 1964) vol. 1, pp. 361–403.

7. Vsevolodsky-Gerngross, *Istoriia russkogo teatra*, p. 243. A detailed comparison of the Byzantine and Russian versions of *The Furnace Play* is found in

for the Russian versions recorded for the period from 1548 to 1643 and described by foreign travelers, such as Adam Olearius and Giles Fletcher. Both the text and the music of the ceremony have been preserved. The early twentieth-century composer Alexander Kastalsky based on them his very attractive reconstruction of the vocal score.[8] Still later, Sergei Prokofiev composed his own version of certain portions of *The Furnace Play* for Sergei Eisenstein's film *Ivan the Terrible* (1944). The subject matter is thus as perennially popular in the Russian tradition as it is in the West, where its currency has extended from various miracle plays derived from the Book of Daniel to the American spiritual about Shadrach ("There were three children from the land of Israel . . .") and to Benjamin Britten's opera *The Burning Fiery Furnace* (1966).

For performances of *The Furnace Play*, a special set representing "the fiery furnace" was constructed in the middle of the church. The *dramatis personae* consisted of the three martyred youths, impersonated by three choirboys who sang in close harmony; their Chaldean tormentors, two speaking actors who wore jesters' garments and recited comical dialogues in rhymed doggerel; the narrator, a singing basso, usually a deacon, supported by a male chorus, the latter also supplying choral interludes on texts from psalms and prayers; and the rescuing angel, whose appearance toward the end of the play would be accompanied by elaborate stage effects, such as thunder and lightning. To avoid blasphemy, the role of the angel was taken by a lifesize, cutout icon, painted on leather and lowered from the ceiling on a rope—a *deus ex machina* in the original sense of the term. A rather sophisticated differentiation was thus achieved between the singing good characters, the speaking comical villains, and the silent, nonhuman angel.

To procure suitable persons to play the comical Chaldean villains, the Church was known to suspend on occasion its traditional hostility to the *skomorokhi* and hire them to play these

Miloš M. Velimirović, "Liturgical Drama in Byzantium and Russia," *Dumbarton Oaks Papers*, no. 16 (Washington, D.C., 1962), pp. 351–85.

8. A. Kastalsky, *Peshchnoe deistvo* (text and score; Moscow and Leipzig, 1909).

parts. In such cases, *skomorokhi* were usually given dispensa-
tion to perform freely all over the town for a few days after
Christmas. At times, they were also required to undergo a bap-
tism so as to wash away the impurity of having impersonated
heathens.

Giles Fletcher, the worldly, well-traveled envoy of England's
Queen Elizabeth I, saw *The Furnace Play* in Moscow in 1588.
He did not think much of it. As he wrote in his book *Of the
Russe Common Wealth*:

> Another pageant they have the weeke before the nativitie of
> Christ: when every bishop in his cathedral church setteth
> forth a shew of the three children in the oven. Where the
> Angell is made to come flying from the roofe of the church,
> with great admiration of the lookers on, and many terrible
> flashes of fire are made with rosin and gun-powder by the
> Chaldeans (as they call them), that run about the towne all
> the twelve dayes, disguised in their plaiers coats, and make
> much good sport for the honor of the bishop's pageant. At
> the Mosco, the emperour himselfe and the emperesse never
> fail to be at it, though it be but the same matter plaid every
> yeare, without any new invention at all.[9]

There is, of course, a profound cultural misunderstanding
involved in Fletcher's comment. What he saw as a play lacking
dramatic invention was for his hosts a religious ritual, which it
would be meaningless to evaluate by literary or dramatic cri-
teria or to judge in theatrical terms. By the middle of the seventeenth century, *The Furnace Play* was no longer performed in
Russian churches. But echoes of it can be found in later oral
folk drama. Literary playwrights, from Simeon of Polotsk in the
seventeenth century (whose works will be described shortly) to
Evgeny Zamiatin in the twentieth (in his play *The Flea*), have
occasionally cited situations or passages from *The Furnace Play*.

9. Giles Fletcher, "Of the Russe Common Wealth," in *Russia at the Close
of the Sixteenth Century*, Hakluyt Society Edition (London, 1856), pp. 137–38.
The "emperour" mentioned by Fletcher (Russian monarchs did not assume the
imperial title until Peter the Great) was Tsar Fyodor Ioannovich, the meek and
pious son of Ivan the Terrible. His "emperesse" was Irina, the sister of Boris
Godunov.

It is owing to this play that the word for Chaldean has come to be a synonym for "buffoon" in modern Russian.

School Drama

In the mid-seventeenth century, while the authorities in Moscow were busy outlawing the *skomorokhi*, banning *The Furnace Play*, and prohibiting singing and the playing of musical instruments in private homes, churchmen in the outlying areas in southwestern Russia began to look gingerly into the possibility of employing theatrical performances for educational and missionary purposes. The Russian Orthodox Church was driven to this by its rivalry with the Roman Catholic Church, whose influence was particularly felt in the regions that bordered Poland. Both countries claimed jurisdiction over large sections of the Ukraine and Belorussia. Many of those territories changed hands repeatedly during the Russo-Polish wars of the fifteenth, sixteenth, and seventeenth centuries, wars that were so vividly portrayed by Gogol in "Taras Bulba." At such times, Polish Catholic missionaries went to work in those areas considered either "occupied" or "liberated," depending on the national viewpoint of the reporting historian.

Its experiences in combatting the inroads of various Protestant heresies taught the Polish Catholic Church the value of a humanist education and of Latin studies. Martin Luther himself favored Latin drama as part of the curriculum of religious schools in Protestant countries. His Catholic opponents, however, were not about to leave such a proven and potent weapon of indoctrination in the enemy's hands. The result was the emergence of Latin Jesuit school drama, which by the second half of the sixteenth century had spread to all the Catholic countries of Europe in which the Jesuits were in charge of religious education.

The Jesuits had become extremely powerful in Poland by the end of the sixteenth century. Their efforts to convert the neighboring East Slavs, as Pushkin did not fail to note in his play *Boris Godunov*, were untiring. Their religious colleges (*collegia*; sing. *collegium*) in areas where Polish and Russian influences overlapped offered a broad European education to the tradition-bound Russians and Ukrainians. Dramatic performances, compulsory in all their schools, proved an irresistible magnet for attracting and eventually converting non-Catholic students. The Orthodox Church in the Ukraine was therefore forced to become more flexible in its traditional attitude toward the theater. In 1629 the Metropolitan of Kiev authorized performances of miracle plays. There were but few such performances in the first half of the seventeenth century, but in the second half the study and performance of drama were receiving considerable attention in the religious schools of the Ukraine and of western Russia. By the beginning of the eighteenth century the phenomenon spread to Moscow.

Just as the Counter-Reformation brought about the development of the Jesuit drama, the reaction of the Orthodox Church to Catholic inroads led to a cultural broadening and growth known as the Southwestern Revival. The theological school called the Kievan Mohyla Academy was the center of this revival. The academy played an incalculable role in the evolution of Russian education, literature, and drama. Peter Mohyla, a Ukrainian educated in Jesuit schools and in Polish universities, brought to the Kievan divinity school he directed (and which was renamed after him) the advanced teaching methods he had learned abroad, as well as Latin studies and the entire wealth of Western post-Renaissance culture. In the wake of his example, Latin became an accepted subject in schools where only Greek and Old Church Slavic had previously been the recognized languages. Mohyla thus made available to Orthodox schools the theory and practice of Jesuit Latin school drama. This entire tradition could now be placed at the disposal of the Russian Orthodox Church. The result was the creation of Russian school drama, whose aim, like that of its Catholic and Protestant Western counterparts, was not entertainment or art but religious teaching and indoctrination.[10]

10. For a convincing demonstration of profound similarities between the propagandistic school drama of the German Jesuits of the sixteenth to eighteenth centuries and the equally propagandistic twentieth-century Marxist theater of

By the time it was introduced in Poland, the Latin school drama of the Jesuits had attained considerable sophistication and complexity. Based essentially on the dramatic theories and practice of the Italian Renaissance humanists, Jesuit drama also kept alive the earlier medieval dramatic genres, such as the passion play, the miracle and mystery plays, and, especially, the somewhat later genre of the morality play, with its custom of representing on the stage personifications of virtues, vices, and abstract qualities. Christian and religious in subject matter, with its plots derived from the Bible or the lives of the saints, Jesuit drama also allowed representations of characters from Greek and Roman mythology, provided they were seen as allegories.

Theory was particularly important because school plays were written to demonstrate to students how theories of drama functioned and how a play was to be written in accordance with those theories. The theoretical basis was supplied by the study of Aristotle and Horace (as understood by the humanists), by the reading of the Roman dramatists Plautus, Terence, and Seneca in the original, and by various scholastic treatises on poetics. The single most important Jesuit theoretical source for Russian school drama was the textbook *Poeticarum Institutionum libri tres*, first published in Ingolstadt in 1594 and written by the German Jesuit Jacob Spanmüller, better known under his pen name of Pontanus. In his book, widely studied and followed at the Mohyla Academy, Pontanus delineated the structure and the suitable types of characters for tragedy, comedy, and tragicomedy, the last being a comedy where high and mighty personages could be introduced, as they were in the plays of Plautus. Plot development, division into acts, methods of staging, and the function of music and dancing were all prescribed; and the prescriptions were supported by references to humanists, such as Julius Caesar Scaliger, and to Roman classics.

Russian school drama took over the tradition of Jesuit drama so comprehensively that when the prerevolutionary scholar Vladimir Rezanov decided to write the history of this genre, he

---

Bertolt Brecht and Erwin Piscator, see Manfred Brauneck, "Das frühbarocke Jesuitentheater und das politische Agitationstheater von Bertolt Brecht und Erwin Piscator," *Der Deutschunterricht* (Stuttgart) 1 (February 1969): 88–103.

found himself simultaneously writing a parallel book on Jesuit drama. His two large volumes,[11] replete with descriptions of hundreds of plays and dozens of treatises on poetics and rhetoric that he studied in the archives of Rome, Paris, Vienna, Prague, and numerous cities in Poland, the Ukraine, and Siberia, document the origins and sources of Jesuit drama and the derivation of Russian school drama from it. Unfortunately, Rezanov restricted himself to cataloguing these plays and refrained from critical interpretations. He did not write—nor has anyone since his time written—a critical study of Russian school drama dealing with the literary, historical, and linguistic problems that the arrival of this genre raises.

Initially, the plays at the Mohyla Academy were performed in Latin. But because Polish Jesuit schools performed religious drama in Polish as well as in Latin, Russian Orthodox educators decided likewise to present plays in the local vernacular. The earliest manuscript of a non-Latin Kievan drama that we have is an anonymous work called *Saint Alexis, the Man of God.* It was performed in 1673 and is written in a strange language that tries to be Ukrainian and/or Church Slavic, but despite its Cyrillic letters ends up being more Polish than anything else.

Such linguistic confusion is understandable. In the seventeenth century, Polish already possessed a secular literary tradition and a highly evolved system of versification. The Russian literary language and modern Russian versification did not take their definitive shape until the eighteenth century. Before that time, only religious literature was taken seriously in Russia, and all of it was in the official language of the Orthodox Church, an archaic South Slavic dialect called Church Slavic. Russian school drama was written by churchmen who strove to adhere to the norms of Church Slavic while at the same time trying to modernize their language so as to communicate with their audience.

11. V. I. Rezanov, *K istorii russkoi dramy. Ekskurs v oblast' teatra iezuitov* (Nezhin, 1910), and *Iz istorii russkoi dramy. Shkol'nye deistva XVII–XVIII vv. i teatr iezuitov* (Moscow, 1910). For conjectures about the methods of staging school drama at the Mohyla Academy, see Paulina Lewin, "The Staging of Plays at the Kiev Mohyla Academy in the Seventeenth and Eighteenth Centuries," *Harvard Ukrainian Studies* 5 no. 3 (1981): 320–334.

Their versification was the syllabic metrical system borrowed from Poland, a system that suits the prosody of the Polish language but sounds clumsy and cumbersome in Russian because it disregards the rhythmic and metrical possibilities of the movable Russian stress. With all these handicaps, school drama managed to attract a whole pleiad of successful practitioners by the end of the seventeenth century, poets and dramatists among whom we find three non-Russian churchmen—one Belorussian and two Ukrainians—who may be considered the earliest Russian literary playwrights.

Simeon of Polotsk

Samuil Petrovsky-Sitnianovich (1629–80) is better known in the history of Russian literature as Simeon of Polotsk, that is, by the name he took as a monk, the name of the city where he was born. Like all better-educated men of his time, he studied at the Mohyla Academy in Kiev, later continuing his studies at a Jesuit *collegium* in Poland. Upon returning to Polotsk, he established himself as a teacher at the local religious school. In 1656 he took his monastic vows. That same year, Simeon caught the eye of Tsar Alexis, who was passing through Polotsk and was greeted by Simeon and his students with a recitation of rhymed acrostics, written for the occasion. This was a new phenomenon and it was graciously received by the young tsar. The monarch remembered the learned monk and when in the early 1660s Polotsk was occupied by the Poles, Simeon made his way to Moscow, learned Russian (his native Belorussian tongue, although closely related, was by no means identical), and eventually rose to prominence at the tsar's court. Widely known and admired for his culture, Simeon served as tutor to the tsar's children and as interpreter for visiting Eastern Church dignitaries from Greece and other countries; and, at the tsar's behest, he participated in several inconclusive debates with the Old Believer leader Archpriest Avvakum ("We separated as if drunk and I was unable to eat after all the shouting," was the way Avvakum recalled his encounter with the man he ironically termed "the all-wise philosopher from Polotsk."[12]) But above all, it was as a literary figure that Simeon of Polotsk left his mark on the closing decades of the seventeenth century.

A very prolific writer, author of huge quantities of verse (much of it unreadable), Simeon of Polotsk has the uncontestable honor of being the first modern Russian poet and the first Russian literary playwright. It was he who systematized and codified Russian syllabic versification, imposing the eleven- and thirteen-syllable couplets with feminine rhymes, and with an obligatory caesura in the middle, that became standard for all later school drama. All of Russian poetry between the 1670s and 1740s is traceable to his pioneering activity. Whereas the other examples of school drama were written for performances by students in schools, the two plays Simeon wrote in the 1670s may have been intended for the court theater of Tsar Alexis.

The first of these plays is an attempt at a literary adaptation of the earlier standby, *The Furnace Play*. Bearing the unwieldy title *Of the King Nebuchadnezzar, the Golden Calf, and the Three Youths Not Burned in the Furnace (O Navkhodonosore tsare, o tele zlate i o triekh otrotsekh, v peshchi ne sozhzhenykh)*, the brief one-act play is not any kind of comedy in the accepted sense of this term, although it is introduced as one to the audience. The subject of Nebuchadnezzar and the three unburned youths had provided the basis for a play by one of the most widely admired playwrights of Neo-Latin drama, the French Jesuit Nicholas Caussin, who published his *Nabuchodonosor* in Paris in 1620. Whether Simeon was familiar with this play is not clear. His own play seems closer to *The Furnace Play* than to any foreign precedent. In addition to the three young would-be martyrs, the executioners, and the rescuing angel of the traditional Russian version, King Nebuchadnezzar himself appears on the stage and is made the central figure. The comical Chaldeans who were such a popular and admired feature of *The Furnace Play* are replaced by a chorus of grim, anti-Semitic warriors. The action proceeds along the lines of the traditional

12. Cited by I. P. Eremin in his afterword to Simeon Polotsky, *Izbrannye sochineniia*, ed. I. P. Eremin (Moscow-Leningrad, 1953), p. 226.

liturgical play; at the end, the king is so impressed by the miraculous rescue of the children that he is converted to monotheism (and, apparently, to Judaism) on the spot and invites his former victims to a party. The play begins and ends with panegyrics to Tsar Alexis, suggesting that it was intended for performance at court.

Somewhat more interesting and better known is Simeon's other play, *The Comedy-Parable of the Prodigal Son (Komidiia pritchi o bludnom syne)*. The biblical parable of the Prodigal Son was a particular favorite with Polish Jesuit playwrights.[13] The traditional story of the prodigal's travels abroad, where he is cheated and reduced to eating with the pigs, and of his penitent return to his father was usually made into an allegory of the Fall from Divine Grace and of the subsequent forgiveness. Simeon, however, preferred to give it a different treatment, also derivable from Jesuit practice: he turned the familiar biblical story into a topical commentary.

It so happened that during the reign of Alexis, a few carefully chosen nobles' sons were sent abroad to acquire a European education. As had been the case with a similar group in the reign of Boris Godunov a century earlier, most of these youths, once they had a taste of Western Europe, decided to stay abroad permanently. The results of such an action in sixteenth- and seventeenth-century Russia were comparable to what happens today when a Soviet citizen decides not to return home from a foreign tour: an outraged and embarrassed government at home and disgrace and persecution for the family left behind.

A loyal Russian of his time, Simeon of Polotsk was disturbed by what was considered treasonable behavior. His play was intended as a moral lesson to those wayward young men. It has the five-act structure favored by Horace and the Jesuit theoreticians but is tagged with a sixth act, an epilogue consisting of a moralizing soliloquy by the prodigal. The familiar story of the Prodigal Son's misadventures is developed at an extremely slow pace, with lengthy speeches and frequent moralizing digressions by various characters. The cadences of Simeon's verse, which

13. Numerous plays on this subject, both in Latin and in Polish, are cited by Rezanov, *Shkol'nye deistva*, pp. 405 ff.

seek to reproduce Polish metrical patterns based on the predictable position of the stressed syllable in that language, sound
either flabby or plodding in Russian. Compounding the stylistic
monotony are the unimaginative grammatical rhymes, consisting
to a large extent of infinitive verbal suffixes. But as this was the
earliest instance of a literary play in verse written in Russian,
Simeon's contemporaries, who had no standards for comparison,
were impressed. The couching of the familiar biblical parable
in unfamiliar theatrical terms, the superimposed topical message, and the provision in the script for interludes of singing,
music, and dancing must all have contributed to this rather
primitive play's popularity.

Considering the low level of general literacy in Simeon's
time, the printed version of *The Comedy-Parable*, published in
1685, was a major publishing success, requiring four additional
printings before the end of the century. Another edition appeared in 1795. Nineteenth-century Russian commentators
tended to regard this play as a rather clumsy affair, with a reactionary, Muscovite message, which the imminent reforms of
Peter the Great were to render meaningless. More recent Soviet
literary historians, however, have found the play's attack on
unauthorized travel abroad both patriotic and "progressive."[14]
Simeon included his two plays in the most comprehensive compilation of his poetry, *Rythmologion* (1679). Because of this inclusion and because *The Comedy-Parable* came out in all those
separate editions, his dramatic work undoubtedly was known to
and studied by all the writers of school drama who came after
him. Thus, even though he is not a very typical practitioner of
the genre, there is some justification for considering him its
founder in Russia.

St. Dimitry of Rostov

The author of the most popular, most influential, and most
widely performed Russian school plays was a Ukrainian Cossack

14. For example B. N. Aseev, *Russkii dramaticheskii teatr ot ego istokov do
kontsa. XVIII veka* (Moscow, 1977), p. 116.

whose original name was Daniil Tuptalo. Born near Kiev in 1651, he became a monk and changed his name to Dimitry at the age of 17. His literary productions include a multivolume *Calendar of Saints (Chet'i minei)*, numerous sermons regarded as exemplary by later Orthodox churchmen, and polemical works directed against the Old Believers and the Schism. In 1702, Peter the Great appointed him the Metropolitan of the city of Rostov, where he founded the Rostov Theological Seminary and where he died in 1709. A kind and saintly man, Tuptalo was canonized by the Orthodox Church in 1751 and then became known as Saint Dimitry (or Demetrius) of Rostov. As a part of his educational activities during his tenure in Rostov, he wrote six plays, of which only two have been preserved.

In the eighteenth century his most popular work for the stage was *The Sinner's Repentance (Kaiushchiisia greshnik)*, widely played at religious schools and, by mid-century, at amateur theatricals. This play retained its appeal even after French-style neoclassical Russian plays became available. Fyodor Volkov's company, the first professional acting troupe in Russia, performed it before Empress Elizabeth in 1752. The text of *The Sinner's Repentance* is lost. All we have are the recollections of this play communicated to the early nineteenth-century playwright Prince Alexander Shakhovskoy by the actor Ivan Dmitrevsky, who, as a member of Volkov's original company, performed it in Iaroslavl and St. Petersburg.

As remembered by Dmitrevsky, the play must have been an austere affair, more like a medieval miracle play than a school drama. The setting is a desert. The Sinner, in a garment covered with black patches bearing the inscriptions of his transgressions, remains at the center of the stage at all times, flanked by his Guardian Angel, a demon, and two opposed choruses of angels and of devils. Doomed to hell, the disconsolate Sinner gradually takes heart and begins to repent and to pray. As he does so, the black patches on his robe gradually fall off, revealing the immaculate white robe underneath.

This description does not provide us with the most essential criterion for imagining or judging this kind of play, for it says nothing about its verbal texture. For this we can turn to Dimitry's two surviving plays. The first of these, *The Nativity Play*,[15] offers such a typical example of Jesuit theater usages as adapted by Russian school drama and is such a seminal work for the later development of the genre that it merits a detailed description.

Chapter 2 of the Gospel According to St. Matthew, which tells of the Adoration of the Magi, of the shepherds, and of King Herod's Massacre of the Innocents, served as a subject for countless religious plays in almost every European country. Dimitry's Western predecessors in dramatizing this story range from anonymous tenth-century priests, to the creators of a version in the German medieval songbook the Carmina Burana, to Margaret, Queen of Navarre (who wrote a sequence of four plays based on the chapter), to various German and Polish learned Jesuits of the seventeenth century. Vladimir Rezanov was the first to demonstrate the formal and structural affinity of *The Nativity Play* to the Polish and Western Jesuit theater.[16] Earlier Russian scholars who wrote of this play without having done any homework on the Jesuits were likely to be baffled by what they took to be an eclectic mixture of the mystery, morality, and interlude genres.[17] All the same, Rezanov could find no play of the Jesuit repertoire that Dimitry might have used as a direct model, and he had to admit that Dimitry's play showed, within the framework of its borrowed conventions, considerable originality and freedom of treatment.

In the first scene, a female character called Human Nature, unsure what course to take after the Fall of Man, is lulled into a false sense of confidence by another allegorical lady, Deceptive

15. This play was first published in N. Tikhonravov, ed., *Russkie dramaticheskie proizvedeniia 1672–1725 godov*, vol. 1 (St. Petersburg, 1874). In that publication it bears the title *Rozhdestvenskaia drama* (*Christmas Drama*) at the beginning, but the sections that follow the antiprologue and the prologue are preceded by the additional title *Komediia na den' Rozhdestva Khristova* (*Comedy for Christmas Day*). Since Russian sources refer to this play under both titles, leading to some confusion, I have chosen to follow the example of D. S. Mirsky's *A History of Russian Literature* (New York, 1960), which translates the title by its traditional English cognate, *Nativity Play*.

The two extant plays by St. Dimitry have been reprinted in *Ranniaia russkaia dramaturgiia XVII–pervaia polovina XVIII v.*, ed. Olga Derzhavina et al., vol. 2 (Moscow, 1972).

16. *Shkolnye deistva*, pp. 94–114.

17. For example, A. Veselovsky, *Starinnyi teatr v Evrope* (Moscow, 1870).

Hope. The Golden Age, Peace (bearing an olive branch), Love, Meekness, Kindness, and Joy (strumming on a harp) all lend credence to Deceptive Hope's assurances that humanity's blissful state will endure forever. But Human Nature makes the mistake of letting in Reason, who immediately opens the door to the Iron Age (who subjugates the Golden Age with his iron bullets), then to Strife (who sinks her sword into the olive branch), Hatred (baring her fangs at Love), Rage, Anger, Weeping, and Envy. The members of this new group assure Human Nature that they shall henceforth follow her wherever she may go.

A new character, Prologue, appears at this point and announces that the coming play will be about King Herod and the Massacre of the Innocents. Heaven and Earth, Life and Death, and, finally, God's Mercy all enter the action. They assure Human Nature that the advent of a Savior is both possible and necessary. But this outcome is opposed by Envy (the Invidia of Neo-Latin plays), an ally of Lucifer. Envy transforms herself into Medusa and calls upon Vulcan and a chorus of singing and hammering Cyclopes[18] to forge the weapons for the coming Massacre of the Innocents in order to prevent Christ from accomplishing his mission.[19] The "Anvil Chorus" of the Cyclopes is written in amphibrachic meter, something that was supposedly not introduced into Russian literature for another four decades. (Russian amphibrach is a three-syllable meter with the stress falling on the second syllable. It is similar to the meter of Anglo-American limericks: "There WAS a / young MAN from / Nan-TUCK-et," and so on.)

The sequence of abstract antiprologues and prologues is followed by a long pastoral interlude. Three unmistakably Ukrainian shepherds named Boris, Avram, and Afonia are directed by angels to go to Bethlehem and adore the infant Christ. This episode was quite justly admired by all the nineteenth-century commentators who wrote about it. There is a fine dif-

18. The representation of Cyclopes as blacksmiths was a regular feature of Jesuit plays.

19. This conceit anticipates, at some distance, Paul Claudel's similar one in his *Le livre de Christophe Colomb* (Paris, 1933), where the Mexican gods call on their colleagues in ancient Greece to join them in destroying the expedition of Columbus in order to prevent him from making America a Christian continent.

ferentiation in character between the crotchety old Avram, the practical-minded, sedate Boris, and the naive, but observant adolescent Afonia. There is also a gentle, appealing humor in the shepherd's supper scene (they have only bread and vodka) and in their matter-of-fact inquiry as to whether the King of Kings would, like their local prince, refuse to receive them without a suitable bribe. Above all, the gradual transformation of simple-minded, wisecracking shepherds into ecstatic worshippers is handled with remarkable style and conviction. The language of this interlude, a relaxed South Russian vernacular, is unique in the drama of the period. It contrasts most favorably with the synthetic stylistic archaism of most other school plays.

After the three extended scenes of the shepherds, the main action of the play is still not ready to begin, for there is an additional short interlude. Still another allegorical character, Astrological Inquisitiveness, a polite, puzzled investigator, visits the tomb of the diviner Balaam and conjures up his ghost in order to find out the significance of the new star, the Star of Bethlehem, not indicated on astrological charts. His fact-finding mission accomplished, Inquisitiveness returns the ghost to its tomb and bustles off to prepare the three Kings of the Orient for their expedition.

The play is almost half over when the principal character, King Herod, finally appears on the stage. He is shown surrounded by a fawning court and is entertained by a chorus invoking Apollo and the muses. A messenger appears, asking for safe conduct for the three Magi and speaking broken Russian, distorted in a manner that makes it sound suspiciously like Chinese but is probably intended to convey a German accent.[20] On the basis of this announcement and after consulting his senators and rabbis, Herod concludes that the Infant Jesus is a pretender to the throne of Judea. He tries to trick the Magi into leading him to his supposed rival. Failing that, he orders a massacre to take place in Bethlehem and is immediately punished by having his flesh disintegrate.

20. English mystery plays of the Christmas cycle traditionally featured a herald who carried messages between Herod and the Magi and spoke with a heavy foreign accent, usually French.

After his physician and his court flee in terror, Herod listens to long, moralizing speeches by Innocence and Vengeance, falls through a trap door, and is last seen in Hell, fettered for eternity. Herod's mournful soliloquy, punctuated by the mocking rhyming responses of an offstage echo, is said by Rezanov to represent a particularly favored device of Jesuit playwrights. The play concludes with a set of brief epilogues. Life and Death return to contend once more for Human Nature, who now, after the birth of Christ, sides with Life. God's Strength recites a soliloquy, gloating over her victory over Lucifer and reviling Herod. Finally, the character Epilogue wishes the audience a Merry Christmas, thanks it for its "affectionate attention," and apologizes for any possible shortcomings in the performance.

In the nineteenth century it was thought that *The Nativity Play* was the only surviving drama by St. Dimitry. Some of his biographers did not consider the attribution to him of even this play sufficiently proven. But in 1907 the literary scholar Mikhail Speransky discovered Dimitry's autograph of another dramatic work, *The Dormition Play* (*Uspenskaya drama*), in the library of the Moscow Synod Printery. Because this manuscript, apparently an early unedited draft of the play, is in Dimitry's own hand and matches the descriptions of this play in early-eighteenth-century sources, its attribution to Dimitry can be considered certain. The numerous similarities in language, style, and poetic method between this play and *The Nativity Play* further serve to dispel any doubts about Dimitry's authorship. In addition, the second half of *The Dormition Play* offers some interesting parallels and correspondences to *The Sinner's Repentance*, as described by Dmitrevsky.

The two surviving plays are, however, also dissimilar in many important aspects. *The Nativity Play* was clearly patterned after the Jesuit dramas; it is somewhat top-heavy in its structure, with the prologues and allegorical scenes taking up almost one half of its length. Yet, in comparison with the other play, it is far more dynamic and dramatic. *The Dormition Play*, on the other hand, has a balanced and elegant structure. Its first half owes very little to the Jesuit tradition and, though its individual scenes are not devoid of dramatic interest, its overall effect is

static. The subject is the announcement of the death and dormition of the Virgin Mary. There did exist a few medieval mystery
plays on this theme, but even the thorough Rezanov could find
no immediate predecessor in Neo-Latin drama for this play.

In the first part of the play, scenes of mortals' encounters
with angels and lamentations for the Virgin's demise alternate
with a group of scenes in which disbelieving characters are told
of her death and dormition. The resultant structure can be
compared to the musical form of double variations, wherein
two related themes are alternately varied (e.g., the Andante of
Beethoven's Fifth Symphony). The first scene, which also serves
as a prologue, tells the story of Jacob's dream of the ladder. It is
written with a verve and charm quite unprecedented in Russian school drama. The young Jacob, enthusiastic and excited
because his father has sent him to marry his cousin Rachel, has
lost his way during his journey. He rushes onstage, bursting
with eagerness, introduces himself to the audience, takes it into
his confidence, and asks for directions to Mesopotamia:

Таковаго есмь рода, простѣте, хвалюся:
Не вам, но да Рахи красной полюблюся.
Не вѣсте ли моего пути, гряду камо?
В Междорѣчие иду, Лаван живет тамо,
Брат матере моея, а в него дщи чиста:
Та ми возлюбися, та будет ми невѣста.

. . . .

Гряду убо в ту страну: кто вѣсть путь скажите,
Хощете ли ис нами на свадбу пойдѣте,
Прошу—рад буду, и Лаван вас приймет,
Яко приятелей своих любезне обиймет.
Но уже от долгого пути утрудихся.[21]

Such is my origin, forgive me for bragging:
It's not for you I brag, but so that lovely Rachel may love me.

21. *Chteniia v Imperatorskom obshchestve istorii i drevnostei rossiiskikh
pri Moskovskom universitete* (Moscow, 1907), vol. 3, p. 1, of the second pagination.
Transcription of this passage into new orthography has to retain the letter ѣ,
because in Russian poetry and drama of St. Dimitry's time it was pronounced as и,
Ukrainian fashion. The text printed in *Ranniaia russkaia dramaturgiia* (see note
15, above) replaces it with *e*, which wrecks the author's rhymes. Moreover, the
last of the cited lines is missing in that edition (vol. 2, p. 73).

You don't happen to know the way to where I'm going,
do you?
I'm headed for Mesopotamia; Laban lives there,
My mother's brother, and he has a chaste daughter.
She is the one I love; she shall be my bride.

. . . .

So I am headed for that country; if anyone knows the way,
tell me.
Would you like to come along to our wedding?
Oh, I beg you, I'll be so happy and Laban will welcome you!
He will embrace you lovingly like his own friends.
But I'm exhausted from my long journey.

The tired Jacob goes to sleep and dreams of angels bearing
the orbs of heaven and earth. To the promises of plentiful
progeny mentioned in the Book of Genesis the angels add some
Apocryphal material, explaining the significance of the ladder
in the dream as a symbol for the Virgin Mary, who is a descendant of Jacob, and her role as an intermediary between man
and God. In subsequent scenes, Tidings (a female character,
whose gender, like that of the other allegorical characters, is
determined by the gender of the noun denoting the quality it
represents) announces the death of the Virgin to a disbelieving
and grief-stricken hermit in the desert; an allegorical figure
of Lament mourns the Virgin's passing and is consoled by another allegorical youth, appropriately named Consolation; and
the Apostle Thomas displays his inveterate skepticism by expressing doubts about the physical fact of the dormition during
a conversation with Faith, Hope, and Charity, and is reassured
by two angels who offer him all the proof he might wish. The
emotional center of the first part of the play is the speech made
by the Date Palm Branch (sent by Christ to His Mother as a
token of their forthcoming reunion in Heaven). Since the Virgin
does not appear on stage in this play, the Branch quotes her
prayer to be reunited with her Son and her recollections of Christ
when He was an infant. The tenderness and sheer lyrical power
of this prayer again raise *The Dormition Play* far above the
usually primitive literary level of Russian school drama.
The second part of *The Dormition Play* is a demonstration

of the Virgin's role as a ladder between man and God. It is also, as mentioned, a variation of the theme treated by Dimitry in *The Sinner's Repentance*. The Sinner is about to face divine judgment. His lawyer is his Conscience, which begs him, at first in vain, to ask for the Virgin's intercession. Divine Wrath is about to smite him, when his Conscience invokes the Virgin. Presently, another allegorical figure, Clemency of the Mother of God, speaks up on the Sinner's behalf.

At the ensuing trial of the Sinner, there is a curious combination of theology and an almost parodistic reconstruction of various legal procedures. Conscience and Clemency are the defenders, with some assistance from Hope. Divine Wrath and Judgment are the prosecutors. Truth appears as an impartial arbitrator to whom both sides may appeal. But even after the Sinner is temporarily incarcerated to give the defense additional time, no new evidence is offered. As he is about to be consigned to the flames, a prayer from the Virgin Mary to Christ on his behalf is submitted to the court (as a highly original added touch, this prayer is in prose). The evidence is reexamined, and the Sinner is reprieved from Hell and handed over to his Guardian Angel. The play ends with an apotheosis of the Virgin, in which Temporal Power recognizes her supremacy and she (presumably, her icon) is offered various emblems and symbols that are associated with her in the Christian tradition.

The study of his two extant plays easily convinces one that St. Dimitry of Rostov was the single most gifted and interesting playwright of the Russian religious tradition. Alone among the writers of that school, he possessed a genuine poetic talent. He used the pageantry and the conventions inherited from Jesuit dramatists more effectively and imaginatively than his successors. He was capable of dramatic invention and of such novel touches as writing the Virgin's prayer in prose, devising a strange foreign accent for the envoy, and representing the Massacre of the Innocents in a pantomime: "inaudibly, but visibly." He did some interesting experiments with line lengths and meters. Above all, he had a remarkable way of humanizing his characters, not only real people such as Jacob, Herod, the Apostle

Thomas, and the shepherds, but the abstract, allegorical figures as well.

Human Nature's exchanges with Life and Death in *The Nativity Play*, for example, are conducted in a tone that suggests an impoverished noblewoman trying to choose one of two powerful princesses as a suitable protectress. Conscience in *The Dormition Play* speaks in the frantic accents of a woman whose son or brother has landed in jail and who is desperately trying to reason with the sullen delinquent. Other examples could easily be found. Dimitry's use of language is also special. Although expectedly archaic and replete with Polonisms, it is close to the South Russian vernacular of his day, and his diction, at its best, has a gentle and seemingly artless directness that makes one think of a Giotto painting.

Russians of the eighteenth and nineteenth centuries honored Dimitry as a revered saint and an important religious poet. But his plays were rarely mentioned. He was admired by Gogol. He was venerated by Wilhelm Küchelbecker, who did a verse adaptation of one of Dimitry's moral parables and addressed a moving poem to him. It is doubtful, however, that either Gogol or Küchelbecker was familiar with Dimitry's plays, available in their day only in manuscript. At the end of the nineteenth century, Dimitry's biographer, Ivan Shliapkin, denied his authorship of *The Nativity Play* and, in fact, did not believe that he wrote any plays.[22] In postrevolutionary times, Dimitry's posthumous canonization made his writings a risky topic for scholars and editors. The plays of the two other principal practitioners of school drama, Simeon of Polotsk and Feofan Prokopovich, were made available in the 1950s and 1960s, respectively, in fine critical editions, prepared by Igor Eremin.[23] Dimitry, however, remained unpublished and, usually, unmentioned until 1972, when his two surviving plays were included in volume 2 of the collection *Ranniaia russkaia dramaturgiia* (*Early Russian Plays*).

22. I. A. Shliapkin, *Sv. Dimitrii Rostovskii i ego vremia* (St. Petersburg, 1891).
23. Polotsky, *Izbrannye sochineniia*; Feofan Prokopovich, *Sochineniia*, ed. I. P. Eremin (Moscow-Leningrad, 1961). For a good account of Feofan's ideas and writings in English, see James Cracraft, "Feofan Prokopovich," in *The Eighteenth Century in Russia*, ed. J. B. Garrard (Oxford, 1973), pp. 75–105.

On the basis of this publication, the Moscow Chamber Musical Theater recently produced an abridged modern version of Dimitry's *The Nativity Play*, the first time it was performed since the early eighteenth century. Renamed *The Rostov Play* (*Rostovskoe deistvo*) for the occasion, the production was prepared and staged by the noted Soviet opera director Boris Pokrovsky, with the assistance of some of the most important literary and musical experts in the Soviet Union. Much of the text was set to reconstructed music by various Russian church composers of Dimitry's time. Premiered on June 30, 1982, *The Rostov Play* proved to be one of the greatest successes in recent Russian theatrical history. At this writing, tickets to the play and copies of the recording of its music are among the hardest items to obtain in Moscow and command astronomical resale prices.

Feofan Prokopovich

The third important writer of school drama was Feofan (or Theophanus) Prokopovich, the Archbishop of Novgorod (1681–1733). Born in the Ukraine, he had an unusual life. After graduating from the Mohyla Academy, he continued his studies in Rome, where he acquired a broad humanist education and outlook and was converted to Roman Catholicism. Feofan read Greek, Latin, and Polish literature in the original and was one of the very few Russians of his time who could talk and write of Spinoza and Descartes. He eventually relapsed into Orthodoxy, returned to Russia, became a personal friend and protégé of Peter the Great, and rose to great heights in the church hierarchy. Much of Feofan's energy and many of his sermons were devoted to championing Peter's reforms, especially his secularization of the Orthodox Church structure, bringing it under greater control by the central government.

Feofan's tireless polemics against Peter's opponents made him some formidable enemies among Russian churchmen. But his powerful position protected him from their frequent denunciations and verbal attacks. He remained a figure of political importance during the reigns of Peter's widow, Catherine I, and of his niece, Empress Anna. In 1730, Feofan was instrumental in influencing Anna to repudiate and tear up a kind of Magna Carta that she had previously signed at the insistence of a group of nobles who wished to limit the absolute autocracy of Russian monarchs. Between his political, ecclesiastic, and polemical activities, Feofan also found time to write some of the more attractive Russian poetry of the first three decades of the eighteenth century.

In 1705 Feofan served as a visiting professor in Kiev at the Mohyla Academy. He taught a course on literary theory in Latin (his lecture notes for that course, a freely abridged paraphrase of Pontanus's text, were subsequently published under the title *De arte poetica* and for a while became the standard textbook in many Russian schools). He wrote his only dramatic work, the tragicomedy *Vladimir* (the complete title is five lines long) as part of his professorial duties, for a performance by his students during the summer recess. In addition to its intended pedagogical uses, the play was very much an extension of Feofan's political and religious polemics.

A carefully organized piece of theater, *Vladimir* tells of the conversion of Russia to Christianity. In both its structure and its location of action, the play outlines the progression of the Russian national soul from Hell to Heaven by way of wisdom and philosophy in accordance with the five-act scheme shown in Figure 1.

FIGURE 1

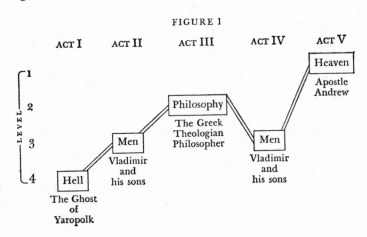

25

The play begins with a long soliloquy by the Ghost of Iaropolk, whom his brother, Prince Vladimir, had murdered in order to get possession of the Kievan throne. Iaropolk has left his abode in Hell at Satan's bidding, outraged at the injustice of his situation. The brother who murdered him is about to convert the country to Christianity and thus is sure to become a saint, while Iaropolk, his victim, will continue to burn for eternity. The Ghost appears to the pagan high priest and advises him on measures to prevent Vladimir from making the final decision. In Act II, three scheming and greedy pagan priests whose descriptive, neologistic names can be rendered into English as Oxenmuncher, Chickeneater, and Drinkhard, set about executing Iaropolk's design. They conjure the Demons of the World, of Slander, and of the Flesh and let them all loose on Prince Vladimir to distract him from thoughts of religion. Then they breathe life into their idols, who dance a ballet to the accompaniment of the priests' singing.

In Act III, Vladimir is discussing his plans with his sons Boris and Gleb (historically not even born at the time of the action), who, mindful of their future roles as venerated Orthodox saints, urge him to open his heart to Christian teachings. The center of this act and, indeed, of the entire play is the debate between the pagan priest Oxenmuncher and the Christian Greek Philosopher, sent by the Byzantine emperor to explain the Christian doctrine. At this point, Feofan deliberately introduced current, eighteenth-century issues into the tenth-century setting of the play. The ignorant pagan priest, who stands for Peter's opponents, is concerned only with maintaining his own privileges and with food. The Greek Philosopher, quoting liberally from the sermons of Feofan Prokopovich, speaks for the kind of secularized Orthodoxy that Peter was trying to bring about.

In Act IV, Vladimir and his sons make their decision for Christianity, but the act ends in uncertainty, for there appears a vision of Seduction (the only female character in the play), who in a singing chorus urges Vladimir not to give up his harem and the pleasures of the flesh. In the final act, the chicken- and beef-eating priests lament the inevitable and mourn the passing of their gods. Two officers sent by Vladimir smash the idols, the Heavens open up, and the Apostle Andrew appears with a host of angels.[24] The Apostle Andrew then recites the future history of Russia and predicts victory over the Turks and the Swedes, to be won by Peter the Great and his loyal and valiant supporter, the Ukrainian hetman Ivan Mazepa. The play was originally dedicated to Mazepa, and he was present at its first performance in Kiev. The dedication was removed after Mazepa betrayed Peter a short time later and went over to Charles XII of Sweden.

The structure and the unities of Feofan's play were classical, as this term was understood in Renaissance drama. He ignored the poetics of French neoclassical drama, which had by his time become the norm in most of Europe and which as a man of wide travels he must have encountered. He preferred to pattern his play after Seneca and the Jesuit playwrights. The similarity of Iaropolk's long soliloquy to the soliloquy of Tantalus in Seneca's *Thyestes* has been frequently noted.[25] Rezanov also found some parallels between *Vladimir* and the Latin plays by the English Jesuit Joseph Simon, which were frequently performed in Italy during Feofan's sojourn there. Although all school drama was didactic and preachy by definition, Feofan, realizing that the most effective propaganda is simplistic, reduced his polemics to the level of a political poster, anticipating in a way the similarly propagandistic use of drama in the twentieth century by a far greater poet, Vladimir Mayakovsky, in his *Mystery Bouffe*.

The contest between the Christian Philosopher and the pagan priests is also, obviously, the contest between Feofan and his adversaries. Lined up on the one side we have God, Heaven,

24. This part of the play was based on the officially fostered legend, found in Russian historical chronicles of the Muscovite period, about the Apostle Andrew coming to Novgorod and preaching there. The aim of this legend was to assert the existence of an earlier Russian Christian tradition, independent of Byzantium. Of course, no such thing as a Russian language and nationality existed in biblical times. To have preached in Novgorod, the Apostle Andrew would have had to come there at least 700 years before that city was founded.

25. The impact of Seneca on Feofan and on other playwrights of Russian and Ukrainian school drama has been studied by Wolfgang Busch, "Die slavische Literaturen," sec. 2, in *Der Einfluss Senecas auf das europäische Drama,* ed. Eckard Lefèvre (Darmstadt, 1978), pp. 451 ff.

St. Vladimir, Peter the Great, the Apostle Andrew, philosophy, and enlightenment. Opposed to them are Hell, paganism, the temptations of the flesh, Sweden, Turkey, and the conservative elements among the Orthodox clergy (whom the pagan priests actually quote). In this respect, Feofan can be contrasted with St. Dimitry of Rostov, whose even most negative characters, such as Envy-Medusa, are given a modicum of human dimension and a chance to state their side of the question.

Nevertheless, the structure of Feofan's play, with its deliberate progression from darkness to light, has considerable style. He was by no means devoid of poetic talent. Some of his play's vivid baroque imagery is exuberant and impressive. It is the play's language that is its most vulnerable component. A quarter of a century later, in the poems he wrote in St. Petersburg in 1730–33, Feofan attained a far greater refinement and fluency of language. His *Vladimir*, however, was written in such a particularly cumbersome blend of Ukrainian and Church Slavic that the text of the play inevitably sounds better in any translation than it does in the original. Here is the invocation of Oxenmuncher, aroused by Iaropolk's soliloquy, first in a verbatim prose translation, then as Feofan wrote it:

I can't bear to hear it, I must have revenge! Help me, O gods! If my songs have power and are effective, let them go to unknown places, to woods, to caves, to rivers, to abysses, to tombs, into the deep bowels of Mother Earth. I shall move the dead, I shall gather the spirits of hell, air, and water, and call together various beasts; hideous serpents will come, reptiles, dragons, boa constrictors, scorpions, vipers; I shall drag the sun down from the heavens, extinguish the planets, transform day into night, and my strength shall be made manifest.

Не могу се слишати, но отмстити мушу!
   О бози, помозѣте! Аще мои пѣсны
Силни сут и могут что, да пройдут в безвѣстны
   мѣста, в дебри, в пещеры, в рѣки, в бездны, в гробы,
В глубокия великой матеры утробы.
   Подвигну мертвых, адских, воздушних и водних

Соберу духов, к тому звѣрей многородных
созову купно, прийдут змии страховидни,
Гади, смоки, полозы, скорпии, ехидны;
совлеку солнце з неба, помрачу светила,
День в нощь претворю: явѣ будет моя сила.

Later School Drama

With the proliferation of religious seminaries and other
institutions of higher learning during the rule of Peter the Great
(reigned 1682–1725) and of his immediate successors, school
drama gradually spread to most of the big cities of European
Russia and Siberia. Dramatic works in this form continued to be
written and performed until about 1750.[26] But none of these
later plays was ever to match St. Dimitry's two surviving plays
for poetic flair or Feofan's *Vladimir* for structural sophistication.
In Kiev, Feofan's successor to the chair of literature at the Mohyla Academy, Lavrenty (or Lawrence) Horka (1671–1727), followed Feofan's example by writing and producing a play to
illustrate *his* lecture course on poetics. Performed in 1708, Horka's *Joseph the Patriarch* (*Iosif patriarkha*) is couched in language and imagery that betray the influence of Feofan's *Vladimir*. The situation between the young Joseph and Potiphar's
wife is handled by Horka in a manner that suggests his acquaintance with plays about Phaedra and Hippolytus by either
Euripides or Racine. In particular, the exchanges between Potiphar's wife and her two allegorical *confidantes*, Conscience and
Seduction (the latter is provided with a *confidante* of her own,
the Friend of Seduction), bear a remote resemblance to the dialogues between Phèdre and Oenone in Racine's play.

26. Manuscripts of Russian school drama were studied and published in
various scholarly journals at the end of the nineteenth and the beginning of the
twentieth century by Ivan Shliapkin, Peter Morozov, Mikhail Speransky, and
others. A good prerevolutionary source is the two-volume collection of early plays
edited by Tikhonravov, *Russkie dramaticheskie proizvedeniia*. Recent editions
are *Pamiatniki russkoi shkol'noi dramy XVIII veka*, ed. Iosip Badalich and Vera
Kuzmina (Moscow, 1968), and vols. 2 (1972), 3 (1973), and 4 (1975) of *Ranniaia
russkaia dramaturgiia*, which contain the texts of most of the plays discussed in
this chapter.

In his later career, Horka served as the Archbishop of Astrakhan in eastern Russia, where he initiated performances of school dramas at the local divinity school. The surviving scripts of school dramas written in Kiev after the second decade of the eighteenth century by Mitrofan Dovgalevsky, Sylvester Liaskoronsky, and other Ukrainian churchmen add little new luster to the genre.

The productions of St. Dimitry's plays at his religious school in Rostov during the first decade of the eighteenth century alternated with those of school plays written by his students—for example, A [Martyr's] Crown for Demetrius (Venets Dimitriiu). Premiered in Rostov in 1704, this play dramatized the account of the martyrdom of St. Demetrius of Salonika as it was told in the Calendar of Saints by St. Dimitry. Scenes from the life of the historical saint are interspersed in the play with debates between allegorical characters, such as Polytheism versus Christianity, or with lyrical dialogues between Faith, Hope, and Charity. In the eighteenth and nineteenth centuries, this play was attributed to St. Dimitry, even though its literary level is considerably below that of his known writings and its text contained a eulogy addressed to him. The author is now assumed to have been Dimitry's disciple Ievfimy (or Euphemius) Morogin.

In Moscow the Slavic-Greek-Latin Academy, founded in 1687, began performing elaborate school dramas in 1701. Initially, these were rather grim, apocalyptic affairs, with titles like The Terrifying Change of Voluptuary Life into Dire and Indigent (1701), The Fearful Depiction of the Second Coming (1702), and God's Humiliation of Proud Scoffers (1710). Written in clumsy language, with a large admixture of Ukrainianisms (most of the teachers at the Moscow Academy were Ukrainians, trained at the Mohyla Academy in Kiev), these plays mingled biblical characters (Lazarus and the rich man, the prophet Daniel) with Latin allegories (Sapientia, Fortuna, Mars) and sought to compel the spectators to observe their fasts and in general to stay on the straight and narrow Christian path by showing them scenes wherein famine, death, and apocalyptic beasts punish those who stray.

To the religious themes of traditional school drama, the

Moscow cycle began adding secular themes: panegyrics to Peter the Great and his policies, assertions of Russian patriotism, and topical allusions to Russia's victories over Sweden or Poland during the Great Northern War of the early eighteenth century. Thus an ostensibly religious play about the Exodus of the Israelites from Egypt, *The Liberation of Livonia and the St. Petersburg Province (Svobozhdenie Livonii i Ingermanlandii,* 1704), of which only a detailed synopsis survives, turns out on closer inspection to be a rather transparent political allegory of Peter the Great's reign. Russia's new-found military might enjoys in this play the support of the usual school drama abstractions such as Fortuna, the Golden Age, and Hope; of Roman deities such as Jupiter, Phoebus, and Mars; and interestingly enough, of the science of astrology. In the astrological subplot, a group of stargazers are shown interacting with personified stars and zodiacal signs: Aquila, Ariadne's Crown, Virgo, and Sagittarius.

In the 1720s the school drama performances at the Slavic-Greek-Latin Academy met strong and unexpected competition from the Moscow School of Surgery. Organized and headed by the Dutch surgeon Dr. Nikolaas Bidloo, who was a learned amateur of music and the theater, the School of Surgery instituted dramatic performances, possibly to lure the students into studying medicine. We do know that between 1719 and 1722 Dr. Bidloo was instrumental in arranging the transfer of at least a hundred students from the Slavic-Greek-Latin Academy to his own school, so that the academy was obliged to complain to the ecclesiastic authorities and ask them to stop his recruiting. In addition to having its own theater, the School of Surgery had its own playwright, Fyodor Zhurovsky (dates not known), the author of one and, possibly, two allegorical plays written for that theater.

The texts of the plays attributed to Zhurovsky survived because of the importance of the occasions for which they were written and on which they were performed. The one attributed with certainty, called *Fama Rossiae* in Latin and *Slava Rossiiskaia (Glory of Russia)* in Russian, was staged in 1724 to celebrate the coronation of Catherine I, the wife of Peter the Great.

The other play, *Slava pechal'naia* (*Funereal Glory*), whose attribution to Zhurovsky is in some dispute, commemorated the funeral of Peter one year later. Both are examples of school drama fully divorced from its original religious themes and aims in that they put the allegorical framework of the genre in the service of secular (in this case, political) purposes. In *Fama Rossiae*, written in a macaronic mixture of Russian and Latin, the protagonist is a personified Russia who secures the help of Neptune (i.e., Peter's fleet building), Mars (his military might), and Pallas (the newly imported sciences) to defeat her adversaries Sweden, Poland, Turkey, and Persia. Other characters in the play, besides the allegorical Olympians and personified countries, are Piety, Truth, Victory, Envy, and Flora.

As we move closer to the mid-eighteenth century, we see secularized school drama appear even in religious seminaries. A good example is the allegorical play *Stephanotokos* (Greek for "deserving a crown"), performed at the divinity school in Novgorod in 1742 on the occasion of a visit there by the Empress Elizabeth. Populated entirely by abstract characters, such as Fatherland, Prosperity, and Conscience, the play is an allegorical account of how Elizabeth, the daughter of Peter the Great, was bypassed in the succession to the Russian throne in favor of her cousins but eventually became monarch. Situated in the middle of the play, several digressive scenes based on the Book of Esther are all that connect *Stephanotokos* with the biblical and Christian essence of earlier school drama.

In addition to school drama proper, there existed in the early eighteenth century brief religious plays in verse performed by amateurs (e.g., at the private theater of Tsar Peter's sister Natalia) that were either based on various episodes of St. Dimitry's *Calendar of Saints*, such as *The Comedy of St. Catherine* and *The Comedy of Chrysanth and Daria*, or, following the example of *The Comedy-Parable of the Prodigal Son*, dramatized other biblical parables, as was the case with *The Play of the Ten Virgins, Five Wise and Five Foolish* (*Deistvo o desiati devakh, o piati mudrykh i o piati iurodivykh*). These were usually clumsy, often semiliterate affairs, without either the style of the best school drama or the charm of the plays of chivalric adventure (see Chapter 2), both of which they occasionally resembled in language and structure.

Beginning with Simeon of Polotsk, writers of school drama often made provisions for comical or choreographic interludes between the acts of their plays. These interludes were either left to the improvisation of the performers or written out. Toward the middle of the eighteenth century, they turned more and more satirical. In an allegorical play performed at the religious seminary in Tver in 1745 in honor of the Empress Elizabeth (*Deklamatsiia ko dniu rozhdeniia*, i.e., *Birthday Recitation*), the satirical barbs are aimed at Old Believers (whose movement was gathering new momentum in the eighteenth century), Jews (Elizabeth was quite outspoken in her detestation of them), and Gypsies. In the Jewish interlude, a grotesque Jew, who intersperses his lamentations with exclamations in Yiddish, gathers an international army of dancing Jews in order to liberate Jerusalem from the Turks. In the ensuing ballet, this dancing Jewish army is scattered by a single Russian policeman wielding a club. Other school drama interludes dating from the 1740s poked fun at bribe-taking officials and at ignorant village priests who refused to let their children learn Latin.

Russian school drama should provide future scholars with a rewarding field of study. Its influence on both the oral folk plays (especially those about King Herod that date from the eighteenth century) and the dramatizations of chivalric tales, such as *Peter of the Golden Keys* (described in Chapter 2), still needs to be elucidated. The popularity of school drama in the first half of the eighteenth century prepared both the language and the audience for the French-based neoclassical drama that succeeded it. If we remember that the two best-known practitioners of French neoclassicism in drama, Pierre Corneille and Molière, were brought up on Latin school drama by their Jesuit teachers, we can better understand the transition that the originators of Russian neoclassicism, Mikhail Lomonosov and Vasily Trediakovsky, both educated at the Slavic-Greek-Latin Academy, made from school drama to the poetics created by their French predecessors.

❧❧II❧❧

Beginnings
of Secular Drama:
Court Theater and
Chivalric Romance Plays

The reigns of Tsar Fyodor Ioannovich (1584–98) and of Boris Godunov (1598–1605) saw a lively exchange of envoys and diplomatic correspondence between Russia and England. Russian envoys aroused much curiosity in London, which was apparently what led Shakespeare to make his Hermione in *The Winter's Tale* the daughter of the Emperor of Russia. Yet none of those Russian visitors showed any awareness of the remarkable theater that Elizabethan London had to offer. Other Russian travelers to European capitals did report their encounters with theater. Thus, Avraamy, the Bishop of Suzdal, attended a church council in 1437–39 in Florence, where he witnessed a miracle play about the Annunciation. Mid-seventeenth century diplomats described attending a play in Warsaw about Judith and what seems to have been an opera on a mythological theme in Florence. In 1668 the Russian ambassador to Paris was taken to see a performance by Molière's company and was then invited backstage to meet Molière himself.[1]

What is striking in these accounts is that they all concen-

1. P. O. Morozov, *Ocherki po istorii russkoi dramy XVII i XVIII stoletii* (St. Petersburg, 1888), pp. 24 ff.

trate on the external elements: settings, stage machinery, the looks of the performers, or the importance of the occasion that the performance celebrated. Nowhere in them can be found an awareness of the script, of the play as a verbal or literary construct. Peter Morozov, who in his pioneering history of early Russian theater compiled a list of such accounts,[2] likened these observers to a dull-witted peasant of his own time, the 1880s, who was by some chance taken to a performance of an Italian opera in St. Petersburg and was both baffled and bored.

The frequent written (and surely oral) reports of the theatrical marvels in the West that Tsar Alexis kept receiving during the 1650s and 1660s must have aroused his curiosity. One of the milder and more humane of the Romanovs, Alexis was passionately interested in falconry and church choir singing, and he caused important treatises on both to be published. As a young man, he was hostile to theater and to other forms of entertainment. At the wedding of his father, Tsar Michael, entertainment was supplied by the *skomorokhi* and balalaika players. But the young Alexis banned the *skomorokhi* and all musical instruments and even prohibited *The Furnace Play* rite in the churches. At the time of his first marriage in 1648, the singing of religious hymns was the only diversion allowed at the wedding.

But in the course of the religious schism (*raskol*) of the second half of the seventeenth century, Alexis had to struggle against both the Old Believers, led by the Archpriest Avvakum, and the author of the reforms against which the Old Believers objected, the Patriarch Nikon. Both the Avvakum and the Nikon factions were essentially conservative and xenophobic. Having them for adversaries rendered Alexis more flexible and more tolerant of new ideas. After his first wife died, a sort of beauty contest was held among the daughters of the higher nobility in order to find a new bride for the tsar. The young woman selected, Natalia Naryshkina, was an orphan, raised as the ward of Artemon Matveyev, the head of the foreign office and one of the most broadly educated and Westernized Russians of his day.

2. Ibid.

35

Of lower class origin (he was the son of a scribe), Matveyev rose to great eminence through his intelligence and diplomatic skills. He was married to a Scotswoman, née Hamilton. Their home contained a library with books in various languages, which made their neighbors suspect that Matveyev was a sorcerer. His diplomatic post put Matveyev and his entire household in daily contact with foreigners. The new tsarina, who grew up in Matveyev's home, was therefore free of the panicky fear and mistrust that were then the typical Russian response to foreign customs and ideas. Natalia's love of entertainment, the literary activities of the tsar's protégé Simeon of Polotsk, and the newly instituted productions of school drama at the Kievan Academy must all have contributed to the decision of Tsar Alexis to organize his own theater.

The ensuing story has been told many times.[3] It begins with the search in Germany for importable theatrical talent. Colonel Nicholas von Staden, who was dispatched for that purpose, was unable to accomplish his mission. Comedians and opera singers, who had initially agreed to come and perform in Moscow, changed their minds. They had heard stories of foreign artisans being denied exit permits or being flogged when they insisted on getting the agreed fee. While negotiations still dragged on, Natalia gave birth to a son, the future Peter the Great. To celebrate the event, the tsar commanded a private theater to be constructed. As no Russian plays or actors were available, Matveyev directed the tsar's attention to the German quarter of Moscow (*Nemetskaia sloboda*), a special ghetto populated by the families of German, English, Danish, and other foreign merchants, soldiers, and artisans.

3. The two most comprehensive and thorough accounts of the origins of the Russian seventeenth-century court theater are I. M. Kudriavtsev's introductory essay to *Artakserksovo deistvo* (Moscow, 1959); and Kurt Günther, "Neue deutsche Quellen zum ersten russischen Theater," *Zeitschrift für Slawistik* (Berlin) 8(5) (1963): 664–75. Willi Flemming's "Deutsches Barockdrama als Beginn des Moskauer Hoftheaters 1672)," *Maske und Kothurn* (Graz-Köln) 4(2/3) (1958): 97–124, is very good on German connections and sources, but full of mistakes whenever it deals with Russian background or names. Flemming's mistakes and misspellings are repeated *verbatim* in Heinz Kindermann's monumental *Theatergeschichte Europas* (Salzburg, 1959), vol. 3, pp. 621 ff.

The Comedy of Artaxerxes

On June 4, 1672, Johann Gottfried Gregori, the cultivated and well-traveled pastor of the Lutheran church in Moscow and an amateur poet, received a written royal order. He was commanded to compose and stage a comedy based on the Book of Esther in the Bible and to take charge of all the preparations for the production, including the construction of the theater. No expense was spared. Surviving receipts and accounts testify to lavish purchases of fabrics, furs, feathers, jewelry, and gold plate for the sets and costumes. The best foreign painters, decorators, and tailors available in Russia were engaged for the project and given large staffs of assistants. A pipe organ was purchased from a foreign resident at an astronomical price and then wrecked by inept transportation. The organist of the Lutheran church was put in charge of a small orchestra composed of whatever instrumentalists were available in Moscow. They were to provide fanfares and other incidental music.

On October 17, 1672, *The Comedy of Artaxerxes (Artakserksovo deistvo)*, written by Pastor Gregori, with some possible assistance from the schoolmaster Lorenz Rinhuber, and rendered into Russian by Artemon Matveyev's translators at the foreign office, was performed for the first time. It was not a part of a religious ceremony or of school instruction. It was simply a play put on for pleasure and entertainment. The idea of drama as drama had finally arrived.

The play was in seven acts of several scenes each, not to mention songs, choruses, a prologue, and lengthy quotations from the Psalms in Hebrew. Apparently there were also improvised comic interludes between the acts. The cast required sixty-four persons. At its premiere, the play took ten hours to perform. According to the testimony of Rinhuber, who also functioned as the production's director, the tsar was so enchanted that he never once got up during the entire ten hours.[4] To show

4. Laurent Rinhuber, *Relation de voyage en Russie fait en 1684* (Berlin 1883), p. 29.

37

his appreciation, he richly rewarded many of the participants. In an entirely unprecedented gesture that shocked his Russian subjects, Alexis later gave a reception for the entire cast and technical staff, all of them foreigners.

Two long-standing misconceptions about *The Comedy of Artaxerxes*, frequently encountered in references, are both traceable to Peter Morozov's 1888 book on Russian drama. One is that all the performers were children.[5] The records do refer to them as "children of foreigners" or as *otroki*, which is the Russian word for either "boys" or "youths." But Paul Berner, who played Esther (all women's parts were taken by males), was a goldsmith, the speaker of the prologue was seventeen or eighteen years old, and several of the other players received commissions as lieutenants in the tsar's army a year or two later.[6] All this indicates that the performers were senior students or recent graduates of the German school in Moscow, that is, young adults between the ages of fifteen and twenty. Nor were they all German. Some of them had names like Goosens, Carr, and Ridder, indicating Dutch or Scottish nationality.[7]

Another persistent misconception was that the text of Pastor Gregori's play was a reworking or adaptation of a drama about Esther and Ahasuerus from the collection *Engelische Comoedien und Tragoedien* published in Germany in 1620. Morozov made this assumption on the basis of contemporary descriptions of Gregori's play, whose text had supposedly been lost, and it was believed by everyone until the middle of the present century. Then, in one of those improbable coincidences that can make literary studies genuinely exciting, two copies of *The Comedy of Artaxerxes* were discovered almost simultaneously in 1954, one in a library in Lyons, France, and the other in a library in Vologda, USSR. Still later, in 1968, a copy of the second act of the play was found at the National Library of Thuringia in Weimar, East

5. Morozov, *Ocherki po istorii russkoi dramy*, p. 148, states: "uchastvovali deti i nemtsy"; that is, "it was performed by children and Germans."

6. See Kudriavtsev, *Artakserksovo deistvo*, and Günther, "Neue deutsche Quellen."

7. Erik Amburger, "Die Mitwirkenden bei der Moskauer Aufführung des 'Artaxerxes' am 17. Oktober 1672," *Zeitschrift für slawische Philologie* (Heidelberg) 25 (1956):304–9.

Germany. The Lyons and Weimar manuscripts contained not only the Russian translations but also the German text.[8] The availability of the original German text has now shown the other surviving plays of the seventeenth-century Russian court theater in a new light and invalidated many assumptions of earlier commentators.

When Tsar Alexis specified that the play that was to open his new theater was to be based on the Book of Esther, he meant this as a compliment to his young wife. Like the biblical Esther, Natalia was an orphan raised by a wise male relative and selected, from a large number of competitors, to be queen for her beauty and virtue. Alexis was not likely to have known that of all the episodes in the Bible, the story of Esther lends itself most readily to dramatic treatment or that it had provided subject matter for every imaginable sort of play in the West since the Middle Ages. Adaptations of the Esther story for the stage continued long after the Moscow version of the 1670s. In France, almost two decades after Gregori's play, there was Racine's *Esther* (1689), written for performance by the pupils at the elegant school for young girls, the Saint-Cyr (it betrays some vestigial connections to school drama by beginning with a prologue spoken by a personified Piety, who alludes to her dear friend and companion, Innocence). In Russia there were later two anonymous plays dating from the first half of the eighteenth century, *The Play of Esther*, a canonical school drama wherein Faith, Virtue, and Malice were shown interacting with Esther, Mordecai, and Haman; and the more secular *Comedy of Queen Esther in Which Are Shown Hatred and Other Things*, which, despite a few allegorical characters that appear at the end, is closer in treatment and format to the chivalric romance plays.[9]

8. The Lyons copy was published by André Mazon and Frédéric Cocron as *La comédie d'Artaxerxes* (Paris, 1954), the Vologda copy by Kudriavtsev (see note 3, above), and the Weimar fragment by Kurt Günther, "Das Weimarer Bruchstück des ersten russischen Dramas 'Artaxerxovo dejstvo' 1672," in *Studien zur Geschichte der russischen Literatur des 18. Jahrhunderts*, ed. Helmut Grasshoff et al. (Berlin, 1968).

9. *Deistvie ob Esfiri* and *Komediia o Esfire tsaritse, v neizhe pokazuet o nenavisti i o protchem* in *Ranniaia russkaia dramaturgiia*, vol. 4: *P'esy stolichnykh i provintsial'nykh teatrov pervoi poloviny XVIII v.*, ed. Olga Derzhavina et al. (Moscow, 1975).

The German text of Gregori's play demonstrates that it was neither a school drama nor an imitation of English-style German comedies of the early seventeenth century. For all its cumbersome length, it shows a good sense of dramatic values. Its language is expressive and has considerable style (Gregori had published some German poetry before receiving the tsar's commission for a play). An expert on German baroque drama has found points of comparison between Gregori's play and the works of the finest baroque playwrights of that time, such as Andreas Gryphius and Joost van den Vondel.[10] Gregori followed the biblical story with considerable fidelity, but he also knew when to develop a seemingly insignificant episode for his dramatic purposes. He was particularly good at providing plausible psychological motivation when it was lacking in his biblical source.

Thus, in the Book of Esther, Queen Vashti refuses to attend her husband's feast when summoned, and no reason for her refusal is specified (1:12). Gregori's Vashti refuses because, anachronistic though it may sound, she has a strong case of what is now called feminist consciousness. She finds it demeaning to have to display her beauty in front of a group of drunken men she does not know. She is abetted in her resolution by her friend and adviser Naomi, who asserts that women should be given the same rights as men and that some women might even be superior to men. In this way, the panicky reaction of the king and his cronies in the Bible and their rapid passing of new laws to control the behavior of women make perfect sense: they are averting a brewing feminist revolt. But within the mores of pre-Petrine Russia, where upper-class women were still cloistered and where the tsarina, for whose pleasure and in whose honor the play was written and staged, had to watch its performance through a slit in a curtain at the back of the theater, the sentiments expressed by Gregori's Vashti and Naomi must have sounded like insanity.

Nor does the Vashti theme disappear in the play with her disgrace and banishment in the middle of the second act. Greg-

10. Flemming, "Deutsches Barockdrama." Blake Lee Spahr, an expert on German baroque drama, found significant textual parallels between Gregori's play and *Leo Armenius* (1650) by Andreas Gryphius (verbal communication).

ori ingeniously connects with her the two disgruntled chamberlains, Bigthan and Teresh, who in his source in the Bible (2:21–23) seek to murder the king for no known reason and are exposed by Esther's guardian, Mordecai. In some of the most effective scenes of his play, Gregori shows these two conspirators as partisans of Vashti, who was earlier their benefactress. Their plotting is motivated by their desire to reinstate her to her former position or, failing that, to kill the king to avenge Vashti's disgrace.

The theme of female dependence and independence, sounded in the early scenes, continues later on in the play. The gentle and docile Esther, ostensibly Vashti's opposite, has to disobey the king's orders if she is to save her people from extermination. Breaking the law, and fainting from fear as she does so, Esther barges into the king's presence without being summoned so as to invite him to the banquet at which she will reveal Haman's genocidal plans. Like other dramatic adaptations of the Book of Esther, Gregori's play dispenses with the public hanging of Haman's children and the massacre of their adversaries with which the Jews, in true Old Testament fashion, celebrated their deliverance.

As the detailed analysis of Ivan Kudriavtsev shows, Gregori drew not only on the Book of Esther for his sources, but also on the writings of Josephus Flavius, the fables of Aesop, and the Psalms, the last incorporated in the text both in translation and in verbatim transcriptions of the Hebrew originals.[11] Gregori's verse—cross-rhymed iambic lines of varying length rather than the usual Alexandrine lines customary for German playwrights of his time—is fluent and sonorous. But none of these virtues and subtleties could possibly have been perceived by the play's Russian audience because it was performed in a translation prepared by people who had no notion of literary style. They rendered the text into the only written Russian idiom they knew, an archaic mix of Church Slavic and the legalese language of official treaties. The result was not only clumsy, but often incomprehensible and unpronounceable.

Here, for example, is a bit of Vashti's dialogue with Naomi

11. Kudriavtsev, *Artakserksovo deistvo.*

41

from the first act in Gregori's original German, followed by the English translation.

VASHTI

Was aber soll dann nun ich endlich sagen?
So irret denn die weiseste Natur,
wie oder soll ich über Unrecht klagen!
Und dass es sei der Welt Gewohnheit nur,
dass Männer allezeit den Vorzug müßen haben,
da wir doch sind von 1000 schönen Gaben,
fürwahr, es ist nicht recht!

NAEMI

Was recht! O Königinne?
Man ruffe die Natur doch selbst zu Zeugin an,
man überleg' es nur mit ungefälschtem Sinne!
Was ist es, dass vor uns sich doch wohl rühmen kann
das männliche Geschlecht?

VASHTI

But what can one finally say?
Should the all-wise Nature herself be in error,
how can I complain of injustice?
For this is merely the habit of the world,
at all times to give preference to men,
whereas we are blessed with 1,000 fine gifts:
truly, this is not right!

NAOMI

What do you mean, right, O Queen?
Let one call Nature herself to witness,
let one ponder this with unclouded reason!
Why should the male sex be glorified above ours?

And here are the plodding couplets in which these lines were recited before Tsar Alexis:

АСТИНЬ

Что ж аз о сем мышлю, хощу же прелагати,
мню, истинно аз мню натуре изменяти.
Что же имам для того признати в том повинна?
Обыклость ли мира, наричю аз, причинна,

42

яко же мужей род нас выпше хощет быти,
идеже мы жены краснейпе украшенны.
Сие же есть неправда.

Наеми

Неправда есть явленна!
Да призовет же ся натура обращенна,
и всячески о сем в сердцах да разсуждают.
И что есть паче нас, иже вси суть восхваляют,
мужей ли убо род?

Much has been written in the Soviet Union about the ideological significance of Gregori's play and of the impression its theme and message produced. But if we consider that the Russian translation, almost incomprehensible to begin with, was recited with heavy foreign accents by young Germans, Dutchmen, and Scots, some of whom had resided in Moscow for two years or less, it becomes doubtful that the text had anything to do with the success of the play. Gregori stayed close enough to the Book of Esther to enable his Russian audience, who knew their Bible thoroughly, to follow the action with ease even if the play were played in German (which some earlier scholars had assumed to be the case). It must have been the lavish costumes and sets, the acting, the music, and the clowning during the comic interludes that so enchanted Alexis and made him such an avid theatergoer during the few years he had left to live.

The premiere of *The Comedy of Artaxerxes* was witnessed only by the tsar and his family. Later performances of this and other plays were attended by the higher nobles of the realm who were ordered to do so.[12] These guests were expected to stand on the two sides of the stage throughout the performance, for it

12. This practice of compelling their subordinates to attend theatrical performances whether they wanted to or not was later continued by Alexis's son Peter and granddaughter Elizabeth; the latter's passion for neoclassical tragedies exacted a great toll of boredom from her courtiers, forced to sit through tragedies on several consecutive days. The last such instance was in the 1830s, when Nicholas I ordered all the high officials of his government to see Gogol's *Inspector General*. After the reforms of Alexander II in the 1860s, Russian monarchs no longer had the power to compel anyone to attend something, nor would the idea have occurred to them.

was considered disrespectful to sit in the tsar's presence. When these nobles were understandably disinclined to come, royal couriers were sent to bring them to the theater.

For later productions of his theater, Alexis ordered Russian actors to be trained. Sons of scribes and clerks were placed in a special school where Gregori and his associates taught them the theatrical arts. It somehow never occurred to anyone to provide these young men with a stipend, so that in a few months they addressed to the tsar a desperate petition saying that in their starving and freezing state they could not study acting. The astonished tsar resolved to give them a daily stipend of four kopecks each, which economic historians tell us was adequate at that period.[13]

For the next three years more plays on biblical subjects were supplied by Gregori and his group and regularly performed for the tsar and his court at two small theaters, one at his summer residence outside of Moscow and the other in his palace in the Kremlin, upstairs from the pharmacy. The episodes these plays dramatized were the favorite ones for centuries in both the sacred and the secular drama in the West: *Judith, The Pitiful Comedy of Adam and Eve*, and *The Small Refreshing Comedy of Joseph.* Unlike *The Comedy of Artaxerxes*, they were in prose. The play about Judith is similar in format and treatment to the one about Esther, except that the comic element is not restricted to the interludes but is incorporated into the main action. Two of the principal characters in this play are clowns: a cowardly soldier and a wisecracking maid, who provide burlesqued commentary on the heroic doings depicted in the play. This was an element typical of English-type German plays of the early seventeenth century.

Only the Russian texts of these works survive. The style and language of these texts are similar to those of the Russian version of *The Comedy of Artaxerxes*, with many Germanisms, such as the use of German-style auxiliary verbs, which are redundant in Russian. There is little doubt that the originals were written by Germans and translated by Matveyev's employees at

13. For details about the apprentice actors' petition and its text, see S. K. Bogoiavlensky, *Moskovskii teatr pri tsariakh Aleksee i Petre* (Moscow, 1914), p. 26, and N. S. Tikhonravov, *Sochineniia* (Moscow, 1898), vol. 2, 73.

the foreign office. There were also plays on nonbiblical subjects, such as *The Comedy of Tamerlane* (*Temir-Aksakovo deistvo*) ascribed to Georg Hübner, the teacher of Russian at the German school, who later settled permanently in Russia and called himself Iury Mikhailov. With its language even more heavily Germanized than usual, this play may have been written by Hübner directly in Russian. Morozov and other earlier scholars thought this play to be an adaptation of Christopher Marlowe's *Tamburlaine the Great*, but recent scholarship has shown them to have been wrong.[14]

Other nonbiblical works, somewhat unexpected within the Muscovite cultural atmosphere, were also performed before Tsar Alexis. One such was a ballet with singing, *Orpheus*, which featured two dancing pyramids brought into motion by the power of Orpheus's song. The music for this production was apparently by Heinrich Schütz, the first instance of a work by a noted Western composer performed before a Russian audience. Another intriguing production, *The Comedy of Bacchus and Venus*, is known only through the list of costumes and props it required. Accounts show that costumes were created for four bears, ten drunkards, and a brothelmaster who had two outsized pasteboard heads and ten horns.[15] The court theater came to an end early in 1676, when Tsar Alexis and Pastor Gregori died within a month of each other. The immediate heir of Alexis, his elder son Fyodor, had both of the theaters closed and dismantled.

Theater Under Peter the Great

The theatrical experiment of Tsar Alexis, interesting as it was historically, remained little more than a private whim of the monarch. His subjects either did not know of the performances or regarded them with sullen hostility. The surviving plays,

14. A. T. Parfenov, "K voprosu o pervoistochnikakh 'Temir-Aksakova deistva,'" *Vestnik Moskovskogo gosudarstvennogo universiteta. Seriia 10, Filologiia,* no. 2 (1969):16–30, shows that the play was based on Jean du Bec's *Histoire du Grand Empereur Tamerlanes,* first published in Paris in 1564 and reissued in 1607.

15. Bogoiavlensky, *Moskovskii teatr,* p. xv.

written for Alexis by Germans in German and then translated into Russian, are not a part of the Russian literary tradition, and it is therefore puzzling why they were included in the collection called *Early Russian Plays* (*Ranniaia russkaia dramaturgiia*) or why *The Comedy of Artaxerxes* is occasionally called "the first Russian play."[16]

The next step for secular drama in Russia came during the Westernizing reforms of Peter the Great. Determined to bring his backward subjects into the modern world by brute force if necessary, this monarch did not hesitate to use, as Lenin aptly put it, "barbarous methods in his battle against barbarity." It was on Peter's orders that a cycle of patriotic school dramas was mounted at the Slavic-Greek-Latin Academy in Moscow. But Peter also realized that secular theaters open to the general public were a part of cultural life in civilized Western countries. So, in 1701, while away at war, he issued a set of orders to have a public theater built in Moscow's Red Square, facing the Kremlin.

The project encountered several kinds of sabotage from his unwilling subordinates, who were particularly shocked by the location of the foreign abomination right in the ancient center of Russian culture.[17] But Peter knew how to break opposition. Within a year his theater was ready, complete with elaborate sets and stage machinery. A provincial German theatrical company headed by an actor named Johann Christian Kunst was imported from Danzig and began to give performances in German. Once again some hapless young Russian clerks were appointed actors and handed over to Kunst for dramatic training. Plays were performed twice a week, and after the first few months most of the performances were in Russian. Access to the theater was not restricted to any particular group. Anyone presentably dressed was welcome. To encourage attendance, the Kremlin gates were kept open especially late on performance nights. Theatergoers were excused from the city gate toll and

16. For example, see the title of Kurt Günther's publication of the Weimar text in note 8, above.

17. See P. O. Morozov, "Russkii teatr pri Petre velikom," *Ezhegodnik imperatorskikh teatrov; Prilozhenia* (St. Petersburg, 1894), vol. 1, p. 55.

from the lantern tax, levied for walking around after dark. Admission to all performances was free.

The venture was the most unmitigated disaster in the history of Russian theater. Performances were well attended only when Peter and his court were expected to be present, and on such occasions the audience would come to see their monarch, not the play. At all other times the theater designed to seat 450 spectators had an average audience of 25. With all the encouragement and subsidies Peter lavished on it, his theater lacked three basic and mutually dependent ingredients essential for any theatrical undertaking: there were no Russian plays, no suitable literary language into which foreign plays could be translated, and hence no interested audience. The plays that Johann Kunst (who died soon after the theater opened) and his successor, Otto Fürst, presented were adaptations of current successes in Germany and Holland.

It was a curious grab bag of cultures and playwrights. *Prince Pickled Herring, or Jodelet, Himself His Own Prisoner*,[18] was taken from a Dutch adaptation of a German version of Thomas Corneille's *Jodelet prince, ou Le geôlier de soi-même* (Jodelet was a well-known comedian of Molière's time for whom the French version of the play was created), but the ultimate source of this play was Calderón's comedy *El Alcaide de si mismo. The Honest Traitor, or Friderico von Papley and Aloysia, His Wife* came from a German adaptation of an Italian play, *Il tradimento per l'honore* by Giacinto Andrea Cicognini, first performed in Bologna in 1668. German drama was represented by the seventeenth-century baroque playwrights Andreas Gryphius (his *Aemilius Paulus Papinianus*) and Daniel Casper von Lohenstein, whose *Sophonisbe* became *Scipio Africanus, Leader of the Romans* in its Russian guise. There were also a few other translated plays in the company's repertoire whose foreign originals have not been identified.

---

18. A poster announcing the performance of this play in Vienna in 1697 by a visiting theatrical company from Saxony (as *Sein selbst eigner Kerker-Meister, oder Der närrische Jodelet und Prinz Pickelhäring*, with no author cited) is reproduced in Margarete Baur-Heinhold, *The Baroque Theatre* (New York and Toronto, 1967), p. 99 (originally published in German as *Theater des Barock*).

Molière was probably the most admired and widely imitated playwright in Europe at the beginning of the eighteenth century. No acting company with pretense to quality, Peter felt, could do without Molière. The Kunst–Fürst group performed his *Le médecin malgré lui* as *Komediia o doktore bitom* (*The Comedy of the Doctor Drubbed*). In the files of the theater and among the papers of Peter the Great, two other Russian versions of Molière were found that date from the Kunst–Fürst period: *Amphitryon* (translated as *The Origin of Hercules, Wherein the Principal Person Is Jupiter*) and *Les précieuses ridicules*. The latter, still untranslatable into either English or Russian with total precision, was rendered all but incomprehensibly as *Dragyia smeianyia*, which means something like "dear ones laughed at."

Whether the plays were translated from the German or, as was the case with Molière, directly from the French, did not much matter. They were all rendered into Russian chancery language, the same hybrid of archaic biblical style and equally archaic legalese into which Pastor Gregori's plays had been translated three decades earlier. The only difference was that in the reign of Peter, many unassimilated foreign words invaded the official language, hampering understanding still further. The partial translation of *Les précieuses ridicules*, published by Tikhonravov,[19] is a good illustration of how unsuitable the written Russian of the time was for any imaginative literature. Molière's comedy satirizes the pretensions of provincial gentry who ape emotional and intellectual fashions they do not quite understand. Not only were there no ways of conveying the notions of pretensions, affectation, flirting, or *préciosité* in Russian, but the concepts themselves had no counterparts in anyone's experience. The translation reads like the collaboration of a monk, who tried to bring Molière's text as close to the language of the Old Testament as possible, and a legal clerk, who sought to reduce it to a lawyer's brief.

Given such scripts, neither the German actors who performed the plays at first nor the Russian ones whom the Germans eventually trained could possibly hold the attention of the

19. In N. Tikhonravov, ed., *Russkie dramaticheskie proizvedeniia 1672–1725 godov*, vol. 2 (St. Petersburg, 1874).

audience, regardless of the quality of the play or of the acting. After four years of failure and general apathy, Peter gave up the idea of a theater open to the public. In 1706, the Kunst–Fürst company in Moscow was disbanded. Its sets, costumes, and scripts were turned over to Peter's younger sister, Princess Natalia, who used them to organize her own private theater at her manor near Moscow. She succeeded, on a much smaller scale, where her father and brother had failed. She took a closer interest in the problem of repertoire than they did. Her theater (which was open to the local public, a policy that was continued when it was moved to St. Petersburg after the new capital was built there) offered religious and school dramas, but it also inaugurated an interesting minor genre that deserves more attention than it has gotten from literary historians. It is at Natalia's private theater that we find the earliest examples of dramatic adaptations of translated foreign tales of love and adventure, which became the most popular form of secular drama in Russia during the first half of the eighteenth century.

Chivalric Romance Plays

The chivalric romances that originated in France and Italy in the twelfth and thirteenth centuries went on inspiring poets, novelists, and dramatists for many centuries to come. On the highest level of literature, these romances provided story lines and characters for such figures as Ariosto, Cervantes, and Shakespeare (in his romance plays, such as *The Winter's Tale* and *Pericles*). On the middle literary level, they evolved in the sixteenth through eighteenth centuries into the interminable courtly adventure novels by such forgettable writers as La Calprenede in France, Duke Anton Ulrich, the author of *Aramena*, in Germany, and Fyodor Emin (ca. 1735–70) in Russia. And on the low-brow level, medieval romances had a new surge of life with the invention of printing, reemerging as inexpensive chapbooks intended for mass consumption. It was in this form of cheaply printed semiliterate fiction that medieval romances reached Russia during the last quarter of the seventeenth century, usually in translations from other Slavic languages, such as Polish, Czech, or Croatian.[20]

Some of these stories, familiar for centuries in Western Europe, came to be widely circulated in Slavic countries, including Russia. Such was the case with the tales about Tristan and Isolde, about Melusine, and about Apollo (or Apollonius) of Tyre. A few retained their popularity long after they were forgotten in their countries of origin. The Carolingian romance of Buovo d'Antona, known in Russian as Bovà Korolevich (it was once current in England as "Bevis of Hampton"), and the Burgundian one of Pierre de Provence ("Peter of the Golden Keys" in Russia) entered Russian national folklore and remained a part of it until the twentieth century. Alexei Remizov, one of this century's most influential and innovative Russian prose stylists, wrote during his old age, when he was slowly going blind in Paris in the 1950s, several highly idiosyncratic narratives based on russified chivalric tales: "Tristan and Isolde," "Buovo d'Antona," "Melusine," "Brunswick," and "Apollo of Tyre."

By about 1710, with the continuing popularity of chivalric romance chapbooks, there appeared dramatic adaptations of some of these stories, written by anonymous authors and intended for performances by amateurs. Productions of school drama at religious academies and the existence of the court theaters of Tsar Alexis (from 1672 until his death in 1676) and his daughter Natalia (from 1707 until her death in 1716) stimulated interest in amateur theatricals among various social groups. These ranged from the private theater of Peter's daughter, the future Empress Elizabeth, to performances by the palace grooms and stable boys, as recorded by the earliest chronicler of the eighteenth-century theater in Russia, Jacob von Stählin.[21] Between about 1710 and 1750, these amateur groups spread from the two capitals to the provinces, culminating in the organization of

20. A thorough study of this phenomenon is Vera Kuzmina's *Rytsarskii roman na Rusi* (*Bovà, Petr Zlatykh Kliuchei*) (Moscow, 1964). See also in Josef Matl, *Europa und die Slaven* (Wiesbaden, 1964), the sections "Ritterromane" and "Romantische Liebesgeschichten" of chapter 2 ("Die internationalen Wander- und Erzählstoffe bei den Slaven"), pp. 103–11.

21. Jakob von Stählin. "Zur Geschichte des Theaters in Russland," in *J. J. Haigolds Beylagen zum Neuveränderten Russland* (Riga and Mittau, 1769), p. 399.

Fyodor Volkov's company in Iaroslavl in 1750, which is traditionally regarded as the beginning of professional theater in Russia.

As for repertoire, the best-documented amateur group is the court theater of Princess Natalia. It offered, as mentioned, some religious plays and it had in its files the translations of German plays written back in the 1670s for her father's theater. Princess Natalia herself was also said to have been an amateur playwright, though no play has been attributed to her with certainty.[22] But what is most interesting about Princess Natalia's theater is that its repertoire included such plays as *The Comedy of Peter of the Golden Keys* (i.e., the dramatization of the romance of Pierre de Provence), *The Comedy of the Italian Marquis and of the Boundless Obedience of his Marchioness* (based on the story of the patient Griselda, possibly derived from Boccaccio's *Decameron*), and *The Comedy of the Beautiful Melusine* (the wandering romance going back to Jean d'Arras, about a woman condemned to be periodically transformed into a serpent). The texts of the chivalric romance plays performed by Natalia's company have not been preserved. We know them through a folder of some separate roles that belonged to one of the actors. But a number of other complete scripts of plays of this type did come down to us. A few were published in various prerevolutionary historical and literary journals (usually designated as "an unknown play of Petrine times"). Since the 1950s, a number of these plays have been included in anthologies of early Russian drama published in the Soviet Union.

22. A slip of the pen in Stählin's account (ibid., pp. 397–98) credits Natalia's much older half-sister, Sophia (the regent during Peter the Great's childhood and later an opponent of his reforms), with having her own theater, writing plays, and even translating Molière into Russian. This version, entirely at odds with Sophia's character and views, was repeated uncritically by various eighteenth- and nineteenth-century commentators. Thoroughly debunked by Morozov in his 1888 book (see note 1, above), the legend of Sophia as a playwright and theater buff is still occasionally encountered—for example, in the catalogue of the Bibliothèque Nationale in Paris, where Pastor Gregori's *Judith* is listed as written by Princess Sophia Alexeyevna, and in Marc Slonim's *Russian Theater: From the Empire to the Soviets* (New York, 1961), p. 19, where we read that after her father's death, "Sophia wrote plays and acted with a group of amateurs from her own court."

Identifying the plays of the chivalric romance provenance is somewhat complicated because their authors were wont to use for their titles any of the three words used in Russian at the end of the seventeenth and beginning of the eighteenth century to designate any kind of play: *deistvo* or, more rarely, *deistvie* (literally "action" and corresponding to the German use of the Latin word *actio* during the same period and in the same meaning); *akt* (also meaning "action," but borrowed from the Polish or German); and *komediia* (literally "comedy," but applied at the time to any kind of play). In the past, dramatizations of chivalric romances have been included in collections of oral folk drama[23] and school drama.[24] The series *Ranniaia russkaia dramaturgiia*, which contains the most comprehensive selection of these plays, whose text has unfortunately been lost, and *The Comaters in the Capitals and the Provinces in the First Half of the Eighteenth Century* and volume 5 (*Plays of Amateur Theaters*).[25]

The literary sources of these plays are diverse. *The Play of Prince Peter of the Golden Keys and the Beautiful Magilena, Daughter of the King of Naples* goes all the way back to the romance of Pierre de Provence and Maguelonne, the Princess of Naples, and it adheres to the plot of the romance with great fidelity. *Eudon and Bertha*, the most widely performed of these plays but whose text has unfortunately been lost, and *The Comedy of Indrik and Melenda* are reworkings of more recent imitation romances that have come down in prose fiction form from surviving chapbooks. The source of the latter play is a translation from the Polish of a romance called "The History of the Mighty Knight Henryk, Prince of Saxony and the Most Gracious Melénda, Daughter of Ludwig, the Prince of Brandenburg."

Two of these plays have recognizable sources in seventeenth-

23. *Komediia o Indrike i Melende*, in *Russkaia narodnaia drama XVII–XX vekov*, ed. P. N. Berkov (Moscow, 1953).

24. *Akt o Petre Zlatykh Kliuchei* was published in *Pamiatniki russkoi shkol'noi dramy XVIII veka*, ed. Iosip Badalich and Vera Kuzmina (Moscow, 1968).

25. Volume 4 of *Ranniaia russkaia dramaturgiia XVII–pervaia polovina XVIII v.*, ed. Olga Derzhavina et al. (Moscow, 1975), reprints the text cited in note 24 above and includes *Komediia o grafe Farsone*. All the other plays discussed in this section are in volume 5 (1976) of the series.

century novels of gallant adventure. *The Spanish Comedy of Hypolite and Julia* dramatizes *Histoire d'Hypolite, Comte du Duglas* by Marie Catherine, Comtesse d'Aulnoy, published in Paris in 1690 (the novel was set in England, with "Duglas" meant to be Douglas; the Russian adapter moved it to Spain as apparently a more suitable locale for a romance). The mammoth *The Comic Play of Caleander, Prince of Greece, and the Courageous Neonilda, Daughter of the King of Trebizond* (1731), a combination of dramatized romance and an allegorical school drama, comes from a German adaptation of an Italian seventeenth-century novel, *Il Calloandro fedele* by Giovanni Ambrogio Marini.

Yet, for all the diversity of their sources, these plays all follow certain thematic and structural patterns that go back to medieval romances. They are all about thwarted romantic love— a theme unknown in pre-Petrine Russian culture and up to that point unprecedented in Russian drama. The protagonists are foreign royalty who live in the Age of Chivalry. The heroine is usually a princess who is somewhat higher on the social ladder than her lover. The hero is a knight-errant, traveling through the countries of Europe and the Near East in search of love and tournaments. Jousts and duels, also unknown in earlier Russian culture, are shown as a form of advanced and civilized behavior. This knightly code of honor is assumed to be operative in all the countries, European or Eastern, through which the protagonists may move.

The plot invariably hinges on the separation of the two lovers or on other obstacles to their union. In some of the plays these obstacles are the result of the misdeeds of the lovers' parents. In such cases the action of the play may cover two generations, with the younger generation settling, through their final marriage, whatever problems their parents had caused by their earlier actions. Caleander's father was once betrothed to Neonilda's mother but broke his troth, and the resultant enmity prevents the two predestined lovers from finding their way to each other until numerous adventures and hardships succeed in uniting them. The father of Hypolite raised Julia, the daughter of his friend, as his own child, and the two lovers, believing themselves to be incestuously in love, are on the verge of taking monastic vows when a lucky accident reveals to them that they are not related. The father of Indrik prevents him from marrying Melenda and through perfidy separates them for many years. The resultant plot pattern is thus not unlike the one found in Shakespeare's romance-derived plays, such as *Pericles* and *The Winter's Tale.*

Another plot formula familiar from the traditions of Western dramatic literature is the strategem of the heroine disguising herself as a male or as a nun, after which her lover or relatives fail to recognize her. Told of the loved one's supposed betrayal or death, the hero or, more often, the heroine, launches into an extended lament, at times in the form of an aria, the music for which is supplied in at least one of these plays, *Peter of the Golden Keys.* No unities of time or place are observed in these plays. The action may extend all the way from the time the parents of the protagonist first meet to the time of his or her old age and death.

The two works that show the genre of Russian chivalric play at its most typical and attractive are *Indrik and Melenda* (dating from the second or third decade of the eighteenth century) and *Peter of the Golden Keys* (the second dramatization of this romance dating from about the 1730s, not to be confused with the earlier treatment, done for the theater of Princess Natalia and now lost except for a copy of one minor role). The action of *Indrik and Melenda* moves through the Danish, Swedish, Saxon, and Austro-Hungarian royal courts (with a few scenes laid in Rome for good measure) and over a period of some thirty years. It tells the story of the separation and reunion of a Danish princess and a Saxon prince, betrothed at birth and kept apart through the machinations of the hero's misguided father, who has been talked into lusting after his son's bride by an evil councillor. When the lovers are reunited despite all of his intrigues, the villain-father dies of grief and at the end of the play is lamented by his dutiful and forgiving son.

The play is written in syllabic verse of varying line lengths, both rhymed and unrhymed, with occasional use of free assonance rhymes of the kind encountered in Russian folk songs.

There is one allegorical character, Lamentation, who appears dressed in mourning and recites a brief soliloquy at the time of the lovers' initial separation. A translated passage from the *Aeneid* serves as one of the hero's speeches, which would suggest that the author was a divinity student, for Latin classics were at the time assiduously studied in religious schools.

The plot of *Peter of the Golden Keys* shows its well-born hero traveling to foreign parts and winning the love of a princess—the daughter of the king of Naples. Some of the developments of the story evoke the fairy-tale world rather than that of chivalric romance. Thus, when the lovers have to flee from Naples, they become separated when Peter pursues in a boat a raven that had stolen some of his loved one's jewelry (the bird was a sparrow hawk, *épervier*, in the French original of the romance). But most of the time in this play we are in the world of chivalry, a rather simple-minded one, to be sure, with its tournaments depicted approvingly in terms of continuous, mindless slaughter and an occasional Arthurian echo, such as naming a minor character Lantsylont (i.e., Lancelot). There is a brief, rather rococo allegorical prologue, in which Cupid and Venus confront and defeat Envy.

The anonymous poet-playwright responsible for this version of *Peter of the Golden Keys* must have been one of the more gifted and accomplished Russian dramatists of his time. He used the old syllabic versification at a time when the more literate poets were introducing the new syllabotonic one (see page 62), and yet he managed to write with greater fluency and assurance than most of his contemporaries. His diction and vocabulary are typical of the immediate post-Petrine age, when numerous recently introduced terms had not yet been assimilated enough to sound familiar and often had a jarring ring. The habit of using the plural form of the second person personal pronoun as a polite form of addressing a single individual had not yet taken hold fully, so that we find characters addressing each other as *ty* and *vy* within the same sentence, which no literate person would do in the second half of the eighteenth century. Indicative of the stylistic confusion of the age is the designation of the lady-in-waiting of the Princess of Naples alternately as *devka* (contextually, a "serving wench") and *dama* (a recently introduced term for "lady"). Here is an exchange between Princess Maguelonne, smitten by Peter of Provence, and her disapproving nurse:

Магилена

Поди в скорости, ищи того ковалера,
    которой вчерась здесь был, где его квартера,
Спроси его имя, спроси о фамилии,
    он мне в моем сердце так показался милы,
Что ни днем, ни нощию покоя не знаю,
    Когда про него вспомню, сердцем умираю.

Мамка

Ах, что, государыня, мыслите такое?
    Напрасно вы здравие тратите златое.
Ей, недостойно чести сие сотворили,
    что иностранново таво полюбили.
Знайте, что вы дочь честна королевска,
    как можешь любовница быти кавалерска?
Не могу я истинно сей ваш приказ зделать,
    чтоб про кавалера итти и проведать.

(По сем королевна упадает на постеле замертва.)

MAGUELONNE

Go in haste, search for that knight
    who was here yesterday; where is his dwelling?
Ask him his name, ask about his family.
    In my heart he seemed so very dear
That I find no peace by day nor by night.
    When I recall him, I die in my heart.

NURSE

Ah, what is it you are thinking of, Madam?
    You are wrong to ruin your precious health.
By God, you've done what is unworthy of honor
    by falling in love with that foreign one.
You should know that you are a king's honorable daughter,
    so how canst thou be a knight's mistress?
I really cannot do this your command,
    to go and find out about the knight.

(At this the princess is to fall into a swoon on her bed.)

The language may be informal and unpolished, but these lines are written in Russian, not in an artificial archaic dialect.

They are expressive in a way that no writer of school drama (with the obvious exception of St. Dimitry) and no translator at the foreign office could match. Not all the plays of this type are quite so colloquial in their language as this one is. *Hypolite and Julia* manages to be both semiliterate in certain passages and unsuitably ecclesiastic in others. *Caleander and Neonilda*, apparently written by a Ukrainian divinity student, has a Ukrainian-influenced diction reminiscent of Kievan school dramas.

If *Peter of the Golden Keys* represents the genre of dramatized romances in its pure form. *Caleander* is a hybrid that quite systematically combines features of school drama (Olympian gods and allegorical characters are given important roles) with the typical plot and action of a seventeenth-century idealistic adventure novel. *Caleander* has survived in a director's copy of the script, with annotations describing actual staging. A play of enormous length, each of whose three acts must have taken an entire evening to perform, it has a cast of hundreds of human, mythological, and allegorical characters. It is assumed to have been performed at the Moscow School of Surgery on three consecutive days, beginning on July 16, 1731.

Three other plays of the early eighteenth century that, like *Caleander*, represent a hybridization of a dramatized romance and some other literary form have been discovered and published. *The Comedy of Count Farson*, the earliest copy of which was made in 1738, may have been performed in the provincial town of Penza. It has the external trappings of a romance, but its source seems to have been an unknown picaresque novel. The amoral French hero of the title wins the love of the Infanta of either Spain or Portugal (the author keeps confusing these countries with each other) but is eventually framed and destroyed by her envious courtiers. The tournament scenes and the courtly atmosphere suggest a dramatized romance. But the sexually aggressive heroine and the explicit depiction of the seduction scenes, which take place in a house of assignations that the Infanta visits disguised by a mask, are a far cry from the world of chivalry. The language of *Count Farson* is genuinely racy and unpretentious, and its verse is the irregular rhymed prose of the carnival barkers, the *raëshnik*, all of which adds up to a piquant and unconventionally attractive combination. The rather clumsy *Play About the King of Spain*, with its large, almost all-male cast (there is only one female character) and its emphasis on military drills, processions, fencing demonstrations, and horn signals, seems to have been a piece of soldiers' theater. A few strands of a chapbook romance provided a pretext for a group of military men to display their martial arts skills.

Finally, the very puzzling and complex play *Of Sarpidon, Duke of Assyria, of Love and of Fidelity* seems to be an adaptation, not of a chapbook romance or an adventure novel, like the rest of the plays in this group, but of a foreign baroque play. It is a drama of court intrigue that pits Orestes and Pylades of the Greek myth against an adversary named Symphon, who is abetted by a conniving royal nurse, in a contest over the affections of Leonora, the daughter of the Duke of Assyria. Both the action and the language of this play are crude and violent, but the text is noteworthy for its ability to convey brutal emotions—fury, anger, outrage—in an expressive way not otherwise found in Russian drama of the seventeenth and eighteenth centuries. A major role is given to a clown (called *gaer*), who participates in the main action and also has his own comical scenes in which he sings scatological ditties about digestion and defecation (causing the recent editors to replace a few words with initials or dots). The clown's role suggests that the original of this play may have been an English-type German tragedy of the early seventeenth century, which permitted interpolations of broad comedy in serious drama.

Russian playwrights did their dramatizations of romances at a time when that form of literature was held in low esteem in culturally advanced countries. Almost a century had to elapse before the young Pushkin based a narrative poem on Buovo d'Antona, Carl Maria von Weber won success with his opera *Oberon* (derived from the romance of Huon of Bordeaux), and Ludwig Tieck did his own treatment in prose and verse of Peter of Provence, from which Brahms took the texts for his song cycle *Die schöne Magelone*. Still farther in the future were Wagner's *Tristan und Isolde* and *Parsifal*. In the late seventeenth and early eighteenth centuries, however, romances were disdained by the literate and enjoyed only by the backward and ignorant strata of the population.

Russian neoclassical poets, such as Antioch Kantemir and Alexander Sumarokov, deplored dramatized romances, referred to them by the contemptuous term *igrishcha* (a very old term, which earlier meant "pagan rites"), and denounced their popularity in their satires and verse epistles. It was in connection with these plays that Sumarokov in 1748 advised aspiring dramatists in his "Second Epistle" (later reworked into "Instruction to Those Who Would Be Writers"):

Для знающих людей ты игрищ не пиши.

For knowledgeable people, don't write *igrishcha*.[26]

It is thus understandable that with the appearance at the end of the 1740s of Russian tragedies and comedies cast in the French neoclassical mold, plays of chivalric romance fell into disrepute and were quickly forgotten.

Yet, these plays are of interest—and not only historically or as belated exotic branches of a tree that had earlier sprouted *Orlando Furioso* and *The Tempest*. They are in their own right worthwhile examples of dramatic literature. They have held up better than some of the competition that replaced them. The unities and the imitation of French models that seemed of such paramount importance to Russian playwrights of the second half of the eighteenth century have now dated many of their plays beyond rescue. No conceivable effort could make a present-day production of a tragedy or comedy by Sumarokov, Mikhail Kheraskov, or Nikolai Nikolev (discussed in the next chapters) even remotely bearable. But an imaginative, wittily designed, and intelligently stylized staging of *Count Farson* or *Peter of the Golden Keys*, which still retain the two-dimensional charm of a gaudy deck of cards, might well turn out to be amusing and enjoyable.

26. This line of Sumarokov's is often quoted in Russian histories of the theater. It is assumed to refer to oral folk drama and/or to skits of peasant life (*intermedii*). But in his epistle, Sumarokov addresses would-be literary men, who neither could nor would want to write works of orally transmitted folklore.

❧ III ❧

Neoclassical Tragedy

The political and military prestige that France enjoyed in the seventeenth century combined with the splendid achievements of that century's French literature to spread the renown and influence of Corneille, Molière, Racine, La Fontaine, and Boileau to every country of Western civilization. By the beginning of the eighteenth century, these writers and the literary genres and theories embodied in their work were universally accepted as the summit of literary art, to be imitated and assimilated by any national culture that aspired to style and refinement.

It took Russian playwrights a while to find their neoclassical bearings. Despite the country's extensive contacts with the West, Russian drama prior to the mid-eighteenth century stayed with the baroque genres of school drama and dramatized romances. As the attempts to translate Molière for the Kunst–Fürst theater in 1702–6 showed, the state of Russian language and versification was unequal to the task at the time. It was the rapid developments in these two areas during the next four decades that enabled Russian drama to catch up with the kind of play that was then current in other countries. By the time it did, the imitated model had undergone alterations on its home ground. The French neoclassical tragedy written by Voltaire at midcentury had acquired a preachy, moralizing tone unknown to Racine. The comedy inherited from Molière and Marivaux was headed in the direction of sentimental drama with Nivelle de la Chaussée and Diderot.

It therefore happened that the neoclassical dramatic genres had no sooner been introduced by Sumarokov, Trediakovsky, and Lomonosov than they began an evolution that reflected the current changes in the West. Yet, with all the changes that these genres sustained, we can speak of a definite neoclassical period in Russian drama that began with the publication of Sumarokov's tragedy *Khorev* in 1747 and reached both its apogee and its natural termination with Alexander Griboedov's *The Misfortune of Being Clever* in 1824. Of the three principal neoclassical types of play, the prose comedy reached its peak with Vladimir Lukin and Denis Fonvizin between the 1760s and 1780s. The tragedy and the verse comedy, however, did not produce their finest achievements until the first quarter of the nineteenth century, by which time these forms were regarded as outmoded in the West.

The emergence of neoclassical drama in Russia was prepared by visits of foreign acting companies and by the introduction of syllabotonic versification. Companies of German comedians and Italian *commedia dell'arte* performers visited St. Petersburg regularly from the 1720s on. Caroline Neuber, called "die Neuberin" and famous in Germany as the popularizer of Corneille and Racine in German translation and of the plays of their German imitator Johann Gottsched, presented a season in St. Petersburg in 1739–40. Two years later she was followed by a distinguished French troupe that performed plays by Molière, Destouches, and Voltaire. By the end of the decade, military cadets of the Infantry Corps of Nobles were putting on performances of plays by Racine in French.

In the meantime, the literary language was undergoing changes. The reign of Empress Anna (1730–40) gave Russia its first important poet who was not a churchman and who wrote on nonreligious subjects. This was Prince Antioch Kantemir, a Moldavian (Rumanian) nobleman in Russian service, who wrote satires patterned after Boileau in syllabic verse. Apart from their considerable literary value, Kantemir's satires are important because the author turned to contemporary Western examples, rather than to forms long obsolete in the West, such as the Jesuit plays and chivalric tales. In 1730, the poet Vasily Trediakovsky, upon returning from his studies at the Sorbonne in Paris, published a translation of an allegorical French novel in prose and in verse, *Voyage de l'Isle d'Amour*, by Abbé Paul Tallemant. The novel was full of abstract allegorical characters familiar from school drama, but instead of religious edification the book preached a hedonistic message of sexual promiscuity. Despite denunciations by prominent churchmen, Trediakovsky's version of Tallemant enjoyed a great popular success and was favorably received at Anna's court.

Its publication resulted in Trediakovsky's appointment as Professor of Eloquence at the Academy of Sciences. Equally significant was Trediakovsky's introductory manifesto to this work, in which he proclaimed his intention to write in colloquial Russian, since Church Slavic was not suitable for a contemporary novel dealing with love and sex. The centuries-old custom of writing in an archaic language was not to be that easily cast off, and Trediakovsky's translation did not quite attain the gracious and fluent manner for which he strove. Still, even though around 1730 the literary Russian was not yet ready for *préciosité*, a comparison of Trediakovsky's Tallemant to the abortive *Précieuses ridicules* of a quarter of a century earlier testifies to the speedy pace at which the literary Russian language was evolving.

In 1735, Trediakovsky initiated the reform of Russian versification by introducing the notion of the metrical foot and by writing some trochaic verses. This innovation brought in the syllabotonic system, which corresponds to the accentual-syllabic one in English and organizes verse into regular two- or three-syllable meters instead of having lines of a certain number of syllables, without regard to stresses, as was done in the syllabic system. By 1739, the prosodic and metrical reform was completed when Mikhail Lomonosov, then studying in Germany, sent to the Russian Academy of Sciences his "Ode on the Taking of Hotin," written in iambic tetrameter and accompanied by a detailed treatise outlining the possibilities of using binary and ternary meters as well as masculine and feminine rhymes in Russian verse. The reform, proposed by Trediakovsky and given its final formulation by Lomonosov, gained almost instant ac-

ceptance, so that within a decade only a few provincial clergy-
men could still be found using the old syllabic versification in
their religious drama and poetry. Both the shift to contemporary
and conversational vernacular and the introduction of an attractive, exciting new kind of versification (in an age when all serious drama was written in verse) were of major import for the
development of Russian drama.

The fun-loving Empress Elizabeth (reigned 1741–62), was
particularly noted for her patronage of theatrical activities of all
sorts, be it school drama, Italian opera, French neoclassical tragedy, or an allegorical pageant eulogizing the virtues of her
reign. In her endeavor to popularize theatergoing, Elizabeth
made theater attendance compulsory for members of her court
and even for visiting foreigners. She also invited members of the
merchant class to attend her private theater. A young German
princess, the future Catherine the Great, brought to Russia to
marry Elizabeth's nephew, described in her memoirs the trapped
feeling and tedium experienced by Elizabeth's courtiers, forced
to sit through nine tragedies on nine consecutive days. When
Alexander Sumarokov wrote the first French-style neoclassical
Russian tragedies and the cadets of the Infantry Corps of Nobles put on a very successful production of one of them in 1749,
Elizabeth had them repeat the performance at her court theater.
She encouraged Sumarokov to write other plays, and she issued
a royal command to the other two leading Russian poets of the
day, Lomonosov and Trediakovsky, to write a tragedy each.

Soon thereafter, rumor reached Elizabeth that a particularly
successful amateur theatrical company, organized in the provincial city of Iaroslavl by a merchant's son named Fyodor Volkov,
was performing plays by St. Dimitry of Rostov, tragedies by
Sumarokov, and a dramatization of a chivalric romance (*Eudon
and Bertha*). Their performances drew large and enthusiastic
crowds. By royal decree, Volkov and his company were brought
to St. Petersburg. They put on four performances, including
Sumarokov's *Khorev* and St. Dimitry's *The Sinner's Repentance*. Their native abilities and enthusiasm were admired, but
the general educational level of the merchants' sons and young

artisans who made up Volkov's company was judged too low. Elizabeth ordered the company disbanded and had its most promising members enrolled in the Infantry Corps of Nobles for the completion of their education. Among those thus retained, in addition to Volkov himself, were the young divinity student Ivan Dmitrevsky and the Iaroslavl barber Iakov Shumsky, destined to become the two most famous Russian actors of the eighteenth century. This association between the provincial artisan-actors and the stage-struck noble cadets of the Infantry Corps gave rise to the first professional and successful Russian acting company, from which all later Russian theaters descended.

When Volkov and his colleagues finished their studies in 1756, Elizabeth issued a command to organize a public theater in St. Petersburg for performances of secular plays in Russian. The efforts of Kantemir, Trediakovsky, Lomonosov, and Sumarokov had brought the Russian literary language to the point where it was ready to accommodate the neoclassical drama, newly popular in Russia. The proliferation of theatrical companies in St. Petersburg, Moscow, and the provinces quickly brought about a galaxy of playwrights who wrote in the new manner. Chivalric romances and school plays were soon relegated to history. Whatever transgressions can be charged to the Romanov dynasty, some of those rulers do deserve credit for their efforts—extending through three generations, beginning with Alexis, continuing with his son Peter and his daughter Natalia, and culminating in the ultimate success of his granddaughter Elizabeth—to get their apathetic subjects interested in theater and drama.

Alexander Sumarokov

Открытель таинства любовныя нам лиры,
Творец преславныя и пышныя Семиры

The discoverer for us of the love lyre's mystery,
The creator of the most renowned and opulent Semira

Ivan Elagin, mid-1750s

Before he wrote his first dramatic work, Alexander Sumaro-kov (1718–77) had already established himself as the third prominent poet of his time. Unlike his older contemporaries Trediakovsky (son of a poor village priest) and Lomonosov (son of a prosperous peasant from the far North), Sumarokov came from a family of impoverished nobility. After graduation from the Infantry Corps, he briefly followed a military career, then worked in the civil service, and, after the establishment of the first permanent Russian theater, became its general manager. His true calling, however, was literature. Sumarokov was the first Russian nobleman to devote himself full-time to professional literary activities. He thus stands at the very beginning of the illustrious line of Russian writers of noble origin who contributed so much to the literature of their country. Beginning as a faithful disciple of Trediakovsky, he later briefly switched his allegiance to Lomonosov, but eventually came to assume a hostile and contemptuous attitude toward both of his mentors. Each of these three poets considered himself the initiator of Russian neoclassicism. But while Lomonosov and Trediakovsky in their individual ways (and at the price of daring experimentation and frequent failure in the case of the second) sought Russia's own path to neoclassical literary art, Sumarokov preferred direct imitation and uncritical transplanting of the standard ideas, forms, and, above all, restrictions, of French and French-influenced German neoclassicism.

In the two programmatic epistles in verse on the subject of language and literature that he wrote in 1748, deriving them from Boileau's "L'art poétique" and Trediakovsky's "Epistle to Apollo from Russian Poetry" of 1735, Sumarokov outlined his program of good literary taste and usage. The basic, eternal, unchangeable literary models were all created in Greece and brought to perfection in Rome and in seventeenth-century France. Each genre has its own laws and rules, based on the immutable properties of the human heart and mind. All a Russian writer needed was to follow carefully the prescribed usages and restrictions. The worst sin was to contaminate one genre with another, "lest you irritate the muses with your ill-gained success: Thalia with tears and Melpomene with laughter." In tragedy, unities of time and place were seen by Sumarokov as essential to verisimilitude. He was quite sure that adherence to these unities would cause the spectator to believe that he was witnessing actual events and not a play in verse.

As unsurpassed models to be imitated by Russian dramatists Sumarokov offered Corneille, Racine, and Philippe Quinault (1635–88), who was the librettist of Jean Baptiste Lully's operas and still very much admired in France in the eighteenth century. But foremost was Voltaire. For Sumarokov and for Trediakovsky, Voltaire was not the free thinker and the libertarian that subsequent generations came to admire, but the supreme playwright of the ages, the principal keeper of the flame of classical purity, already somewhat threatened by the inevitable processes of literary evolution. Comedy recipes were available from Molière and (characteristically overlooking Marivaux) from Destouches, whose *Le philosophe marié* and *Le glorieux* Sumarokov considered "immeasurably good."

The theme of French neoclassical tragedy (and, by the early eighteenth century, of all neoclassical tragedy) had to be, in the apt formulation cited by Francis Fergusson, "a heroic action performed by persons whose ideal is the triumph of will over instinct."[1] The conflict between instinct and will, between love and duty, between passion and reason that Pierre Corneille placed at the center of the French stage in *Le Cid* in 1636 was to remain at that center until the premiere of Victor Hugo's *Hernani*, almost two centuries later. The normative poetics of the age prescribed both the theme of the tragedy and its canonical five-act structure. The psychological motivations of the characters were the main object of interest. Violent actions implicit in the plot (wars, murders, suicides) occurred offstage and were narrated at length, while the psychological reactions of queens and heroes to these events could be examined in detail.

By the time Sumarokov got the chance to try his hand at this form, the poetic splendor and psychological depth that Corneille and Racine had brought to it were things of the past. In the present, Voltaire in France, Scipione Maffei and Pietro

1. Francis Fergusson, *The Idea of a Theater* (Princeton, 1949), p. 44.

Metastasio in Italy and Gottsched in Germany kept repeating the gestures and the unities of neoclassical tragedy. The literary and theatrical world of Europe, still hypnotized by the achievements of the seventeenth century, believed that there was not, nor would there ever be, any other way of writing serious plays. The tone and the verbal texture of Sumarokov's tragedies imitated this later variety of neoclassical form, *opera seria* by now rather than tragedy (Giambattista Varesco's libretto for Mozart's *Idomeneo* would be a good, still-familiar example). For his plots, he borrowed certain time-tested situations from Racine (especially from *Britannicus*) and Corneille (*Cinna* and *Horace*).

Also from Corneille came Sumarokov's standardized heroine, the kind of haughty princess known in the French tradition as *la belle inhumaine*, an appellation that Sumarokov himself disliked. Patterned by Corneille after the heroine of Honoré d'Urfé's once popular novel *L'Astrée* (1632), *la belle inhumaine* (Emilie in Corneille's *Cinna* is perhaps the most typical example) is morbidly obsessed with her posthumous reputation. For the sake of this abstract *gloire* she is likely to indulge in feats of self-denial, cruelty to her lover, and other kinds of sadistic and self-destructive behavior. Sumarokov's audience, like that of d'Urfé a century earlier, was expected to admire the character's mastery of her emotions. The protagonist of Sumarokov's *Semira* declares to her *confidante*, who bears the improbable participial name of Izbrana ("The Chosen One"):

Избрана, я хочу любовника оставить
И, одолев себя, на век себя прославить.

Izbrana, I wish to leave the man I love
And, by mastering myself, cover myself with eternal glory.

The five tragedies Sumarokov wrote between 1747 and 1751—*Khorev, Hamlet, Sinav and Truvor, Artistona,* and *Semira*—were originally performed by the cadets at the Infantry Corps and at the court theater of Empress Elizabeth. For the next two decades these five plays formed the backbone of the Russian repertoire. Three of them are set in pre-Christian Kievan Russia. *Artistona* (more correctly *Artystone*) takes place at the court of Darius in ancient Persia and *Hamlet* in Shakespeare's Denmark. The names of the characters, however, make the only discernible difference. What these plays show us are the same French courtiers, disguised as ancient Romans, that we know from *Cinna* and *Britannicus*. Hans-Bernd Harder, who did a study of Sumarokov's first five tragedies in his book on Russian neoclassical tragedy,[2] was able to formulate the plot structure of the five plays very simply. In all of them, a pair of lovers is involved with a ruler of the state. The conflict between duty and passion is caused either by the lovers' belonging to opposing sides in a dynastic struggle or by the ruler forcing his unwanted attentions on the heroine. Sumarokov's adaptation of *Hamlet* can illustrate how the scheme works.

Out of some three dozen great writers Sumarokov mentioned in his "Second Epistle," Shakespeare was the only one given a derogatory epithet: "albeit unenlightened." In a footnote to this opinion, Sumarokov revealed that his judgment of Shakespeare (whom he did not read either in the original or in a complete translation) relied on that of Voltaire: "Shakespeare, English tragic and comic writer, in whom there is both much that is bad and much that is exceedingly good."[3] Using a French prose paraphrase as his source, Sumarokov retained only five characters from the original play: Hamlet, Gertrude, Claudius, Polonius, and Ophelia. Dispensing not only with the unsuitably comic gravediggers and the undesirably fantastic ghost, but with the multitude of lesser characters and episodes that offended against unity of action, Sumarokov added three characters of his own invention so that Hamlet, the Queen, and Ophelia could all have their individual *confidants*.

The first act introduces one crucial correction into the Shakespearian situation: it was Polonius in this version, rather than Claudius, who killed Hamlet's father. Thus, in one stroke, *Hamlet* is changed into Corneille's *Le Cid* and Sumarokov can feel at home. To avenge his father, Hamlet, like Rodrigue, has to kill the father of the woman he loves, while Ophelia is put

2. Hans-Bernd Harder, *Studien zur Geschichte der russischen klassizistichen Tragödie 1747–1769* (Wiesbaden, 1962).

3. Quoted from A. P. Sumarokov, *Izbrannye proizvedeniia* (Leningrad, 1957), pp. 117 and 129.

in the situation of Chimène and reacts as can be expected. In the middle acts, Sumarokov's *Hamlet* moves away from both Shakespeare and Corneille: a situation from Racine's *Britannicus* is introduced when Claudius, the usurper, tries to force his love on the bride of the rightful heir Hamlet, recapitulating in considerable detail the triangle of Nero, Junia, and Britannicus. The end of the play reverts back to *Le Cid*, and Ophelia is permitted to marry Hamlet because by seeking revenge against him she had discharged her filial obligation toward her villain-father.[4]

The formal structure of French seventeenth-century tragedy was copied by Sumarokov almost photographically. What is conspicuously missing is the poetry, the human depth and the psychological subtlety that Corneille and Racine brought to the structure that Sumarokov so adroitly borrowed. Another sorely lacking dimension is the elegance and suppleness of the language of the French originals, which Sumarokov (unlike Voltaire, whose literary style still provides a saving grace for his hopelessly faded tragedies) was simply not able to match. Although adequate for the 1750s, Sumarokov's style was very soon overtaken by the rapid linguistic evolution of his century and became antiquated within a few decades. His nineteenth-century heirs in the sphere of neoclassical tragedy, such as Ozerov and Küchelbecker, were stylistically far more fortunate, because the literary language of their epoch proved much more durable. And, of course, Sumarokov's tragedies are quite innocent of anything resembling literary originality.

Yet, for his contemporaries those early works came as a revelation. The French classics and the German neoclassical tragedies of Gottsched, which the more cultivated members of St. Petersburg audiences grew to appreciate through performances by visiting and resident French and German companies in the 1740s, suddenly had a Russian equivalent. The idea of a Russian play depicting human passions and concentrating on

4. For highly enthusiastic (and to my mind, misguided) appraisals of Sumarokov's *Hamlet*, see D. M. Lang, "Sumarokov's *Hamlet*: A Misjudged Russian Tragedy of the Eighteenth Century," *Modern Language Review* 43(1) (1948): 67–72; and Joyce S. Toomre, "Sumarokov's Adaptation of Hamlet and the 'To Be or Not to Be' Soliloquy," *Newsletter of the Study Group on Eighteenth-Century Russia* (Norwich), no. 9 (September 1981) 6–20.

the characters' inner emotions (earlier dramatized romances took a far more external approach) must have seemed irresistibly attractive. Sumarokov was immediately proclaimed the Racine of Russia. His plays were translated into French and written about in French and German journals (Sumarokov himself published Russian translations of his favorite foreign reviews). Gottsched in Germany and Jean François de La Harpe in France hailed him. Voltaire entered into correspondence with him.

Not all of his Russian contemporaries were fooled. Lomonosov, a far greater man, to whom Sumarokov owed so much and whom he so viciously denigrated and ridiculed, declared quite truthfully that "whatever is good in [Sumarokov's] plays is copied from the French." Fonvizin, the finest Russian playwright of the age, considered Sumarokov ridiculous and in his letters from Paris compared him to the most absurd and pedantic of the French writers he met there. And Ivan Barkov (ca. 1732–68), that secret prince of Russian eighteenth-century poetry, whose pornographic poems were so much admired in the Age of Enlightenment, circulated amusing obscene parodies of Sumarokov's tragedies in which all the roles were taken by personified sex organs.[5]

Still, the myth of Sumarokov as the Racine of Russia survived for decades. No one took it more seriously than Sumarokov himself. Only Voltaire and Metastasio were deemed by him his equals in all of Europe. An irascible man with a vastly inflated idea of his own importance, he was forced to resign from his position as general manager of the St. Petersburg Russian public theater after five years, having quarreled with a large number of influential people. Catherine the Great, bored with Sumarokov's constant complaints and denunciations of his contemporaries, wrote to him to save his dramatics for the stage, "where they are far more amusing." At the end of the 1760s, alarmed at the appearance of rival playwrights and disgusted with the success of the new genre of sentimental drama (which to his classical sensibilities was a revoltingly bastardized form), Sumarokov returned to writing tragedies.

5. See A. A. Morozov, Introduction to *Russkaia stikhotvornaia parodiia* (Leningrad, 1960), pp. 21–24.

In this new group, comprising four works, Sumarokov strove to break out of the Corneillian structure that had served him so well in the past and to achieve a more diffuse one, rather in the manner of Racine's *Bérénice*, with the result that his plots failed to develop and the action kept returning to its point of departure with monotonous regularity. Another new feature of his later tragedies was that he now followed the example of Voltaire in preaching rather abstract civic virtues and indulged in overt moralizing about the dangers of not overcoming private passions. The most successful play of this later period, *Dimitry the Impostor (Dimitrii Samozvanets*, 1771), occupies a rather special place in his work. Renewing his interest in Shakespeare, possibly owing to the impact of Catherine II's own Shakespearian plays, Sumarokov attempted to pattern his hero after the protagonist of *Richard III*. He created a rather pallid villain who keeps trying to examine the causes for his own villainy. It was in this play that Sumarokov achieved some of his few memorable and ringing verses. It remained in the repertoire of Russian theaters until the second decade of the nineteenth century, by which time his other works had long ceased to be performed.

Sumarokov died in 1777, widely disliked and in poverty. His funeral was paid for by the actors who had appeared in his plays. Realizing that his work was gradually disappearing from the stage, in his last poems he expressed confidence that future generations would come to recognize his importance. The hope had a hollow ring at the beginning of the nineteenth century. The seventeen-year-old Pushkin, denouncing the uncritical veneration of eighteenth-century reputations in a polemical poem he dedicated to Vasily Zhukovsky, addressed the following youthfully vehement apostrophe to Sumarokov's ghost:

> Ты ль это, слабое дитя чужих уроков,
> Завистливый гордец, холодный Сумароков,
> Без силы, без огня, с посредственным умом,
> Предрассуждениям обязанный венцом
> И с Пинда сброшенный и проклятый Расином?[6]

6. A. S. Pushkin, *Polnoe sobranie sochinenii v desiati tomakh* (Moscow, 1956), vol. I, p. 202.

Is it you, you feeble child of others' lessons,
Envious snob, cold Sumarokov,
Without strength, without fire, with a mediocre mind,
Owing your crown to prejudice
And shoved off Mt. Pindus and damned by Racine?

A century later, a poet almost as great as Pushkin, Osip
Mandelshtam, in his eulogy of Ozerov (1914) mentioned Sumarokov in similarly derogatory terms as "pitiful Sumarokov [who]
mumbled a role he had learned by rote" (see pages 214–15). In
the mid-nineteenth century, Ivan Goncharov, wishing to suggest
the backwardness and God-forsaken provinciality of his protagonist's upbringing, has the father in *Oblomov* pick off the shelf
a volume of Sumarokov's tragedies and read them with awe and
wonder. None of Sumarokov's plays was published between
1787 and 1893. At the beginning of the twentieth century, he
was relegated to histories of Russian theater. People could hardly
believe that he was ever taken seriously as a writer.

When Soviet scholars began to reevaluate eighteenth-century
writers in the 1920s, Sumarokov came in for his share of redress
and was given his due for the innovations he did in fact introduce. By the 1940s, when much of Soviet literary studies turned
nationalistic, it came to be assumed that earlier Russian literature never owed anything to any foreign influences. With his
French models thus removed from the scene, Sumarokov was
suddenly given the kind of credit he could never have hoped
for during his lifetime. His theories (which came from Boileau)
and his tragedies (which came from Corneille and his followers)
were seen as original and enduring contributions to a native and
totally independent Russian classicism. A study of Sumarokov's
plays published in 1949 in the series *Russian Playwrights* and
written by the eighteenth-century specialist P. N. Berkov managed to avoid all mention of Sumarokov's French models or of
French literature.[7]

7. The detailed discussion of Sumarokov's tragedies in Boris Aseev, *Russkii
dramaticheskii teatr ot ego istokov do kontsa XVIII veka* (Moscow, 1977) (a revised edition of the same author's *Russkii dramaticheskii teatr XVII–XVIII vekov*
[Moscow, 1958]), strives to turn the loyal monarchist Sumarokov into the leading
antimonarchist dissident of his age. An ingenious new approach has been tried

Sumarokov's tragedies were undeniably a pivotal event in the history of Russian drama. They inaugurated the Russian neoclassical tragedy, and in them he codified the five-act structure and the couplets of iambic hexameter in which all subsequent plays of this genre were written in Russia. Sumarokov was also the first Russian playwright to write Western-style prose comedies (they will be discussed in the next chapter).

But it is also true that apart from his epistles on language and literature and his pseudopopular love songs, which can still be read with pleasure, all of his dramatic and poetic writings became outmoded and absurdly (rather than quaintly) antiquated before the eighteenth century was over. Like Simeon of Polotsk a century before him, Sumarokov was a minor literary talent, who succeeded by importing and naturalizing foreign literary forms on which later playwrights could build. To give him credit for more is to substitute what is desired for what really existed.

Trediakovsky and Lomonosov as Playwrights

The order Elizabeth issued in 1750, in her first flush of enthusiasm over the cadets' performance of Sumarokov, for "Professors Trediakovsky and Lomonosov to compose a tragedy each" enriched Russian literature with four new plays: Trediakovsky's tragedy *Deidamia* and his adaptation of *The Eunuch* by Terence, and Lomonosov's tragedies *Temira and Selim* and *Demophon*.

Vasily Trediakovsky (1703–69), a very important innovator in Russian versification and literary language, spent a lifetime wrestling with the form and spirit of a language not advanced

---

by Iu. V. Stennik ("Dramaturgiia petrovskoi èpokhi i pervye tragedii Sumarokova," *XVIII vek* (Leningrad) 9 [1974]: 227–49), who seeks to derive the characters and situations of Sumarokov's tragedies from the chivalric romance plays of the early eighteenth century. In this way his roots in Corneille and Voltaire can be minimized and his native Russian ones stressed. The awkward fact that Sumarokov detested the romance dramatizations and is not likely to have known them well is passed over in silence.

enough to perform as he desired. His fate was to go down to one valiant defeat after another. Hidden under the verbal knots and contortions of Trediakovsky's tortured style—he was trying to impose Latin syntax on Russian—was a genuine lyric poet who now and then pushed himself to the surface in occasional dazzling flashes. Ridiculed by Sumarokov in the comedy *Tresotinius*, viciously slandered in Ivan Lazhechnikov's popular historical novel *The Ice Palace* (1835), Trediakovsky, despite the esteem and affection in which Pushkin held him, became for the nineteenth century the very epitome of an absurd, ridiculously untalented eighteenth-century pedant. In line with this unfair legend, Adam Mickiewicz in one of the lectures on Slavic literature that he gave at the Collège de France in 1841–42 subjected a scene from Trediakovsky's *Deidamia* to a derisive, almost contemptuous analysis.[8] Seeking for understandable reasons of his own to discredit Russian social institutions in the eyes of his French students, Mickiewicz quoted Trediakovsky's Greek characters' description of a palace ceremony to demonstrate the supposed Russian fondness for superficial pomp and hierarchy.

Trediakovsky's tragedy is derived from *Achille in Sciro* (1736), an opera libretto by Pietro Metastasio. The plot is a variation on the Iphigenia story. Trediakovsky prejudiced any possibility of its performance by showing the heroic Achilles, disguised as a woman, hiding out during much of the play on the island of Scyros to avoid going to the Trojan War. A sense of the ridiculous was not, unfortunately, one of Trediakovsky's stronger points. The comic implications of his feminine-attired hero carrying on a romance with the Princess Deidamia, with both roles actually taken by young men (Elizabeth's cadets, for whom the play was written), apparently did not present themselves to the poet.[9]

8. *Pisma Adama Mickiewicza* (Paris, 1860), vol. 3, pp. 429–32. Whatever the merits of the great Polish poet's opinions on Trediakovsky are, three things are made abundantly clear by his analysis: (1) Mickiewicz did not read the play beyond the one scene he translates and discusses; (2) his understanding of the Russian text was very imperfect; and (3) his transcription of proper names indicates difficulties with reading the Cyrillic alphabet.

9. The comic possibilities of this situation were not wasted on the young

The dialogue of *Deidamia* is couched in Trediakovsky's usual convoluted style. But, as in all his longer works, there is a nugget of pure poetry now and then (particularly in the letter from Thetis to her son Achilles, written in quatrains of lilting iambic hexameter, perforated by elegantly placed caesurae) that seems written by some forgotten or undiscovered twentieth-century Futurist poet attempting an eighteenth-century stylization. The play was never staged and it was published only after Trediakovsky's death. In a touching gesture of posthumous reconciliation, Trediakovsky's testament directed that it be dedicated to Sumarokov, the erstwhile disciple who did so much to discredit him and to besmirch his reputation.

The cadets did perform Lomonosov's *Temira and Selim* on several occasions, but it did not remain in the repertoire for long. Mikhail Lomonosov (1711–65) was a major figure in the development of Russian culture. He was a distinguished scientist, an important grammarian, and a genuinely gifted poet. Lomonosov was vastly superior to Sumarokov in every possible way except one: he had no sense of dramatic structure. His verse tragedies have the finest verbal texture, the purest and most convincing diction of any Russian work in that form written in the eighteenth century. But dramatically they go nowhere.

A lack of dramatic focus is inherent in the plot of *Temira and Selim*. An "Oriental" classical tragedy set among the Moslems in the Near East (following such Western precedents as Racine's *Bajazet* and Voltaire's *Zaïre*), the play has a plot that deals ostensibly with a love affair between a princess of the Crimean Tatars and a young prince from Baghdad. The lovers are threatened with separation because the leader of the Golden Horde, Mamai, has designs on the heroine. But the author's and

---

Denis Fonvizin, who on December 14, 1763, wrote to his sister from St. Petersburg: "Incidentally, the thing to do these days is to read *Deidamia*, a tragedy by Mr. Trediakovsky. There is nothing funnier. I would have gladly copied it and sent it to you, but it is very long. Please imagine Achilles, who in his tragedy wears women's clothes. And the verses are frightfully bizarre and funny. Adieu. I'm sleepy." (D. I. Fonvizin, *Sobranie sochinenii* [Moscow, 1959], vol. 2, p. 328). A far more appreciative twentieth-century view of Trediakovsky's role and significance is conveyed by Vera Panova in her play *Trediakovsky and Volynsky*, written in the 1960s. See her collection of plays *Pogovorim o strannostiakh liubvi . . .* (Leningrad, 1968), pp. 369ff.

his characters' interest remains riveted on the offstage struggle between the Mongols and the Russians led by Dimitry of the Don, culminating in the battle of Kulikovo. The fight for the liberation of Russia from the Mongols is not really integrated into the plot. The news from the battlefield is invariably given more dramatic and poetic emphasis than the other elements of the play, thus sporadically converting it into the kind of baroque historical ode that Lomonosov knew how to write so well.[10]

Demophon, like Trediakovsky's *Deidamia,* turns to the post-Homeric legends about the adventures of the lesser participants of the Trojan War.[11] Since Sumarokov wrote no plays dealing with classical antiquity, Trediakovsky and Lomonosov here inaugurated the ancient Greek theme in Russian drama. But again, in this story of a four-cornered love entanglement set during the aftermath of the Trojan War, the play comes to life only in the *récits* about offstage battles and holocausts. Both Trediakovsky and Lomonosov strove for originality by minimizing the inevitable love-versus-duty conflict and altering the strict French structural disposition of the five acts. Both were original and innovative poets. But Sumarokov's servile, imitative path, his uncritical adaptation of the structural and verbal clichés inherited from Corneille and Racine, turned out to be more productive for the later course of Russian tragedy than the more original, but less influential efforts of his two predecessors and teachers.

Between them, Lomonosov, Trediakovsky, and Sumarokov (Kantemir should also be mentioned) changed the Russian idea of what literature and drama should be. As a group, they amply

10. *Temira and Selim* is not written in couplets, but uses cross-rhymes. In this respect it is unique in Russian neoclassical tragedy. Lomonosov found some highly interesting possibilities for subdividing his quatrains among several characters to good poetic and dramatic effect. But subsequent practitioners of the genre preferred to follow Sumarokov's example. Russian tragedy continued to be written in couplets of iambic hexameter until the time of Pushkin's *Boris Godunov,* when Shakespeare replaced Corneille as the model and rhymeless iambic pentameter became the norm.

11. The play combines the myths of Demophon and Phyllis and of Priam's younger son, Polydorus, being given refuge by Polymnestor and Iliona (cf. Robert Graves, *The Greek Myths* [Baltimore, 1955], vol. 2, secs. 168*l* and 169*i* and *j*). Lomonosov treated these two legends with considerable poetic license.

deserve the following handsome and knowledgeable tribute by
Hugh McLean:

> The more one studies Russian literature of the eigh-
> teenth century, the more admiration one comes to feel for
> that remarkable series of devoted, bitterly contentious, in-
> defatigable men who with so much dedication carried out
> for Russian literature the great work that Peter had accom-
> plished for the country as a whole: they made it a part of
> Europe. If one compares the state of Russian literature in
> 1725 with that a mere half century later, the contrast is in-
> deed staggering: in fifty years the Russians had successful-
> ly assimilated all the major forms of contemporary Euro-
> pean literature—translated them, adapted them, and gone
> on to create independently in them. Where there had been
> only a few labored imitations of already antiquated European
> forms—for example, the school dramas of Simeon Polotsky
> or Feofan Prokopovich—now there was a flourishing and
> up-to-date original literature. Perhaps few major artistic
> masterpieces had as yet appeared; but there was already a
> substantial body of both verse and prose of high quality, and
> even more important, the indispensible ground work had
> been carried out which made possible the magnificent
> achievements that were to follow.[12]

Sumarokov's Successors

Neoclassical tragedy continued to reign as the most popular
and respected dramatic genre throughout the second half of the
eighteenth century. Following the examples of Sumarokov and
Lomonosov, many of the poets of the period felt they had to try
their hand at it. Thus, Vasily Maikov (1728–78), who retains
his place in Russian literature as the author of two witty mock-
heroic epics, also wrote two Voltairian tragedies. His *Agriope*
(1769) attempts a slow-motion psychological closeup of a Greek
princess who gradually realizes that the man she loves has used

---

12. Hugh McLean, "The Adventures of an English Comedy in Eighteenth-
Century Russia: Dodsley's *Toy Shop* and Lukin's *Ščepetil'nik*," *American Contributions to the Fifth International Congress of Slavicists* (The Hague, 1963), p. 201.

and betrayed her. *Themistes and Hieronyma* (*Femist i Ieronima*, 1773) is an "Oriental" tragedy, set in a Turkish seraglio. It has a plot that resembles Mozart's opera *Die Entführung aus dem Serail* transposed into a tragic key.

Hieronyma Paleologue, a Byzantine princess, is imprisoned in the seraglio of the Sultan of Turkey, who is in love with her. Her fiancé, Themistes, who has entered the sultan's service in disguise, hopes to rescue her. Their escape is thwarted by a palace guard named Osman, corresponding to Osmin in Mozart's opera. What Maikov produced was a tragic variant of the numerous eighteenth-century comic operas and vaudevilles about a foreign, usually Christian woman who is imprisoned in a seraglio by an amorous Turk and manages to escape. Traceable to *Les pèlerins de la Mecque* by Lesage and d'Orneval, first presented at the *théâtre de la foire* in Paris in 1726, these works include operas by Gluck, Haydn (*L'incontro improvviso*), and Mozart.

Maikov may also have known a play based on a similar situation, *Les trois sultanes, ou Soliman II* by Charles Simon Favart, which premiered in Paris in 1761 and was performed in St. Petersburg in French in 1765.[13] The similarities between Maikov's and Favart's plays involve not only the names of Osman (which reproduces the French pronunciation of Osmin) and Soliman (the name of Favart's sultan is the name under which Maikov's Themistes enters Turkish service), but also the closely reproduced scene wherein the sultan tells Osman that the fair Christian captive has caused him to lose interest in the other women of his harem. In Favart, as later in Mozart's opera, the seraglio situation serves as the pretext for regaling the audience with the fashionable *turquerie* of the period: opulent harem costumes, the janissary music of tinkling triangles or clashing cymbals, and polite mockery of quaint Moslem customs (e.g., the subjugation of women or the fear of wine).

Maikov chose to convert this plot into a grim tragedy of national oppression, revenge, and perfidy. Hieronyma is a Sumarokov-style *belle inhumaine*, longing for death and posthumous glory. Themistes is a Machiavellian freedom fighter, who resorts

13. R.-Aloys Mooser, *Annales de la musique et des musiciens en Russie au XVIII siècle* (Geneva, n.d.; ca. 1950), vol. 2, p. 41.

to betrayal and deceit in the cause of political liberation. These self-destructive lovers do not get to escape from the seraglio. Their plans are discovered by Osman, Hieronyma is stabbed by the jealous sultan, and Themistes kills himself. Maikov's language, so lively and sparkling in his mock epics *The Ombre Player* and *Elisha, or Bacchus Enraged*, is ploddingly monotonous in the tragedies, owing to slavish imitation of Sumarokov. Still, his tragedies were performed in their day by celebrated actors and actresses and enjoyed by the public.

The same fatal reliance on Sumarokov can be seen in the one surviving tragedy by Alexei Rzhevsky (1737–1804), *The False Smerdius (Podlozhnyi Smerdii*, 1769),[14] a variation on the popular False Dimitry theme. Rzhevsky, a poet of genuine ability, who brought a rococo elegance to the short Russian lyric, might have achieved something original in the field of Russian tragedy had he not chosen to give up literature quite early in life and become a bureaucrat instead.

In the 1780s, Sumarokov's tragic torch passed on to his son-in-law, Iakov Kniazhnin, who was, however, far more important for his contributions to comedy and comic opera (see the section on him in Chapter 5). The two other authors of widely performed neoclassical tragedies were Mikhail Kheraskov (1733–1807) and Nikolai Nikolev (1758–1815). Kheraskov, an unbelievably prolific writer, practiced every genre of prose, verse, and drama that was known in his age. Possessor of a negligible literary talent, he was acclaimed and honored by his contemporaries as the author of the unwieldy, unreadable epic poem *The Rossiad*, seen as the Russian equivalent of the equally forgotten *Henriade* by Voltaire. A friend and protégé of the arch-classicist Sumarokov, Kheraskov utilized both the literary forms sanctioned by Boileau, such as the tragedy and the epic, and the new ones that outraged Sumarokov's traditionalist sensibilities: the didactic novel and the sentimental drama in prose.

Kheraskov's earliest tragedy, *The Nun of Venice (Venetsianskaia monakhinia*, 1758), must have seemed a daring departure from the Sumarokov-Voltaire model. In three acts instead of the traditional five, it incorporates features of West-

14. First published in *Teatral'noe nasledstvo* (Moscow, 1956).

ern sentimental drama, a genre that had not yet been introduced in Russia at that time. In its denunciation of religious in-
tolerance, *The Nun of Venice* shows Kheraskov as a faithful
disciple of Voltaire. But in his later tragedies, Kheraskov not
only reverted to the standard five-act format but took up preaching Christian virtues and glorifying Christian martyrs in the
manner of Corneille's *Polyeucte*.[15] These tragedies were received
with respect, but Kheraskov's wooden characterizations and unimaginative way with language prevented them from becoming
popular successes along the lines of Kniazhnin's *Dido* or Nikolev's *Sorena and Zamir*.

Nikolai Nikolev was the adopted son of Princess Ekaterina
Dashkova, Empress Catherine's intimate friend who helped her
engineer the coup that deposed Peter III. Nikolev wrote comedies and comic operas, but his greatest success as a playwright
was his tragedy *Sorena and Zamir*, written in 1784 and premiered
in Moscow in 1785. Because its temporary difficulties with censorship brought it a *succès de scandale*, this became the best-
known work of its genre between Sumarokov and Ozerov. The
play is an instance of transferring a popular foreign play to Russian soil, a procedure known as "adaptation to our customs"
(*sklonenie na nashi nravy*), of which more presently. The foreign
original was Voltaire's *Alzire, ou les américains* (1736),[16] which
in the next century provided Giuseppe Verdi with the libretto
(and title) of his eighth opera.

The action of Voltaire's play, which was set in Peru after its
conquest by the Spaniards, was moved by Nikolev to medieval
Russia. The ferocious nomadic Polovtsy (later known mainly
through the "Polovtsian Dances" from Borodin's *Prince Igor*)
took the role of Voltaire's humane and noble Indians. The Russian Prince Mstislav (it is not clear which of the several medieval

15. See Michael Green, "Kheraskov and the Christian Tragedy," *California
Slavic Studies* 11 (1976): 1–25.
16. As demonstrated in exhaustive detail in A. Kadlubovskii, " 'Sorena i
Zamir' Nikoleva i tragedii Vol'tera," *Izvestiia otdeleniia russkogo iazyka i sloves-
nosti Imperatorskoi akademii nauk* (St. Petersburg) v 12, bk. 1 (1907): 185–204.
Kadlubovsky also shows that the few scenes and plot elements in Nikolev's play
that cannot be traced to *Alzire* were taken from Voltaire's other tragedies, namely
Eryphile, *Sémiramis*, and *Mahomet*.

Russian rulers of that name Nikolev had in mind) replaced Voltaire's vengeful Christian Spanish viceroy. The setting was moved to the Belorussian city of Polotsk, which from the sound of its name Nikolev took to be the ancient capital of the Polovtsy, medieval studies being what they were in his time. The villain, Mstislav, lusts after the captive Polovtsian princess, Sorena, but she remains faithful to her husband, Zamir. Unable to control his unreasonable passion, Mstislav eventually causes the deaths of Sorena and Zamir after trying to convert them to Christianity. He then comes to his senses and curses his own villainy. The specific anti-Catholic tendency of Voltaire's play was mechanically transposed by Nikolev to Russia, although there is no record of the medieval Russians trying to christianize their Mongol invaders by force. It was not until the play's revival in the Napoleonic age, in 1810, that the Russian press noticed, with disbelief, the play's anti-Christian and antipatriotic outlook.

The monarch as a villain was, of course, a standard fixture in tragedies by Corneille and Voltaire with which eighteenth-century Russian audiences were widely familiar in translation. Nevertheless, at the time of the premiere of *Sorena and Zamir*, the commander-in-chief of the Moscow garrison, Count Iakov Bruce, became alarmed at the play's appeal for religious tolerance and at some of the tirades denouncing tyranny. He ordered further performances of the play discontinued and sent a copy of the script to the empress, with the supposedly offensive passages underlined. Catherine, who was more tolerant than many of her officials (this was before the events in France had alarmed her), refused to become concerned. "I am astounded, dear count," she wrote to Bruce, "that you stopped the performances of the tragedy which was apparently received with pleasure by the entire audience. The meaning of the verses you indicated has no relation to your sovereign. The author protests against the abuses of tyrants, and you yourself have called Catherine mother."[17]

A writer almost as prolific as Kheraskov and possibly even more mediocre, Nikolev took up literature when his military

17. The last sentence, refers to Nikolev's line "We do not always find a father in our monarch", which Bruce found subversive.

career was interrupted by progressive blindness. Throughout the remainder of the eighteenth century, Nikolev's tragedies, comedies, and comic operas were regularly performed. His collected poetry and plays were published in 1796 in five volumes. But his plays lost their popularity even during his lifetime. When the eighteen-year-old literary enthusiast Sergei Aksakov, the future author of *The Family Chronicle*, was taken by an actor friend to see the aged Nikolev in 1812, most of the younger playgoers had no idea who Nikolev was. In his later memoirs, Aksakov drew a touching portrait of the blind and forgotten playwright still sure of his own greatness. His plays were by then hopelessly eclipsed by the recent achievements of Ozerov and Shakhovskoy. Surrounded by a small group of faithful followers, Nikolev read to them his new Sumarokov-type tragedy, incongruously based on a sentimentalist novel by the then fashionable Mme Cottin.[18]

18. S. T. Aksakov, *Sobranie sochinenii* (Moscow, 1902) vol. 4, pp. 4–14.

❧IV❧

The Age of Catherine: Prose Comedy and Sentimental Drama

In the twentieth century, Sophie Auguste Fredericke von Anhalt-Zerbst has frequently been impersonated on stage and screen by actresses as diverse as Pola Negri and Marlene Dietrich, Elisabeth Bergner and Mae West. None of these portrayals ever bothered with her intellectual dimensions or the complexities of her personality. They were all too busy documenting her sexual exploits. The erotic fantasy of the popular imagination about a woman insatiable enough to need a male harem and powerful enough openly to provide herself with one has almost eclipsed from our view the historical reality of the astute politician, the enlightened eighteenth-century skeptic, the patron and correspondent of Voltaire, Diderot, and other fine minds of the age.

The provincial German princess who took the name Ekaterina Alekseyevna to marry the unbalanced Peter III of Russia, who became the absolute ruler of the country after arranging to have him assassinated (it was a question of her own survival), and who got to be known as Catherine the Great even during her lifetime, was in fact head and shoulders above any of her Romanov descendants in culture, intellectual independence and imagination. It was during her reign that the drastic and mostly beneficial changes in Russian society, education, and the arts, initiated by Peter the Great half a century earlier, came to fruition.

During Catherine's long reign (1762–96), the theatrical and musical life of Russia began to rival that of Western European countries. Italian, French, German, and, for a brief period, English operatic and theatrical companies performed regularly in the two Russian capitals.[1] Renowned composers, such as Cimarosa, Paisiello, Galuppi, and Sarti, stayed in Russia over long periods (Mozart's planned visit was prevented by his untimely death).[2] New theaters and concert halls were constructed all over the country. Secularization of the church, continued by Catherine with great energy, did away with the vestiges of clerical opposition to theatrical entertainments. The spread of education and increased foreign contacts assured that there was a receptive and informed audience for the generation of Russian dramatists that appeared in the 1760s.

Catherine as Playwright

The very art of writing plays acquired in the reign of Catherine an entirely new prestige, because the sovereign herself was a prolific and widely performed playwright. Not that she took her plays all that seriously. According to the memoirs of Princess Dashkova, her close personal friend, the empress regarded writing plays as a form of therapy. Once, when Dashkova happened to succumb to acute mental depression, Catherine cured her by ordering her to compose a comedy, with the assurance in advance that it would be performed at the Hermitage Theater and published in an annual collection of the best Russian plays (*The Russian Theater* [*Rossiiskii featr*], edited by Dashkova herself). To her friend's protestations that she lacked the necessary talent, Catherine replied by stressing the value of

1. On the English troupes, see A. G. Cross, "Mr. Fisher's Company of English Actors in Eighteenth-Century Petersburg," *Newsletter of the Study Group of Eighteenth-Century Russia* (Norwich), no. 4 (1976): 49–56.

2. On musical theater in eighteenth-century Russia and foreign composers and artists who contributed to it, see R.-Aloys Mooser, *Annales de la musique et des musiciens en Russie au XVIIIme siècle*, 3 vols. (Geneva, n.d.; ca. 1950).

playwriting for relaxation and distraction. The poet and critic Prince Peter Viazemsky, who gives this account of the origin of Princess Dashkova's play in his biography of Fonvizin,[3] concludes his story with the remark: "The history of this work [i.e., the play] is far more noteworthy and entertaining than the work itself."

The plays written by Catherine in Russian fill three thick volumes (there is also a volume of French plays).[4] As could be expected from the episode just cited, the literary quality of these plays is low. As drama they are amateurish and unoriginal. But as facts of Russian intellectual and cultural history her plays and opera libretti are not devoid of interest. They raise a number of questions begging answers that Russian scholarship has so far failed to provide. The first of these is the problem of authorship. By all available evidence, Catherine spoke Russian unidiomatically to the end of her days and she never learned to write it correctly. It is accordingly assumed that she needed the aid of her literary secretaries, Ivan Elagin and Alexander Khrapovitsky, both of them minor playwrights, to compose her Russian plays. Professor Alexander Pypin, however, who published her collected plays, spoke of working with Catherine's own manuscripts and saw the function of the secretaries as that of editorial assistants.

The Soviet historian of Russian theater Vsevolod Vsevolodsky-Gerngross, on the other hand, flatly asserts that "the empress provided the ideological outlook, but the composition of the plays and the development of their themes belong to her co-authors."[5] An examination of the published diaries of Khrapovitsky[6] and of the numerous biographical and epistolary sources on Elagin,[7] while providing a wealth of material on Cath-

3. Peter Viazemsky, Fon-Vizin (St. Petersburg, 1848), pp. 199–200.

4. Sochineniia Imperatritsy Ekateriny II, ed. A. A. Pypin (St. Petersburg, 1901), vols. 1–3 (Russian plays) and vol. 4 (French plays).

5. V. Vsevolodsky-Gerngross, Russkii teatr vtoroi poloviny XVIII veka (Moscow, 1960), p. 137. Reprinted in Istoriia russkogo dramaticheskogo teatra, (Moscow, 1977), vol. 1, pp. 252–53.

6. Dnevnik A. V. Khrapovitskogo, ed. N. Barsukov (Moscow, 1901).

7. For example, Alexander Kruglyi, "I. P. Elagin," in Ezhegodnik Imperatorskikh teatrov (St. Petersburg, 1895), suppl. 2, pp. 96–118.

erine's involvement in theatrical and literary affairs, supplies no clue as to her actual share in the composition of the plays. At the same time, the copious details of Russian provincial life and the familiarity with Russian folklore, proverbs, and provincial dialects displayed in these plays strongly suggest that the German-born monarch must have had outside help that went beyond simple editing.

Most of Catherine's plays fall into groups (or perhaps "nests" is a more suitable term), each group containing several plays that are variations on the same theme and plot. The earliest set, all subtitled "Composed in Iaroslavl During the Plague" (which Pypin considers a hoax), are the comedies *O Times!*, *Mrs. Grumbler's Name Day*, and *Mrs. Newsmonger and Her Family* (respectively, *O Vremia!*, *Imianiny gospozhi Vorchalkinoi*, and *Gospozha Vestnikova s sem'eiu*), written in 1772. These are full-length prose comedies, with plots revolving around the arrangement of a suitable match for a passive and obedient young noblewoman (usually named Christina), waited upon by an improbably learned and well-read maidservant (usually named Mavra). The heroine and her marriage provide the basic plot mechanism in these plays, but most of the interest is centered on the elderly female characters, the heroine's mother or guardian and her cronies. These characters serve as the butt for Catherine's satire. In them, she attacks such obvious targets as gossiping, hypocrisy, hypochondria, and parental tyranny. Less expected is the attack on religious bigotry in the first play, where as a faithful disciple of Voltaire, Catherine equates excessive religiosity with superstition.

The satire turns nasty in the group of comedies Catherine wrote in 1785–86, during her persecution of Russian Freemasons and other groups of *illuminati*. These comedies reflect her conflict with some of the prominent writers and journalists of the day. The first two plays, *The Deceiver (Obmanshchik)* and *The Deceived (Obol'shchennyi)*[8] are variations on the theme

---

8. There were several French and German translations of each of these plays. *The Deceiver* was performed in St. Petersburg in German and Russian, and also in Hamburg (see Pypin's notes to these plays in *Sochineniia Imperatritsy Ekateriny II*, vol. 1).

of Molière's *Tartuffe*; under the guise of ridiculing Cagliostro, they suggest that anyone interested in the mystical and the occult must be a dupe. The indictment of mysticism is even more sweeping in the third play of this set, *The Shaman of Siberia* (*Shaman Sibirskii*), which takes swipes at Freemasons and Neoplatonism, as well as Buddhism and other Oriental religions. The ultimate point of this comedy is that to search for ecstatic religious experience or revelation is to expose oneself to fraud. There is some unusual ethnographic material in *The Shaman of Siberia* that may be of interest to specialists in that area. The customs and religions of Siberian native peoples, as represented by the alien tribal culture of the play's hero, are viewed with a Westerner's contempt.

Catherine's satirical comedies of the 1770s follow the canons of the standard foreign or Russian neoclassical comedies of the period. Her imitations and adaptations of Shakespeare and her opera libretti based on Russian folklore, while unsuccessful artistically, do constitute new departures in their genre. Since Russia remained a French cultural colony almost until the romantic age, in the eighteenth century Shakespeare was regarded as unsuitable for the stage in his original form. His plays could be staged only in neoclassical adaptations. As late as the first quarter of the nineteenth century, *Othello* and *King Lear* were played in Russia in translations not from the original English but from simplified and "regularized" French versions by Jean François Ducis. A translation of the complete text of *Julius Caesar* published by the young Nikolai Karamzin in 1787 was perceived by his contemporaries as an act of willful eccentricity.

In this situation, it took both audacity and vision for Catherine to offer the Russian public her adaptations of *The Merry Wives of Windsor* (the Russian title, *Vot kakovo imet' korzinu i bel'ë* [This 'Tis to Have Linen and Buck-Baskets], comes from Ford's "Is this a vision?" speech, III, 2) and of *Timon of Athens* (as *Rastochitel'* [*The Spendthrift*]). They appeared in 1786, one year before Karamzin's *Julius Caesar*. The action of both plays was moved to contemporary Russia. Characterizations were in some cases drastically altered. Falstaff emerged as an affected Russian Gallomaniac, so very usual in Russian comedy of the time and so unlike his original in Shakespeare. *Timon of Athens* was provided with a happy ending, with the protagonist repenting his misanthropy and planning to marry the sister of the character who corresponds to Alcibiades in Shakespeare.[9]

The russified *Merry Wives of Windsor* was quite correctly subtitled by its author "A Free but Feeble Adaptation." It was a diluted and distorted Shakespeare, but a version that was at least allowed to keep the original shape. For once, his plays were not cut in the neoclassical pattern, as was the custom in that age. The same concern for Shakespearian form may be observed in Catherine's two "imitations of Shakespeare." These are original works patterned on Shakespeare's historical plays. The first of them bears the self-consciously provocative title *An Historical Representation Without Observance of the Usual Dramatic Rules. From the Life of Riurik. Imitation of Shakespeare.* The second one is called *The Beginning of Oleg's Reign (Nachal'noe upravlenie Olega).* Here, Catherine demonstratively dispensed with the unities of time, place, and action to depict in a series of flat and pompous tableaux the deeds of early Kievan rulers, as reflected in the *Primary Chronicle.* There is a great deal of historical inaccuracy about her portrayal of these medieval rulers as spokesmen for the eighteenth-century brand of enlightened absolutism. As writing for the stage, these plays are inept. But this did not prevent the empress from getting them staged at her court theater, with much pomp and pageantry. The 1791 production of *The Beginning of Oleg's Reign,* with choruses provided for the occasion by the court composer Giuseppe Sarti, was by all accounts the most lavishly mounted stage presentation in the history of Russia.

Catherine's opera libretti, the music for which was written by various Russian and foreign composers in her employ, date from 1786 to 1790. Some of them make use of Russian folklore in ways that are truly striking for their time. Thus, *Ivan Tsarevich*[10] explores the world of Russian magic folktales, complete

---

9. For a detailed comparison of Catherine's adaptations with Shakespeare's originals, see Ernest J. Simmons, "Catherine the Great and Shakespeare," *PMLA* 47 (September, 1932): 790–806.

10. The libretto is published in Pypin's *Sochineniia Imperatritsy Ekateriny II,* vol. 2, as *Opera komicheskaia: Khrabroi i smeloi vitiaz' Arkhideich,* pp. 403–37.

with wood demons, the witch Baba-Yaga with her hut on fowl's legs, and the hero's final marriage to the Tsar-Maiden, after he liberates her from the evil dragon. The text is full of quotations of traditional Russian folklore formulae and imagery, subsequently made familiar through their utilization in nineteenth- and twentieth-century works of literature and theater, ranging from Pushkin's *Ruslan and Liudmila* and Ershov's *The Little Humpbacked Horse* to Stravinsky's *The Firebird*. In a libretto written in the 1780s and coming from the author in question, all this is unexpected indeed.

Similarly, the libretto of *Boeslaevich, the Hero of Novgorod* (*Novgorodskii bogatyr' Boeslaevich*)[11] draws on the Novgorod cycle of *byliny*, the ancient folk poems that folklorists were only beginning to collect in the eighteenth century. The opera includes among its characters the standard *byliny* heroes Vasily Buslaev (with his mother Amelfa Timofeyevna) and Sadko (a century before Rimsky-Korsakov's opera), recognizable despite an odd spelling of his name (Satko). The last and most popular of Catherine's libretti, *Fedul and His Children* (*Fedul s det'mi*, 1790), is a straightforward compilation of Russian peasant song texts, gleaned from folk-song collections available at the time. Their arrangement and harmonization were entrusted by Catherine, somewhat perversely, to the visiting Spanish composer Vicente Martín y Soler.

Finally, there is a large group of shapeless later comedies (some of them published in the Pypin edition for the first time from Catherine's own manuscripts), with titles like *What Tricks Are These?*, *Misunderstandings*, and *Planned One Way, Done Another* (respectively, *Chto za shtuki?*, *Nedorazumeniia*, and *Dumaetsia tak, a delaetsia inako*). These plays are set in the milieu of the landed gentry. Their relatively realistic and un-

---

Evaluation of the music composed to this libretto by Ernest Wanzhura (or Vanchura) is found in N. Findeizen, *Ocherki po istorii muzyki v Rossii* (Moscow, 1928), vol. 2, pp. 245–47. R.-Aloys Mooser (*Annales*, vol. 2, pp. 410–11) portrays this Wanzhura, who pretended to be a Czech baron, but wasn't, as a shoddy confidence man.

11. *Sochineniia Imperatritsy Ekateriny II*, vol. 2, pp. 371–99. The music for this opera was composed by one of the finest Russian eighteenth-century composers, Evstignei Fomin.

flattering portrayal of that class is remarkable. Like Catherine's other experiments with dramatic genres, these plays all contain features that point, in vague and fumbling terms, to future literary tastes and styles.

For example, in *What Tricks Are These?* the tyrannical matriarch Mrs. Tverdina (Mrs. Hard), who is surrounded by female spongers (*prizhivalki*) and assorted schemers and who banishes a serf to a remote manor for showing kindness to a child, is a type that would come up frequently in the nineteenth century in Alexander Ostrovsky's plays. In *Misunderstandings*, the impractical noblewoman discussing with her wise peasant major-domo some inept scheme for improving her fortunes and saving her estate seems to be an eighteenth-century ancestress of Chekhov's equally impractical Mme Ranevsky, with Gogol's Manilov from *Dead Souls* occupying an intervening branch on the family tree. *Planned One Way, Done Another*, a story of a young widow courted by some grotesque country bumpkins (their probable derivation from Fonvizin's comedies is the only instance of a clear contemporary Russian influence in Catherine's plays), seems to strive for the structure and mood of one of Turgenev's proverb plays, such as *It Breaks Where It Is Thinnest*.

Catherine was well aware of the literary insignificance of her dramatic efforts. "I consider all my writings to be trifles," she wrote to her Parisian correspondent Melchior Grimm. "It pleases me to experiment in various genres, but it seems to me that everything I've written is mediocre, and therefore I have never ascribed any importance to it, other than as a means of distraction."[12] But she was vain enough to arrange publication, productions, and translations into other languages of most of her plays. She sent copies of them to her foreign correspondents, including Voltaire, at times disguising her authorship under a transparent cloak of pretended anonymity. Because these plays were widely performed and otherwise circulated throughout her reign, they remain a fact of the social and cultural scene of the period.

12. *Ēntsiklopedicheskii slovar'*, ed. F. A. Brockhaus and I. A. Ēfron (St. Petersburg, 1894), vol. 11, p. 575.

Had almost anyone else written them, it is quite certain that these comedies and libretti would have attracted major attention in the burgeoning field of eighteenth-century literary studies in the Soviet Union. Catherine did almost everything in her plays that orthodox Soviet scholars want their eighteenth-century writers to do. She ridiculed mysticism, cast a jaundiced eye on the official religion, and explored native Russian folklore long before the romantics made this fashionable. She tried to break out of the neoclassical structural straitjacket and to introduce authentic Shakespearian dramatic forms, thus anticipating the course Russian historical drama would take after Pushkin's *Boris Godunov*. Furthermore, she steadily ridiculed the Russian nobles in her plays and treated the lower classes (serfs, servants, and an occasional merchant) with sympathy, repeatedly showing them as smarter, kinder, and more human than their owners or employers.[13]

Now, none of these traits could ever make Catherine's clumsy plays any better as drama or more valuable as literature. But they *are* the sort of traits on which Soviet scholars based their reevaluation of Russian eighteenth-century art and literature. In any other author's play, a hypocritical domestic tyrant, such as Catherine's Mrs. Tverdina, would inevitably have been interpreted as an indictment of serfdom and of Russian nobles and as a satire on Catherine herself. Characters in plays by conservative Russian writers from Sumarokov to Gogol are explicated in this manner on far flimsier pretexts.

Were Catherine's plays to be given the same sociological treatment as the rest of Russian drama of the period (which supposedly did nothing but criticize the abuses of Catherine's rule), the entire official view of the period would collapse.[14] The em-

13. This attitude probably owed more to the Western theatrical tradition of Molière's Scapin and the Figaro of Beaumarchais than to any actual observation of the social realities of the period or the author's own social sympathies.

14. Recent Soviet scholars have obliterated the important distinction made by earlier historians, including Soviet ones, between the early part of Catherine's reign, when, while extending serfdom and increasing the privileges of the nobility, she still tried to bring as much of the Enlightenment to Russia as she thought practicable, and the later stage of her reign, when, terrified by the French Revolution and the fate of Louis XVI, she indeed turned oppressive and censorial in the cultural sphere.

press herself simply cannot appear as one of the more audacious social critics of the day. Therefore all the principal recent Soviet studies of the drama and literature of the period reduce their comment on her plays to an absolute minimum.

"Adaptations to Our Customs"

Catherine's literary collaborator, Ivan Elagin (1725–94), was responsible for a significant Russian theory of drama that came to be known (in the formulation of the playwright Vladimir Lukin) as the theory of "adaptation to our customs" (*sklonenie na nashi nravy*). A man of considerable literary culture, Elagin was educated at the Infantry Corps of Nobles at the same time as Sumarokov and Kheraskov. He formed a friendly relationship with Catherine while she was still the wife of the heir presumptive, and he served as an intermediary between her and her lover Stanisław Poniatowski, the future king of Poland. This brought him under suspicion of conspiracy, and he was banished from the capital by the Empress Elizabeth. His loyalty to Catherine was rewarded during her reign by a succession of official posts in which he could indulge his literary and cultural proclivities. In addition to heading Catherine's personal secretariat, Elagin in 1766 replaced the quarrelsome Sumarokov as the director of the Imperial Theaters. Among the secretaries and translators who worked under Elagin's supervision we find the future playwrights Fonvizin, Lukin, and Elchaninov.

A much admired literary translator (his translation of Abbé Prévost's *Mémoires d'un homme de qualité* was particularly valued by his contemporaries), Elagin was especially concerned with the problem of repertoire for the expanding Russian theater of the 1760s. Sumarokov's tragedies and comedies were still widely performed; new playwrights were appearing. In the meantime, there was an obvious pressing need for translations of foreign playwrights. The genre that was in short supply was comedy. To facilitate the advent of an authentic and contemporary Russian drama, Elagin and the young writers of his circle conceived the idea of selecting suitable foreign comedies and then transposing their action to Russia, substituting Russian names, customs, and situations for those depicted in the foreign original, but keeping the plot and the action intact. Elagin himself set the first example for this procedure by producing in 1764 a russified adaptation of *Jean de France*, a topical satire on fashionable Gallomania by the Danish playwright Ludvig Holberg.

Elagin's idea of russifying successful foreign plays may not strike us as a particularly unusual idea now, when European films are matter-of-factly converted into Broadway musicals and forgettable hits of the Paris boulevard theaters are carefully retooled by knowledgeable play-doctors into studies of American *moeurs*. Nor was it a new or original idea in Elagin's time, for adaptations of foreign plays to local customs had been widely practiced in various countries of Western and Eastern Europe since at least the seventeenth century.[15] For Russian conditions, however, it was a clever and timely concept. Within one season and in the face of considerable adverse criticism in literary journals, it deflected Russian comedy from the purely imitative path that Sumarokov had charted for it.

The beginning of the new age of Russian comedy can be dated from the season of 1764–65, when, in addition to Elagin's adaptation of Holberg, there appeared Denis Fonvizin's verse comedy *Korion* (a russification of *Sidnei* by J. B. L. de Gresset), Bogdan Elchaninov's adaptation of Voltaire's *L'écossaise* (itself an adaptation of a play by Carlo Goldoni), and the first full-length original Russian prose comedy, Vladimir Lukin's *The Wastrel Reformed by Love*. All these authors were at that time Elagin's protégés and disciples, and it was their work that pointed the way for the subsequent development of Russian comedy.[16] Although the practice of "adaptation to our customs" could on occasion be applied to tragedy (e.g., by Nikolev, or in Catherine's misguided use of it in her adaptation of *Timon of Athens*),

15. The modern Russian term for this practice is *peredelka*. See *Teatral'naia Entsiklopediia* (Moscow, 1965), vol. 4, cols. 312–13.

16. On the circle around Elagin, see the section "Die Jelagingruppe (1764–66)" in Hilmar Schlieter, *Studien zur Geschichte des russischen Rührstücks 1758–1780* (Wiesbaden, 1968).

it was in prose and verse comedy and in sentimental drama that its impact was most fruitful and most durable. By the 1770s, it became common for Russian theaters to produce russified versions of comedies by Holberg and Goldoni. In the transposed version of Lessing's *Minna von Barnhelm*, Minna and the other characters became landowners in the province of Iaroslavl.[17] The practice of adaptation was still current at the beginning of the nineteenth century, as can be seen from Alexander Pisarev's russification of Sheridan's *The School for Scandal* in 1823. The more successful Russian vaudevilles of the mid-nineteenth century often followed the same procedure. Later in that century, a playwright of Alexander Ostrovsky's stature saw nothing wrong with converting a successful French melodrama into a play set in Russia.

Prose Comedy: Sumarokov, Lukin, and Elchaninov

As already noted, Sumarokov was the earliest writer of literary prose comedy in Russia. According to the theatrical customs of the day, presentations of tragedies had to be preceded by brief comic curtain-raisers. In 1750 Sumarokov composed three such plays: *Tresotinius, Monsters (Chudovishcha)*, which was later renamed *The Court of Arbitration (Treteinyi sud)*, and *A Pointless Quarrel (Pustaia ssora)*. The aims, form, and method of writing comedies offered no difficulty to Sumarokov. They had all been prescribed by neoclassical normative poetics, for which he had made himself the official spokesman in Russia. In his "Second Epistle" of 1748, he outlined those aims: "It is comedy's property to correct mores by means of mockery; to make one

17. See R. Iu. Danilevsky, "Lessing v russkoi literature XVIII veka," and R. M. Gorokhova, "Dramaturgiia Gol'doni v Rossii XVIII veka," both in *Èpokha prosveshcheniia*, ed. M. P. Alexeyev (Leningrad, 1967). Allardyce Nicoll, in *A History of Late Eighteenth Century Drama, 1750–1800* (Cambridge, 1927) (despite its title, the book is about drama in England only), lists hundreds of French, German, and Italian plays whose action and characters were transposed to England during that period in a manner identical to the one practiced by the Elagin circle in Russia.

laugh and to heal is its true law."[18] As models, Sumarokov recommended the comedies of Molière and the "immortal" Destouches, and as suitable targets for comedy he listed inept judges, soulless law clerks, vain fops, pedantic Latinists, misers, and compulsive gamblers—that is, not anything rooted in Russian reality, but the stock-in-trade types of traditional French and Italian comedy.

With his earliest comedy, *Tresotinius*, Sumarokov inaugurated the custom of presenting onstage a vicious caricature of some contemporary adversary. *Tresotinius*, for example, was a lampoon directed against Trediakovsky. Later Sumarokov comedies satirized the novelist Fyodor Emin and one of Sumarokov's own sons-in-law, with the actors instructed to impersonate the victim during the performance. This method of personal caricature (*lichnost'* in eighteenth-century terminology) was continued by other Russian playwrights, and it persisted until the time of Griboedov.

Because Sumarokov ascribed a lesser importance to comedy than to tragedy, his works in this form, including the later group written in the 1760s and 1770s, are mechanical transpositions of French and Italian conventions reduced to a common denominator. The action of the comedies is said to be set in Moscow or St. Petersburg, but the characters bear such names as Geronte, Dorante, and Isabelle. They own serfs with names like Finette and Pasquin whom they must have abducted bodily from the Comédie Italienne in Paris. The dialogue strives for local color by introducing Russian proverbs and folk sayings, but much of the writing is labored and actually reads like a bad translation from another language. The social situations depicted in Sumarokov's later comedies aimed at a more plausible reflection of Russian reality. But the elegance, gaiety, and wit of the brief French and Italian comedies Sumarokov sought to imitate were hopelessly beyond his reach. During the 1750s his comedies held the stage simply because they were the only existing and performable Russian plays in that form.

With the appearance of the group of playwrights around

---

18. A. P. Sumarokov, *Izbrannye proizvedeniia* (Leningrad, 1957), p. 121.

Elagin, Sumarokov's monopoly was broken. Elagin and his protégés—especially Lukin, Fonvizin, and Elchaninov—had a more up-to-date conception of drama than the orthodox classicist Sumarokov. They were free of his rigidity and thus more receptive to the new forms of drama evolving in the West and more willing to incorporate recognizable aspects of Russian reality into their plays. Prose comedy was the genre that interested them the most. For all the importance of Fonvizin's subsequent production in this form, it is Vladimir Lukin (1737–94) who is revealed by recent Soviet scholarship as the pivotal figure in the development of Russian prose comedy in the early 1760s.[19]

Lukin's father was a court lackey, who at the end of his life somehow managed to purchase a small landed property with sixty serfs attached to it. This acquisition enabled the future playwright to enter the civil service, but his father's past saddled him with the serious handicap of ambiguous social origins. Even before he came to Elagin's attention, Lukin was one of the growing group of young civil servants and army officers who dabbled in translating French dramatists. Some of his early translations were published in 1763. After entering Elagin's service as his personal secretary in 1764, Lukin became the prime exponent of the "adaptational" theory as well as its most articulate theoretician.

Elagin's friendship and good will brought down upon Lukin the lasting hatred of Elagin's other secretary, Denis Fonvizin, the young nobleman of German descent also possessed of playwriting ambitions. Several passages in Fonvizin's published letters to his parents leave no doubt that Lukin's lowly origins were the crux of the matter and that Fonvizin found it intolerable to be on an equal footing with a man "whose father and ancestors never held any rank in their lives and were born to serve and not to rule."[20] For his part, Lukin wrote of Fonvizin's early

19. For a reevaluation of Lukin's significance, see the following publications by P. N. Berkov: *Vladimir Ignat'evich Lukin* (Moscow-Leningrad, 1950); the introductory essay to *Russkaia komediia i komicheskaia opera XVIII veka*, edited by Berkov (Moscow-Leningrad, 1950); and *Istoriia russkoi komedii XVIII v.* (Leningrad, 1977), chaps. 4 and 5.

20. Quoted, together with several other similar passages from Fonvizin's

efforts with respect and kindness, at least during the first few years of their association.[21]

Of the ten works for the theater published by Lukin during the decade of the 1760s, some are straightforward translations of plays by such then-admired French authors as Jean François Regnard and Jean Galbert de Campistron. Somewhat less expected is his abbreviated and rather clumsy translation of *La seconde surprise d'amour*, produced at a time when Marivaux was going out of fashion in France and had not yet caught on in Russia. Of his "adaptations to our customs," the most interesting ones are *Constancy Rewarded* (*Nagrazhdennoe postoianstvo*, a russification of Campistron's *L'amante amant*) and *The Trinket Vendor* (*Shchepetil'nik*). The first of these is an improbable comedy of disguises in which a forsaken mistress recaptures her fickle lover by disguising herself as an army officer and humiliating him in front of her rival, while her maid impersonates a valet. Ivan Dmitrevsky wanted to produce this play, but could find no actresses willing to appear in it. The first Russian actresses had made their debuts only a few years earlier. Before that time, female roles were taken by men, including Dmitrevsky himself, who had once played Osnelda in Sumarokov's *Sinav and Truvor*. The reverse disguise required by Lukin's play seemed both scandalous and unbecoming to the women, and production plans had to be abandoned.

The Trinket Vendor (Lukin's use of the rare regional word *shchepetil'nik* for the title of this play obliged him to explain its meaning in the preface to the printed version) was adapted from *The Toy Shop* (1735) by Robert Dodsley, via an intermediate French version by Claude Pierre Patu. It is interesting as an example both of English literary influence, unusual in Russian comedy of the eighteenth century, and of the growing trend,

---

correspondence, by K. V. Pigarev, *Tvorchestvo Fonvizina* (Moscow, 1954), pp. 60–61.

21. See the Introduction to the play *Nagrazhdennoe postoianstvo* (originally published in 1765), in *Sochineniia i perevody Lukina i El'chaninova*, ed. P. A. Efremov, (St. Petersburg, 1868), pp. 113–14, where Lukin defends Fonvizin's *Korion* against its critics and states that both Fonvizin and Elchaninov surpass him in talent and knowledge.

also ultimately traceable to England, toward open preaching and moralizing in the second half of the century.[22] The almost plotless play consists of a series of vignettes in which the vendor, a retired government official, confronts a succession of customers at a public masquerade, and while selling a trinket to each, insults and chastises them for their vices.

The customers are personifications of definite social types: a fop, a snob, an old man trying to act young, two dizzy society belles, a haughty poet, and the like. Some of these customers were meant as personal satires against Lukin's literary opponents (e.g., Sumarokov and Rzhevsky) and were easily recognized as such by his contemporaries. To the characters and situations he found in the English and French plays he was adapting, Lukin added a nobleman named Chistoserdov (Mr. Pureheart), who acts the *raisonneur* and explains the moral of the proceedings to his nephew, recently arrived from the provinces. He also added two peasant lads, employed by the vendor in his storeroom, who speak a provincial Russian dialect and are supposed to mark the earliest appearance of realistically depicted peasants on the Russian stage. If this is so, the debut was not auspicious, for Lukin seems to sneer at their coarseness and stupidity and uses the phonetic transcription of their northern dialect (*tsokanie*) only to ridicule their simplicity.

Lukin's one fully original dramatic work is the sentimental comedy *The Wastrel Reformed by Love* (*Mot liubov'iu ispravlennyi*). This was the first full-length, five-act modern comedy written in the Russian language (Sumarokov's comedies were one- or two-act curtain raisers), and one of the more interesting Russian plays of the entire eighteenth century. It was apparently written prior to Lukin's association with Elagin. Betraying a close study of Destouches and Nivelle de la Chaussée, the play has a well-intentioned but weak hero named Dobroserdov (Mr. Goodheart) who has squandered away most of his estate. Under

---

22. See Hugh McLean's ground-breaking study of these problems with specific reference to *The Trinket Vendor* (referred to above in Chapter 3, note 11), and also Thursten Wheeler Russel, *Voltaire, Dryden and Heroic Tragedy* (New York, 1946), on Voltaire's role in transmitting to France the English tendency to preach and moralize in dramatic works.

the influence of his false friend Zloradov ("happy about the misfortune of others," i.e., Mr. Schadenfreude), Dobroserdov takes up residence at the home of an elderly rich noblewoman he pretends to court. He is actually in love with the niece of his hostess, a pure and honorable young woman named Cleopatra. The hero's virtuous tutor, the serf Vasily, tries to save his master from wrong influences, but the evil Zloradov keeps embroiling Dobroserdov deeper and deeper with his hostess and his assorted creditors. The hero is about to be led off to a debtors' prison, when a *deus ex machina* in the form of his younger brother appears with the news of an unexpected inheritance that saves the hero from his creditors and unites him with Cleopatra.

There is much preaching in *The Wastrel Reformed by Love*. Some of its scenes are pointedly emotional, thus justifying the contention of certain scholars that this play is the earliest Russian sentimental drama. And indeed, the evil behavior of the play's villain is unmotivated, and money is the mainspring of all the action, in the manner of a nineteenth-century melodrama. The well-paced structure of the play is probably its strongest point, though this is vitiated by the occasional crudity of the dialogue.

The single most successful characterization is that of the serf Vasily, who is offered his freedom at the end of the play, but refuses to leave his repentant master. This was one of the earliest literary portrayals of the serf as a devoted family retainer, to be made familiar later by similar types in Pushkin and Tolstoy. Another interesting character is Cleopatra (she was named after the Orthodox saint of that name and not for the Egyptian queen), a curious hybrid of the standard dutiful daughter of neoclassical comedy and the tragic heroine, torn between her love for the hero and her duty to comply with the last will of her dead parents, who charged her to obey her hostile aunt.

Against the background of the 1760s and in comparison with Sumarokov's comedies, Lukin's plays represented a genuine breakthrough. Russian life was reflected in them more fully and with greater dramatic know-how than ever before. It was Lukin who introduced to Russian drama characters who had believable Russian names (albeit broadly symbolic ones) and lived in recognizable Russian surroundings. The social customs of the period, including serfdom, appeared on the Russian stage for the first time in this play. So did the forms of personal address, complete with patronymics and affectionate nicknames. Without Lukin's pioneering efforts, the somewhat later dramatic and literary discoveries of Fonvizin would be hard to imagine.

The Wastrel Reformed by Love had a triumphant first performance on January 19, 1765, with the participation of almost all the important Russian actors and actresses of the period. Lukin was particularly pleased with Iakov Shumsky, a specialist in roles of roguish French valets, giving a believable performance as the sedate and reasonable serf Vasily, and with Avdotia Mikhailova's "experimental" treatment of the role of the wise serving maid.[23] The resounding success came despite the efforts of a cabal of Lukin's enemies (possibly encouraged by Novikov and Sumarokov) to discredit the play by circulating rumors that it was actually an inept translation of *Le dissipateur* by Destouches.[24]

Encouraged by the play's success, Lukin proceeded to publish his collected plays and translations in two volumes. The very act of doing so (Lomonosov was the only writer whose collected plays had been published up to that time) was received as an act of unprecedented insolence by Sumarokov and other senior literary noblemen. They were already angered by Lukin's contributions to a literary dictionary, published in Leipzig, in which his portraits of his Russian contemporaries were not flattering. In addition, Lukin provided each play with a detailed preface, and in some of these he ridiculed Sumarokov's comedies and even doubted that Molière was at his best in every one of his plays, citing *Le mariage forcé* as an example of a rather stupid play. Such *lèse majesté* (Sumarokov was still revered by many as

23. *Sochineniia i perevody*, p. 15.

24. Despite Lukin's own disclaimer of any similarity to Destouches beyond the basic theme of a young man losing his fortune, Hilmar Schlieter (*Studien*, pp. 67–68) takes the view of Lukin's enemies in his otherwise admirable study of Russian sentimental drama and insists at some length that Lukin's play is in fact an adaptation of *Le dissipateur*. But most of Schlieter's parallels are unconvincing, because the comparison of the two plays reveals little similarity in plot, treatment, or characterization.

the Racine of Russia) turned most of the literary establishment of the day against the lowly-born upstart Lukin. Lukin's interest in folk theater and popular entertainments, so unusual for a literary man of his period, and his desire to see on the stage a believable representation of Russian reality (as outlined in several of his prefaces) were plainly ahead of his time. His views on these subjects provided additional fuel for his adversaries.

In the satirical journals of the day, the aristocratic critics of the late 1760s started a concentrated campaign of vilification against Lukin.[25] The aim of the attack was nothing less than the annihilation of the offending writer. Literate public opinion was mobilized and controlled in such a way that the victim of the attack had no way of replying or defending himself. Lukin chose to withdraw from playwriting and literature altogether and to concentrate on his civil service career, where he eventually rose to an important rank. His plays, despite the initial success of *The Wastrel Reformed by Love*, disappeared from the Russian stage for good. Pushkin was apparently not aware that such a man as Lukin had ever lived. When Viazemsky unearthed him in the 1830s in the course of his research on the biography of Fonvizin, Lukin was a totally forgotten writer. It is due to the efforts of Alexander Pypin in the nineteenth century and particularly to those of more recent Soviet scholarship that we have become cognizant of Lukin's considerable historical significance.

Of the original members of the Elagin circle, the playwright who was personally closest to Lukin was Bogdan Elchaninov (1744–70). This is evidenced by Lukin's admiring mention of Elchaninov in his introduction to *The Wastrel Reformed by Love*, and especially in the essay "A Letter to Mr. Elchaninov," which served as a preface to *The Trinket Vendor*, where their friendship and the community of their literary interests are dis-

25. See V. B., "Vladimir Ignat'evich Lukin," in *Ezhegodnik Imperatorskikh teatrov* (St. Petersburg, 1893–94), suppl. 2, pp. 147–60, for a good account of the press campaign against Lukin. The leading instigator of the campaign was the editor of the better satirical journals, Nikolai Novikov, who was also an admirer of Sumarokov and the publisher of his works. It is possible that some of the anti-Lukin articles credited to Novikov were actually written by Fonvizin (see P. N. Berkov, *Istoriia russkoi zhurnalistiki XVIII veka* [Moscow-Leningrad, 1952], pp. 288–90).

cussed at some length.[26] Little is known of Elchaninov's background, except that he was an army officer educated at the Kiev Mohyla Academy (which would suggest clerical origins). During the mid-1760s, Elchaninov was connected with the Infantry Corps of Nobles and, of course, with the group of writers around Elagin. His russification of Voltaire's *L'écossaise* and his translations of *comédies larmoyantes* by Diderot made his name known in literary circles. His single most notable contribution was his one-act comedy *The Giddypate Undone (Nakazannaia vertoprashka)*[27] which was produced at the Imperial Theater in St. Petersburg in 1767, with Tatiana Troepolskaya in the principal role and with Dmitrevsky, Shumsky, and Alexei Popov in the cast. The initial premise of this play may have been suggested by the French comedy *La coquette corrigée* (1756), by Jean-Batiste de la Noue, but upon it Elchaninov built an attractive and wholly original dramatic work.

Set in Russia, but frankly French in style, the play may perhaps be described as an "adaptation to our customs" of Célimène's final humiliation in Molière's *Le misanthrope*. Despite this debt to the heroine's predicament in Molière, Elchaninov wrote a fresh and original play. His flirtatious young widow, maliciously amusing herself at the expense of her numerous admirers (she was to serve as the prototype for Shakhovskoy's Countess Leleva in *The Lipetsk Spa* half a century later), is quite believably Russian, and so are the assorted fops, intellectuals, and dignitaries who surround her. Elchaninov demonstrated, possibly for the first time in Russian drama, the art of writing elegant, witty dialogue, superior in its way to anything his friend Lukin had achieved. All of a sudden, in the 1760s the Russian language was shown to be capable of subtlety and ready for *marivaudage*.

The confrontation between the heroine and her disapproving aunt, with both ladies' tempers barely below the boiling point throughout the scene; the cruel mockery of an amorous elderly judge by some heartless young noblemen; the literary

26. See *Sochineniia i perevody*, pp. 183–89.
27. Published in the Efremov edition of Lukin and Elchaninov, *Sochineniia i perevody.*

discussion in which a high-minded nobleman tries to explain the value of Feofan Prokopovich and Lomonosov to a pair of frenchified popinjays who have never heard of these writers; and the final dramatic exposure of the heroine's perfidy by her masked lover—all these show that in Elchaninov eighteenth-century Russia possessed one of her more gifted dramatists. Much was expected of this young man by his contemporaries. But the playwright's military duties took him off to one of the Russo-Turkish wars, where he was killed at the age of 26.

Apart from Fonvizin's two prose comedies and Vasily Kapnist's *Chicane*, *The Giddypate Undone* is the only conceivable Russian play of the second half of the eighteenth century that one could look forward to seeing in a modern production, in Russian or in another language. Both nineteenth- and twentieth-century Russian critics chose to ignore this play because they could not pin a simplistic sociological or political moral on it. Its literary art makes it a play that deserves to be known.

Sentimental Drama of the 1770s

Inaugurated by the international success of two English plays, George Lillo's *The London Merchant, or The History of George Barnwell* (1731) and Edward Moore's *The Gamester* (1753), European sentimental drama took its definitive form in the 1750s in the plays of Denis Diderot and, on a higher literary level, of Gotthold Ephraim Lessing. Known as *comédie larmoyante* or *comédie sérieuse* in French, subsuming the categories of *bürgerliches Trauerspiel* and *Rührstück* in German and of melodrama and sentimental comedy in English, this new form of drama abandoned both the unities and the rationalistic frame of mind of neoclassical tragedy and comedy. Instead of appealing to the spectators' reason, it aimed at their tear ducts. In the second half of the eighteenth century, playwrights learned that the flow of tears could be a source of both pleasure and profit.

In their search for touching situations, the writers of sentimental drama discovered that audiences could be more easily affected by the exposure of the protagonists' children to hunger, seduction, and assorted other dangers than by the psychological inner conflicts of neoclassical tragedy. They rediscovered the principle, known to Elizabethan playwrights, that comic scenes, interspersed with tragic ones, serve to heighten audience response. Their plays were consequently family-centered and allowed for the inclusion of both heroic and ridiculous characters. Actual representation of pain or danger was what produced the dramatic effect in this form of drama, not the characters' reactions to them. With the lessening of interest in psychological motivation, there appeared the unmotivated villain of sentimental drama, a man (though in the progenitor of the genre, Lillo's *George Barnwell*, it was a woman) who enjoys inflicting suffering on others for no reason at all.

The intended impact of sentimental drama on the audience was unabashedly didactic, preachy, and moralizing. In his unpublished dissertation on the plays of Kheraskov,[28] Michael Green points out that the plays of Diderot and the didactic canvases of Diderot's contemporary Jean Baptiste Greuze (the counterpart of sentimental drama in the visual arts) seem embarrassing today because of their "painfully contrived sentimentality." "They are filled," Green goes on, "with virtuous old gentlemen wringing their hands over erring but fundamentally dutiful children; weeping is frequent and there is much lifting of hands and eyes heavenward, while the characters are so prompt to throw themselves on their knees that one wonders whether the actors were provided with protective knee padding." [29] There follows a tabulation of the stage directions for the characters to kneel or fling themselves at other characters' feet, gleaned from one single play by Kheraskov, *The Friend of the Unfortunate* (which will be described shortly).

Traces of sentimental drama began seeping into Russian

28. Michael Green, "Mikhail Kheraskov and His Contribution to the Eighteenth Century Russian Theater" (Ph.D. diss., University of California, Los Angeles, 1972). On the importance of Diderot's plays and theories for the origin of sentimental drama in Russia, see Michael Green, "Diderot and Kheraskov; Sentimentalism in Its Classicist Stage," *Russia and the West in the 18th Century*, ed. A. G. Cross (Newtonville, Mass., 1983), pp. 206–13.

29. Green, "Mikhail Kheraskov," in his chapter on sentimental drama, pp. 5–6.

plays within a decade after the introduction there of neoclassical forms. They first appeared in Kheraskov's irregular early tragedy *The Nun of Venice* (1758) and even more so in his "heroic comedy" in verse *The Atheist (Bezbozhnik,* 1761), with its arch-villain protagonist who betrays his beloved, his brother, and his father and intends to commit a series of murders without any discernible psychological motive. Hilmar Schlieter begins his book on sentimental drama in Russia[30] with these two plays and he also includes Fonvizin's *Korion* and Lukin's *Constancy Rewarded* and *The Wastrel Reformed by Love* in his purview. But while these plays of the 1760s do feature undoubted traits of sentimental drama, it is only in the 1770s that we get Russian sentimental drama in its full-blown form.

The legitimization of the genre in Russia can be dated roughly from 1770, the year of a highly successful production in Moscow of *Eugénie* by Beaumarchais, staged by Ivan Dmitrev-sky, who also played the principal male role. This early effort by the author of *The Marriage of Figaro* is a typical sentimen-talist play in which a spoiled, wealthy English nobleman seduces an impoverished gentlewoman by deceit and trickery, leaves her pregnant in order to marry a rich bride, but eventually, touched by her continuing love and devotion, returns to her. The pro-feminist attitudes expressed in the play, the plight of the seduced and abandoned heroine shown without equivocation, and the denunciation of all neoclassical tragedy in the introductory essay that accompanied the play—all this alarmed Sumarokov, who responded by devoting the introduction to his own play, *Dimitry the Impostor* (1771), to an extended attack on *Eugénie.*

Sumarokov's essay vividly conveyed the alarm of a confirmed neoclassicist at the idea of combining tragic and comic elements in the same play and of extending theatrical conventions to the point of presenting on the stage problems and situations never treated in Greek or seventeenth-century French classics. Suma-rokov appealed to the authority of Voltaire, to whom he had written on the subject and whose reply he quoted in his in-troduction *in toto.* Voltaire agreed that sentimental drama was a bastardized genre, but he added that "when you have no

30. See note 16 above.

horses, you are happy to have your carriage drawn by mules."[31] Seemingly unaware that Voltaire was writing his own sentimental dramas and getting them staged, Sumarokov denounced the new genre in his own and Voltaire's name and concluded:

> I could praise such a taste when people shall eat cabbage soup with sugar, drink tea with salt and coffee with garlic, and combine the inauguration mass with the requiem. The difference between Thalia and Melpomene is the same as between day and night, between heat and cold, and between reasonable spectators and mindless ones. The value of something is affirmed not by a majority vote, but by its quality; and quality is based on truth.[32]

Sumarokov's vehement protests notwithstanding, *Eugénie* opened the way for native Russian sentimental drama. Its principal authors were Mikhail Kheraskov, Mikhail Verevkin, and Pavel Potemkin. Kheraskov emerged from his neoclassical closet temporarily in the 1770s to produce two sentimental dramas, *The Friend of the Unfortunate* (*Drug neschastnykh*, 1774) and *The Persecuted* (*Gonimye*, 1775). The former is a compendium of melodramatic and sentimentalist clichés, in which the father of a starving family is driven by desperation to commit an armed robbery. His victim, a young judge, forgives him upon seeing the domestic situation of "this most virtuous of criminals, most sentimental of fathers" and falls in love with his elder daughter, who later turns out to be not his daughter but the heiress of a wealthy noble. The characters are, to quote Michael Green, "not only virtuous, but exquisitely conscious of being so, forever congratulating themselves and each other on their moral sensibility; the word *dobrodetel'* (virtue) and its derivatives occur no less than thirty-two times in the course of the play."[33]

The Persecuted, whose action is set on an uninhabited island—an unusual setting for a sentimental drama, to be sure—has been until recently regarded as an original play. Michael

31. A. P. Sumarokov, *Polnoe sobranie vsekh sochinenii v stikhakh i proze* (Moscow, 1787), vol. 4, p. 66.

32. Ibid., p. 64.

33. Green, "Mikhail Kherasov," in his chapter on sentimental drama, p. 14.

Green has shown that it is an adaptation or, more exactly, a plagiarism (the debt was neither acknowledged nor discovered for exactly two centuries) of Shakespeare's *The Tempest*, deprived of Ariel, Caliban, and Prospero's magic, dressed in Spanish garb, and stripped of its poetry.[34] The result is a play every bit as lachrymose and contrived as *The Friend of the Unfortunate*.

Kheraskov's sentimental dramas are deployed in a neutral, abstract world, not unlike the one in which much of neoclassical tragedy is set. On the other hand, the plays of Mikhail Verevkin (pronounced Veryovkin; 1732–95) have emphatically contemporary, even topical themes and settings. Verevkin had a varied career as a naval officer, university professor, and, after 1759, director of the *gymnasium* in Kazan, where the future poet Gavriil Derzhavin was among his pupils. He wrote a total of five works for the stage, of which only three survive.[35] His comedy of intrigue, *The Name-Day Celebrants* (*Imeninniki*, 1774), is about the defeated scheme of an envious stepmother to wreck her stepdaughter's courtship by a young man the stepmother desires for herself. Verevkin's two sentimental dramas bear idiomatic, hard-to-translate titles: *Tak i dolzhno*, meaning approximately *As It Should Be*, published in 1773 and first performed in 1777;[36] and *Toch'-v-toch'*, contextually translatable as *True to Life*, written in 1774 but not published or performed until 1785.

As It Should Be shows the plight of Captain Doblestin (Val-

34. Michael Green, "Kheraskov's *Gonimye*: Shakespeare's Second Appearance in Russia," *Slavic Review* 35, (2) (1976): 249–57.

35. For Verevkin's biography and a good, informative analysis of his plays, see N. M. Tupikov, "Mikhail Ivanovich Verevkin (Istoriko-literaturnyi ocherk)," in *Ezhegodnik Imperatorskikh teatrov* (St. Petersburg, 1893–94), suppl. 3, pp. 130–60.

36. An eyewitness account in English of a 1778 Moscow performance of Verevkin's *As It Should Be*, recorded in the unpublished diaries of Katherine Harris, the sister of the British ambassador to St. Petersburg, Sir James Harris, is cited by A. G. Cross, "The Eighteenth-Century Russian Theater Through British Eyes," *Studies on Voltaire and the Eighteenth Century* (Oxford, 1983), vol. 219, p. 230. Miss Harris called the play *Il doit être* and provided a fairly accurate summary of its plot. She expressed a particular admiration for the performance of the actor Vasily Pomerantsev (she spelled his name Pomeranci) in the role of Doblestin's aged uncle.

orous), whose plans to marry his beloved Sophia are jeopardized by a chance meeting with an old derelict, kept in the local jail and periodically released to beg for alms. In this pathetic beggar, Doblestin recognizes his uncle who was declared missing during the Battle of Hotin in the reign of Empress Anna and whose estate Doblestin had inherited. The uncle had been captured by the Turks, it turns out, and sold into slavery. Released and allowed to return to Russia in his old age, he was unable to prove his identity to the officials of his home town and was imprisoned for vagrancy. In a brutal and violent scene, Doblestin confronts the corrupt municipal administrators and, by first bullying them and then bribing them, secures his uncle's release. When he tries to return to his uncle the lands and the serfs that were his, Sophia's greedy grandmother withdraws her consent to their marriage because without his uncle's property Doblestin is considerably poorer than he was when he made his initial proposal. The impasse is resolved when Sophia and Doblestin agree to renounce their claims on the dowry that the grandmother had earlier promised them.

In the two big dramatic climaxes of the play, the scene at the city hall and altercation about the dowry, Doblestin has to sacrifice his principles and resort to bribery, which he despises, in order to secure happiness and justice. The comical subplot, which involves Sophia's serf chambermaid Malania, shows an innocent victim of another form of chicanery, this time of the ecclesiastical variety. Malania's earlier marriage had been declared invalid on an absurd technicality when the priest who officiated at her wedding was denounced by an envious colleague and defrocked. Long separated from her one-time husband, Malania finds herself neither married nor single and thus has difficulty accepting the proposal of Doblestin's valet, who has fallen in love with her. *As It Should Be* belongs to the long line of eighteenth- and nineteenth-century plays that denounce corruption in the administrative system of the country. Unlike such later examples as *Chicane* by Kapnist (1796) and Alexander Sukhovo-Kobylin's *The Affair* (*Delo*, 1861), Verevkin's play was published and widely performed without any trouble from the censor.

108

Corruption and bribery are also an important theme in *True to Life*, which, however, casts a much wider net in its examination of contemporary issues. The play is set in a small town in the eastern part of European Russia during the immediate aftermath of the peasant rebellion of 1773–74, led by the Cossack deserter Emelian Pugachov, who claimed to be Tsar Peter III. Pulcheria, the daughter of the town commandant, had been captured by the rebels, raped, and forced to serve as the concubine to their leader. The dramatic opening scene shows Pulcheria after she has been freed and returned to her father. She feels debased and polluted and sees no other course but to enter a nunnery. Her insensitive father Trusitsky (Cowardly) refuses to understand her despair.

Pulcheria is loved by an impetuous young officer named Voin Miloy (Lt. Warrior Darling—the *noms parlants* characteristic of much eighteenth-century drama tended to be particularly obvious in sentimental drama). She feels unworthy of Miloy after her ordeal, but he insists on restoring her honor by marrying her, so that "innocence, beauty, and virtues wronged by the enemies of mankind may be given redress by my hand." He then points a drawn sword at his heart, threatening suicide unless she consents to marry him. The contest in generosity between Pulcheria and Miloy is contrasted with the parallel situation of a more prosaic married landowning couple named Lezhebokov (Mr. and Mrs. Lazybones).

Mrs. Lezhebokov, who had also been raped by the rebels, was forced to go through a marriage ceremony with one of them. Her husband is not sure if he wants her back or if they are still legally married. She wins him over by pointing out that had *he* been threatened with floggings and hanging, the way she was, he might have consented not only to marry another woman but even to offer himself as a concubine to the rebels. Surrounding these two couples are the corrupt officials, headed by Pulcheria's father, who all return to their business-as-usual lives of graft and bribe-taking as soon as the rebellion is suppressed. Comic relief of sorts is provided by three mutilated ex-soldiers who comment on the proceedings from the no-nonsense, practical point of view of working-class people.

Set in the same historical moment and dealing with some of the same themes as Pushkin's novel *The Captain's Daughter* and written by a playwright who was personally involved in the events of the Pugachov rebellion, *True to Life* is a fascinating historical document. Verevkin had an excellent ear for racy, colloquial dialogue and a good sense of dramatic values. What doomed his plays to oblivion was the pompous, inflated dialogue of his lovers, whose artificial rhetoric must have sounded unbearably melodramatic by the beginning of the nineteenth century. The moral purity of his young heroes and heroines makes for a good dramatic contrast with the corruption of their surroundings. But it also gives both *As It Should Be* and *True to Life* a blurred moral focus. Why do Captain Doblestin and Lieutenant Miloy defend the status quo with such ardor when they see how oppressive and dishonest it is?

Count Pavel Potemkin (pronounced Potyomkin; 1743–96) was distantly related to Catherine's powerful favorite of that name. He served in the army, taking part in the Russo-Turkish wars and in the suppression of the Pugachov rebellion. In the 1780s, he held gubernatorial posts in Saratov and in the Caucasus. He returned to active military service in 1790 and was placed under Suvorov's command. For the bravery he displayed during the taking of the fortress of Ismail from the Turks in 1790 and in the campaign against the Poles (led by Tadeusz Kościuszko) at the time of the partitioning of Poland, Potemkin was awarded the title of count. He was also the first translator into Russian of *Julie, ou La nouvelle Héloïse* and other texts by Rousseau, and he wrote poetry, comparable in its fluency with the work of the more elegant of the eighteenth-century predecessors of Pushkin.

Hilmar Schlieter has likened the first of Potemkin's two works in dramatic form, *Russian Heroes in the Archipelago* (*Rossy v arkhipelage*, 1771) to the earlier German genre of *Staatsaktion*,[37] a type of court theater that depicted actual historical persons of the recent past, usually monarchs, performing acts of sublime heroism. But perhaps the term devised by American television two centuries after this one-of-a-kind play was

37. Schlieter, *Studien*, p. 96.

written describes it better: it was a docu-drama. What Potemkin did was to write a play in verse about the battle of the Bay of Chesme, which had taken place only one year earlier and during which the Russian navy defeated and sank the fleet of the Ottoman Empire. The characters in the play are Alexei Orlov, Admiral Greig, and other generals and admirals who participated in the battle. They appear under their real names and they all express themselves in couplets of iambic hexameter, couched in the archaized diction of neoclassical tragedy.

Features of neoclassical tragedy are also prominent in Potemkin's equally unusual second play, the sentimental drama in verse *The Triumph of Friendship* (*Torzhestvo druzhby*), first performed in St. Petersburg in 1773 and revived in Moscow in 1778. Once again the Russo-Turkish war provides the background. Modest, a Russian officer, had rescued the Turkish maiden Zaida from violence and dishonor under battle conditions by making her his personal captive. Out of gratitude she followed him to Russia, where he placed her at the home of his closest friends, the young judge Milon (Darling) and Milon's sister Chestana (another artificial name, derived from *chest'*, "honor"; its English equivalent would be Honoria). To afford Zaida his further protection, Modest is planning to make her his wife.

These four characters comprise the entire cast of the play. All four are given equal prominence. They are united by a tense network of emotional interrelationships—love, friendship, and possessiveness—and Potemkin deployed this network with a sure hand, making one think of a similarly intricate emotional quadrangle in Racine's *Andromaque* or the triangle in his *Bérénice*. The initial premise of the play—a Turkish captive involved in cross-cultural and erotic interaction with her Christian captors—may seem like just a clever reversal of the basic plot of all those popular eighteenth-century comedies and operas about a Christian woman imprisoned in a Turkish seraglio. But Potemkin claimed that his play was based on an actual event, and, indeed, during those Russo-Turkish wars marriages or liaisons between Russian soldiers and captive Turkish women were known to have occurred. The great romantic poet Vasily Zhukovsky (1783–1852) owed his existence to just such an alliance.

The very first scene in *The Triumph of Friendship* shows it to be a curious hybrid between the elevated, abstract universe of the traditional love-versus-duty eighteenth-century tragedy and the domestic milieu and overheated emotional climate typical of *comédie larmoyante*. Judge Milon refuses to see petitioners and cancels his appointments so as to be alone and meditate on his emotional predicament. His sense of duty and his friendship with Modest are the two most important things in his life. Both are threatened by Milon's growing attraction for Modest's prisoner and intended bride, Zaida. In a soliloquy that foreshadows the eulogies to emotional friendships in Ozerov's *Dimitry of the Don* (1807), Milon outlines his principles for the audience:

Коль горестна была разлука та для нас.
Прощаясь с другом, я вещал ему в тот час:
Служи отечеству, пренебрегая веком;
Служи ты ближнему, будь прямо человеком.[38]
Мне в горести мой друг лобзая отвечал.
Расставшись, три года его я не видал.

. . . .

Наш первый в жизни долг есть обществу служить,
Любить отечество, Монарху верным быть,
Всем жертвовать для них.

How sorrowful that separation was for us.
Bidding farewell to my friend, I proclaimed to him at that
time:
Serve the Fatherland, disregarding all that is transitory;
Serve thy neighbor, be a true human being.
In his sorrow, my friend replied to me with kisses.
After parting, I did not see him for three years.

. . . .

Our primary duty in life is to serve society,
To love our Fatherland, to be loyal to our Monarch,
To sacrifice everything for their sake.

38. Italicized in the original.

Chestana, an instantly recognizable neoclassical *belle inhumaine*, is even more fanatical on the subjects of duty and honor than is her brother. She has loved Milon's friend Modest for years but she kept her feelings hidden because "Благопристой-ность нам скрывать любовь велит" ("Decorum commands us to conceal love," wherein the Russian *blagopristoinost'* represents the *bienséance* of seventeenth-century French tragedy). Chestana considers her failure to overcome her love for Modest a sign of weakness. Instructing her new friend Zaida in the ways of Western civilization, Chestana tells her:

> Но рассуждением страсть должно побеждать,
> И крайность всякую пороком почитать.

> But passion should be vanquished by reason
> And everything extreme regarded as a vice.

But Zaida, who during her brief stay in Russia has somehow learned to speak fluent and elegant Russian, rejects rationalism and neoclassical heroics. Hers is the voice of nature as perceived and described by Jean Jacques Rousseau. She refuses to wear Western clothes, feeling that her Turkish costume is more appropriate to the human shape. Having fallen in love with Milon, Zaida sees no reason to suppress this love or to be ashamed of it. She owes Modest a debt of gratitude for rescuing her, but this does not oblige her to marry him. When Chestana promises her that by overcoming her feelings for Milon she will earn the admiration of posterity, Zaida vehemently rejects this neoclassical *gloire*:

> Какой ты славы мне желаешь преужасной?
> Не славу, смерть сулишь Заиде ты несчастной.

> What is this most horrendous glory that you wish on me?
> It's not glory, but death that you promise the unfortunate
> > > > > > > > > Zaida.

The internal battle that Milon, Chestana, and Zaida have to fight with their own selves during the three acts of *The Triumph of Friendship* is actually the battle between the right to emotional fulfillment that sentimentalism had postulated (and the later romanticism was to take up as its cause) and the rigidity of Cartesian rationalism. It is a battle, fought in an eighteenth-century play, between the seventeenth and nineteenth centuries. Chestana represents the views of Corneille, and behind him, paradoxically, there looms pre-Petrine Russia. Zaida's outlook starts from that of Rousseau and goes forward all the way to George Sand.

Modest's position is the simplest of all. His attitude toward Zaida is mostly proprietary. He is at first outraged to learn of Milon's love for her, seeing this solely in terms of Milon's betrayal of their friendship. But learning of Milon's suffering, of Zaida's love for Milon, and of Chestana's hopeless passion for his own person, Modest relinquishes Zaida and offers to marry Chestana, simply, one gathers, in order to do the decent thing. If these three people, who are dear to him, will be made happy by the arrangement, Modest is prepared to go along with it.

Philosophically, if not quite dramatically, *The Triumph of Friendship* is an enthralling work. It occupies a halfway point between two basically incompatible genres. Out of this incompatibility arises the paradox at the core of the play: friendship and love, seen as the highest good, are also constant sources of pain. Further, as Hilmar Schlieter has observed, there is the absurd situation that four essentially virtuous people are made to suffer every time they try to act in a virtuous manner.[39] The inner dialectic of the play is thus of considerable complexity. The rationalist sermons preached by Milon and Chestana with so much conviction appear not quite so obvious once we see the effect on their lives of practicing what they preach. The philosophical seriousness and the implicit moral ambiguity of this play, combined with the fluency and elegance of Potemkin's verse, raise it high above the level of the simplistic, imitative productions of Sumarokov and Kheraskov.

Initially well received, Potemkin's plays were forgotten by the end of the century. His translation of Voltaire's tragedy *Mahomet* went on being performed in the early nineteenth century, but it was usually ascribed in the playbills to the actor Ivan Dmitrevsky. In an oft-recorded instance of the inferior

39. Schlieter, *Studien*, p. 102.

pushing out the good, the place that *The Triumph of Friendship* should have occupied by virtue of its literary art in the repertoire of turn-of-the-century Russian theaters was taken instead by a far less subtle or interesting sentimental drama in verse by one Dimitry Efimiev (1768–1804), *A Criminal Through Gambling, or a Sister Sold by Her Own Brother (Prestupnik ot igry, ili Bratom prodannaia sestra)*. This lachrymose offering tells of a crazed gambler who sells his sister into serfdom after gambling her estate away and of the love that then blossoms between the betrayed young woman and her purchaser. Premiered in 1788 and published in 1790, it went on being played in both Russian capitals until around 1820.

In human interest and literary worth the plays of Verevkin and Potemkin seem more attractive now than the popular tear jerkers of the prolific German playwright August von Kotzebue (1761–1819), whose numerous sentimental dramas began their reign on the stages of Russia and of the Western world in the 1790s. By the start of the nineteenth century, Kotzebue supplanted most of Russian sentimentalist drama and much of eighteenth-century neoclassical tragedy in Russian theaters. His plays were ubiquitous. In 1811, he was big enough in England to have one of his dramas cause a major crisis in the plot of Jane Austen's *Mansfield Park*. The protagonist of Gogol's *Dead Souls* (1841) saw an announcement of the performance of a Kotzebue play upon arriving in the God-forsaken provincial town in which the action of the novel is laid. When the heroine of Alexei Pisemsky's novel *A Thousand Souls* (1858) decided to become an actress, she made her debut in *Misanthropy and Repentance* by Kotzebue. His weepy dramas went on being played in Russia even after the advent of romanticism and then of realism had relegated almost all the other native and foreign eighteenth-century playwrights to mothballs.[40]

40. Gerhart Giesemann's *Kotzebue in Russland*, Frankfurter Abhandlungen zur Slawistik, vol. 15 (Frankfurt am Main, 1971), is a book-length study of Kotzebue's impact on Russian culture. The author's inclination to exaggerate the admittedly important influence of his subject makes his account not always reliable. See also Michael Green, "Kotzebue and Kheraskov: Sentimentalism in Its Pre-Romantic Stage." *Newsletter of the Study Group of Eighteenth-Century Russia.* (Norwich), no. 10 (1982): 20–29.

※V※

The Age of Catherine:
Comic Opera
and Verse Comedy

Comic opera was introduced in Russia in the early 1770s. It remained one of the favorite dramatic forms until the end of the century. The term "comic opera" may perhaps be misleading in this case. We are not talking of *La serva padrona* or *Le nozze di Figaro* or of any other eighteenth-century comic opera that requires opera singers to perform. Russian comic opera of the age of Catherine was essentially a literary rather than a musical-dramatic genre. It was a brief (one- or two-act) play that included songs, vocal ensembles, and occasionally choruses. The performers were actors with some singing ability rather than trained singers. The music for these productions was at times composed by Russian or resident foreign composers, but equally often there would be no original musical score, the performers being instructed to sing their vocal numbers to the tune of this or that popular air of the day.

In its native France, this form of drama had a more appropriate name: *comédie mêlée d'ariettes*. Its main practitioner was Charles Simon Favart (1710–92). During his four decades of writing musical comedies, Favart bridged the transition from the *comédie en vaudevilles*, associated with the theatricals at the two annual Paris fairs (*théâtre de foire,* in which Favart did his playwriting apprenticeship in the 1730s), to the true French *opéra comique* at the end of the century. Favart's comedies treated a variety of themes and social situations, but some of his most lasting successes depicted peasant life in the countryside. The plot invariably showed two young peasant lovers overcoming obstacles to their union, be it parental opposition or interference by a villainous bailiff. A favorite plot device was to involve a naive, inexperienced peasant girl with a man above her on the social scale and in a position to hold her in his power. This was the situation in Favart's *Le caprice amoureux, ou Ninette à la cour* (1755), *Annette et Lubin* (1762), and *Les moissonneurs* (*The Reapers*, 1768), the latter being a musical comedy version of the Book of Ruth in the Bible, of all things.

Favart's manner of presenting peasant life on the stage has been compared to the idealized and bucolic canvases of Boucher and Watteau. Because of his enormous popularity, these plays were soon exported to other countries and adapted to local tastes and conditions.[1] Thus *Ninette à la cour* reappeared in Germany as *Lottchen am Hofe*, in England as *Phoebe at Court*, in Italy as *La contadina in corte*, and in Sweden as *Lantflickan på hovet*. In 1783, it was incarnated as *La villanella rapita*, a comic opera with libretto by Giovanni Bertati and music by Francesco Bianchi, with two additional scenes composed by Mozart (K. 479 and 480) for the 1785 production in Vienna. Similar transformations occurred with other successes of Favart, leading to a great vogue for rustic settings and for peasant girl—peasant boy—nobleman (or bailiff) triangles in comedy and comic opera throughout the Western world.

By the time Lorenzo da Ponte used this theme in his libretti for Mozart's *Le nozze di Figaro* (the Susanna, Figaro, and the Count imbroglio) and *Don Giovanni* (Zerlina, Masetto, and the Don), in 1786 and 1787, respectively, he was offering his own version of possibly the most widespread comedic plot situation of the century. The famous Don Giovanni–Zerlina duet "Là ci darem la mano" is a rare survivor of hundreds upon hundreds

---

1. On the impact of Favart on the whole of Europe (with the exception of the Slavic countries), see Alfred Iacuzzi, *The European Vogue of Favart* (New York, 1932).

of duets of similar content and tone that resounded for half a century in every theater in Europe.

Another work whose international success helped enhance the fashion for *paysannerie* in musical comedies was Jean Jacques Rousseau's *Le devin du village*, premiered in Paris in 1752. Considered the first genuine French comic opera (i.e., unlike the earlier *comédies d'ariettes*, it was provided with a musical score of its own), Rousseau's brief idyll about a peasant couple brought together by a kindly quack consolidated the custom of letting the musical theater voice a preference for the wholesome rustic life over the supposedly corrupt life of the cities. *Le devin du village* became the object of innumerable imitations, one of the most popular of which was Favart's parody of Rousseau, *Les amours de Bastien et Bastienne* (1753), also widely copied and imitated. Its progeny included the brief opera *Bastien und Bastienne*, composed by the twelve-year-old Mozart for a performance at the home of Dr. Anton Mesmer, the originator of the notion of animal magnetism.

A third French name essential for tracing the origins of the comic opera in Russia is Michel-Jean Sedaine (1719–97), author of comic-opera libretti for such popular composers of the second half of the eighteenth century as Philidor, Pierre Monsigny, Egidio Duni, and André Grétry. Follower and personal disciple of Denis Diderot, Sedaine carried out in the libretti of his earlier period Diderot's behest that theater deal with all occupations and social classes. Thus the protagonists of Sedaine's *Blaise le savetier* (1759, music by Philidor) are a poor village cobbler and his wife; in *Le jardinier et son seigneur* (1761, also with Philidor), a kitchen gardener is humiliated and his wife and daughter are insulted during a visit from an inconsiderate noble and his entourage; and in *Le roi et le fermier* (1762, music by Monsigny), King Henri IV of France finds refuge in a hut of a peasant whose fiancée has been abducted by neighboring nobles.

Sedaine's most popular comic opera, *Le déserteur* (1769, also with Monsigny), deals with the adventures of a simple army private who got into trouble because of a practical joke played on him by his future father-in-law. Through their great currency, these early libretti of Sedaine (his later ones, including the one for Grétry's *Richard Coeur de Lion*, 1784, dealt mostly with royalty) greatly expanded the social purview of comic opera.[2] Between them, Favart, Rousseau, Sedaine, and a host of their contemporaries and imitators made the poorer and humbler classes the expected and accepted protagonists in comic opera. Servants, peasants, artisans, or gardeners who could appear in subsidiary or episodic roles in neoclassical comedy and sentimental drama were now shown to have love lives of their own and interesting, at times paradoxical emotions. Although the surviving conventions of the dramatic pastorale could at times force the rustic protagonists of the new genre into the poses and attitudes of Arcadian shepherds and shepherdesses, the extended social purview of the *opéra comique* did represent a step in the direction of a more democratic theater.

Russians became acquainted with this new genre during the guest appearances of a French touring company in St. Petersburg in 1764–68.[3] Because of the continuing orientation toward Parisian tastes and the widespread practice of "adaptation to our customs," it was inevitable that Russian comic opera would materialize. The earliest chronologically was *Aniuta*, a one-act comedy with music, which was performed for Catherine by the members of her church choir at Tsarskoe Selo on August 26, 1772. *Aniuta* is generally considered the ancestress of all Russian operettas and musical comedies. The text was written by Mikhail Popov (1742–ca. 1790), otherwise known as a journalist and folklore collector. The music for this piece is lost. It is not

2. On the significance of Sedaine, see Louise Parkinson Arnoldson, *Sedaine et les musiciens de son temps* (Paris, 1934).

3. R.-Aloys Mooser, *L'opéra-comique français en Russie au XVIIIe siècle* (Geneva, 1954), pp. 45 ff. The same author's *Opéras, intermezzos, ballets, cantates, oratorios joués en Russie durant le XVIII siècle* (Geneva, 1955) is a useful tabulation of foreign and Russian works for musical theater during the period in question. Soviet studies of Russian comic opera as a literary genre have either ignored its dependence on its French models or gone to the extent of denying this dependence. Soviet musicologists offer a somewhat more factual and historically balanced account of the genesis of the genre in Russia; see, for instance, Iu. V. Keldysh, *Russkaia muzyka XVIII veka* (Moscow, 1965), chap. 6. But even they have not yet ventured a full-dress comparison of the Russian texts with Favart and Sedaine, which is the crux of the matter.

clear whether there was an original score composed for it or, as was often the practice with Favart, the musical numbers were simply sung to the melodies of currently popular songs (known as *timbres* in France).

Popov's play follows closely the mode of representing peasant life developed by Favart and Rousseau. The heroine, the adopted daughter of a poor peasant, is being forced into a distasteful marriage with a hired hand. A handsome young nobleman named Victor falls in love with her and, upon investigating her origins, discovers that Aniuta is a noblewoman by birth, the daughter of a colonel and thus a suitable match for himself. The disappointed foster father and the hired hand are easily placated by small sums of money. The concluding ensemble chants the praises of the stratified social system: "Do not try to possess things you were not meant to own. . . ./ He who is pleased with his lot / Is the most fortunate man in the world!" While their extreme poverty and very hard life are made explicit in the play, Aniuta and the two peasant men are shown as crude, grasping, foul-mouthed creatures. Only the noble Victor is endowed by the author with some semblance of dignity and humanity.

For all its lack of dramatic polish and human insight, Popov's *Aniuta* did set the pattern for the numerous comic operas that were written and produced in Russia during the following three decades. Popov's incorporation of native folk songs into his text led his followers to feature such songs, either authentic or imitations, in their plays. The name Aniuta (probably inspired by Favart's *Annette et Lubin*, known as *Aniuta i Liubim* in Russian and widely performed in the 1760s and 1770s both in versions set in France and in "adaptations to our customs") became as canonical for peasant heroines in comic operas as Sophia was for young gentlewomen in serious comedy.

In the wake of successful productions of imported comic operas with texts by Favart and Sedaine and of *Aniuta*, Russian playwrights and poets took to writing comedies with music that reflected, with greater or lesser fidelity, the situation of the humbler classes of the time: peasants (both enserfed and free), artisans, lower ranks in the army and the navy, and, eventually, the merchant class and even the clergy. The comic opera was thus the dramatic genre that encompassed a social range broader than any other of its time.

A basic fact of Russian lower-class life of the time was the form of slavery known as serfdom. For all her enlightenment and oft-reiterated opposition to tyranny, Catherine not only supported this archaic institution, but even extended it to areas where it did not previously exist, such as the Ukraine. When the popular successes by Favart that portrayed free peasant farmers in France were transplanted in Catherine's Russia, the result was the first full-scale portrayals on the Russian stage of serfs as protagonists. Now, criticism of mistreatment of serfs by their owners and of other abuses of serfdom was permitted and expected in that age to a degree that would seem unbelievable in the early nineteenth century. But it was permitted only provided that the abuses were attacked, not the institution itself. Catherine herself offered an example of such permissible criticism in her comedy *What Tricks Are These?*

Therefore no eyebrows were raised when Nikolai Nikolev presented his "drama with voices" *Rozana and Liubim* (premiered in Moscow in 1778 and regularly played in both capitals until the end of the century), with music composed by one of the members of the Kerzelli family. It was a comic opera about a peasant maiden, abducted by an amorous nobleman who eventually repents and returns her to her father, so that she can marry the young fisherman she loves. Nikolev's libretto was a russification of two of Favart's greatest successes: *Annette et Lubin* and *Ninette à la cour*. He followed these two texts with so much fidelity, in fact, that he anticipated by seven years Bertati's libretto for the Bianchi–Mozart *La villanella rapita*, which, had it not postdated Nikolev's effort, might have easily been mistaken for its model.

No one in the eighteenth century would have thought Nikolev's text incendiary, nor would the ruling classes (royalty and nobility), who were the principal audience of comic opera performances, have ever tolerated a work they thought was directed against themselves or their interests. Both the authors of comic operas and the spectators considered the institution of serfdom a given of Russian life, which, like all human institutions, was capable of being abused. Commentators in later centuries, however, have often chosen to see such works as *Rozana and Liubim* not as russifications of Favart and his contemporaries, but as denunciations of serfdom based on the playwright's observations of concrete social realities.[4] The rationale for such readings is usually the unsympathetic portrayals of serfowners in the comic operas in question. Conversely, Vasily Maikov's *The Village Feast, or Virtue Crowned (Derevenskii prazdnik, ili Uvenchannaia dobrodetel', 1777)*, with music by Mikhail Kerzelli, has at times been assaulted as a reactionary, pro-serfdom tract, merely because it shows the relations between the serfowner and his serfs as amiable.[5] But one could easily turn this around, because on a deeper level it can be shown that Maikov's portrayal is far more grim than Nikolev's.

Styled as "a pastoral drama with music in two acts," Maikov's play begins with the mannered wooing of a coy shepherdess by an eloquent shepherd. They seem to have stepped right off a delicate Sèvres teacup. These rococo porcelain creatures are intended to represent Russian serfs living in the environs of Moscow. In the second act, the lovers are duly betrothed, with the kindly aid of their owner. Other assembled serfs chant the praises of their wise master. An ideal relationship thus seems to exist between serfs and their owners. The benevolent squire expresses his concern for the welfare of his subjects to a visitor and in a solo accompanied by a peasant chorus sings:

4. P. N. Berkov's *Istoriia russkoi komedii XVIII v.* (Leningrad, 1977) is unique among the Soviet literary and musicological studies of the last three decades in denying that Nikolev's *Rozana and Liubim* and Kniazhnin's *Misfortune from a Coach* are antiserfdom tracts (pp. 190 ff. and 207 ff.).

5. For example, Boris Aseev, *Russkii dramaticheskii teatr XVII–XVIII vekov* (Moscow, 1958), p. 315 ("a typical example of a reactionary comic opera"; in the revised edition of the book, *Russkii dramaticheskii teatr ot ego istokov do kontsa XIII veka* [Moscow, 1977], the adjective "reactionary" was changed to "pseudopopular"); and Iu. Keldysh, *Russkaia muzyka*, p. 259 ("a reactionary feudal idyll"). Because of this reputation, *The Village Feast* has been excluded from the collections of Maikov's poetry and plays that have appeared in postrevolutionary times. It can be found in *Sochineniia i perevody V. I. Maikova*, ed. L. N. Maikov (St. Petersburg, 1867).

If my peasants are pleased with me
Then I am pleased with myself.
If they are wealthy and free,
Therein lies all my joy.

But the chieftain of a transient band of gypsies (who are treated in this play with the kind of racist contempt that late nineteenth-century Russian melodrama reserved for the Jews, and Soviet drama of the 1950s for Americans) gives the squire some sharp arguments. To his preaching of honor and virtue, the gypsy, in a tone reminiscent of Brecht's *Three-Penny Opera*, rejoins with the following sung argument:

He who has something in his pocket
Will be honored even by the Heathen.
But he whose pocket is empty
Will buy nothing with his honor.
He will be indeed vanquished by hunger
And allowed to die among the Christians.

The gypsy's pretended astuteness at reading palms (which helps unite the lovers) so frightens the squire's bailiff that he confesses having instituted a system of bribes in the village, thereby bringing some serfs to the verge of ruin. And even though the virtuous serfowner promises to set everything right, the play's most striking point has been made: Maikov's happy peasants, who do not have to contend with the cruel voluptuary of *Rozana and Liubim* and are not owned by the irresponsible and silly Gallomaniacs of Kniazhnin's *Misfortune from a Coach* (discussed later in this chapter), are still not protected from oppression and exploitation even though their owner happens to be a benevolent singing philosopher. It can thus be seen that *any* eighteenth-century comic opera can be used to demonstrate the inhumanity of slavery if one looks at it from the viewpoint of later, more enlightened times.

It is a measure of the freedom of Russian literature from censorship pressure in the reign of Catherine II prior to the French Revolution that the social issues raised by serfdom could be reflected in comic opera as openly as they were. Certainly, the more outspoken examples of this genre could not have been published or performed in the reigns of Alexander I or Nicholas I half a century later. Yet in the 1770s and 1780s these works were produced at Catherine's court and in open public theaters and were performed by serf actors in the private theatres of wealthy magnates. Nor is there any indication that the empress and the upper hierarchy felt themselves indicted by the depiction of the abuses of serfdom in comic opera, any more than an American politician or banker today feels himself personally indicted by a portrayal of a corrupt politician or a dishonest banker in a Hollywood film.

The single most popular comic opera on a peasant subject, however, ignored serfdom altogether. It owed its huge and lasting success to the charm of its music and to the wit and gaiety of its dialogue, written in an authentic-sounding peasant dialect. This was *The Miller: A Wizard, a Cheat, and a Matchmaker* (*Mel'nik—koldun, obmanshchik i svat*)[6] by Alexander Ablesimov (1742–83), otherwise known as a minor journalist of the period and the author of several other, forgettable libretti. Initially performed in Moscow in 1779, *The Miller* had for a musical score a pastiche of Russian folk songs arranged by the conductor Mikhail Sokolovsky and later revised by Evstignei Fomin.

One of the numerous progeny that Rousseau's *Le devin du village* engendered all over Europe (a not unillustrious lineage, since it also includes Mozart's *Bastien and Bastienne*),[7] *The Mil-*

---

6. This title is usually rendered into English with the four nouns separated by commas (e.g., D. S. Mirsky, *A History of Russian Literature* [New York, 1960], p. 59). This creates the impression that the title refers to four characters: a miller, a wizard, a cheat, and a matchmaker. In the original Russian, the last three nouns serve as epithets, qualifying the miller. All four nouns refer to the same character.

7. This obvious dependence of Ablesimov on Rousseau, recognized by prerevolutionary commentators and by Nikolai Findeizen (*Ocherki po istorii muzyki v Rossii* [Moscow, 1928], vol. 2, pp. 213 and 216), has been either flatly denied in recent Soviet scholarship (Keldysh, *Russkaia muzyka*, pp. 287–88) or else challenged. Aseev, *Russkii dramaticheskii teatr* (1977 ed.), pp. 425–26, admits the similarities between Rousseau and Ablesimov, but denies that Ablesimov imitated his French predecessor: "The contrast between the natural and pure

ler shows the unlikely predicament of a free peasant who is married to an impoverished noblewoman and of their daughter, named of course Aniuta, who is in love with a neighboring farmer. Each of the parents wishes the daughter to marry into his or her own social class. The miller of their village, who moonlights as a quack magician, helps the young couple by convincing the parents that the young man is fatally predestined to be Aniuta's husband. The miller subdues the parents' social prejudices with the argument that an independent farmer who owns his own homestead (*odnodvorets*) is a peasant and a nobleman at the same time.

The racy arguments among the characters and the abundance of popular peasant songs (including some that were taken from the traditional wedding ritual), plus such novelties as having a live horse onstage and real Russian balalaikas in the orchestra, all added up to an overwhelmingly successful work. *The Miller* brought about a host of imitations, spread the renown of the genre of comic opera throughout Russia, and became a favorite for amateur theatricals (Vissarion Belinsky, the future critic, played the part of the father in an amateur student production in the late 1820s). It retained its popularity well into the nineteenth century and has occasionally been revived in Soviet times.

The only other eighteenth-century Russian comic opera to enjoy a success comparable to *The Miller* was *The St. Petersburg Bazaar (Sankpeterburgskii gostinyi dvor)*[8] by Mikhail Matinsky

---

country life and the corrupting influence of the city, which is present in Rousseau's opera, are replaced in Ablesimov's play with the contrast between peasants and noblemen and, most importantly, with glorification of free peasant labor."

8. This work exists in two versions. The second version, revised by Matinsky and with its music rearranged by the court composer Vasily Pashkevich, was performed in 1792 under the title *You Shall Be Known by the Way You Live* (*Kak pozhivesh', tak i proslyvesh'*). The first version of the text remained the better known one, but the musical contributions of Pashkevich were incorporated into it in subsequent performances. The first version (i.e., *The St. Petersburg Bazaar*) is also the one found in various recent collections of eighteenth-century drama, for example, the Berkov anthology and (in excerpts) in *Khrestomatiia po russkoi literature XVIII veka*, ed. A. V. Kokorev (Moscow, 1961). On the differences between the two versions of the play, see Findeizen, *Ocherki po istorii muzyki*, vol. 2, pp. 224–30, and Keldysh, *Russkaia muzyka*, pp. 315–24.

(1750–ca. 1820). Matinsky was born a serf, possibly an illegitimate son of his owner. Aware of his intelligence and talents, the owner sent him to study in Italy (in this he followed a widespread custom during Catherine's reign; some of the best Russian painters and musicians of the period were Italian-schooled emancipated serfs). Upon returning to Russia, Matinsky was given his freedom and became a teacher of mathematics and geography at the exclusive boarding school for the daughters of the highest nobility, the Smolny Institute. His later writing efforts were devoted to textbooks on geography and geometry. It was during his stay in Italy that Matinsky wrote what is certainly the most original Russian comic opera of the eighteenth century. Matinsky was thought to have also composed the music for this piece. More recent research casts serious doubts on the assumption that Matinsky ever composed any music at all.[9]

The St. Petersburg Bazaar seems to owe less to a recognizable foreign model than does any other work of this genre. There is no young peasant heroine and, in fact, no love story at all. Matinsky turned his attention instead to the "dark kingdom" of the tradition-bound Russian merchant class. In so doing, he discovered an entirely new social and dramatic dimension that nineteenth-century Russian drama was to explore and populate. The central character is the wealthy but miserly merchant Skvalygin (Mr. Tightwad), a greedy and unprincipled moneylender, who is shown both in his family life, with his doting, alcoholic wife and his stupid daughter, and in his varied business practices.

Skvalygin forms an alliance with his prospective son-in-law, an equally corrupt retired civil servant named Kriuchkodey (Mr. Hook-and-Crook), who makes a practice of involving transient out-of-town peasants in horse-cart accidents and then extorting money from them for imaginary damages. Skvalygin and Kriuchkodey cook up a complicated financial swindle designed to victimize an army officer and two society ladies who had been careless about getting their dealings with Skvalygin certified and documented. In the second act, the victims invade Skvalygin's home during the engagement party (*posidelki*) for his

9. See Keldysh, *Russkaia muzyka*, for a summary of this research.

daughter and Kriuchkodey, but can obtain no satisfaction. Owing to a clumsy blunder of the daughter, the two crooks believe themselves mutually betrayed and their misdeeds are exposed in the end.

From the very first two scenes, one showing Skvalygin putting the squeeze on the other merchants in the bazaar arcade and the other bringing in the two subsequently victimized noblewomen to bargain in a vocal sextet with four of the merchants, Matinsky displays a truly admirable grasp of the milieu and a profusion of dramatic invention. One original scene follows another throughout: the bargaining of the crafty merchants with their capricious customers; the indignant aria of the peasant (in the northern *tsokanie* dialect), forced to pay damages for the accident he knows was caused on purpose; Skvalygin's stingy dispositions for the engagement party refreshments, clashing with the hospitable inclinations of his wife; the carousing of the previously prim and sedate merchants' wives who are briefly left alone with the liquor supply; and the complex and ingenious plot strategem that brings the villains to justice.

All these scenes achieve a genuine dramatic impact. None of them seems to have any precedent in foreign or Russian comic traditions. Matinsky managed to make even the moralizing scene between Skvalygin and his remonstrating virtuous nephew (an enlightened young merchant given to charitable works), interesting, lively, and believable. Musically, the work is also one of the finest of its kind, with very successful female choruses in the engagement party scene, pointing the way for future treatment of similar material by Glinka, Tchaikovsky, and even Stravinsky (there are phrases in the betrothal scenes of both *The Miller* and *The St. Petersburg Bazaar* that have their exact counterparts in the text of *The Wedding*). Matinsky's use of an urban middle-class dialect for literary purposes was a pioneering event, leading in a direct line, via the merchant-class plays of Peter Plavilshchikov, Alexander Shakhovskoy, and Gogol's *Marriage* to the plays of Alexander Ostrovsky.

The tendency of comic opera to depict a wide range of social groups led Russian playwrights of the period into some unusual paths. The ubiquitous Kheraskov tried his hand at comic opera, with *The Good Soldiers (Dobrye soldaty,* 1780). The result was closer to sentimental drama than to comic opera. The heroine of the work is unjustly accused of theft while wandering about like Micaela in search of her missing soldier-lover. There are a phenomenal number of scenes in which people find their long-lost relatives. The novelty of the piece was in its regimental milieu, for which the music by Hermann Raupach (the same composer who had, back in 1758, turned Sumarokov's *Alcestis* into one of the earliest Russian *opere serie*) provided an appropriately military background, with bugle calls and sung marches. One of these marches, "We Love You from the Heart" ("My vas lyubim serdechno"), entered folklore; it became a favorite song of Russian soldiers in the 19th century and was still popular as late as World War I. The Russian equivalent of the Anglo-American "For He's a Jolly Good Fellow," it was cited as such in a highly ironical context in Gogol's comedy *The Gamblers* (1842), where it is sung in honor of a stooge who is helping a band of confidence men swindle the protagonist out of his fortune.

Nikolai Lvov (1751–1803), a good minor poet of the period, art critic, and collector of folk songs (he collaborated in the famous Prach-Lvov collection of 1790), as well as the brother-in-law of both Derzhavin and Kapnist, was responsible for *Postal Coachmen at the Relay (Iamshchiki na podstave,* 1788). It utilized the traditional musical lore of those drivers who transported travelers across the vast Russian plains and whose singing was to inspire so many of the later Russian poets, from Pushkin to Annensky. The musical score for this work, composed by Evstignei Fomin, is one of the most successful and attractive in the entire range of Russian comic opera.

A totally unexpected turn was taken by comic opera with the production of *The Candidate Priest (Stavlennik),* which was first performed by divinity students in the city of Iaroslavl, the "cradle of Russian theater," in 1780. The text was written by Iakov Sokolov, of whom nothing is known except that he was "a student of philosophy." Nor is anything known about the music, for the score has been lost. With *The Candidate Priest*, comic opera invaded the realm of the Russian clergy, who were a separate caste in prerevolutionary times. The story deals with a competition for a job left vacant by the death of a parish priest. The leading candidate is Foma (Thomas), son of a wealthy priest, whose main qualifications for the job are a sonorous, low-pitched voice and a large supply of money his father has provided for bribes.

Other characters in the all-male cast are Foma's rival for the job, the poor bell-ringer's bright son Provor (a nonexistent, invented name, conveying the idea of agility and adroitness), whose family home has burned down and who needs the job desperately, but lacks funds for bribes; a nobleman at whose house Foma is a lodger and who fawns on and flatters the priest's son, his social inferior, so long as the latter provides the liquor; the mercenary secretary of the local administration; the incorruptible city official who has to judge at the candidates' competition; and a comical peasant who disrupts the examination scene when he mistakes Foma's voice for the lowing of his lost cow. The clumsy web of intrigue woven by Foma comes to naught when the well-prepared Provor bests him at reading and singing; but in defeat, Foma does not give up and puts up a spirited defense for the right of the untalented and the unlearned to fend for themselves by whatever means they can.

Unlike other comic operas of the time that had prose dialogue between the sung numbers, *The Candidate Priest* follows the example of Popov's *Aniuta* in having its dialogue in iambic hexameter throughout. The writing is lively and witty, the characterization vivid, and the versification expertly done. There is no record of this work's performance in either of the capitals, but it did enjoy a lasting and deserved provincial success. There exists an account of an open-air performance of this piece staged in 1814 to celebrate Napoleon's defeat. Handwritten copies of the text were still circulated in Iaroslavl in the 1830s. What makes this work particularly interesting is its portrayal of members of an important social class that traditionally remained outside the scope of Russian literature until the late nineteenth century, when Nikolai Pomialovsky, Nikolai Leskov, and Chekhov made the members of the clerical class the protagonists of some of their finer stories and novels.[10]

The growing success of comic opera in Russia induced the two leading lyric poets of the 1780s, Bogdanovich and Derzhavin, to try their hand at it. Their libretti were not set to music or performed, but they were published and read. Ippolit Bogdanovich (1744–1803) is remembered for his humorous narrative poem on the subject of Psyche and Eros, *Dushen'ka* (1783), which was a landmark in the development of light verse in Russia. His attempt at comic opera was the ineptly anachronistic "drama with choruses and ballet" *The Slavs* (*Slaviane*, 1788). It shows an encounter between Alexander the Great and some ancient Slavs with whose princess he has a platonic relationship of sorts. The Greeks represent corrupt, decadent city culture, while the Slavic nobles are Rousseauist sages, championing simplicity and natural wisdom, inherited by them, through an apparent time warp, from a female ruler who sounds very much like Catherine II. For comic relief there are a sociable gardener and his wife, typical eighteenth-century comic-opera peasants who have Russian Christian names and patronymics centuries before the birth of Christ.

Gavriil Derzhavin (1743–1816) possessed the biggest poetic talent in eighteenth-century Russia. He did not, unfortunately, possess a dramatic one. This did not prevent him from writing the numerous tragedies, dramatic prologues, magic operas, and comic operas that fill more than six hundred pages of the fourth volume of his collected works.[11] These plays are almost never mentioned in critical and scholarly writings on this poet. And indeed, put next to his splendid poetry, they seem unworthy of him. His two comic-opera libretti were published posthumously, and there is no agreement among scholars wheth-

---

10. The text of *The Candidate Priest* (*Stavlennik*) was published in *Russkaia starina* (St. Petersburg) 13 (June 1875): pp. 277–300. The work was discussed in prerevolutionary histories of Russian drama. In Soviet times, because of its non-satirical portrayal of clergy, it has usually been relegated to an occasional footnote; in fact, it was hardly mentioned at all until Berkov ventured a brief discussion of it in his *Istoriia russkoi komedii XVIII v.*, pp. 208–11.

11. *Sochineniia Derzhavina*, ed. Iakov Grot (St. Petersburg, 1874), vol. 4.

er they were written in the early nineteenth century or date from the heyday of Russian comic opera in the 1770s and 1780s.

Both libretti are obviously derivative. *A Foolish Girl Outsmarts the Smart* (*Durochka umnee umnykh*) is patterned after Ablesimov's *The Miller*, with additional features drawn from *True to Life* by Derzhavin's one-time teacher Verevkin and, less expectedly, from the oral folk play *The Boat*. The play shows the family of a civil servant captured by Volga river pirates and rescued by a vivacious granddaughter who pretends to be a simpleton in love with the pirate leader. Like the play by Verevkin that served as its model, Derzhavin's play anticipates some of the scenes and situations in Pushkin's *The Captain's Daughter*, a parallel that ought to be examined by Pushkin scholars. Derzhavin's setting of his other comic opera, *The Miners* (*Rudokopy*), in Ural Mountain gold and silver mines and metallurgical laboratories might have constituted an original stroke were it not patterned on a popular Viennese *Singspiel, Die Bergknappen* (1778) by Ignaz Umlauf. Other ingredients of *The Miners* were provided by Molière (*Le bourgeois gentilhomme*) and Beaumarchais (*Le mariage de Figaro*).

Before the eighteenth century was over, there were some 150 Russian comic operas written and performed. The popularity of this genre had its impact on the relaxation of the three classical unities, on the acceptance of Russian folk song as raw material for Western-style musical composition (a practice that became even more popular in the nineteenth and twentieth centuries), and on the mode of representing peasants and merchants on the Russian stage by later playwrights. Modern understanding of the historical importance of this genre began with Nikolai Findeizen's pioneering study published in 1928.[12] But some of the recent Soviet scholarship on comic opera, by saddling the form with anachronistic ideological content and ignoring its Western sources and parallels, has produced as much obfuscation as understanding.[13]

12. Findeizen, *Ocherki po istorii muzyki*, chap. 1, note 6.
13. This comment is not meant to minimize the useful information on Russian eighteenth-century comic opera that can be found in the work of such literary historians as P. N. Berkov. Two musicological works dating from the ultra-repressive Zhdanov period offer a wealth of valuable documentation through

The Fate of Iakov Kniazhnin

Following closely in importance behind the two high points of Russian comic opera, Matinsky's *St. Petersburg Bazaar* and Ablesimov's *The Miller*, are two very successful works by Kniazhnin, *Misfortune from a Coach* and *The Hot-Mead Vendor*. These comic operas are best examined in conjunction with their author's tragedies and verse comedies. The vicissitudes of the literary reputation of Iakov Kniazhnin (1742–91) constitute the greatest paradox in the entire history of Russian drama. In his lifetime he was admired for his very first play, the tragedy *Dido*, and for his later comic operas. Posterity knows him primarily through the controversy after his death over his least original play, the tragedy *Vadim of Novgorod*. Kniazhnin is least known for his most durable and substantial contribution, the inauguration of viable Russian comedy in verse.

Because much of his work was of the "adaptation to our customs" variety, Pushkin in *Eugene Onegin* applied to Kniazhnin the epithet "imitational" (*pereimchivyi*), leading many people whose only knowledge of this playwright comes from that one mention in Pushkin to dismiss him as an untalented imitator of foreign models. But a closer study of his work and of its historical significance reveals him as a pivotal figure.

Born into a family of provincial nobility (his father was the vice-governor of the province of Pskov), Kniazhnin received a thorough education at the *gymnasium* attached to the Academy of Sciences in St. Petersburg and at a private boarding school. He acquired not only the good knowledge of French language and literature that was customary for all Russian writers of his

the haze of their compulsory Stalinist clichés and falsifications: A. S. Rabinovich, *Russkaia opera do Glinki* (Moscow, 1948), and T. Livanova, *Russkaia muzykal'naia kul'tura XVIII veka*, 2 vols. (Moscow, 1953).

A good presentation of the musical aspects of the topic in English can be found in Gerald R. Seaman, *History of Russian Music* (New York and Washington, 1967), vol. 1. See also Miriam Karpilow Whaples, "Eighteenth-Century Russian Opera in the Light of Soviet Scholarship," *Indiana Slavic Studies* 2 (1958): 113–34.

time (Fonvizin and Maikov being the prominent exceptions to this), but, far less typically, also a knowledge of Italian literature. He was eventually to translate into Russian Giambattista Marino's narrative poem *The Massacre of the Innocents* and several of Goldoni's comedies, as well as four tragedies by Corneille and Voltaire's early epic *La Henriade*.

Kniazhnin entered the civil service as an official translator at the age of seventeen. Five years later, in 1762, he transferred to the military, where he was to remain for a number of years. He made his debut as a playwright in 1769 with the tragedy *Dido*, a free adaptation of Pietro Metastasio's popular opera libretto *Didone abbandonata*, which served as the basis for numerous operas and neoclassical tragedies throughout Europe. In addition to Metastasio's libretto, Kniazhnin's *Dido* drew on some of Metastasio's now forgotten French imitators, as well as directly on the *Aeneid*, and, in its structural aspects, on the example of Sumarokov's tragedies.

According to the memoirs of Kniazhnin's one-time pupil, the sentimentalist playwright Sergei Glinka, *Dido* was staged in St. Petersburg at Catherine's command after it was read privately before her by the author. Kniazhnin himself would have preferred to submit the manuscript of the play to "the father of the Russian theater," Sumarokov, for his approval before offering it to the theaters. In Glinka's account (considered somewhat unreliable by later commentators), Kniazhnin left for Moscow immediately after the first sensationally successful performance of *Dido* to present his manuscript and apologies to Sumarokov.[14]

Sumarokov, who was usually alarmed by the appearance of new Russian playwrights, was touched and gratified by this act of homage. He instantly designated Kniazhnin as his disciple and heir. It was during that visit, Glinka tells us, that Kniazhnin made the acquaintance of Sumarokov's elder daughter, Ekaterina, who was later to become his wife. As Russian eighteenth-century tragedies go, Kniazhnin's *Dido* followed the Sumarokov model faithfully and almost mechanically. It was to remain his most widely performed play, with most of the noted Russian

14. *Zapiski Sergeia Nikolaevicha Glinki* (St. Petersburg, 1895), pp. 82 ff.

actors between 1770 and about 1820 trying their hand at the roles of either Aeneas or Iarbas. As late as 1839, the provincial actor-hero of Lensky's popular vaudeville *Lev Gurych Sinichkin* keeps looking back to the days when he used to play Iarbas opposite his late wife's Dido and quoting the ringing, now half-forgotten verses from Kniazhnin's tragedy.

Kniazhnin was the husband of Ekaterina Sumarokova, a father, and a recognized playwright when, in an uncontrollable access of gambling fever, he gambled away not only his own estate, but some 6,000 rubles from the funds of his regiment. As a result of the nasty scandal that ensued, Kniazhnin was tried, deprived of his nobility, and demoted to army private. After serving for a time as a common soldier, Kniazhnin was dismissed from the military service. It was during his period of disgrace that he did most of his literary translations from French and Italian. Within five years after his trial, he was fully pardoned and reinstated with the rank of captain.

Soon after his reinstatement in 1778, Kniazhnin was given a new civil service position as an aid to Ivan Betsky, the official in charge of Catherine's educational reforms. He also taught Russian literature at the Infantry Corps of Nobles, where among his students were the future playwrights Sergei Glinka and Ozerov. This was the period of his greatest productivity as a dramatist. Between 1779 and his death in 1791, he wrote seven tragedies, four comedies, five comic operas, and a considerable body of lyric and satirical poetry. Unlike his first tragedy, *Dido*, which retained the locale of the foreign plays on which it was based, the subsequent Kniazhnin tragedies often followed the example of Sumarokov in selecting their protagonists from medieval Russian chronicles.

Kniazhnin used his exceptional "adaptational" faculties to transplant these Russian medieval rulers into the borrowed plot and framework of the better-known French and Italian tragedies of his time. Thus the historical source for his tragedy *Vladimir and Iaropolk* was the chronicle account of St. Vladimir's assassination of his older brother, the same event that served as the theme of the first act of Feofan Prokopovich's *Vladimir* in the

first decade of the eighteenth century. But the names of Vladimir, Iaropolk, and Vladimir's spurned first wife, Rogneda (or
Ragnhild) of Polotsk, were used as a mere pretext for moving
Racine's tragedy *Andromaque* to medieval Kiev—plot, structure,
dialogue, and all. It took some ingenuity to convert Racine's
jealous and vengeful Hermione into the jealous and vengeful
Rogneda of the Russian chronicles and to equate Vladimir's dy-
nastically motivated fratricide with the murder of Pyrrhus by
the love-crazed Orestes.

Since the chronicle account of the Vladimir-Rogneda-Iaro-
polk triangle provided no figure corresponding to Andromache
in the love quadrangle, Kniazhnin had to invent, rather lamely,
a historically nonexistent captive Byzantine princess, Cleomena,
for whose sake Iaropolk abandons his erstwhile fiancée, Rogneda. Despite the considerable success of *Vladimir and Iaropolk* at
its public performances, in St. Petersburg in 1775, the play's
unexpected transformation of the famous Russian prince, who
had been canonized by the Orthodox Church as a saint, into
Racine's passionate murderer did not go unchallenged.

When a Moscow production was planned in 1789, fourteen
years after its St. Petersburg opening, the irrepressibly zealous
censor Khariton Chebotarev, Professor of History, Morals, and
Eloquence at Moscow University, who six years earlier had un-
successfully attempted to censor Fonvizin's *The Minor*, de-
manded that the mayor of Moscow ban the play as both sac-
rilegious and hostile to the principle of monarchy. But the
mayor, after ascertaining that Catherine had no objections to
the play, which had been freely available in printed form for
more than a decade, overruled Chebotarev, who thereupon resigned in a huff from his self-appointed position as censor.[15]
Professor Chebotarev found an ally in the person of Ivan Krylov, the future playwright and fable writer, who in his satirical
journal *The Correspondence of Spirits* greeted the Moscow open-

---

15. On the history of the censorship of Kniazhnin's *Vladimir and Iaropolk*
and of his *Vadim of Novgorod*, the most reliable and factual source remains
Baron N. V. Drizen's "Ocherki teatral'noi tsenzury v Rossii v XVIII veke,"
Russkaia starina (St. Petersburg) 90 (April–May–June 1897): 539–68.

ing of *Vladimir and Iaropolk* with shrill accusations of plagiarism and charged Kniazhnin with insulting the memory of a saint.[16]

Two of Kniazhnin's other tragedies, *Vladistan* and *Olga*, were inspired by various aspects of Scipione Maffei's tragedy *Merope* as well as by Voltaire's play of the same name that was adapted from Maffei. In *Olga*, the historical grandmother of St. Vladimir was placed in the situation of a typical neoclassical heroine and had to reject love and marriage to safeguard the throne for her little son Sviatoslav. Soviet commentators on this play have repeatedly attributed the fact that it alone among Kniazhnin's tragedies was never performed during the author's lifetime to the possible parallels between the situation of its heroine and Catherine's relationship with her son Paul and her continued usurpation of the throne after Paul had attained his majority.

The Clemency of Titus (*Titovo miloserdie*), Kniazhnin's conversion of Metastasio's *La clemenza di Tito* into a Russian tragedy *en grand spectacle*, with sung choruses and ballets, was written on direct commission from Catherine.[17] The situation depicted in Metastasio's celebrated libretto and the

16. "Pochta dukhov," letter 30, in I. A. Krylov, *Sochineniia v dvukh tomakh* (Moscow, 1969), vol. 2, 171–74. On Krylov's feud with Kniazhnin, see the section on Krylov in the next chapter.

17. This is, of course, an adaptation of Pietro Metastasio's most famous libretto, *La clemenza di Tito* (translated earlier into Russian by Derzhavin), which served as the text for innumerable eighteenth-century operas, including Mozart's magnificent and unfairly underrated last opera. Caterino Mazzola's adaptation of Metastasio's text, which Mozart had set to music, retained large chunks of the original text intact, as did Kniazhnin's, with the result that several of the speeches in his tragedy are exact textual counterparts of some of the arias and choruses in Mozart's opera. *The Clemency of Titus* breaks with Sumarokov's practice, followed by Kniazhnin in all his other tragedies, of writing the entire work in couplets of iambic hexameter. Instead, Kniazhnin wrote this play in iambic verse of mixed lengths, with an equally mixed system of rhyming, which Russian poets from Sumarokov to Krylov had traditionally reserved for didactic fables. This is the разностопный ямб, subsequently used with great effectiveness in Russian high classical comedy by Shakhovskoy and Griboedov and in the romantic drama of Lermontov and Küchelbecker. Kniazhnin's *The Clemency of Titus* apparently marks the introduction of this popular verse form into Russian dramatic literature.

parallel one in Corneille's *Cinna,* which Kniazhnin had earlier translated into Russian, must have fascinated him, for it was on these two related plays that he based his last and best known tragedy, *Vadim of Novgorod.* This play became famous in the history of Russian literature, not for its artistic merits, which are negligible, but for its role in the inauguration of a full-fledged censorship over Russian drama, exercised in ways that were previously not known.

In both Corneille and Metastasio, a Roman emperor (Augustus and Titus, respectively) befriends an impetuous young nobleman who falls in love with a woman bent on wreaking vengeance against the monarch. Under her instigation, the hero repays the sovereign's friendship by organizing a republican conspiracy against him. In both plays the emperor escapes when the conspiracy fails, and wins his adversaries over by magnanimously forgiving their hostile actions. In Metastasio, the causes for the conspiracy are mainly emotional, but Corneille's play is a political tragedy, which treats its audience to a full-scale debate on the respective virtues of absolute monarchy versus those of a republic.

In line with his adaptational method, Kniazhnin imposed his borrowed plot on an episode from the Russian chronicles, in this case a brief and obscure account of the unsuccessful uprising in the ninth century of the native Novgorod leader Vadim against the Scandinavian prince Riurik, the originator of the dynasty that ruled Russia from the ninth to seventeenth centuries. One of Catherine's Shakespearian imitations utilized the same historical material. Since the chronicles provided no concrete information about Vadim's person, Catherine chose to show him as an immature and selfish youth who attacked the lawful sovereign for reasons of personal ambition. In Kniazhnin's play, Vadim is an elderly military leader, who returns after a three-year absence to find that the people of Novgorod have given up their republican form of government and have elected Riurik as their absolute monarch (thus, in a hopelessly anachronistic manner, the Russians' ninth-century invitation to the Scandinavian princes, Riurik and his brothers, to come and rule Kievan Russia, is fused here with the suppression of the republican city-state of Novgorod by Moscow at the end of the fifteenth century).

The principal female character in *Vadim of Novgorod* is Vadim's daughter Ramida, a typical Corneillian *belle inhumaine*, who corresponds to Emilie in *Cinna* and Vitellia in *La clemenza di Tito*. She had become Riurik's fiancée during her father's absence. Vadim's conspiracy to overthrow Riurik enables Kniazhnin to build much of his play on the most tired of all neoclassical plot strategies, the heroine's inner conflict caused by divided loyalties to her father and her lover. In the manner of Corneille's *Cinna*, the virtues of the monarchic and the republican forms of government are defended and debated by various characters. In the last act, Vadim's uprising is defeated by Riurik, who, just like Metastasio's Titus, forgives his enemy.

Going even further, Kniazhnin's Riurik offers Vadim both his crown and himself as an obedient son-in-law. As still another show of good will, Riurik orders a plebiscite to be held. Vadim sees the entire population of Novgorod unanimously voting to retain Riurik as their monarch rather than to go back to their previous republican ways. The grimly fanatical Vadim then curses his native city for its slave mentality. His daughter, fired by her father's pro-republican sermon, stabs herself rather than marry the man she loves, whom she now sees as a tyrant.

Vadim of Novgorod was written in 1789. In 1790, it went into rehearsals for a production that was to feature two celebrated actors of the day, Iakov Shusherin and Peter Plavilshchikov, in the roles of Riurik and Vadim. But while the monarchy-versus-republic debates in Corneille's *Cinna* pertained to ancient Rome and had a strictly academic interest in the earlier part of the eighteenth century, in 1790 the rapidly developing events of the French Revolution suddenly lent this theme an unexpected contemporary relevance. Realizing this, Kniazhnin requested that the projected production of his play be abandoned. He died the next year—of a respiratory disease, by all contemporary accounts. Two years after his death, his widow applied to the president of the Russian Imperial Academy, Princess Dashkova, a personal friend of the playwright to whom he had dedicated his tragedy *Rosslav*, for help in publishing several of Kniazhnin's posthumous works, including *Vadim*.

After clearing the matter with the official censor, Princess Dashkova authorized publication of the tragedy in the annual collection of plays, *The Russian Theater*. It was published separately as well, with the proceeds going to Kniazhnin's family. A few months after the publication, a zealous courtier brought the play to the attention of Count Platon Zubov, the youngest, the handsomest, and the most vacuous of Catherine's kept young men. In an apparent act of personal malice directed against Princess Dashkova, Zubov proceeded to denounce the play to the empress as subversive.

Ekaterina Dashkova had a long history of refusing to pay homage to favorites whose position at court derived from their bedroom activities. In the brief reign of Peter III, she had a clash about this with her older sister, Elizaveta Vorontsova, who was Peter's mistress. Following her estrangement from her sister, Dashkova gave her allegiance to Peter's wife, Catherine, and helped her win the throne. During Catherine's reign, Dashkova was appointed the director of the Academy of Sciences and elected president of the Russian Imperial Academy, of which she was one of the founders. She also edited several scholarly journals and initiated the publication of the first Russian academic dictionary.

Her intellectual interests, her independent stance, and her refusal to assume with Catherine's lovers the sycophantic tone they expected caused considerable resentment at court. Kniazhnin's posthumously published tragedy and Platon Zubov's hostility to Dashkova were used by the anti-Dashkova party to orchestrate her fall from Catherine's good graces. The timing of Zubov's denunciation of *Vadim of Novgorod* could not have been better chosen. By 1793, the once liberal Catherine had been sufficiently frightened by the events in France to suppress the Russian Freemasons, to incarcerate without trial Nikolai Novikov, the leading publisher of satirical journals, and to banish Alexander Radishchev to Siberia for having published his critique of serfdom, *A Journey from St. Petersburg to Moscow.* The death by guillotine of Louis XVI and Marie Antoinette that occurred just before Zubov's denunciation had brought Catherine to the point of hysteria. Her reaction to Zubov's accusations was spectacular indeed. She ordered a copy of *Vadim of Novgorod* burned by an executioner in a public ceremony. All copies of *The Russian Theater* that contained the play were ordered destroyed. All purchasers of the play were directed to turn their copies in to the authorities. Private homes were searched to ensure that no copy of the play survived. Several booksellers who had unwittingly stocked the volume suffered reprisals.[18] Princess Dashkova's perfectly reasonable suggestion that Catherine at least read the play and compare it to translated French tragedies, freely performed all over Russia, went unheeded.[19]

Catherine's hysterical reaction created for Kniazhnin's creaking, derivative tragedy a celebrity that was out of all proportion to either its literary worth or its importance within the playwright's work. While the rest of Kniazhnin's plays went on being published and performed in the nineteenth century, *Vadim of Novgorod* remained officially banned during the reigns of Paul, Alexander I, and Nicholas I. In his memoirs written in the 1850s, Sergei Aksakov recalled how the text of this tragedy was privately read and recited during his student days in Kazan in about 1808:

> It [*Vadim of Novgorod*] enjoyed great fame, not only because it had been banned, but because it contained, in everyone's opinion, many audacious, profound ideas, harsh truths, and powerful lines of verse. That was what the older generation of writers and amateurs of literature thought at the time. I must confess that we, the younger men, were also carried

---

18. See note 15, above.

19. Princess Dashkova's involvement in the publication of *Vadim of Novgorod* and her views on this play are to be found in her memoirs (*Memoirs of the Princess Daschkaw, Lady of Honour to Catherine II, Written by Herself* [London, 1840], pp. 361–67). Various Russian editions of these memoirs are clearly translated from the English of this edition.

away by this opinion, whereas in actual fact this entire tragedy is nothing but an array of empty, loud phrases and inflated emotions, frequently lacking all logical sense.[20]

The romantic narrative poems by Pushkin, Kondraty Ryleyev, and Mikhail Lermontov about Vadim of Novgorod as the last defender of republican freedoms in medieval Russia had their probable source not in the text of Kniazhnin's tragedy, but in its seductive reputation.

The same reputation gave rise in the 1820s to a legend, to which Pushkin subscribed, that Kniazhnin died not of natural causes but from a flogging he received during an interrogation connected with the banning of his play. This was easily disproved by subsequent nineteenth-century scholarship. Not only did Kniazhnin die two years before anyone made objections to the play, but had there been such an interrogation and a death by flogging, it would have been sheer insanity for Kniazhnin's widow to publish the play that had supposedly caused her husband's death or for Dashkova to authorize the publication.

The appearance of the memoirs of Princess Dashkova in Russian in 1859 and of several comparative studies that established the play's derivation from Corneille's *Cinna* in the second half of the nineteenth century brought a more rational dimension to the earlier view that Kniazhnin's play represented a subversive or revolutionary statement. The text of *Vadim of Novgorod* was finally reissued in 1871 with four lines deleted by censorship and republished in full in 1914. Although the endorsement of the monarchic system at the end of the play is unequivocal, there was a renewed debate about the play's political significance in the early twentieth century and in the first two decades of the Soviet rule.

From the 1950s to the 1970s, Kniazhnin studies in the Soviet Union were the private preserve of Professor Liubov Kulakova (1903–73).[21] With single-minded determination, she proceeded

---

20. S. A. Aksakov, *Sobranie sochinenii* (Moscow, 1952), vol. 1, p. 255.

21. See L. I. Kulakova, *Ia. B. Kniazhnin* (Moscow-Leningrad, 1951); her essay "Ia. B. Kniazhnin" in *Russkie dramaturgi*, ed. G. P. Berdnikov et al. (Leningrad-Moscow, 1959), vol. 1, pp. 293–337; and her introductory essay and detailed commentary to Ia. B Kniazhnin, *Izbrannye proizvedeniia* (Leningrad, 1961).

to build up the image of Kniazhnin as a revolutionary figure feared and persecuted by Catherine, as a nineteenth-century-style critical realist, and as an ardent Russian patriot. In this scheme of things, *Vadim of Novgorod* was given pride of place as Kniazhnin's most original and successful work. The Kulakova version of Kniazhnin's biography and significance is generally, though not universally, accepted in the Soviet Union, with the result that two widely used reference works published in the 1960s offer two drastically different versions of Kniazhnin's biography and of the meaning of his work.[22]

Almost two centuries after Catherine's ban, *Vadim of Novgorod* keeps on concealing Kniazhnin's far more important plays from view. Thus, when Vladimir Nabokov needed to gloss Kniazhnin's name for his annotated edition of *Eugene Onegin*, he wrote that Kniazhnin was the "author of tragedies and comedies awkwardly imitated from more or less worthless French models." "I have tried his *Vadim of Novgorod*," Nabokov went on, "but even Voltaire is more readable."[23] By restricting his research to this one tragedy and failing to have a look at his comedies and comic operas, Nabokov obviously formed an inadequate notion of Kniazhnin. The verse comedies, in particular, are essential links in the development of that natural and graceful diction that Nabokov admired so much in the verse of Pushkin and Griboedov.

Kniazhnin's Comic Operas

One year after he was rehabilitated following his embezzlement and disgrace, Kniazhnin produced his first comic opera, *Misfortune from a Coach* (*Neschastie ot karety*; this title is sometimes mistranslated as *Accident with a Carriage* by commentators not familiar with the plot.)[24] The text was set to

22. Cf. the entry on Kniazhnin in *Teatral'naia èntsiklopediia* (Moscow, 1964), vol. 3, cols. 91–93, and the one in *Kratkaia literaturnaia èntsiklopediia*, (Moscow, 1966), vol. 3, cols. 615–16.

23. Alexander Pushkin, *Eugene Onegin*, translated from the Russian with a commentary by Vladimir Nabokov (New York, 1964), vol. 2, p. 82.

24. Mirsky, *History of Russian Literature*, p. 54, calls it *An Accident with a*

music by Vasily Pashkevich. The premiere took place in November of 1779 at the Hermitage Theater in St. Petersburg, a few months after the opening there of Ablesimov's *The Miller*. The empress and her son were present and their manifest pleasure and approval contributed to the work's resounding success.

In its first few scenes, *Misfortune from a Coach* looks very much like one more adaptation of Favart's *Annette et Lubin*. A pair of peasant lovers, named, expectedly enough, Aniuta and Lukian, are prevented from getting married by another stock character from Favart, the jealous bailiff Klimenty, who wants Aniuta for himself. Then a grim and specifically Russian motif is introduced. Aniuta, Lukian, and Klimenty are all serfs, belonging to a silly Gallomaniac couple named Firiulin (Mr. and Mrs. Ninny), whose aim in life is to ape whatever new fashions appear in Paris.

Owners of many carriages, the Firiulins have decided that they must have a new model of coach that is all the rage in France. To raise the money for the coach, they want to sell some of their serfs into military service. This type of transaction was one of the ugliest ways of abusing the serfowners' privileges, because the drafted peasant would still remain their slave, but would in addition be parted from his family and friends for the next twenty-five years. Deplored as this practice was by all decent people, there were instances of men as enlightened as the satirist Novikov, the great poet Pushkin, and the radical political thinker Peter Chaadaev resorting to this form of fund-raising for personal expenses.

Klimenty is authorized by his owners to call himself by the French version of his first name, Clément, which other peasants think is a new rank to which Klimenty has been promoted. They accordingly offer Klimenty their congratulations. To get rid of Lukian as a rival for Aniuta's hand, Klimenty nominates him to be drafted into the army. On the advice of the Firiulins' house jester, Aniuta and Lukian make a plea to their owners not to be parted, speaking in exaggeratedly sentimental terms and using French forms of address. This ploy serves to establish the

---

Carriage (Mirsky did not know it was a comic opera, for he listed it as a verse comedy); Mooser, in *Opéras*, p. 2, translates the title as *Accident de voiture*.

proper literary point of reference for arousing the Firiulins' sympathy. As long as they saw the young couple as Russian peasants and serfs, the Firiulins were impervious to pity. But sentimentalist clichés and French words put everything in a different perspective. Now the owners are horrified that they were about to separate two loving hearts. The bailiff's decision is overruled. Aniuta and Lukian will marry and join their masters in the city as their new chambermaid and valet.

Two centuries later, in an age that thinks of slavery as a horror of the past, the situation of the protagonists of *Misfortune from a Coach* may strike us as a powerful denunciation of serfdom. But there is no contemporary evidence for such a perception. Empress Catherine repeatedly had this opera performed at her court theater, on one occasion even selecting the costume for the actress who played Aniuta. It went on being produced throughout the country well into the second decade of the nineteenth century. There were even performances by serf actors at private theaters owned by wealthy nobles. One cannot help wondering whether those audiences perceived the illusory nature of the supposed happy outcome: even though Lukian escapes the draft and gets to marry Aniuta, the Firiulins make it clear that they still want their Parisian coach. Some other hapless peasant will have to be sold to the army after the final curtain.

Kniazhnin's other successful comic opera, *The Hot-Mead Vendor (Sbiten'shchik)*[25] enjoyed an even more enduring popularity than *Misfortune from a Coach*. First performed in 1784, it was still being revived in the two capitals and in the provinces as late as the 1850s. In this case, Kniazhnin's text had to share the acclaim with the music composed by the Czech bassoonist Anton Bullandt, who lived in Russia from 1780 until his death in 1821 and whose only important composition was this comic

25. *Sbiten'shchik* was an itinerant vendor, who went around in the winter selling *sbiten'*, a nonalcoholic hot drink consisting of an infusion of honey and spices in boiling water. With the spread of the popularity of tea in the early nineteenth century, *sbiten'* went out of favor and the word that designated it became obsolete. For a history of this drink and of customs connected with it (and for some interesting recipes), see V. Sorokin, "Za kruzhkoi sbitnia," *Nauka i zhizn'* (Moscow), no. 1 (1970): 131.

opera. It was in *The Hot-Mead Vendor* that Kniazhnin's adaptational ability showed itself at its most ingenious.

Just as he was later to base *Vadim of Novgorod* on the realization of a fundamental similarity between seemingly disparate tragedies by Corneille and Metastasio, Kniazhnin based this comic opera on Molière's *L'école des femmes* (1662) and its two eighteenth-century descendants, *On ne s'avise jamais de tout* by Sedaine (1761) and *Le barbier de Séville* by Beaumarchais (1775). Able theatrical craftsman that he was, Kniazhnin perceived that all these three works about the escape of a sheltered young ward from the tutelage of her elderly guardian were variations on the same theme.

Moving the action to contemporary Russia, Kniazhnin turned the barber Figaro into the mead vendor Stepan. Molière's Arnolphe, who out of vanity changed his name to Monsieur de la Souche (he corresponds to Tue in Sedaine and to Bartholo in Beaumarchais), becomes the Russian merchant Makey, who took the name Voldyrev (Mr. Blister) because he thought it would make him sound like a nobleman. The Russian officer Izved, in love with Voldyrev's ward, disguises himself as an old woman in order to get to speak to her, just as his predecessor Dorval did in Sedaine's play. For all the seamless surgery with which Kniazhnin joined these three models to form his libretto, there is not very much Russian authenticity in the final result. The merchant milieu is not reflected with anything like the vividness and specificity we find in Matinsky's *St. Petersburg Bazaar* or in the somewhat later sentimental comedy *The Salesclerk* by Peter Plavilshchikov. In comparison to these works, *The Hot-Mead Vendor* does not really russify Molière, Sedaine, and Beaumarchais, but merely adds to them a few touches of *couleur locale*.

Kniazhnin's Verse Comedies

Kniazhnin's tragedies and comic operas, for all their popularity with his contemporaries, added nothing substantially new to the development of these two genres in Russia. It is his two high comedies in verse, *The Braggart* (*Khvastun*, 1786) and *Odd Fellows* (*Chudaki*, also called *The Eccentrics* in English, which was premiered after Kniazhnin's death in 1791 and written presumably one year earlier) that constituted a new departure in Russian drama. Prior to *The Braggart*, comedy was written in prose. Earlier attempts to create a Russian comedy in verse consisted of four or five untypical works that were either unperformable (Trediakovsky's adaptation of *The Eunuch*, styled as "a five-act comedy, from the Latin of Terence, purged of the more revolting obscenities" or Nikolev's clumsy and interminable satire on Sumarokov, *The Vain Poetaster* [*Samo-liubivyi stikhotvorets*]) or were sentimental dramas palmed off as comedies because they were written in verse (e.g., Fonvizin's *Korion* and Kheraskov's *The Atheist*).

It can therefore be said without fear of exaggeration that *The Braggart* and *Odd Fellows*, with their lively action and witty dialogue in verse, are the true point of departure for that illustrious line of Russian verse comedy that leads to Kapnist's *Chicane*, to the verse comedies of Shakhovskoy and Khmelnitsky in the second and third decades of the nineteenth century, to Griboedov's *The Misfortune of Being Clever* and, in a different medium, to Pushkin's sparkling verse tales couched in a manner reminiscent of eighteenth-century verse comedy, such as "Count Nulin" and "The Little House in Kolomna." Kniazhnin's contribution to originating this whole tradition has not been always perceived or sufficiently valued.

Kniazhnin wrote his verse comedies after Lukin and Fonvizin had brought considerable verisimilitude and authenticity to Russian prose comedy. But he chose to ignore their innovations and discoveries. He followed instead the earlier precedent of the prose comedies by his father-in-law, transposing to Russia mores and customs typical of French and Italian eighteenth-century comedy, but having no counterpart in contemporary Russian reality. Thus intermarriage between servants and employers, usual in Italian comedy and comic opera (Pergolesi's *La serva padrona*, Goldoni's *La cameriere brillante*), but hardly imaginable in Catherine's Russia, is a plot component in both *The Braggart* and *Odd Fellows*.

Instant marriage by signing a contract, severely criticized by Lukin in Sumarokov's comedies as a patent impossibility in Russia, is also mechanically adapted by Kniazhnin. Some characters in his comedies bear recognizable Russian Christian names or symbolic last names morphologically consistent with the possibilities of Russian name formation. But mostly their names are either composite nicknames unimaginable in reality, such as Verkholyot (Flying-High) or Vysonos (Nose-in-the-Air), or else frank foreign importations: the officer Zamir, the valet Poliste, and the odic poet Trompetin (from the French *trompette*).

The central character in *The Braggart* is the impoverished young nobleman Verkholyot, who, in order to marry a rich heiress, impersonates a count and pretends to have good connections at court.[26] His serf valet Poliste impersonates a noble who is the count's secretary and, to further his master's suit, promises to marry the heroine's chambermaid and to make a noblewoman of her. Verkholyot is exposed by his rival's father, the wise old nobleman named Cheston (i.e., Honorius), delivered to the mercies of his creditors and arrested by the authorities for fraud.

Odd Fellows features a totally improbable recently ennobled commoner Lentyagin (Mr. Lazybones), a Rousseauist "philosopher" of sorts or perhaps a Tolstoyan a century ahead of his time. Lentyagin refuses to recognize social distinctions of any sort and is willing to share his considerable fortune with anyone who claims to be free of social prejudices. The plot hinges on the conflict between Lentyagin and his haughty, highborn wife over the choice of husband for their daughter. Among the daughter's suitors are an impoverished, conceited Gallomaniac nobleman, two silly poets, and the daughter's true love, a sentimental ninny named Priyat (a truncated form of "Pleasant").

26. Kulakova and other recent Soviet commentators have repeatedly interpreted Verkholyot's pretended court connections to mean that he claims to be the paramour of the empress. The comedy is thus represented as Kniazhnin's pointed satire of Catherine's immorality. The proponents of this view never bother to explain why Catherine not only tolerated performances of *The Braggart* throughout the country but had it played at her own court theater on several occasions.

One of the most important roles in the play is that of Priyat's valet Prolaz (a coined name that implies the ability to horn in where one is not wanted), who so delights Lentyagin by playing on his dislike of social distinctions that the latter decides to make this servant his son-in-law. But the modest Prolaz has been humoring Lentyagin only in order to help his master Priyat and to sabotage the marriage between the daughter and the pompous young Gallomaniac rival, whose equally pompous servant Vysonos is his personal enemy. He steps aside in the end, leaving the bride free for his swooning and ineffectual young master.

Lentyagin's egalitarianism was clearly viewed by Kniazhnin as a cranky eccentricity. It was only after the advent of Slavophile philosophy and, even more, after the liberation of the serfs in the 1860s that educated Russians would come to see such an outlook as admirable and democratic. While most of *Odd Fellows* was derived from two comedies by Destouches (*L'important* and *L'homme singulier*), the character of Lentyagin and his scenes with Prolaz are based on the unconventional Venetian gentleman Florindo and his exchanges with a chummy servant in Carlo Goldoni's *La cameriere brillante*.[27]

Despite their derivative qualities, their improbable plots and characters, their sly Pasquins and Harlequins masquerading as Russian serfs, and their obligatory scenes of young lovers' spats (*le dépit amoureux*, familiar from Molière), Kniazhnin's two verse comedies brought to Russian drama new and, as it turned out later, important dimensions. The plays are genuinely lively and amusing (something Sumarokov was never able to accomplish despite frequently similar material). The language is wittier and brighter than anywhere else in Russian eighteenth-century drama. There are successful attempts to incorporate proverbs and folk sayings into the verse texture and a gift for the kind of terse, aphoristic formulations that are one of the glories

27. As demonstrated by B. V. Neiman, "Komediia Ia. B. Kniazhnina," in the collection *Problemy realizma v russkoi literature XVIII veka* (Moscow-Leningrad, 1940), pp. 121–82. The dependence of Kniazhnin's verse comedies on French sources, established by nineteenth-century Russian scholars, can at times be rather tenuous. But their possible dependence on Italian sources, so highly likely in view of his close involvement with Metastasio and Goldoni, remains uninvestigated and undocumented to this day.

of Griboedov's comedy. Compared to the verbal texture of Griboedov or even Shakhovskoy, Kniazhnin's comedies may appear unpolished. But it was his tentative solution of the problems of verse dialogue and of light, entertaining repartee that made the achievements of these later playwrights possible.

The Braggart and Odd Fellows remained in the repertoire of Russian theaters until the 1830s. They were favorites for amateur productions, and such Russian writers as Ivan Krylov, Sergei Aksakov, and Pavel Katenin performed in various private stagings of The Braggart. Even after the appearance of The Misfortune of Being Clever, the foremost Romantic critic, Viazemsky, still considered The Braggart the best all-around Russian comedy. Pushkin drew on both of Kniazhnin's verse comedies for epigraphs that helped re-create the eighteenth-century atmosphere in his The Captain's Daughter, and used other quotations from these plays in his literary criticism and in the story "The Coffin-Maker." Gogol, as has been occasionally asserted, may well have drawn on Kniazhnin's compulsive liar Verkholyot for some of the features of his Khlestakov in The Inspector General. All in all, Kniazhnin's comedies give him a modest, but indispensable place in the history of Russian drama. Posterity is not justified in remembering his name only through Pushkin's casually flung, derogatory epithet.[28]

28. In Pushkin's juvenile poem "Small Town" ("Gorodok," 1815), Kniazhnin's plays are placed on the bookshelf right next to Fonvizin and "the gigantic Molière."

❧ VI ❧

Russian Comedy
Comes of Age

The last two decades of the eighteenth century witnessed the further spread of professional theater from the capital to the more remote provinces. Amateur theatricals became popular among the gentry, among the educated merchants, at the Imperial court, and, in rare instances, even among the urban proletariat.[1] The 1780s saw the beginning of the uniquely Russian theatrical institution of serf theater, which was to attain considerable currency before its decline in the 1820s. Stage-struck wealthy nobles, whose serfs often numbered in the thousands, would organize their own domestic acting companies in which actors, musicians, stage designers, the crew and occasionally the playwright were human chattels.

As an institution, serf theaters became economically untenable and morally repugnant several decades before serfdom itself was abolished.[2] Their prevalence in the 1780s, however, testifies to how widely the idea of theater as entertainment be-

1. See V. N. Vsevolodsky-Gerngross, *Russkii teatr vtoroi poloviny XVIII veka* (Moscow, 1960), pp. 52–53, for a description of some of these proletarian theatrical ventures, including a company consisting of employees of a printer's shop.

2. Among the numerous sources on serf theater, one can recommend N. N. Evreinov, *Krepostnye aktery* (St. Petersburg, 1911; Leningrad, 1925); V. N. Vsevolodsky-Gerngross, *Istoriia russkogo teatra* (Leningrad, 1929), vol. 1, pp. 519–34; and the entry "Krepostnoi teatr" in *Teatral'naia èntsikopediia* (Moscow, 1964), vol. 3, pp. 264–67, which includes a useful bibliography.

came accepted only a quarter of a century after Elizabeth had established the first successful public theater. By the time the earliest serf actors were scoring their first successes, Russian drama already possessed at least one original play that was destined to remain in the repertoire to this day. That play was *The Minor (Nedorosl')*[3] by Denis Fonvizin (1745–92).

Denis Fonvizin

Fonvizin was born in Moscow, in a family of Russian nobles of German origin, whose surname was originally spelled von Wiesen. A precocious child, the future playwright learned to read and was taught grammar at the age of four. He acquired a good knowledge of earlier Russian religious literature at home and then began his studies at Moscow University at the age of fourteen. Selected as one of the best students for a university-sponsored trip to St. Petersburg, the fifteen-year-old Fonvizin was taken to meet Lomonosov and to see Fyodor Volkov perform in several plays, including *Henrich and Pernille* by Ludvig Holberg. This journey and his subsequent friendship with the actor Ivan Dmitrevsky determined Fonvizin's life-long love affair with the theater. University graduation was followed by a brief military career, and then Fonvizin entered the civil service as a translator at the foreign office and was assigned as personal secretary to Ivan Elagin. In the Elagin circle, Fonvizin's playwrighting ambitions were given the fullest possible encouragement. In 1762 he rendered Voltaire's *Alzire* into rather clumsy, archaic Russian verse. The translation was remembered mainly for the several unintentionally funny howlers it contained.[4]

In 1764, the year in which Elagin and Lukin launched the "adaptation to our customs" form of drama, Fonvizin adapted

---

3. The Russian title, *Nedorosl'*, originally meant a young nobleman, not yet legally of age and completing his education in preparation for military or civil service. Under the impact of Fonvizin's comedy, the term acquired new derogatory and ironic connotations that it still retains.

4. Unlike the majority of educated Russians of his day, for whom French was their second language, Fonvizin was more proficient in German. He learned French as an adult, shortly before undertaking the translation of *Alzire*.

Jean Baptiste Louis Gresset's sentimental drama in verse *Sidnei*, which received the name of *Korion* in its Russian incarnation. Although styled a comedy, *Korion* is a very static and lugubrious play. Like his prototype in Gresset (whose play was first performed in 1745 and had its action situated in a country house in England), Korion is a nobleman who has withdrawn from society and settled on his country estate. It takes most of the first two of the three acts for the audience to learn the cause of this retirement.

After endless prodding by his faithful valet and by his best friend, Menander, Korion confesses that he is overcome by remorse because of his infidelity to his beloved Zenobia, whom he had betrayed with another woman. Even though Zenobia herself appears in the last act, protesting her devotion and forgiveness, the repentant Korion insists he has to kill himself to atone for his transgression. But he is cheated out of his final death scene when the valet announces that the poison his master has drunk was secretly replaced by a glass of water.

Fonvizin's *Korion* is partly a translation and partly a free adaptation of Gresset's play.[5] In its attempts to transfer the action to a Russian locale, the play is far more timid than the similar efforts of Fonvizin's contemporary and rival, Lukin. The Greek-derived names Korion, Menander, and Zenobia (with which Fonvizin replaced Gresset's Sidnei, Hamilton, and Rosalie) may all appear in the Orthodox calendar of saints, as Pigarev points out,[6] but they are not in any way usual. Taken in conjunction, they sound as neoclassical as Molière's Alcestes and Philintes. Moscow and St. Petersburg are mentioned where Gresset's characters spoke of London.

The most recognizably Russian feature of *Korion* is that two of its characters are serfs: the loquacious valet Andrei, the only character with a familiar Russian name,[7] and the nameless

5. For a detailed comparison of *Korion* to its French original, see K. V. Pigarev, *Tvorchestvo Fonvizina* (Moscow, 1954), pp. 82–88.

6. Ibid.

7. In Gresset's play, the English gentry have recognizably English names, while their servants seem to be French: Dumont, Henri, and Mathurine. Fonvizin, in an oddly parallel procedure, has classically named gentry and servants who bear common Russian names.

comical peasant messenger who makes an appearance in the first act. Andrei, who has one of the longest roles in the play, seems quite satisfied with his serf status. Like the servant in Lukin's *The Wastrel Reformed by Love*, Andrei is offered his freedom. Unlike Lukin's Vasily, who turns the offer down only once, Fonvizin's Andrei rejects emancipation repeatedly throughout the play. But the nameless rustic (who speaks the same northern *tsokanie* dialect that Lukin and Matinsky had also found hilarious and used for broadly comic characterizations of *their* peasants) makes a brief, vehement speech about his lack of rights and the hardship of his life.[8]

The brief scene between Andrei and the peasant messenger is the only foretaste *Korion* offers of Fonvizin's future mastery of colloquial dialogue. The rest of the play is as clumsy as anything in Sumarokov or Kheraskov. The play's historical distinction lies in its being one of the earliest examples of Russian comedy (such as it is) in verse. Since it is based on one of the earliest French *comédies larmoyantes*, it also helped usher in Russian sentimental drama.[9] The language and versification are old-fashioned for their time. A few of the more archaic-sounding passages would not have seemed out of place in a play by Simeon of Polotsk. Fonvizin did well to switch from verse to prose in his subsequent plays.

Along with other efforts by the Elagin group playwrights, *Korion* was produced on the stage and had a modest success.[10] But Fonvizin's clashes with Lukin, in which Elagin took the side of his rival, eventually led to his departure for Moscow, where he was to remain for several years. It was there that, five years after *Korion* (and several years after the banishment of Lukin from Russian literature), Fonvizin wrote his next play, *The Brigadier* (*Brigadir*), which not only incorporated everything he had

8. One of this peasant's lines served as an ironic epigraph to a witty poem written by Georgy Ivanov in 1950. See *Modern Russian Poetry*, ed. Vladimir Markov and Merrill Sparks (Indianapolis, 1967), pp. 420–21.

9. See the section on *Korion* in Hilmar Schlieter, *Studien zur Geschichte des russischen Rührstücks 1758–1780* (Weisbaden, 1968), pp. 42–51.

10. Catherine's son, the ten-year-old future Paul I, showed good literary judgment when he singled out the episode with the peasant messenger as the best part of the play (the journal of Paul's tutor, as quoted by Pigarev, *Tvorchestvo Fonvizina*, p. 85).

learned from the plays of his deposed enemy, but easily surpassed Lukin or any other Russian playwright of the period in originality and literary quality.

In its dramatic action, *The Brigadier* is almost as static a play as *Korion*. The Brigadier of the title, his wife, and their son Ivanushka (Little Ivan) are visiting the country estate of the Councillor so as to arrange a match between Little Ivan and the Councillor's daughter Sophia. Sophia finds the prospect distasteful, for her heart already belongs to a virtuous neighboring landowner named Dobroliubov (Mr. Lovegood), unacceptable to her father because his property is tied up in a lawsuit.

Little Ivan, who has become a raging Gallomaniac after a brief visit to Paris, is, for his part, bored with the level-headed Sophia and attracted to her frivolous, frenchified stepmother, the Councillor's youthful second wife. The Brigadier himself is also taken with her; and to complete the amorous entanglement, the pious and corpulent Councillor becomes captivated with the Brigadier's stupid, penny-pinching wife (mainly because of her economical ways of household management) and attempts to seduce the confused lady by citing appropriate quotations from the Bible and the catechism. The repetitive, cross-purpose web of courtships is broken only in the last act, when the two fathers catch Little Ivan and the Councillor's wife in a compromising situation. All the hidden motivations come to the surface in the ensuing uproar. Sophia is now left free to marry Dobroliubov, whose estate and serfs are restored to him by an opportune court decision.

What *The Brigadier* lacks in plot and structure it more than makes up in rich characterizations and the remarkable quality of its dialogue. On one level, its characters are humors or masks, personifying particular qualities or vices. The Brigadier himself stands for military crudity and gruffness, his wife for stupidity and avarice, the Councillor for religious hypocrisy, chicanery, and greed, Little Ivan and the Councilor's wife for mindless, unreasoning worship of everything French combined with disdain for their own country. But Fonvizin has managed to imbue each one of these humors with a modicum of individuality and depth, so that they can be seen as believable representations of actual eighteenth-century Russians, rather than as abstractions. Even the frigid Sophia is endowed with a certain opportunistic turn of mind, which saves her from being a stereotype of the virtuous, obedient daughter of neoclassical comedy.

Russian nineteenth-century critics, who rarely knew eighteenth-century cultural history in depth, usually read *The Brigadier* as an indictment of Gallomania. At the end of the nineteenth century, it became common to describe this comedy as an adaptation of Ludvig Holberg's anti-Gallomaniac play *Jean de France, or Hans Frandsen*. Although there is a probable similarity between the triangle of Little Ivan, Sophia, and Dobroliubov in Fonvizin and their counterparts Jean, Elsebet, and Antonius in Holberg, the two works could otherwise not be more dissimilar.[11] Besides, *Jean de France* was frequently played on the Russian stage in the 1760s, both in translation and in Elagin's "adaptation to our customs." Surely, the appearance of one more adaptation of Holberg's play would not have caused the stir that *The Brigadier* immediately did. Satire of Gallomania was a common ingredient of many plays of the period. We meet it in comedies by Sumarokov, Lukin, Elchaninov, and a few others, all of which antedate *The Brigadier*.

The contemporary record and, above all, Fonvizin's own *Confessions* make it abundantly clear that what struck the first audiences about *The Brigadier* were not its views on Gallomania, but the unprecedented verisimilitude of its characters.

11. For an account of scholarly assertions that *The Brigadier* is either an imitation or an adaptation of Holberg's play, followed by a debunking of these assertions, see Evgeny Cherniavsky's dissertation "Dramaturgiia Khol'berga" (Moscow University, 1950), chap. 3 ("Khol'berg i Fonvizin"); and Marvin Kantor, "Fonvizin and Holberg: A Comparison of *The Brigadier* and *Jean de France*," *Canadian-American Slavic Studies* 7 (Winter 1973): 475–84.

Though it is true that Fonvizin did not derive *The Brigadier* from Holberg's play, there does exist an affinity between these playwrights that ought to be studied. Oscar James Campbell, Jr., in his *The Comedies of Holberg* (Cambridge, 1914), pp. 72–73, outlines the typical Holberg family constellation, centered around a mother who dotes on her adult son but is indifferent to or estranged from her husband. This situation is of course also significant for Fonvizin. Fonvizin's dramatic method is closer to that of Holberg than to that of any of his foreign predecessors or contemporaries. So, though it makes little sense to speak of copying or borrowing, there is still the issue of affinity or general influence to be examined.

The playgoers hardly mentioned the Gallomaniac characters (there *was* an anonymous epigram about a lady in the audience who was upset because she thought she recognized herself in the Councillor's wife[12]), but Fonvizin's early readers and his friends were unanimous in their acclaim of the characterization of the Brigadier's wife, Akulina Timofeyevna. Based on a real-life personality (according to his *Confessions*, that of the mother of a young girl Fonvizin had tried to seduce during his university years), the role of this cheerfully stupid female tightwad is humanized by the suffering she experiences and the compassion she shows for others.

Patronized and mocked by her own son, cursed and beaten by her brutal husband, naively unable to understand the Councillor's lecherous designs on her virtue, Akulina Timofeyevna has appealing streaks of forgiveness and of genuine wit. Kirill Pigarev's point that, after all is said and done, the Brigadier's wife is the only real human being in the play, is well taken.[13] Nor is it surprising that Fyodor Dostoevsky, in the course of several enthusiastic evocations of *The Brigadier* in his *Winter Notes on Summer Impressions*, was particularly drawn to the humanity and humility of Akulina Timofeyevna. And indeed, her riposte to Sophia's refusal to hear her story of the wife-beating Captain Gvozdilov—"There now, my dear, you refuse to listen; what was it like for the captain's wife to endure it?" —does have an unexpectedly Dostoevskian ring.[14]

Fonvizin brought *The Brigadier* to St. Petersburg in the

12. See Pigarev, *Tvorchestvo Fonvizina*, p. 96.

13. Ibid., p. 99. Some eighteenth-century references list this play as *The Brigadier and His Wife* (cf. Vsevolodsky-Gerngross, *Russkii teatr*, p. 74), further testifying to the popularity of the character of the wife with Fonvizin's contemporaries.

14. Dostoevsky made Fonvizin's offstage Captain Gvozdilov (Captain Pummel or Hammering) a generic type, representing all crude and violent military men, and the captain's name is repeatedly mentioned in *Winter Notes*. In line with his own Slavophile ideology, Dostoevsky interprets Sophia as "a representative of the aristocratic, humanitarian, and European development in the comedy," while the Brigadier's wife is seen to derive her compassion from being a simple Russian *baba* (see F. M. Dostoevsky, *Sobranie sochinenii* [Moscow, 1956], vol. 4, pp. 71–85). On the involvement of Dostoevsky with Fonvizin, see G. M. Fridlender, "Dostoevskii i Fonvizin," *XVIII vek*, (Leningrad) 10 (1975): 92–97.

summer of 1769. By his own admission, he could read it master-
fully. After reading it in a number of aristocratic homes, he was
invited to read it at court before the empress. Catherine's approval was the final cachet that established *The Brigadier* as
one of the most popular Russian plays of the period. The play
brought Fonvizin the patronage of Count Nikita Panin, the
head of the Commission of Foreign Affairs who was also the
preceptor of the heir to the throne, Grand Duke Paul. Fonvizin
soon became Panin's secretary, and he retained that position for
many years.

Fonvizin's wife, a lady of merchant-class origins previously
married to another nobleman, suffered from a severe infestation
of intestinal parasites. During the next decade he took her on
several prolonged journeys through Western Europe in search
of a cure. The collected letters he wrote during those travels to
his sister and to his friend Count Peter Panin (Nikita Panin's
brother) are classics of Russian eighteenth-century literature.
They show Poland, Germany, France, and Italy as seen by a
cultivated Russian, brought up on the ideas of the Enlightenment tempered by a fierce nationalistic pride.

Fonvizin's first biographer, the worldly Prince Viazemsky,
was clearly shocked by the chauvinistic bias of some of these
letters. "Most of his observations abroad," Viazemsky wrote,
"are marked with prejudice, with a spirit of extraordinary intol-
erance and condemnation, regrettable in an intelligent man. A
scourge of prejudices at home, a champion of education and
of the victory of reason, Fonvizin the traveler sees everything
with prejudiced eyes, and while not saying so out loud, he all
but allows his negative thinking to preach the advantages of
ignorance."[15]

Actually, some of Fonvizin's typical statements about the
West, such as "Everything in Russia is better and we are more

15. Peter Viazemsky, *Fon-Vizin* (St. Petersburg, 1848), p. 117. Viazemsky
quotes extensive material proving that Fonvizin's letters describing life in
France are full of verbatim passages from various books by French moralists,
which Fonvizin passed off as his own observations. Viazemsky's evidence was ignored by Dostoevsky in *Winter Notes*, and Fonvizin's borrowings are never
mentioned in the vast Soviet literature on his work.

human than the Germans,"[16] or "We are beginning, but they [i.e., the West] are finished," inaugurate the vast chip-on-the-shoulder tradition of Russian literary travelers, extending throughout the nineteenth and into the twentieth century. Dostoevsky in Paris and London in the middle of the nineteenth century, Maxim Gorky in New York at the beginning of the twentieth, and Boris Pilnyak in Hollywood in the 1920s all deliberately sought out the ugliest aspects of the incomprehensible foreign culture that surrounded them, drew sweeping generalizations from incidental or trivial occurrences, and yearned for the comforts of the familiar Russian reality they had left behind—no matter how grim and flawed that reality may have appeared in their own writings.

The opposing tradition, exemplified by Nikolai Karamzin on his grand tour of Western Europe in 1789, by Turgenev on his numerous foreign sojourns, by Chekhov in his letters from Vienna and Venice, and, in our own time, by Viktor Nekrasov's travel impressions of America and Italy, shows the writer as an inquisitive and sympathetic observer, anxious to understand foreign ways before he condemns them and not suffering from the compulsion to justify the current Russian social forms by finding life in other countries a nightmare by comparison.

Fonvizin's letters from abroad are important not only as a primary document in the continuing love-hate relationship between Russian intellectuals and the West. They contain a wealth of fascinating impressions and observations, including a description of the impact of the American Revolutionary War on the Continent, an eyewitness account of Voltaire's "apotheosis" on the occasion of his final visit to Paris in 1778, an intriguing account of an invitation to attend a meeting of a French learned society where Fonvizin was to meet Benjamin Franklin, "the minister of the United American Provinces,"[17] and sarcastically acid portraits of some of the French Encyclopedists.

16. "У нас все лучше, и мы больше люди нежели немцы." The last part of this much-quoted statement has often been mistranslated as "and we are a greater people than the Germans," which is of course wrong.

17. For the background material on Fonvizin's encounter with Franklin, see W. B. Edgerton, 'Znakomstvo Fonvizina s Lablansheri v Parizhe," in the collec-

The Minor

It was between his two extended tours of Europe that Fonvizin wrote his dramatic masterpiece, the satirical comedy of manners *The Minor*, completed in 1781, but begun some time in the late 1770s.[18] After a few public readings of the text by the author, the play was performed in a private theater in St. Petersburg on September 24, 1782. It immediately became recognized as an achievement with no rival in the preceding Russian dramatic literature. There were no less than 46 different productions of *The Minor* staged in Russia in the next two decades. It was performed for Catherine by her court troupe, by serf actors at aristocratic magnates' estates, by an amateur company of Moscow University students and by almost every professional theater in the country. *The Brigadier*, despite its great success in the eighteenth century, disappeared from the active repertoire of Russian theaters with the onset of romanticism (there were a few scattered nineteenth-century revivals that commemorated various Fonvizin anniversaries). But *The Minor* remains the earliest Russian play that has retained a permanent place on the Russian stage to this day. It is, by common consent, the best Russian play of the eighteenth century, and in this case, for once, common consent is not wrong.

---

tion *Rol' i znachenie literatury XVIII veka v istorii russkoi kul'tury*, ed. D. S. Likhachev et al. (Moscow-Leningrad, 1966), pp. 165–73.

18. Although all sources agree about the date of completion of this work, there is some disagreement among scholars about the time the comedy was begun and whether there were earlier plays by Fonvizin subsequently reworked into *The Minor*. Around 1900, there was discovered an eighteenth-century manuscript of an unfinished play bearing the title *The Minor* and using some of the situations of Fonvizin's play. It was somehow immediately assumed to be Fonvizin's own autograph of an earlier draft of his play and was eventually published as such in *Literaturnoe nasledstvo*, vols. 9–10 (Moscow, 1933). This so-called first version of the play was uncritically accepted by several Fonvizin experts and included in the writer's canon until 1954, when Pigarev's book (*Tvorchestvo Fonvizina*, pp. 281–84) conclusively proved that it could not possibly be by Fonvizin and that, in fact, there was never *any evidence* for supposing that it was. What was mistaken for Fonvizin's draft was one of the numerous imitations of the play that proliferated at the end of the century.

Because Russian criticism of the second half of the nineteenth century and of the postrevolutionary period in the twentieth accepted as an axiom the proposition that the realistic mode is the be-all and end-all of literary expression, a great deal of ingenuity and ink have been expended to build up for *The Minor* the reputation of a fully realistic play, thus giving Fonvizin the priority of originating realism half a century before it was heard of in other countries. These efforts may have obscured, but could not change, the awkward fact that *The Minor* was and remains an eighteenth-century neoclassical comedy *par excellence*. The unities are scrupulously observed. The action begins on the morning of one day and terminates early on the morning of the next day, fitting into the required twenty-four-hour period. All the diverse activities and confrontations in which the characters participate take place in one single room of unspecified nature.

Physical violence is either threatened onstage, but does not materialize, or occurs offstage (the physical fight between Mrs. Prostakov and her brother or the attempted kidnapping of Sophia) and is only discussed onstage. The characters, for all their vividness, are personifications of one or two basic humors, be it avuncular wisdom, the sullen selfishness of a teen-aged boy, or the doglike devotion of an abused servant. The structural device of having the characters leave the stage at the end of each act (except for the final moralistic tableau), does not contribute much to the illusion of realism.

The action of the comedy takes place on the country estate of the meek and timid landowner Terenty Prostakov (Mr. Terence Simpleton). The estate and everyone on it are tyrannized by Prostakov's violent, domineering wife, née Miss Brute (Skotinina). Their son Mitrofan, the minor of the title, is a lazy sixteen-year-old lout, spoiled and pampered by his doting mother, rude and insensitive to everyone except her, and with only one ambition: "I don't want to study, what I want is to be married." Also staying at the estate is the traveling nobleman Pravdin (Mr. Truthful), ostensibly a visitor, but in fact a government spy, sent by the benevolent authorities to investigate Mrs. Prostakov's reported abuse of her serfs.

At the beginning of the play, Mrs. Prostakov has usurped the neighboring estate of a young woman, Sophia, left orphaned by the death of her mother. After divesting Sophia of her personal belongings, Mrs. Prostakov is planning to marry her off by force to another member of the family—Mrs. Prostakov's pig-loving, coarse brother Skotinin (Mr. Brute). However, Sophia soon receives a letter announcing the return of her long-lost uncle Starodum (Mr. Oldsense), who has amassed a considerable fortune in Siberia. With the prospect of Sophia as a rich heiress, Mrs. Prostakov decides that she would now make a suitable match for her son rather than for her brother, with some highly comical squabbling between uncle and nephew ensuing.

Sophia, however, has already pledged her troth to an impetuous young officer named Milon (Lt. Darling) whom she had met before her abduction by the Prostakovs. Presently, Milon himself appears on the scene, commanding a platoon of soldiers quartered on the estate. After Starodum's arrival, both Mitrofan and Skotinin advance their suits and are rejected. Thwarted in her plans, the enraged Mrs. Prostakov resolves to kidnap Sophia and to marry her to Mitrofan whether she wants him or not. Next morning, Milon rescues the screaming and kicking Sophia as she is about to be led off. When Mrs. Prostakov decides to vent her irritation by having some of her serfs flogged, Pravdin confronts her husband with a government order, relieving him ("because of your wife's inhumanity") of any further jurisdiction over his serfs or property. By a typically eighteenth-century coincidence, Milon turns out to be the nephew of Starodum's old friend, and it was to Milon that Starodum had hoped to marry Sophia all along. Mrs. Prostakov gets her full comeuppance when her adored son turns against her with hostility and ingratitude once she is divested of her power.

On this framework, Fonvizin built a full-blooded and dramatically exciting play. The clash between the ignorant and crude provincial gentry (the Prostakovs and Skotinin) and the civilized spokesmen for the Enlightenment (Starodum, Pravdin, and Milon) is a fair match, because although the good characters have truth and justice on their side, the bad ones, with their dynamic energy and colorful language (usually lost in translations), are far more arresting dramatically. In his characterization of these two contrasting groups, Fonvizin relied, perhaps excessively, on certain nondramatic literary genres of his day. Skotinin, Mitrofan, and Mrs. Prostakov often unwittingly condemn themselves out of their own mouths (this was also the case with many of the characters in *The Brigadier*), as was the fashion in the eighteenth-century satirical journals, where the vehicle of satire was usually a letter attributed to the satirized character.[19]

The social and moral disquisitions of Starodum, Pravdin, and Milon are very much in the style of the philosophical treatises of the eighteenth-century moralists, not only in content, but in actual wording. Eighteenth-century audiences had an appetite for such moralistic speeches, but directors of nineteenth- and twentieth-century productions of *The Minor* have often preferred to delete them as dramatically cumbersome. Even Starodum's dialogue with Pravdin about the difficulties of a courtier's life, which is sometimes taken by later commentators for a daring attack on Catherine's court, is very much within the tradition of similar topics treated in numerous Russian poems (Kantemir's satires, for example, or Derzhavin's semihumorous odes) and tragedies of that age, which considered it one of the basic duties of the writer "to give lessons to sovereigns."

Very important for an understanding of the total conception of the play are two groups of lesser characters who appear in *The Minor*: the enserfed retainers of the Prostakov family and Mitrofan's tutors. Fonvizin was unique among the playwrights of his age in his ability to achieve memorable characterizations even with his secondary or incidental characters. The

19. From 1769 on, the journalist and publisher Nikolai Novikov brought out a series of satirical journals, patterned on Addison and Steele's *The Spectator* in England. In keeping with its English prototype, the satirical format consisted of letters from intelligent characters who bore names such as Priamikov (Mr. Straightforward) and from vicious or stupid ones, with telltale names on the order of Skudoum (Mr. Poormind). The unattractive characters were made to condemn themselves out of their own mouths. See G. Gareth Jones, "Novikov's Naturalized Spectator," *The Eighteenth Century in Russia*, ed. J. G. Garrard (Oxford, 1973), pp. 149–65.

two serfs in *The Minor* are overwhelmingly vivid. They are Mitrofan's devoted peasant nanny Eremeyevna and the plucky peasant lad Trishka, who appears briefly in the opening scenes. Eremeyevna is known by her patronymic alone, a usage that indicates respect for an elderly person of humble origin. She was earlier Mrs. Prostakov's nurse and is now looking after the son of her nurseling. The reward she gets for her hard work and loyalty are, as she puts it, "five roubles a year and five boxes on the ear each day." Old Eremeyevna meekly accepts whatever insults come her way, but Trishka (a contemptuous diminutive for Trifon), forced by his mistress to be a tailor even though he lacks all skill or training, dares to talk back and defend himself.

The reason for having three tutors in the Prostakov household was the new legislation, passed in the second half of the eighteenth century, according to which young noblemen had to be trained for either military or civil service duty by acquiring a proper education. Mrs. Prostakov, who thinks she is preparing her dull-witted Mitrofan for a brilliant future in government service, has hired the retired soldier Tsyfirkin (Sgt. Numberkins) to teach him arithmetic and the seminary dropout Kuteikin (the name refers to a kind of rice gruel served at wakes and offered to the clergy) for catechism and Russian lessons. Their best efforts to teach Mitrofan are foiled by the meddling of the indulgent mother and by the German head tutor Vralman (Herr Fibbermann), who speaks Russian with a phonetically transcribed Saxon accent and who owes his privileged position in the household to pleasing the doting mother by excusing Mitrofan from his lessons. At the end of the play, Vralman is exposed as Starodum's former coachman who pretended to be a qualified teacher since he could find no job in his own line of work (in *The Brigadier*, Little Ivan was educated by a French coachman). The scenes with the tutors, among the most successful and enjoyable in the play, point to the basic concern of Fonvizin's two original plays with the importance of education in the formation of human character.

The romantic era bequeathed to later generations the Rousseauist image of the child as the natural sage, the repository of all human virtues, who may later on in life be corrupted by false civilization. It is difficult for most of us to grasp the opposite idea of childhood, the one that was widely held prior to the advent of Rousseauism and the one to which Fonvizin subscribed. "It is not natural for man to remember his earliest infancy," Fonvizin says in his *Confessions* written at the end of his life. "I have no knowledge of myself before the age of six. But I, too, doubtless had in me all the evil that can be observed in other infants, namely: anger, impatience, avarice, and duplicity, in a word, the rudiments of all those vices that later on take root and grow owing to education and bad examples."[20]

It is the basic thesis of both *The Brigadier* and *The Minor*, repeatedly reiterated and brought home by various characters, that bad people are what they are because of bad education. Absence of education (as exemplified by the Brigadier, by Skotinin, and by Mrs. Prostakov) is as harmful as is bad, misdirected education (illustrated by Little Ivan, the Councillor's wife and Mitrofan). Only those who have benefitted from the civilizing teachings of the Enlightenment are shown as worthy and admirable persons in Fonvizin's plays. In this sense, the playwright's purpose is ill-served by the contrast between the noisy scene that Mitrofan has with his tutors at the end of Act III of *The Minor* and the interminable one in which Sophia eagerly listens to the moral and social preaching of her uncle at the beginning of the next act.

This central preoccupation with the formative function of education gives *The Minor* its deserved place as one of the links in the chain of pedagogical comedies that we find in most European literatures in the second half of the eighteenth century. In a remarkably perceptive and highly audacious article, the Soviet scholar Boris Reizov has pointed out numerous parallels between *The Minor* and such Western predecessors as Goldoni's *Il padre di famiglia*, Nivelle de la Chaussée's *L'école de mères*, Oliver Goldsmith's *She Stoops to Conquer*, and Jakob Lenz's *Der Hofmeister*. All of them share with Fonvizin's play some basic plot elements, depict a pampering mother and a

20. D. I. Fonvizin, *Izbrannye sochineniia i pis'ma* (Moscow, 1947), p. 192.

spoiled son, and draw the same general conclusion about the issues the play raises.[21]

Another concept that is basic to both *The Brigadier* and *The Minor* is the idea of duty: the duty of the gentry to serve their country (this is where Little Ivan, the bribe-taking Councillor, Skotinin, and Mitrofan all fail); the duty of landowners to look after and protect their serfs (Mrs. Prostakov and her brother are clear failures in this area); the duty of children to obey their elders (the lack of filial piety in Little Ivan and Mitrofan is contrasted with the docility of the two Sophias, willing to obey their parent or guardian to the point of accepting a distasteful marriage). Most of Fonvizin's manifold satirical thrusts—his attacks on corruption in the civil service (the Councillor), on lack of patriotism, on abuse of parental authority, on mistreatment of the serfs, on heartlessness and greed—are ultimately reducible to either failure of education or insufficient comprehension of duty.[22]

None of the targets that Fonvizin singled out for satirical attack in *The Minor* was particularly exceptional or novel for its time. Much of what he criticized had already been denounced in numerous comedies and comic operas of the preceding two decades, as well as in Catherine's own plays. It was Fonvizin's unique literary and dramatic skill, his instantly recognizable portrayal (within the neoclassical stage conventions of

21. B. G. Reizov, "K voprosu o zapadnykh paralleliakh 'Nedoroslia,'" in the collection *Rol' i znachenie literatury*, pp. 157–64.

22. The extremes to which Fonvizin's own notions of duty could go can be illustrated by the story of his own father's first marriage that he tells in the introductory chapter of his *Confessions*. To save his brother from debtors' prison, the playwright's father, taking advantage of his good looks, sold himself into a marriage with a wealthy woman nearing seventy, who agreed to pay the brother's debts. "Obeying the dictates of fraternal love alone, my father did not hesitate to sacrifice himself," the admiring son wrote. "He married that old lady, being himself eighteen at the time. She lived with him for twelve more years. And he did everything to cherish her old age, as a Christian should. It must be confessed that in our age we no longer encounter such examples of fraternal love, in which a young man would sacrifice himself, as my father did, to the welfare of his brother" (Fonvizin, *Izbrannye sochineniia i pis'ma*, pp. 191–92). After the death of his first wife, whose fortune he inherited, Fonvizin Senior married the playwright's mother, by whom he had eight children.

his time) of actual aspects of Russian reality, and the wit and humor of the characters' speeches that made the satire so stinging and the play so exceptionally popular with his countrymen. As the age of Catherine receded into the past, *The Minor* frequently came to be misinterpreted by critics and scholars, either unconsciously or deliberately, and it remains to this day, with the possible exception of Gogol's *Dead Souls*, the single most widely misunderstood masterpiece of Russian literature.

Already by the 1820s, the relative liberality of Russian censorship that had existed before the French Revolution was largely forgotten. Against the background of the further tightening of the reins that followed the Decembrist uprising, many of Fonvizin's satirical passages began to look quite daring. Viazemsky, for example, writing in the 1830s, was puzzled by what he thought was Fonvizin's audacity in portraying Kuteikin (Mitrofan's teacher of religion who had dropped out of the provincial theological seminary after becoming "affrighted by the abyss of wisdom"), and by the liberality of the censorship that did not object to this figure. For all his wide research, Viazemsky clearly did not realize that comical depiction of Russian clergy on the stage, unthinkable in the nineteenth century, was common during the reigns of Elizabeth and Catherine II.[23]

In the age of Nicholas I, Pushkin's celebrated epithets in *Eugene Onegin*, "satire's audacious sovereign" and "friend of liberty,"[24] which are what most literate Russians first hear of

23. Viazemsky, *Fon-Vizin*, p. 46. Viazemsky goes on to say that the comedy *O, Times!* is equally astonishing, "especially when one remembers who wrote it." And indeed, Catherine's satire of religious hypocrisy would not have been passed by the censor during her grandson's reign.

24. Fonvizin is thus qualified by Pushkin in stanza 18 of *Eugene Onegin's* first chapter. In chapter 5 of that novel, Mitrofan's uncle, Skotinin, appears as one of the guests at Tatiana's name-day party, accompanied by his grey-haired wife and a group of children ranging in age from two to thirty. From Pushkin's youthful poem "Fonvizin's Shade" (1815), in which the ghost of the playwright returns to earth in the second decade of the nineteenth century to pass judgment on the current literary scene, to some of the poet's letters written at the end of his life, there is a steady stream of Fonvizin quotations, references, and allusions in Pushkin's work and in his correspondence. It was Pushkin who encouraged Viazemsky to undertake the writing of the earliest complete biography of Fonvizin. For more details on the reflection of Fonvizin in Pushkin's work, see Pigarev, *Tvorchestvo Fonvizina*, pp. 260–64.

Fonvizin, made good sense, though they would have sounded exaggerated and undeserved in Fonvizin's own day. Later on in the nineteenth century, during and after the emancipation of the serfs, it became common to draw on the characters from *The Minor* to illustrate the inhumanity of the landowners to the peasants and the general corruption of life in tsarist Russia. These references, used in various abolitionist tracts and in editorials denouncing provincial backwardness, have gradually built for *The Minor* the reputation of a daring and revolutionary work, which has the indictment of serfdom and perhaps of autocracy as its central subject.

Fonvizin may have condemned the abuse and mistreatment of serfs in his comedy, but there is no indication anywhere in the play or in his other writings that he perceived the injustice of the institution of serfdom as such. Mrs. Prostakov oppresses her serfs, just as she oppresses her own husband and the defenseless young noblewoman Sophia. She does this because she is an uneducated and cruel harridan, not because she is a landowner. The virtuous and admirable characters—Pravdin and Milon in *The Minor* and Dobroliubov in *The Brigadier*—are all serfowners. As educated people, they can presumably be trusted to treat their serfs in a decent manner. Of course, it goes without saying that Fonvizin, his family, and all his associates were serfowners.

When Fonvizin's patron, Count Nikita Panin, was relieved of his duties as Grand Duke Paul's preceptor upon the latter's coming of age, Catherine lavished rewards and gifts on him, among them the title of ownership to 9,000 enserfed peasants. Panin generously shared a part of this largess with his three secretaries. Fonvizin, in particular, was given 1,180 of those "souls," who lived on a remote estate in Belorussia. Instead of taking any interest in his new subjects, Fonvizin sublet them and the land on which they lived to an unscrupulous nobleman, whose mismanagement and abuse of the peasants led to their rebellion and embroiled Fonvizin in lawsuits that eventually cost him his fortune and left his widow a pauper.[25] On his trips

25. See Fonvizin's biography of Nikita Panin in his *Sobranie sochinenii*, (Moscow-Leningrad, 1959), vol. 2, p. 287; Viazemsky, *Fon-Vizin*, pp. 248–49; the

abroad, Fonvizin found the lot of the free Western European peasants lamentable when compared to that of the "fortunate" Russian serfs.[26] It can be seen that Fonvizin's reputation as an enemy of serfdom has no historical or biographical basis.

From the supposition that *The Minor* was a subversive play there was born the widespread legend that it was initially censored or banned and that its first performance took place despite government objections. The assertion that *The Minor* must have had censorship troubles was already made by the prerevolutionary scholars Alexei Veselovsky and Boris Warnecke, who had simply taken it for granted that the censorship conditions in the reign of Catherine must have been identical with those of the nineteenth century. The claim is repeated to this day. However, the only historically attested attempt to censor the play did not come from Catherine or anyone connected with her government. It was made instead by the self-appointed Moscow censor, Professor Khariton Chebotarev, who six years later would attempt to ban Kniazhnin's *Vladimir and Iaropolk*.

Chebotarev's move to censor *The Minor* occurred some months after the triumphant St. Petersburg opening of the play, when the English-born impresario Michael Maddox was preparing its Moscow premiere. Informed by Maddox that Chebotarev had expressed a wish to examine the text of *The Minor* to see if it contained any objectionable passages, Fonvizin wrote him to tell Chebotarev that since the play had already been performed in a public theater in St. Petersburg by the actors of the Imperial Theater and with the written permission of the government, it made no sense to subject it to further scrutiny in Moscow. "You may assure the censor that in my entire play,

---

memoirs of Fonvizin's financial factotum, H. J. Klostermann (*Russkii arkhiv* (Moscow, 1881), vol. 3, pp. 291–99), which give a shattering picture of the depths of poverty and misery to which Fonvizin's serfs were reduced through his callousness and extravagance; and Pigarev, *Tvorchestvo Fonvizina*, p. 252. Apart from Pigarev's oblique reference to this episode, Soviet scholars writing on Fonvizin avoid mentioning this aspect of his biography lest it contradict their carefully constructed image of an abolitionist and libertarian Fonvizin.

26. For example, his description of the French peasants in Languedoc and Provence in his letter to Count Peter Panin of March 31, 1778, *Sobranie sochinenii*, vol. 2, p. 466.

and therefore also in the passages that so frightened him, not a single syllable has been changed," the letter concluded.[27]

The Minor became widely known and achieved a word-of-mouth success even before it was premiered.[28] It was staged less than a year after the script was completed. Various letters and memoirs of the period indicate that the opening night was postponed, but they all ascribe this to insufficient time allowed for rehearsals. At the first performance, the cast included some of the finest actors and actresses of the time. The illustrious Ivan Dmitrevsky played Starodum, and the other surviving member of Fyodor Volkov's original Iaroslavl company, Iakov Shumsky, scored a great personal success as the peasant nanny Eremeyevna (after him, it became traditional to have Eremeyevna played by men). The remarkable character actress Avdotia Mikhailova created the role of Mrs. Prostakov. As Fonvizin wrote soon thereafter to Michael Maddox, "Le succès était complet."

And indeed *The Minor* quickly became one of the most widely performed plays in Russia and also one of the most frequently performed at Catherine's court. Both her view of the play and that of her entourage have been epitomized by the semiapocryphal remark reportedly made to Fonvizin by Catherine's powerful favorite, Prince Gregory Potemkin, after a performance at the court theater: "You might as well die, Denis, you'll never write anything better!" The phrase has become a popular proverb in Russian, cited to convey the high-

---

27. Ibid., vol. 2, p. 496. The historical background of the first productions of *The Brigadier* and *The Minor* is outlined in M. P. Troianovsky, "K stsenicheskoi istorii komedii D. I. Fonvizina 'Brigadir' i 'Nedorosl' ' v XVIII veke." *Teatral'noe nasledstvo* (Moscow, 1956), pp. 7–23. The facts are all there, but the a priori assumption that the plays were subversive turns every delay, postponement, or criticism into proof of governmental censorship. Granted this initial approach, all testimony of Catherine's approval or enjoyment of Fonvizin's plays can be dismissed as evidence of her hypocrisy or demagoguery.

28. See P. N. Berkov, *Istoriia russkoi komedii XVIII v.* (Leningrad, 1977), pp. 224–25; and also *Istoriia russkogo dramaticheskogo teatra* (Moscow, 1977), vol. 1, p. 310 (The first volume of the latter is a revised reprinting of Vsevolodsky-Gerngross's two volumes on Russian theater of the eighteenth century, previously published in 1957 and 1961, respectively).

est possible accolade.[29] In its own time, *The Minor* was perceived and acclaimed as a brilliant topical play that attacked ignorance, abuse of authority, and inhumanity to others. Only people who saw themselves as embodiments or champions of the play's targets could be offended by the play's message, and such people were few in the Age of Enlightenment, even in Russia.

During the last two years of his life, after he had suffered several strokes and had become partially paralyzed, Fonvizin was working on a rather shapeless three-act comedy, *The Selection of a Tutor* (*Vybor guvernera*, written in 1790–92, first published in 1830), of which the first and third acts and a portion of the second act are extant. Even in its incomplete form, this is clearly the weakest play Fonvizin wrote, lacking any semblance of plot or dramatic action. It consists of a series of discussions between an aristocratic couple and various advisers about the best way to educate the couple's young son. While *The Brigadier* satirizes the military and corrupt civil servants, and *The Minor* has the ignorant landed gentry as its target, *The Selection of a Tutor* is aimed at snobbery based on birth and lineage among Russia's aristocracy.

The wealthy and improbably stupid Prince and Princess Slaboumov (Feebleminded), whose main aim in life is to be addressed as "Your Excellency" by everyone in sight, are looking for a tutor who will flatter their child and instill in him an exaggerated idea of the importance of his lineage. The local Marshal of Nobility, named Seum (Mr. Here's-a-Mind), recommends an honest retired Russian officer as a prospective tutor. But the pompous parents prefer a Frenchman named Monsieur Pélican, who eventually turns out to be a fugitive medical orderly. The play is, of course, one more variation on Fonvizin's basic theme of good and bad education. Almost totally devoid of the literary distinction of Fonvizin's other plays, it does offer some further documentation of the playwright's social and political

---

29. Quoted by Viazemsky, *Fon-Vizin*, p. 219, in an apparently garbled version that reads: "You might as well die, Denis, or else don't bother to write anything more!"

views. Especially telling is the discussion between the *raison-neurs* (Seum and the retired officer), attacking the equality of classes proposed by the French Revolution and advocating the necessity of social stratification.[30]

The long-range impact of Fonvizin's plays on the subsequent development of Russian drama is problematic and open to debate. But the immediate impact of *The Minor* on the lesser playwrights of the end of the eighteenth century is beyond any doubt. No other Russian play had ever brought forth so many imitations, adaptations, and sequels by other authors. For the next three decades, as the comical characters of *The Minor* entered popular lore, there was a steady flow of comedies, comic operas, and even ballets in which Mitrofan, Skotinin, and other Fonvizin creations appeared in principal or subsidiary roles.

There was a sentimental drama outlining the emotional life of Pravdin (who was shown in *The Minor* only in his official capacity). The nanny Eremeyevna was featured in a number of plays in a new role, that of a matchmaker, and several comedies were devoted to the subsequent fate of Kuteikin. Other plays of the period kept referring to the Prostakov family or had characters who claimed to be their relatives. Although there was no play called *The Son of the Minor*, the phenomenon amounted, of course, to a set of rather simple-minded attempts to capitalize on the play's renown and produced no work of real interest. The last of these imitations dates from about 1810.[31] By that time *The Minor* had become a permanent component of Russian culture and national tradition.[32]

30. *The Selection of a Tutor* was performed on the stage of the Empress Alexandra Theater in St. Petersburg on December 1, 1892, to commemorate the centenary of Fonvizin's death; a distinguished cast was headed by the great Maria Savina playing the Princess Slaboumova (*Ezhegodnik Imperatorskikh teatrov* [St. Petersburg, 1892–93], pp. 131–32).

31. See Pigarev, *Tvorchestvo Fonvizina*, pp. 203–08, for a detailed description of these imitations and sequels. Several of these plays are included in P. N. Berkov's anthology, *Russkaia komediia i komicheskaia opera XVIII veka* (Moscow-Leningrad, 1950).

32. Fonvizin was more fortunate than most Russian playwrights in his biographers. The two fine studies of his life and work (on which much in the preceding pages was based) are those of Viazemsky (1848) and Pigarev (1954). Both were written and published in periods of maximal repression, and both managed to deal with their subject originally and in depth. Viazemsky's book suffers

Kapnist's *Chicane*

Kniazhnin's demonstration that it was possible to write viable and successful comedies in Russian verse moved one of the better-known lyric poets of the end of the eighteenth century, Vasily Kapnist (1757–1823), to try his hand at this genre.[33] The resultant work, the satirical verse comedy *Chicane* (*Iabeda*),[34] was the play that achieved the synthesis between Kniazhnin's verse comedy of intrigue and the prose comedies of Lukin, Fonvizin, and Elchaninov, with their more recognizable Russian milieu, down-to-earth characterizations, and reflection of actual Russian social customs and problems.

Kapnist was a Ukrainian landowner of Greek descent. His grandfather, whose name is variously spelled Kapnisos and Kapnissi, came from the island of Zante, where he got into trouble with the occupying Turkish authorities, fled to Russia, and was given rich landholdings in the Ukraine by the Empress Elizabeth as a reward for his military exploits against the Turks while in her service. Kapnist's literary bent was encouraged by Nikolai Lvov and by Derzhavin, his close friends from the time of his military service in St. Petersburg. Derzhavin, Lvov (the folk-song collector and the author of the libretto for *Postal*

---

from an oddly chaotic structure and from the author's inexplicable hostility to all Russian drama (he seems to value Kotzebue higher than Griboedov or Gogol). Pigarev's book includes all the standard nationalistic, patriotic, and Marxist clichés without which it could not have been published where and when it was. But this author refrained to an amazing degree from falsifying history or the meaning of Fonvizin's work, and he brings a deeper understanding to his subject than anyone writing about Fonvizin before or since has managed to do. A thorough recent study in English of Fonvizin's life and writings is Charles A. Moser's *Denis Fonvizin* (Boston, 1979).

33. In the introduction to his later tragedy *Antigone*, Kapnist admitted that "I will say with gratitude that had the most esteemed Mr. Kniazhnin not proved by the example of his excellent *The Braggart* the possibility of composing a comedy in verse using simple conversational language, I would not have dared to undertake writing *Chicane*" (V. V. Kapnist, *Sobranie sochinenii v dvukh tomakh* [Moscow-Leningrad, 1960], vol. 1, p. 447.)

34. The traditional English translation of the title is in accord with the playwright's own rendition in the French dedication to the first printed edition, *La chicane*.

Coachmen at the Relay), and Kapnist eventually consolidated their friendship with family ties when all three married the three Diakov sisters.

For a poet known mainly for his Horatian odes and rococo lyrics, the choice of subject of *Chicane* was unexpected. The play is an energetic attack on corruption in the Russian judiciary. Kapnist found the basis for his play in the antiquated set of laws on personal property holdings. Promulgated in the reign of Tsar Alexis, they were still operative at the end of the eighteenth century. In their vagueness and ambiguity, in combination with a corrupt system of courts based on written, secret procedures, these laws opened a wide field for legal chicanery and fraudulent lawsuits. Beginning with school drama interludes of the early eighteenth century, through Sumarokov's comedies, Verevkin's sentimental dramas, and Matinsky's *The St. Petersburg Bazaar*, corrupt legal officials supplied one of the most frequent targets of satire in Russian drama. But Kapnist's comedy outdid them all in its violent and single-minded indictment.

The play's principal villain is a retired civil servant named Pravolov (Mr. Lawcatcher; the name is formed by analogy with such compound words as *rybolov*, fisherman, *ptitselov*, birdcatcher, and *krysolov*, ratcatcher), who, by employing a network of spies and by liberal use of bribery, is amassing a fortune through embroiling other noblemen in fraudulent lawsuits that usually result in his getting his victims' property confiscated in his favor. Pravolov's current target is an upright young military man Bogdan Priamikov (Lt. Col. Dieudonné Straightforward), who returns from the wars to find his family property tied up in complex litigations initiated on a trivial pretext. The case is to be judged by the president of the Civil Court Chamber Krivosudov (Judge Crooked), who is influenced by his greedy and rapacious wife, Fyokla, and decides cases not on the basis of the evidence, but rather on the amount of bribes that the contending sides offer.

Pravolov showers the judge's family with gifts, while the inexperienced Priamikov naively expects the case to be judged on its merits and offers no bribes to anyone. To strengthen his hand, Pravolov makes a marriage proposal to the judge's pure and innocent daughter, named, as could be expected, Sophia, although he does not really intend to marry her. Sophia, for her part, loves Priamikov, whom she has met while away at a boarding school. The Sophia-Priamikov romance, clearly patterned after the Sophia-Milon encounter in *The Minor*, was allotted considerably more space in the earlier drafts of *Chicane*, but was cut down to the barest minimum in the final version, where Sophia appears only to fulfill the plot requirements and is never given a chance to develop as a character.

The five acts of the play outline the progress of Pravolov's scheme to seize Priamikov's family estate. A whole array of lesser government officials with names like Kokhtin (Claws), Khvataiko (Grabbit), and Radbyn ('d-Beglad-To), the last a stutterer whose every extra syllable is carefully worked into the iambic hexameter verse texture, are bribed and bought by the villain. They help him and the crooked judge to make an honest army officer appear a usurper of his own family home. The only piece of evidence on which the entire case is built is Priamikov's use of the Slavic form of his Christian name (Bogdan) instead of the Greek form (Theodotos) that is entered on his birth certificate. Because court proceedings were transacted in written form and the record kept secret, Priamikov has no way of defending himself or even knowing the exact nature of the charges. Both as a party in a lawsuit and as a suitor, he is repeatedly rebuffed and even thrown out of the house by the tempestuous mother of his beloved. Finally, a *deus ex machina* in the form of a senate investigation exposes Pravolov's misdeeds and vindicates his victims.

Though it lacks the vividness of Fonvizin's plays and though its verse texture may appear unpolished when compared to the better verse comedies of the early nineteenth century, Kapnist's *Chicane* is still in many ways a remarkable play. It is a *pièce à thèse*. The cause it pleads—the reform of antiquated laws and unfair procedures of jurisprudence—is unequivocally and eloquently stated. Its dramatic structure is sound within the neoclassic poetics of its time, with its insistence on the traditional unities. The hero and the villain may be on the lifeless side and resemble cardboard cutouts, but the corrupt and dishonest judge, apprehensive and vacillating in the midst of his bribe-taking, and his loud, violent wife, who is given to throwing tantrums whenever contradicted or not given an explanation, are convincing theatrical creations.

The informative aspects of the play—the complex juridical procedures and the ways of manipulating them—are worked into the dramatic structure and entertainingly presented. The satire is at times amazingly daring, with the high point reached in the scene of a drunken brawl at the judge's house. The sweet Sophia strums her harp and sings a hymn praising the charity and generosity of Catherine Regina, while her father's tipsy friends chime in with a prayerful refrain: "Blind the people, O Lord, so they go on feeding the appointed officials!"

Chicane had a censorship history that is almost as famous as that of *Vadim of Novgorod*. Kapnist began writing it the year Kniazhnin's *Odd Fellows* was published. He finished it when Catherine II was still alive (hence the eulogy of the empress in the carousing scene). With the accession to the throne of Catherine's son Paul, Kapnist thought it best to dedicate the comedy to him, apparently on Lvov's advice.[35] The dedication was graciously accepted. In 1798 *Chicane* began a successful run in St. Petersburg. After four performances, several high officials denounced the play to Paul as seditious. He promptly had it banned and ordered all printed copies confiscated.

Nineteenth-century scholars cite a semilegendary account of subsequent developments, which, although not authenticated, is very much in keeping with Paul's frequently paranoid behavior. According to this story, the emperor was so enraged after the play was denounced to him that he ordered on the spot that Kapnist be banished to Siberia. However, he had misgivings one day later and asked that the play be performed in a closed theater, with himself as the only spectator. The play supposedly so delighted Paul that he sent messengers to inter-

35. For Derzhavin's account of the dedication of *Chicane* to Paul, see S. P. Zhikharev, *Zapiski sovremennika* (Moscow, 1955), pp. 303–4.

cept the playwright, who was already on his way to Siberia, and to offer him a full pardon and a gift of a diamond-studded snuff-box (or some other piece of costly jewelry).

Whether this story is true or not, the play was not performed for the rest of Paul's brief reign. After the assassination of this half-mad monarch in 1801, his successor, Alexander I, quickly authorized public performances of *Chicane*, and the play became one of the staples of the Russian repertoire for the entire first half of the century. Its popularity outlived the success of the comedies of Kniazhnin, and with the exception of Griboedov's one masterpiece, it outlasted its progeny, the neoclassical verse comedy of the first two decades of the nineteenth century. *Chicane* continued being played until the evil against which it pleaded—the antiquated and unjust legal system—was done away with by the reforms of Alexander II in 1864. Since that time it has not been performed, but it is regularly reissued to this day. Literary tradition considers this play to be a bridge that joins Fonvizin's *The Minor* to Griboedov's *The Misfortune of Being Clever*. The metaphor is an apt one, provided it is understood that the stepping stones to this bridge were Kniazhnin's *The Braggart* and *Odd Fellows*.

Peter Plavilshchikov

A number of lesser playwrights, with names beginning for some reason invariably with *K* (e.g., Klushin, Kolychev, Kopiev, and Kropotov, to say nothing of Kniazhnin, Kapnist, and Krylov), were active in the last decade of the eighteenth century. Their plays, mentioned in histories of Russian theater, followed the various trends noted in the last three chapters and added nothing significant to the art of playwriting in Russia. In comparison with those writers, Peter Plavilshchikov (1760–1812), one of the most popular actors of the turn of the century and who also dabbled in playwriting and published articles on the theory of drama, stands out as a figure of some originality. As a very young actor, Plavilshchikov appeared in the world premiere of *The Minor*, playing Pravdin. In his later career he was particularly noted for his performances in Kniazhnin's tragedies (Iarbas in *Dido*, Titus and Sextus in *The Clemency of Titus*) and in tragedies by Ozerov.

In his capacity as a theoretician of the theater (his articles appeared in the early 1790s in Krylov's journal *The Spectator*), Plavilshchikov pleaded for a more recognizable representation of Russian reality on the stage than was customary at the time. He hoped for new plays that would show the Russian middle classes in serious and believable drama. He rejected most of the "adaptation to our customs" comedies for mechanically transposing to Russia the saucy soubrettes and impudent valets of the French comedy. Instead of the semimythical Kievan princes of Sumarokov's and Kniazhnin's tragedies, he wanted tragedies to depict Russian leaders of more recent epochs, so that Russian audiences could relate more spontaneously to the heroes and heroines.

Assuming a superpatriotic stance, Plavilshchikov rejected most of the foreign models that his countrymen were likely to emulate, Voltaire as well as Kotzebue. He wanted Russian drama of the future to follow its own uncharted path, free of the classical unities and conventions and guided only by native good taste. Nor did he have much sympathy for imitating the favored dramatists of the preromantics, Schiller and Shakespeare. "The celebrated Shakespeare," Plavilshchikov wrote (spelling it Cheksper), "placed in his tragedies such persons and actions as would disgrace even the most vulgar comedy; and even though he knew how to redeem these coarse parodies by the noblest tragic sublimities, enlightened good taste has never approved such strange variety in depiction. The beautiful things in Shakespeare are like lightning, flashing in the darkness of the night. Everyone can see how far their glitter is from the radiance of the sun, shining upon a clear day."[36]

---

36. Quoted from the section on Plavilshchikov's critical views in *Istoriia russkoi kritiki* (Moscow, 1958), pp. 105–10. The text, part of a longer article written by P. N. Berkov, offers a concise, if slanted, summary of Plavilshchikov's ideas, but it does not do justice to their originality.

Plavilshchikov the playwright tried to live up to these positions in his writings for the theater. In his tragedy *Ermak, the Conqueror of Siberia* (*Ermak, pokoritel' Sibiri*), he dispensed with the standard unities and the five-act structure and made the Cossack chieftain who conquered Siberia his tragic hero. In his sequel to Fonvizin's *The Minor*, a brief comedy called *Kuteikin's Engagement Party*, (or *Kuteikin's Betrothal* [*Sgovor Kuteikina*]), he left out the noblemen and concentrated his attention on the divinity student Kuteikin and the serf nanny Eremeyevna. The comedy *The Miller and the Hot-Mead Vendor as Rivals* (*Mel'nik i sbiten'shchik soperniki*), an exercise in dramatized literary criticism, praised Ablesimov's protagonist for his national and down-to-earth qualities and condemned Kniazhnin's popular adaptation of Molière and Beaumarchais for not being sufficiently close to Russian realities. Plavilshchikov's most interesting plays are, by common consent, his two sentimental comedies in prose, *The Landless Peasant* (*Bobyl'*, 1790) and *The Salesclerk* (*Sidelets*, 1804).

In the first of these comedies, a young landless peasant comes into conflict both with the well-off peasant parents of the woman he loves and with the sycophantic flunkies who work at his owner's manor as servants and consider themselves superior to the local peasants. But once the friendly and equally youthful nobleman who owns the village realizes the protagonist's predicament, he immediately comes to his aid and sets things right. In the plot structure of this comedy, Plavilshchikov reversed the conventional Western subplot of the valet romancing the chambermaid of his master's lady love by having the romance between the young landowner and a sentimental neighboring noblewoman take a subordinate position to the central courtship of a peasant girl by a peasant lad.

The Salesclerk continued the exploration of the "dark kingdom" of Moscow merchant families that was initiated by Matinsky. The play, which deals with a corrupt merchant's cruel attempts to frame for theft a virtuous young salesclerk whom his daughter loves, is remarkably similar both in dramatic structure and in the depicted milieu to several of Alexander Ostrovsky's mid-nineteenth century merchant-class dramas. Some prerevolutionary scholars have considered *The Salesclerk* to have been the model for Ostrovsky's popular play *Poverty Is No Crime* (1854).

Plavilshchikov's comedies are not strikingly original, but they do represent a historically significant effort to look at unfamiliar social situations in fresh, dramatically valid ways. Plavilshchikov is careful to avoid blaming moral shortcomings on a particular social class. His appealing peasant hero clashes with other peasants rather than with his master. His merchants in *The Salesclerk* come in all moral varieties: some are honest, some are crooked, some are kind and some are not. The refusal of Plavilshchikov to connect moral values with a particular social or economic group and his determination to represent all social classes with equal sympathy offer certain parallels with a far greater playwright, born exactly one hundred years after him, Chekhov. Like Plavilshchikov, Chekhov was the son of a shopkeeper of peasant origin, and like him, he saw the characters he depicted as individuals rather than as social types or spokespersons for their social class.

To complete the parallel with Chekhov: Plavilshchikov has now been labeled an "ideologue of the bourgeoisie," which is exactly what happened to Chekhov in the early postrevolutionary years and for the very same reasons. But Anton Chekhov was too famous and important a figure to have been left permanently in such an inconvenient category. By the end of the 1920s, ingenious ways were thought up to remove him to the "progressive" literary camp. Plavilshchikov, who lacks an international reputation, has been left with his "bourgeois" label to this day. This explains the continuing obscurity of this unique figure. Neither his theoretical articles nor his plays (with one single exception) have been republished in recent times.[37]

Krylov as a Playwright

Ivan Krylov (1769–1844) owes his place of honor in the history of Russian literature to his moralizing fables, which have

37. *The Landless Peasant* is included in Berkov's *Russkaia komediia i komicheskaia opera*.

enjoyed tremendous popular favor since the beginning of the nineteenth century and have contributed countless proverbs and popular sayings to the Russian language. Because of the prestige of Jean de La Fontaine in the neoclassical tradition, the genre of the fable was widely practiced by Russian eighteenth-century poets. But the racy, colloquial language of Krylov's fables and his unique gift for apt, pithy formulation instantly rendered the entire fable output of Sumarokov, Trediakovsky, Maikov, and so many others obsolete. His fables marked both the climax of that genre in Russian literature and its natural end (despite sporadic and unsuccessful efforts to revive the moralizing fable in Soviet poetry). To this day, Krylov's fables are what most Russian children learn as soon as they begin to speak.

Krylov was forty years old and had behind him a quarter of a century of literary activity before he found, as he put it, "his true shelf" and wrote his first fables. He made his debut as a writer at the age of sixteen with the comic opera *The Fortune-Teller* (the original title, *Kofeinitsa*, indicates that the lady used coffee grounds as the tool of her trade). For the next two decades he was active as a playwright and as a translator of foreign plays, in addition to publishing satirical journals and drama criticism. Because of the Russian custom of issuing the national classics in sets of "the complete collected works of . . . ," Krylov's plays are regularly reissued to this day. But it is clear that they owe this honor to their author's fables rather than to their own intrinsic worth. The earlier comedies are all connected with Kniazhnin in one way or another. *The Fortune-Teller* is an imitation of *Misfortune from a Coach*, even though the unpleasant and tyrannical noblewoman who replaces Kniazhnin's landowner in this play is obviously patterned on Fonvizin's Mrs. Prostakov. Krylov's several neoclassical tragedies, of which the text of *Philomela* survives, were likewise conventional reflections of the Sumarokov-Kniazhnin model.

According to the memoirs of Sergei Glinka, the young Krylov was received as a house guest by Kniazhnin and his wife when he first arrived in St. Petersburg from the provinces and was introduced by them into literary circles.[38] This might account for the derivative orientation of Krylov's early plays, but it does not explain the causes of Krylov's subsequent literary vendetta against Kniazhnin. Not content with accusing Kniazhnin of plagiarism and blasphemy in his satirical journal *The Corre-spondence of Spirits*, Krylov in 1788 wrote a comedy-lampoon, *The Mischief-Makers (Prokazniki)*, in which Kniazhnin appears under the name of Rifmokrad (Rhyme-Stealer) and his wife is called Taratora (Chatterbox).[39]

The action takes place in Kniazhnin's house, with some of his friends and associates depicted as subordinate characters. Kniazhnin is accused of, among other things, sexual impotence, his wife of promiscuity, and doubt is cast on the legitimacy of their children. The crudely explicit sexual allusions in this play remind us how tolerant the eighteenth century was toward this sort of thing. The play became unprintable in the early decades of the nineteenth century. Lest anyone miss the point of his satire, Krylov composed and circulated an open letter ad-dressed to Kniazhnin in which he ironically denied that any character in *The Mischief-Makers* had a real-life model.[40]

Krylov's single really interesting play, the burlesque tragedy published variously as *Trumf* or as *Podshchipa* and written for a private amateur performance in 1799, is also connected with Kniazhnin. This is a parody of the entire genre of neoclassical tragedy, and it bears the same relationship to that form that the numerous eighteenth-century mock-epics and burlesques bear to the epic poem. The direct object of parody is Kniazh-nin's most popular tragedy, *Dido*, which supplies the basic re-lationships between the characters and several direct quotations (there are also burlesqued quotations from other tragedies by Kniazhnin and by Nikolev in the text).

38. *Zapiski Sergeia Nikolaevicha Glinki* (St. Petersburg, 1895), p. 87.

39. The play was circulated privately from the time of its writing, but it was first published in 1793, after Kniazhnin's death.

40. I. A. Krylov, *Sochineniia v dvukh tomakh* (Moscow, 1969), vol. 2, pp. 409–11. For other hypotheses on this feud, see the sources quoted by A. V. Zapa-dov, "I. A. Krylov," in *Russkie dramaturgi* (Leningrad-Moscow, 1959), vol. 1, p. 413.

The action is moved from Carthage to the world of Russian folktales. Aeneas is replaced by a slobbering ninny, whose lisping, phonetically transcribed speech lacks all *r*'s and *l*'s. The African conqueror Iarbas becomes a German invader named Trumf, whose Russian has a German syntax and a Saxon pronunciation (the characteristic Saxon reversal of the voiced and unvoiced consonants). In this play the devices of the eighteenth-century mock-epic and burlesque are deliberately and cleverly mixed with native Russian folklore traditions, including some borrowing from the oral folk drama.

For all that, Krylov made no real effort to break out of the classical canon in this play. He merely incorporated his folklore ingredients into the accepted mold of eighteenth-century poetics. Its burlesque features and folklore elements attracted to *Trumf* the attention of Russian theaters at the beginning of the twentieth century, when there were several productions that stressed its colorful buffoonlike possibilities. The play acquired an additional lease on life during World War II, when it became popular in amateur theatricals of the Red Army. By that time its neoclassical antecedents were either forgotten or disregarded, and it was seen as a currently relevant satire on a tyrannical German invader who is rebuffed by the Russian woman he loves and is eventually expelled by the populace.

Krylov's earlier plays were either not produced on the stage or were played in private homes by amateurs. In 1807 he wrote two prose comedies, *The Fashion Shop* (*Modnaia lavka*) and *A Lesson to Daughters* (*Urok dochkam*), and the libretto for a "magic opera" *Ilya the Hero* (*Il'ia bogatyr'*). All three were produced and had some success with their audiences. The magic opera, which draws on Russian *byliny* in a rather unimaginative way (almost as unimaginative as the similar efforts of Catherine in her folklore-based libretti on which it was patterned), must have owed its success to the music of the Venetian-born composer Catterino Cavos and to its spectacular scenery changes and transformations in the manner of *The Magic Flute*.

The two comedies of 1807 are both satires on Gallomania. Written at the time of Krylov's association with the Archaist group of Admiral Alexander Shishkov, these plays display an anti-French bias that is more violent than the similar attacks in earlier Russian plays (e.g., those of Sumarokov and Fonvizin). This was owing both to the nationalistic position of the archaists (seen also in the anti-French passages in the plays of Shakhovskoy and Griboedov) and to the menacing stance of Napoleon's France during the period. *A Lesson to Daughters* utilizes a russified version of the plot and the characters of Molière's *Les précieuses ridicules*—a rather odd choice of model, considering that the aim of the play is to discourage admiration for French culture. Equally paradoxically, this adaptation of Molière turned out to be Krylov's most popular play, remaining for decades in the repertoire of provincial theaters (Gogol played a peasant nanny in one such production while he was a schoolboy in the Ukraine). It has occasionally been revived in Soviet times.

After 1807, Krylov found his true calling as a fable writer. For the rest of his life he did not bother to return to playwriting. He lived long enough to witness the advent of the romantic and the realistic trends in Russian drama, but he remained a confirmed eighteenth-century classicist to the end. He thought Pushkin's *Boris Godunov* an atrocious play, "something like a hunchback with two humps,"[41] and considered even Griboedov's classically structured comedy, *The Misfortune of Being Clever*, to be some sort of unnatural monstrosity.[42] His own plays added nothing to Russian drama that had not been done earlier and better by other eighteenth-century playwrights. Krylov's real contribution to the development of Russian drama lies in his fables. It was in them that he helped to bring about the literary use of conversational and colloquial Russian and perfected multilength iambic verse, paving the way for the later achievements of Pushkin and Griboedov.[43]

41. P. Viazemsky, *Sobranie sochinenii*, (St. Petersburg, 1878), vol. 1, p. 184.

42. Cf. Griboedov's letter to Viazemsky, in *Literaturnoe nasledstvo* (Moscow, 1946), vol. 47–48, p. 229.

43. For a more detailed account of Krylov's career as a playwright, see Tadeusz Kołakowski's book *Dramaturgia Iwana Kryłowa* (Warsaw, 1968), a remarkably balanced and informative survey of Krylov's relationship to the Russian drama of his period. See also chap. 1 (by I. Z. Serman) and chap. 5 (by S. A. Fomichev) in *Ivan Andreevich Krylov*, ed. Il'ia Serman (Leningrad, 1975), for additional information on Krylov's playwriting career.

❧VII❧

"The Last Ray
of Tragedy's Sunset"

In January of 1805, a seventeen-year-old named Stepan Zhikharev, obsessed with theater and hoping to become a playwright,
began his studies at Moscow University. A year later, bored
with his studies, he moved to St. Petersburg, where he obtained
a position as a clerk in one of the government offices. Equally
at home in Russian, French, and German, possessed of a good
knowledge of dramatic literature and a phenomenal memory
that enabled him to retain in his mind entire scenes from the
plays he saw and long stretches of literary conversations he heard,
the young Zhikharev sought out and met a wide array of literary
and theatrical celebrities of the day. They ranged from the
great poet Derzhavin and the patriarch of Russian theater
Dmitrevsky (who was seventy-two when Zhikharev conversed
with him) to actor-playwright Plavilshchikov, playwright-direc-
tor Shakhovskoy, and an elderly prompter who remembered
much theatrical lore of the end of the eighteenth century. From
1805 to early in 1807, Zhikharev kept a detailed record of his
conversations with those people and of his theatergoing experiences. His diaries were eventually published in the 1850s.[1] They
provided Lev Tolstoy with many concrete details of the period
during his work on *War and Peace* in the 1860s.

1. A good annotated edition of Zhikharev's diaries is S. P. Zhikharev,
Zapiski sovremennika, ed. B. M. Èikhenbaum (Moscow, 1955).

At the time Zhikharev's diaries break off in 1807 (their continuation that went up to 1819 was unfortunately lost), another very young theater buff, Sergei Aksakov, three years younger than Zhikharev, obtained a letter of introduction to the well-known neoclassical actor Iakov Shusherin (stressed on the first syllable). The friendship between the youthful enthusiast of literature and the well-connected older actor led to Aksakov's meeting a number of playwrights, poets, and actors Zhikharev had also met and several he hadn't.

Aksakov did not keep diaries. But when he was in his sixties and the author of the much acclaimed *Family Chronicle* and of widely read books on hunting and fishing, he wrote a series of important memoirs[2] about Russian theatrical life between the years 1807 and 1826. A third member of that generation, Pimen Arapov (1796–1861), who, like Zhikharev and Aksakov, dabbled in playwriting in his early youth, but who had to settle for a career as a theater administrator and publisher of theatrical memorabilia, compiled, at the end of his life, his posthumously published *Chronicle of the Russian Theater*. It covers the period 1673–1825 and it has become an indispensable source for subsequent literary historians. Between them, Zhikharev, Aksakov, and Arapov (helped by the memoirs of some of their contemporaries[3]) open up for us a panorama of the vibrant and usually neglected period of Russian drama that was the first quarter of the nineteenth century. This was the period that formed Griboedov, Pushkin, and Gogol. Without knowing about it, we cannot hope to understand their works for the stage.

After the death of the unpredictable, often paranoid Tsar Paul, the ascent to the throne of his eldest son, Alexander I, aroused hopes for a better future, hopes that were reflected in

2. S. T. Aksakov, "Znakomstvo s Derzhavinym" and "Iakov Emel'ianovich Shusherin i sovremennye emu teatral'nye znamenitosti," in his *Sobranie sochinenii*, vol. 2 (Moscow, 1955); and "Literaturnye i teatral'nye vospominaniia" in vol. 3 of the same edition, which also contains his memoir of Gogol and his theatrical and literary reviews of the 1820s and 1830s.

3. Among the more informative memoirs on the theater of the first quarter of the nineteenth century are those of Sergei Glinka, Philip Vigel (or Wiegel), Rafail Zotov, Nikolai Grech, the actor and playwright Peter Karatygin, and his sister-in-law, Alexandra Karatygina, née Kolosova.

heightened theatrical activity. The first two decades of the new century saw frequent productions of the greatest successes of the previous one: comedies by Fonvizin and Kniazhnin, tragedies by Kniazhnin, Nikolev, and occasionally Sumarokov, and comic operas by Ablesimov, Matinsky, and Kniazhnin. But the high literary quality attained by Ozerov in the new sentimentalist form of neoclassical tragedy and by Shakhovskoy and the playwrights who followed him in verse comedy led to the eventual eclipse of the work of their eighteenth-century predecessors. Sentimental drama, however, did not maintain the level of interest it had reached earlier with Verevkin and Potemkin, its relative decline being attributable to the combined impact of Kotzebue and of the New Sensibility, popularized in Russia by Nikolai Karamzin. And though the best examples of eighteenth-century comic opera remained in the repertory, new works of this genre abandoned the philanthropic and egalitarian trends it represented in the eighteenth century. Instead, the early-nineteenth-century comic opera divided into two branches: the fantastic comic opera, featuring supernatural beings and magic transformations; and the vaudeville comedy (to be described in the next chapter). The first of these was imported from Vienna, the second from Paris.

Machinery and Magic:
the Fantastic Comic Opera

The production in St. Petersburg in 1803 of the "magical" comic opera *Das Donauweibchen* (*The Water Sprite of the Danube*, 1785) by the Viennese composer Ferdinand Kauer, called *Dneprovskaia rusalka* (*The Water Sprite of the Dnieper*) in Russian, was the biggest theatrical hit of the decade, perhaps even of the half-century. Additional musical numbers, based on Russian folklore and composed by Stepan Davydov, may have added to the appeal of this tale of a love affair between a water sprite and a prince and her interference with his later marriage to a mortal woman. But the main drawing card was "transformations," the elaborate stage effects that were so admired that entire families traveled from the provinces just to see the Moscow or St. Petersburg productions of *The Water Sprite*.

Sequels to *The Water Sprite* were concocted by various hands, with music composed by Davydov, over the following five years. They were known as *The Water Sprite*, parts 2, 3, and 4 (the last with text by Shakhovskoy). All enjoyed long runs. One or more of the four parts was sure to be playing somewhere in Russia till the 1840s. All serious playwrights and critics deplored the success of *The Water Sprite*.[4] Actors and singers who performed it in the capitals or toured with it in the provinces often hated it.[5] But the public could not have enough of it.

Tunes from *The Water Sprite* were heard all over the country for decades: children sang them, dance bands played adaptations of them, and one of them found its way into Pushkin's *Eugene Onegin*. That was the sentimental air "Pridi v chertog ko mne zlatoy" ("Come into My Golden Mansion"), which a provincial miss whose parents hope to snag Lensky for a son-in-law is forced to squeak to her own guitar accompaniment by way of enticing him.[6] It took all of Pushkin's genius to strip *The Water Sprite* of its excesses and absurdities and to convert it into his hauntingly poetic unfinished drama *Rusalka*, which

4. See the contemporary negative views of *The Water Sprite of the Dnieper* in Abram Gozenpud, *Muzykal'nyi teatr v Rossii* (Leningrad, 1959), pp. 283 ff.

5. Ivan Dmitrevsky expressed his regret to Zhikharev that young actresses were wasting their time playing water sprites: "What is there to be done? Everything has its day, so the water sprites must have theirs too!" (Zhikharev, *Zapiski*, p. 311). The popular comic actor Iakov Vorobyov eloquently conveyed to Zhikharev his disgust with the magical operas, including Krylov's *Ilya the Hero* (p. 315). Popular demand forced Vorobyov to play buffo servants in works of this genre, though he personally preferred high comedy and light operas by Giovanni Paisiello.

6. "Then the guitar (that, too) is brought,/ And she will start to shrill (good God!): / "Come to me in my golden castle!" *Eugene Onegin*, chap. 2, stanza 12. The English version is from Vladimir Nabokov's translation, which in the commentary to this passage tells us that the sheet music for this aria was found everywhere—"on the pianoforte of a provincial miss, in the attic of an amorous clerk, and on the window sill of a whorehouse" (as mentioned in the poem "The Dangerous Neighbour" by Alexander Pushkin's uncle Vasily Pushkin) (*Eugene Onegin*, translation and commentary by Vladimir Nabokov [New York, 1964], vol. 1, p. 107, and vol. 2, pp. 246–47). In Vasily Pushkin's poem, *The Water Sprite* shares the windowsill with two plays by Kotzebue, an adventure novel, and some chapbook romances.

in turn served as the basis for Alexander Dargomyzhsky's lovely opera of the same name.

The phenomenal acclaim for *The Water Sprite* with its quasi-folkloric names of characters and folklore-derived music induced several noted Russian poets to follow the example of Catherine II in making dramatic use of *byliny*, the traditional folk poems about the heroes of olden days. As noted in Chapter 6, Ivan Krylov scored one of his greatest successes with *Ilya the Hero* (1806, music by Cavos), derived from the cycle of folk poems about Ilya of Murom. Gavriil Derzhavin's *Dobrynia* (1804) combined the Dobrynia Nikitich cycle of *byliny* with elements of chapbook romances. The respective treatment of folklore material by Krylov and Derzhavin retained a number of features inaugurated by Catherine, especially the comic cowardly servant called Tarop, a name unknown in folklore but present in her libretti. Tarop is also found in Vasily Zhukovsky's comic-opera libretto on themes from *byliny*, *The Hero Alyosha Popovich, or The Fearful Ruins* (1804–8). But Zhukovsky's treatment placed the folk heroes of Kievan times into the setting of a Gothic horror novel à la Ann Radcliffe—a good distance away from the *byliny*. (The Derzhavin and Zhukovsky libretti were published but never set to music or performed.)

Karamzinian Drama

Nikolai Karamzin (1766–1826) was above all an important innovator of literary language. By drawing on phraseological patterns of contemporary spoken Russian and also French (rather than on Church Slavic or Latin, as many earlier writers did), he simplified the syntax of written Russian, a reform that was as essential for the language of Shakhovskoy, Griboedov, and Pushkin as Lomonosov's and Trediakovsky's earlier reforms of style and versification were for the Russian playwrights of the eighteenth century. Karamzin tried to introduce Lessing and unabridged Shakespeare in Russia, but the playwright he loved above all others was Kotzebue. He described the crying jag to which a performance of Kotzebue's *Misanthropy and*

Repentence reduced him as one of the unforgettable experiences of his life. Karamzin's one work for the stage, the sentimental drama *Sophia* (published in 1791 and never performed) is a pallid imitation of Kotzebue.

In his travelogue *Letters of a Russian Traveler* (1791–92) and in his extremely popular novellas of the early 1790s (especially "Poor Liza," "Natalia, the Boyar's Daughter" and "The Isle of Bornholm"), Karamzin launched Russian sentimentalism. Descended from Rousseau, Diderot, and such Russian figures as Kheraskov and Verevkin, this new movement attenuated the earlier exploitation of tears for tears' sake into a cult of sensitivity. Two new words coined by Karamzin, *chuvstvitel'nost'* (sensitivity, French *sensibilité*) and *sentimental'nost'* (sentimentality, but with no negative connotations) served notice to his contemporaries that some people have more subtle and ethical reactions than others to their fellow humans and that this was a desirable capacity to have. To experience emotions, even painful ones, was revealed by Karamzin to be preferable to unfeeling placidity.

Karamzin's novellas were liked by both the critics and the general reading public (he was the first Russian writer of prose fiction to have achieved this consensus). By the early nineteenth century, there were numerous attempts to bring to the stage both the situations that his novellas depicted and the emotional states these situations embodied. His "Poor Liza," a simple story of a poor peasant girl abandoned by her aristocratic lover, was so widely admired that people made pilgrimages to the pond where, according to Karamzin's description, Liza drowned herself. Nikolai Ilyin turned this story into a complex, Kotzebue-style, three-act drama *Liza, or The Triumph of Gratitude* (*Liza, ili Torzhestvo blagodarnosti,* 1802). One year later, Vasily Fyodorov produced his even more elaborate dramatization, the five-act *Liza, or The Consequences of Pride and Seduction* (*Liza, ili Sledstviia gordosti i obol'shcheniia*). Different from each other in most ways, both plays undermine the central point of Karamzin's novella by ending with the happy marriage of Liza to her lover. And both plays subvert the story's oft-quoted motto, "Even peasant girls have feelings," each by making Liza the daughter of aristocrats, a girl who, owing to unavoidable circumstances, is raised as a peasant but then shown to be noble enough to be accepted by her lover's family. For all their distortions of Karamzin, the two plays went on being performed for the next two decades. Ilyin's other much-performed play, *Magnanimity, or The Selection of Recruits* (*Velikodushie, ili Rekrutskii nabor*, 1803), was set entirely in the peasant milieu, viewed through a prism of rosy sentimentality.

Karamzin's historical novella "Marfa the Mayoress" was converted by Fyodor Ivanov into a five-act neoclassical tragedy with choruses. The original story was a straightforward account of Marfa Boretskaya, who inherited her husband's job as one of the elective aldermen in the city-republic of Novgorod, and who led the resistance of her fellow citizens against the subjugation of the city by the Grand Prince of Moscow in the 1470s. Ivanov dedicated his tragedy "To the Great Women of Russia" and wrote it with the laudable aim of showing the important contribution that women can make to the political process. But he superimposed on the historical characters and on the simple action of Karamzin's story an operatically melodramatic plot (familiar from such later works as Halévy's *La juive* and Verdi's *Il trovatore*), involving switched children, raised by their parents' enemies for purposes of revenge. He thereby reduced Karamzin's story to absurdity and implausibility of the worst kind.

Ivanov's *Marfa the Mayoress, or The Subjugation of Novgorod* (*Marfa-posadnitsa, ili Pokorenie Novgoroda*), with its heroine who is an eloquent partisan of political freedom and of the elective form of government, could not be represented on the stage. Yet, interestingly enough, despite its outspoken sympathy for republicanism, it was published in book form in 1809 and openly sold, while Kniazhnin's *Vadim of Novgorod*, banned by Catherine some two decades earlier, was still prohibited, even though in the debate between monarchy and republic, Kniazhnin's tragedy clearly sided with monarchy. Denunciations of "foes of liberty" and of Moscow rulers as "tyrants of free souls," which the censor pointed out in this play, in no way impeded the circulation of its text or the production of other plays by this mediocre author on the stage.[7]

Karamzin's "Natalia, the Boyar's Daughter," an adventure tale that projects Rousseauist and sentimentalist attitudes back to pre-Petrine Muscovite Russia, was turned into an opera with a text by Sergei Glinka and music by the gifted serf composer Daniel Kashin (1770–1841). A concert version of this opera was performed to celebrate the coronation of Alexander I, and the composer was granted his freedom in consequence. In 1805, the librettist Glinka, who otherwise wrote conventional neoclassical tragedies, returned to "Natalia" and reworked it into a "heroic drama in four acts with choruses," in which form it was more widely performed than Kashin's opera.

Stepan Zhikharev caught a performance of this drama in Moscow and made the following entry in his diary:

> They were playing *Natalia, the Boyar's Daughter* by Glinka. I was bored and I yawned. I just cannot become accustomed to these dramas taken from Karamzin's novellas. The novellas themselves are ravishing, but on the stage they are tiresome and boring to the extreme. Why is it? I honestly do not understand. Besides the inept adaptations, there must be some other reason. Fyodorov's *Liza* is a bore, but to my mind, *Natalia* is an even greater bore. The characters are all on stilts, and they talk such trite rot that I can't stand it.[8]

The "some other reason" was that all these adapters draped Karamzinian sentimentalism over jerry-built melodramas that imitated Kotzebue. Since Kotzebue's own plays were amply in evidence (between the beginning of the century and about 1820, up to half of the plays performed in any given season in

---

7. For the censorship history of *Marfa the Mayoress*, see *Stikhotvornaia tragediia kontsa XVIII–nachala XIX v.*, ed. V. A. Bochkarev (Moscow-Leningrad, 1964), p. 612. The text of this play is included in this volume, pp. 369–447. A rival dramatization of Karamzin's tale by the sentimentalist writer Pavel Sumarokov, published in 1807, bore the same title as Ivanov's play, but it depicted Marfa Boretskaya as a treacherous villainess.

8. Zhikharev, *Zapiski*, p. 212.

Moscow or St. Petersburg were likely to be by him), native competition must have looked redundant.

Elizaveta Titova

One more dramatist strongly influenced by Karamzin and Kotzebue should be mentioned at this point: the somewhat elusive Elizaveta Titova (b. 1780), the first Russian woman playwright since Catherine II and the only one in the first half of the nineteenth century to have her plays performed. Neither her maiden name nor the date of her death is known. Her husband was Sergei Titov (1770–1825), a member of the astounding Titov clan whose men for several generations combined careers as high-ranking military officers, usually as generals, with full-time activities as composers and instrumentalists. Titova's brother-in-law, Major General Alexei Titov, was a concertizing violinist and the composer of a number of popular comic operas; her husband, a lieutenant general, was a cellist and the composer of the music for the ballet *The New Werther* (1799, with choreography by Ivan Valberg) and for the vaudeville opera *The Peasants* by Shakhovskoy (1814); and her son Nikolai, also an army officer, composed several popular songs, among them a setting of Pushkin's text "Toward Evening, in Rainy Autumn" ("Pod vecher osen'iu nenastnoi"), which was later to be quoted in the first scene of Stravinsky's *Petrushka*.

At the age of seventeen, Titova published her adaptation of the one-act comedy *The Blind Woman of Spa* by Comtesse de Genlis, an author of sentimentalist romances whose books enjoyed a great popularity in Russia at the beginning of the nineteenth century. In 1809, Titova's sentimental drama in five acts with choruses and ballet, *Gustav Vasa, or Innocence Triumphant (Gustav Vaza, ili Torzhestvuiushchaia nevinnost')*, was performed in St. Petersburg in the presence of Tsar Alexander I, who asked to meet the playwright and presented her with a gift. Two years later, in 1811, there was a production of another sentimental drama by Titova, *Adelaide and Volmar*, which, according to Pimen Arapov, brought her a considerable renown with her contemporaries. Titova's last published work was the sentimental novel, *Olga, or the Triumph of Faith* (1813), which dressed the account of the early Kievan princess recorded in the *Primary Chronicle* in the fashionable garb of Karamzinian sentimentality, Ossianic melancholy and Christian apologetics in the manner of Chateaubriand's *Le génie du christianisme*. She also wrote a one-act comedy called *The Peasant Theater* (*Krest'ianskii teatr*), of which nothing is known except its title and the dates of its three performances. For a brief period between 1809 and 1815, Elizaveta Titova's writings were mentioned in the Russian and foreign press, after which both her work and her name lapsed into obscurity.

Judging from her two published works, *Gustav Vasa* and *Olga*, Titova was a derivative writer, suiting her play and novel to currently popular trends, as represented by Karamzin, Kotzebue, Genlis, Chateaubriand, and James Macpherson's purported translations of Ossian, but adding no ingredients of her own. Her two sentimental dramas owed their brief success to her imitation of current literary fashions and to the appreciation of her plays by the famous actor Alexei Iakovlev, who is known to have enjoyed playing in them. Like her namesake and counterpart, Elizabeth Inchbald, the English adapter and imitator of Kotzebue, Titova followed the literary fads of her time too closely and doomed her writings to oblivion as soon as those fads died.

Vladislav Ozerov

И для меня явленье Озерова —
Последний луч трагической зари.

But for me, the appearance of Ozerov
[Was] the last ray of tragedy's sunset.

Osip Mandelshtam, 1914

Despite the inroads of Kotzebue and of Karamzinian dramas, eighteenth-century neoclassical tragedy remained the most prestigious form of serious drama in the first quarter of the nineteenth century. It went on retaining its five-act structure, its central emotion-versus-duty conflict, and its monotonous coup-

lets of iambic hexameter inherited from Sumarokov and Kniazhnin. So it was an act of considerable audacity for the nineteen-
year-old Vasily Narezhny (1780–1825) to write and publish in
1800 his tragedy *A Night of Blood, or The Final Fall of the
House of Cadmus* (*Krovavaia noch', ili Konechnoe padenie
domu Kadmova*), which consisted of only one act and was
couched in unrhymed iambic pentameter (and, occasionally,
trimeter).[9] The one act is broken into four scenes, with a change
of setting for each new scene.

A compression of two famous ancient tragedies, *The Seven
Against Thebes* by Aeschylus and *Antigone* by Sophocles, Narezhny's youthful tragedy was based on a study of the original
Greek texts. It represented an effort to return tragedy to its
ancient origins, with strophic choruses and unvarnished emotions. For all of its odd, stuttering diction and lack of structural
balance, Narezhny's play does possess a disconcerting power and
is capable of arousing pity and terror in a way that no other
Russian neoclassical tragedy could ever do. The prolonged
dialogue of the fratricidal twins, Eteocles and Polyneices, who
intersperse their tirades of murderous rage with endearments
and plead for each other's love in the midst of their mutual
slaughter, is astounding in its sustained sadomasochism. Narezhny wrote several other plays besides *A Night of Blood*, of which
his *Dimitry the Impostor*, published in 1804, was given two
performances in Moscow in 1809. This was Narezhny's only
dramatic work to see the stage. He eventually found his niche
as a novelist, the author of *The Russian Gil Blas*, *The Semi-
narian*, and *The Two Ivans, or A Passion for Lawsuits*. The
last two novels are usually mentioned for having provided
Nikolai Gogol with the points of departure for his "Viy" and
"The Story of How Ivan Ivanovich Quarrelled with Ivan Niki-
forovich," respectively.

But no other neoclassical tragedy of the period was as
adventurous as *A Night of Blood*. Otherwise, about the only
new departure from the eighteenth-century norms was the addition of one more foreign model to be imitated in addition to
the canonical quartet of Corneille, Racine, Voltaire, and Meta-

9. The text is included in *Stikhotvornaia tragediia*, pp. 133–207.

stasio. The "tragedies of horror" by Prosper Jolyot Crébillon (1674–1762) were translated into Russian and read in the original in the eighteenth century. But only in the first decade of the nineteenth century were there performances in Russian of his *Atrée et Thyeste* (translated by Stepan Zhikharev) and *Rhadamiste et Zénobie.*

In his own oft-quoted self-description, Crébillon resolved to specialize in depictions of horror because "Corneille took heaven, Racine the earth, and all that was left for me was hell." His scenes of torture, poisonings, and drinking of human blood became acceptable on the Russian stage on the eve of romanticism, exactly a century after Crébillon's heyday in his native France. This new fashion for Crébillon had its impact on such Russian tragedies of the early nineteenth century as Sergei Glinka's *Sumbeka, or The Fall of the Kingdom of Kazan* (1806), a dramatization of an episode from Kheraskov's epic *The Rossiad* (1779) and Derzhavin's *Herod and Mariamne* (1809).

It was not the belated arrival of the "tragedy of horror" that rejuvenated the neoclassical tragedy in Russia, however, but Karamzinian sentimentalism. Ruinous for sentimental drama, it proved salutary in tragedy. This became apparent on November 23, 1804, the St. Petersburg opening night of Ozerov's *Oedipus in Athens.* Brought to Moscow in September of the following year and played everywhere in Russia for the next three decades, the play was regarded by its contemporaries as an epochal event, as precedent-setting for its time as the first neoclassical tragedies were for the middle of the eighteenth century. It was also recognized that unlike Sumarokov's by now faded tragedies, the new play was a work of real literary and poetic stature. After seeing the Moscow premiere, Zhikharev agreed with his friend the elderly prompter, who had assured him during the rehearsals that the Russian stage had not seen the likes of this play. There were a few literary "old believers" who maintained that the tragedies of Sumarokov and Kniazhnin were as well written and as effective on the stage, but Zhikharev and his friends could only describe such an attitude as self-imposed blindness.[10]

Of all Russian writers, Vladislav Ozerov (1769–1816) has

10. Zhikharev, *Zapiski,* pp. 95 and 98 ff.

the least complete and most mysterious biography. The few biographical facts about him in literary reference works and in introductory essays to collections of his writings would fit into one page. He was born on his family's estate in the province of Tver. He was Sergei Glinka's classmate at the Infantry Corps of Nobles, where Kniazhnin taught him Russian literature. Upon graduating with the highest honors, he received a commission as a lieutenant. After a brief stint in the army, he was appointed an aide to the head of his alma mater, General Anhalt. Four years later, after Anhalt's death, Ozerov was asked to leave the Infantry Corps under unexplained circumstances. He then obtained an appointment in the civil service as an inspector in the Department of Forestry, in which capacity he served from 1794 to 1808.

Ozerov's occasional poetry, which includes a funereal ode on the death of Catherine II and some didactic fables, is of no distinction. In 1794, however, he produced a striking long poem, "Heloise to Abelard," a free adaptation of "Lettre amoureuse d'Héloïse à Abailard" by the eighteenth-century French elegiac poet Charles Colardeau, itself a reworking of Alexander Pope's "Eloisa to Abelard" (1716). In his introductory essay to this poem, Ozerov wrote that he had seen another translation of the same work (of Pope's original, it seems), which contained more reason than emotion. Ozerov was inspired to do his own version in which this balance would be reversed.

What is remarkable about his poem is the contrast between the conventional alexandrine couplets of its form and the seething sensuality it conveys, which occasionally spills into an erotic frenzy uncommon in eighteenth-century Russian poetry. Aware that her desire for Abelard is both thwarted by their physical separation and impossible to consummate because of his castration, Heloise goes into transports of sensuous longing, all the more irresistible to her because their reunion is unrealizable. Nothing anywhere as intensely carnal can be found in the treatment of this material by Ozerov's models, Pope and Colardeau.

In 1798, four years after "Heloise to Abelard," Ozerov wrote the first of his five tragedies, *Iaropolk and Oleg*. The protagonist of this tragedy was the same older brother of St. Vladimir who had already been featured in Feofan Prokopovich's school drama and in Kniazhnin's russification of Racine's *Andromaque*. Instead of being a victim of assassination as he was in these two earlier plays, Ozerov's Iaropolk is himself a potential assassin, scheming to murder his younger brother Oleg over the love of a Bulgarian princess with whom both brothers are infatuated. *Iaropolk and Oleg* copied all the neoclassical conventions of its time. It caused no stir when it was presented on the stage and it gave no foretaste of the originality of *Oedipus in Athens*, which followed it six years later.

An idiosyncratic reworking of *Oedipus in Colonus*, Ozerov's second play did not go back to the Sophoclean original for its model. Its immediate source was apparently Antonio Sacchini's 1785 opera, *Oedipe à Colone*, which was performed in St. Petersburg in 1799 and whose French libretto was published there the same year. Ozerov's is a Greek tragedy rethought along sentimentalist lines. His blind Oedipus is a dignified old man who has long since expiated whatever unwitting crimes he had committed and who deserves a respite from his never-ending misfortunes. Antigone is a compassionate young woman whose one desire is to comfort and protect her long-suffering father.

Seeking refuge in Athens, the two are joined by Antigone's repentant brother Polyneices, who for reasons of political ambition had helped drive his father out of Thebes, but who can empathize with him now that he himself is an exile. The homeless Oedipus and his two children are at the mercy of two powerful rulers, the compassionate Theseus of Athens who wants to grant them asylum, and the heartless Creon, capable of persecuting his niece and her helpless father to gain political advantage. Ozerov offered a view of Greek mythical characters with which audiences could become involved emotionally in an intimate way not possible with the tragedies of fate of the ancients or the rationalistic tragedy of the seventeenth and eighteenth centuries.

The intimacy and the direct emotional appeal of the play were enhanced by the melodious lilt of Ozerov's lines. He kept the five-act structure and the alexandrine couplets of his predecessors, but his relaxed and expressive diction made all earlier

Russian neoclassical tragedies, including his own *Iaropolk and Oleg*, sound stilted and contrived in comparison. Ozerov did not entirely dispense with the syntactic inversions and archaic lexicon of the eighteenth century—that was left for Shakhovskoy and his followers to do. Still, compared to the diction of Sumarokov, Kniazhnin, or Nikolev, the fluency of his poetic language must have been irresistible:

Антигон а

Прохлады в жаркий день в моей ты ищешь тени,
Я сяду, ты главу мне склонишь на колени.
Среди густых лесов, в жестокость бурных зим,
Ты согреваем мной, дыханием моим.

. . . .

Ко мне ты проливай свою сердечну боль,
Но мне защитою твоею быть дозволь.
Не позавидую в моей тогда я доле
И братьев участи, седящих на престоле.

ANTIGONE

On a hot day, you seek coolness in my shadow.
I will sit down, so you may rest your head on my lap.
Amidst dense forests, in the harshness of stormy winters,
You are warmed by me, by my breath.

. . . .

Pour out to me the ache of your heart,
But allow me to be your protection.
Then I would not envy in my fate
Even the lot of my brothers who sit on thrones.

Ozerov submitted the text of *Oedipus in Athens* to fellow playwright Alexander Shakhovskoy, who was attached to the Imperial Theaters in St. Petersburg and often acted as the director of their new productions. Realizing the importance of this new work, Shakhovskoy was determined to give it a gala treatment. When the theater management found his estimate for production costs excessive, Shakhovskoy had so few doubts about the play's success that he offered to foot the bills out of his own pocket and be reimbursed out of future receipts. The sets were designed and executed by Pietro Gonzaga, the celebrated Italian architect and stage designer who had settled in Russia. There was an overture for a full orchestra and also choruses, the music of which was composed by the Polish-born Osip Kozlovsky (alias Józef Kozłowski) in a manner reminiscent of early Beethoven.

Oedipus was played by Iakov Shusherin. The mercurial matinee idol Alexei Iakovlev, gifted as both a poet and an actor, strikingly handsome, but often personally untidy, was Theseus. But the most important contributor to the overall success of the production was Ekaterina Semyonova, who as Antigone attained instant stardom and inaugurated an acting career that made her one of the two most charismatic actresses in the entire history of Russian theater (the other being Vera Komissarzhevskaya at the beginning of the twentieth century). Forced otherwise to waste her talent on Kotzebue and on adaptations of Shakespeare that altered his plays beyond recognition or to play the heroines of Racine and Voltaire in mediocre, tone-deaf translations, Semyonova found in Ozerov the playwright who gave her the parts that made her the foremost Russian tragedienne of all time. It was only just that Pushkin linked their names when he wrote in *Eugene Onegin* about Ozerov and Semyonova sharing "the spontaneous tribute of the nation's tears and applause."

Ozerov's next two plays, *Fingal* (1805) and *Dimitry of the Don* (1807), were eagerly awaited. They were jubilantly acclaimed when produced, and they provided Semyonova and Iakovlev with showy roles to play. But as works of literary art they are a letdown in comparison with *Oedipus in Athens*. In them Ozerov sought to capitalize on the artistic (*Fingal*) and political (*Dimitry of the Don*) trends of his day.

Fingal, Ozerov's three-act "tragedy in verse with choruses and pantomime ballets," dramatized an episode from James Macpherson's *Fingal*.[11] Ossian's misty poetry, faked by Macpherson in the 1760s and palmed off as a translation from the Gaelic of the songs by an ancient Scottish bard, was as popular in Russia as in the rest of Europe. Derzhavin, Zhukovsky, and Karamzin all quoted or translated Ossian. Pushkin began his

---

11. For a thorough account of the Ossianic impact on Russian literature and a detailed discussion of the sources of Ozerov's *Fingal* in Macpherson, see Iu. D. Levin, *Ossian v russkoi literature* (Leningrad, 1980).

"Ruslan and Liudmila" with a citation from Ossian's "Carthon."

Fingal was given a highly elaborate production: leading opera singers and ballet dancers of the day performed alongside the actors; and music by Kozlovsky accompanied many of the characters' speeches. The result must have been more like a spoken opera than a play. Deprived of its music and pageantry, Ozerov's *Fingal* is reduced on the printed page to a pallid love story, with two cardboard lovers separated by the heroine's melodramatically vengeful father. Ozerov's melodious verse and sentimentalist sensibility are present in *Fingal*, but they are squandered on bloodless characters and hackneyed situations.

Dimitry of the Don hypnotized its first audiences with its ringing patriotic tirades. At the time when a Napoleonic invasion of Russia seemed imminent (it did, in fact, occur five years later), Ozerov dipped into Russian history for a parallel. He found a suitable one in the battle of Kulikovo of 1380, when the Russians led by the Grand Prince Dimitry defeated the Mongol occupiers on the banks of the river Don, a victory that spelled the beginning of the end of the Mongol occupation. With the leader of the Mongols, Mamai, clearly standing in for Napoleon and with the Grand Prince Dimitry representing Alexander I, Ozerov's play aroused a patriotic fervor that swept away all critical judgment. Even the usually level-headed Zhikharev went into ecstasies in his diary and proclaimed the *récit* about the battle of Kulikovo in *Dimitry of the Don* superior to the famous *récit* in Racine's *Phèdre*.

Actually, apart from the very unusual subplot about Dimitry's relationship with his squire (of which more later), the play is a standard love-versus-duty eighteenth-century tragedy. Dimitry has to choose between the woman he loves and a military alliance he needs to secure the victory, while his beloved Xenia has to choose between Dimitry and a marriage of convenience that is needed to save her country. That Ozerov could reduce the momentous historical events he was depicting to such a stock situation shows to what extent he and his contemporaries were still dependent on the conventions of Corneille, Racine, Sumarokov, and Kniazhnin.

The success of *Dimitry of the Don* was so huge (Tsar Alex-

ander I expressed the wish to meet Ozerov and presented him
with a jeweled snuffbox) that it made the playwright a national
idol. His appearances attracted crowds, and he was given ova-
tions whenever he attended the theater. Yet even people who
had known him for years, such as Sergei Glinka, knew nothing
about him. His private life, his friends, any love life were (and
were to remain) shrouded in mystery. With three plays running
successfully in various parts of the country, Ozerov decided to
resign his post at the Department of Forestry, where he had attained a rank equivalent to major general, in order to devote
himself full-time to writing for the theater. He had a spotless
service record and sufficient seniority to have earned a lifelong
pension on which he expected to live, in addition to the earnings
from his plays. Against all expectations, he was denied the pension. The decision to deny it was motivated by a trivial technicality and came from the tsar himself.

At about the same time there appeared a flurry of anti-
Ozerov epigrams and lampoons, including a nasty parody of
Dimitry of the Don penned by the future playwright Alexander
Griboedov and called *Dimitry Drianskoy* (i.e., *Dimitry of the
Trash*, instead of *of the Don*). The literary attacks came from
the camp called the Archaists by twentieth-century critics. These
were writers opposed to Karamzinian influence and grouped
around Derzhavin, Krylov, and the linguistic theoretician Admiral Shishkov. Hurt by the denial of the pension and the literary sniping, Ozerov withdrew to his father's estate in the
provinces and concentrated on writing his last and best play,
Polyxena.

Ozerov knew *The Trojan Women* and *Hecuba* by Euripides in French translation. But he avoided rereading them when
he undertook the writing of *Polyxena* and was later pleasantly
surprised that only one scene in his play corresponded in a recognizable way to a scene in Euripides. Nor did Ozerov seem to
know any of the now obscure French eighteenth-century tragedies on the subject of *Polyxena*. Apart from traces indicating
study of the *Iliad* and Racine's *Iphigénie*, Ozerov's reworking
of the myth was his own conception. As in *Oedipus in Athens*,
the central relationship of the play is not between a pair of lovers

(there is *no* pair of lovers in either play) but between parent and child, Polyxena and her mother, Hecuba, in this case.

The initial premise is the same one as in *Hecuba* by Euripides. The Trojan queen and her two surviving children, Polyxena and Cassandra, are prisoners of the Greeks after the fall of Troy. Cassandra has become the concubine of Agamemnon, the leader of the Greeks, who intends to take her home and marry her after disposing of his faithless wife, Clytemnestra. Polyxena was to be married to the Greek hero Achilles, who was slain just before their wedding. Now, the ghost of Achilles has appeared to the Greek camp, demanding that Polyxena be offered as a propitiatory sacrifice and threatening that unless this is done, there will be no wind for the ships that are to take the Greeks home from the war.

Ozerov's play opens with a long scene of the Greek chieftains' council. Pyrrhus, the hot-blooded young son of Achilles, demands that Polyxena be sacrificed to his father's ghost. It eventually becomes clear that Pyrrhus is seeking Polyxena's death because he sees her as a wily seductress who came between him and his father and was the cause of his father's death. Agamemnon is opposed to the sacrifice of Polyxena, in part because he has come to regret the earlier similar sacrifice of his own daughter, Iphigenia, and in part because Polyxena is the sister of the woman he intends to marry. The aged Nestor offers what he thinks is wisdom, but what is really perplexity that all his experience has given him no answers to life's dilemmas. The practical Ulysses is willing to go along with whatever decision will benefit the majority.

The women appear only in the second act, and their motivations are as clearly and strikingly delineated. Having lost her husband and sons, Hecuba is determined to save the life of her daughter. She plans strategies, pleads for pity, clutches at straws. But to Polyxena, the sacrifice that her mother sees as the ultimate catastrophe is a fulfillment of an erotic dream of reunion with the man she loved but did not get to marry. As Irina Medvedeva has pointed out, Ozerov's Polyxena is a romantic, not a neoclassical, heroine, the counterpart of the maidens in Gothic ballads by Gottfried August Bürger and Vasily Zhukovsky, in which the heroine loves a dead bridegroom and longs to join him in his grave.[12] Polyxena had wanted to stay alive only to comfort her bereaved mother. Now the plans for the sacrifice offer her an honorable escape from that duty. Thus, for all the touching mutual love between the mother and the daughter, their respective aims are at cross-purposes.

As the likelihood of the sacrifice to the ghost rises and falls, it becomes evident that the two young people who seem to be implacable adversaries, Pyrrhus and Polyxena, are really united in the same purpose—the death of Polyxena. They both seek it, ostensibly out of conflicting motives, but actually out of love for the same person: Pyrrhus for his dead father, Polyxena for her dead lover. In the last act, when the discord in the Greek camp brings the situation to the brink of civil war, Polyxena resolves the conflict by voluntarily offering herself to the sacrificial knife. Her plea for understanding and reconciliation rejected by Pyrrhus, Polyxena cheats him out of his final triumph of putting her to death by stabbing herself.

Her prophetic sister Cassandra then predicts the subsequent fate of the other characters who were involved in planning Polyxena's sacrifice: the assassination of Pyrrhus by Agamemnon's son Orestes, the long odyssey (the original one, of course) of Ulysses, and the murder of Agamemnon and of herself by Clytemnestra and her lover. Borrowing his final lines from *Oedipus in Colonus* by Sophocles (as Ozerov pointed out in a note in his manuscript), the old Nestor sums up the action of the tragedy:

> Какой постигнет ум богов советы чудны!
> Жестоки ль были мы иль были правосудны?
> Среди тщеты сует, среди страстей борьбы
> Мы бродим по земли игралищем судьбы.
> Счастлив, кто в гроб скорей от жизни удалится;
> Счастливее того, кто к жизни не родится.

What mind can perceive the wondrous counsels of the gods!
Were we cruel or were we just?

12. I. N. Medvedeva, introductory essay "Vladislav Ozerov," in V. A. Ozerov, *Tragedii. Stikhotvoreniia* (Leningrad, 1960), pp. 45–46. See also Irina Medvedeva, *Ekaterina Semenova* (Moscow, 1964), pp. 65–66, on Semyonova's realization of this aspect of Polyxena's character.

Amidst vain cares, amidst the passions of struggle
We wander over the earth as a plaything of fate.
Happy is the one who soon withdraws from this life into a
grave;
Happier than that is the one who was never born.

Polyxena is a complex, powerful poem about death and the death wish. Its central paradox is that the advocates of life are the aged—Hecuba and Nestor—while the youngest characters are the ones who embrace death. The structure is elegant, the characterizations are well delineated (far better than anywhere else in Russian neoclassical tragedy), and the verbal texture shows Ozerov at his most expressive and melodious. D. S. Mirsky was right to call *Polyxena* the best play by Ozerov and "no doubt the best Russian tragedy in the French classical manner."[13] Mirsky also pointed out that the play is "genuinely evocative of the atmosphere of the *Iliad*."

Ozerov remained at his family estate when *Polyxena* was premiered in St. Petersburg in May of 1809. The production had another beautiful set by Gonzaga and a notable cast. Ekaterina Semyonova was Polyxena, the distinguished older actress Alexandra Karatygina played Hecuba, and a promising beginner, Maria Valberg ("Valberkhova"), later to develop into a fine comedienne in plays by Shakhovskoy and Griboedov, took the smaller part of Cassandra. Alexei Iakovlev, the *jeune prémier* who usually played Semyonova's lovers, had to content himself with playing Agamemnon.

But the play arrived at the wrong historical moment. With the Napoleonic threat looming even more ominously, the public expected from Ozerov more upbeat patriotic fervor in the manner of *Dimitry of the Don*. One year before *Polyxena*, Ozerov's imitator Matvei Kriukovsky scored a huge success with his tragedy about the repulsion of the Polish invasion of Russia at the beginning of the seventeenth century, *Pozharsky*. The play made Kriukovsky the bright new hope of the Russian theater and moved Alexander I to award him with a stipend for

13. D. S. Mirsky, *A History of Russian Literature* (New York, 1960), p. 66.

travel abroad to study foreign drama. It was still playing to full houses when *Polyxena* opened.

The hopeless view of life expressed in Ozerov's last play was not what audiences wanted. After the respectfully received opening night, the second performance was poorly attended. Someone brought this fact to the attention of the tsar, who thereupon ordered further performances discontinued. The promise of 3,000 rubles, made to Ozerov for the opening night rights, was withdrawn, with the excuse of poor box office receipts. The news of this decision, on top of the recent denial of pension, had a shattering effect on Ozerov. In the throes of acute depression, he destroyed the already completed new tragedy *Medea* and sketches for three other plays on which he was working. He also burned all his letters and other personal papers. He soon fell into paralysis and catatonia, was placed in his father's care, and died six years later, at the age of forty-seven, without ever regaining his reason.

There are so many unanswered questions about the life and death of Vladislav Ozerov, so many loose ends, that the circumstances of his sudden descent from the height of fame and popularity into madness and death gave rise to speculations about a conspiracy of enemies who had set out to destroy him. This view was expressed by the seventeen-year-old Pushkin in his verse epistle "To Zhukovsky" (1816), where he wrote: "Look: stricken by enemies' arrows, / His torch extinguished, his wings immobile, / The ghost of Ozerov calls unto you: 'Friends! Avenge me!' "[14] Pushkin's words reflect the rumors that the antisentimentalist literary reactionaries had hatched a plot against Ozerov. The playwright Shakhovskoy, who supposedly envied Ozerov's laurels, was said to be the principal culprit. Widely repeated in the nineteenth century, this allegation besmirched Shakhovskoy's literary reputation and helped put his comedies, which were otherwise quite popular with actors and audiences, in disfavor and drive them off the stage.

In the 1850s, Stepan Zhikharev in his "Recollections of an

14. A. S. Pushkin, *Polnoe sobranie sochinenii* (Moscow, 1956), vol. 1, p. 203.

Old Theatergoer" cited an impressive amount of factual evidence to show that Shakhovskoy had been slandered and that, far from persecuting Ozerov, he was a major promoter of his plays. But other contemporaries, such as Pimen Arapov and Viazemsky, kept maintaining for years that Shakhovskoy had destroyed Ozerov, claiming in support of their view that this was general knowledge. In her fine (if necessarily slanted) introduction to the 1960 edition of Ozerov's plays and poetry, Irina Medvedeva finally exculpated Shakhovskoy and demonstrated that if there was an intrigue against Ozerov, its instigator was none other than Derzhavin.[15]

The most important poet of the eighteenth century, Derzhavin devoted the first decade of the nineteenth to writing plays, especially tragedies in the manner of Crébillon. Ozerov revered Derzhavin, addressing a long ode to him in 1798 and dedicating *Oedipus in Athens* to him. But the success of this play alerted Derzhavin to the possibility that the new sentimentalist-inspired type of tragedy was about to supplant the didactic tragedy of Voltaire and the violent tragedy of Crébillon. So the aged poet wrote his tragedies *Herod and Mariamne* (1807), *Eupraxia* (1808) and *[Vasily the] Blind (Temnyi, 1808)* to counteract Ozerov's impact and influence. Only the first of these tragedies saw the stage (a total of five performances). Derzhavin had no talent for writing drama. The baroque language, so splendid in his poetry, turned cumbersome and bombastic when he attempted to write for the stage. His characters imitate those of Crébillon, and there was no way actors could make them anything but ludicrous. Both Aksakov and Zhikharev, who knew Derzhavin during precisely this period, have recorded his efforts to get his plays staged and the desperate maneuvers to which Derzhavin's theater-connected friends had to resort to avoid becoming involved in his dramatic projects.

Ozerov soon became aware of the hostility of the great poet he admired. Their personal contacts ceased. As Medvedeva has shown, Derzhavin was behind the lampoons and the critical attacks directed against Ozerov. But Derzhavin's enmity, while possibly contributing to the playwright's depressed state, does

15. Medvedeva, "Vladislav Ozerov," pp. 51–65.

not explain the main catastrophic events of Ozerov's life: the unmotivated dismissal from his administrative position at the Infantry Corps of Nobles in 1794, the denial of pension, and the discontinuance of the performances of *Polyxena* in 1809. Especially puzzling is the role of Alexander I in the last two events. We know of no personal or political motive that could cause the sovereign to treat in such a manner the dramatist whose plays he frequently attended, whom he had met, and from whom he had graciously accepted the dedication of *Dimitry of the Don*.

Perhaps an examination of Ozerov's writings as a whole will help us, if not explain his enigmatic life, at least shed some light on his work and personality. For critical purposes, Ozerov's *oeuvre* consists of one unusual long poem ("Heloise to Abelard"), one imitative tragedy (*Iaropolk and Oleg*), two topical dramatic works of little permanent significance (*Fingal* and *Dimitry of the Don*), and two plays that constitute the culmination of the entire genre of neoclassical tragedy in Russia, *Oedipus in Athens* and *Polyxena*. Varied as this output is in its literary quality, the theme of love is central to all of it, with the possible exception of *Iaropolk and Oleg*, where love is incidental and the interest is concentrated on the rivalry of the two brothers and Iaropolk's vacillations about whether to commit a murder or not.

What is striking is Ozerov's inability to write of reciprocal love. In *Fingal*, the weakest of the mature plays, the mutual love declarations of Fingal and Moina have a monotonous, insipid ring. As Ozerov's biographer Rafail Zotov has pointed out: "All of their phrases could have been reduced to three. Fingal and Moina say 'I love you,' 'Me too,' while her father would like to say to her lover 'I hate you,' but is afraid to do so. Without the tragic end of Moina and Starno, the whole affair would resemble an opulent vaudeville."[16] Similarly, the love interest in *Dimitry of the Don* is its least interesting or original feature.

But Ozerov becomes a true poet whenever he writes of unrealizable love. Both "Heloise to Abelard" and *Polyxena* end with impassioned assertions of a love that can be fulfilled only

16. R. Zotov, "Biografiia Ozerova," *Repertuar i panteon* (St. Petersburg, 1842), vol. 6, p. 10 (2nd pagination).

beyond the grave. Much of Ozerov's finest dramatic writing is about nonsexual love within the family, such as Antigone's love for her father. In *Polyxena*, Agamemnon and Cassandra are living together and hope to be married. Yet, nothing is shown of their emotional involvement with each other; instead, we find in the foreground Hecuba's love for her daughter and Polyxena's love for her mother and her yearning for a dead bridegroom. Another passion convincingly projected by Ozerov is the hatred of Pyrrhus for Polyxena, but once again it is predicated on his love for his late father.

Ozerov's inability to write convincingly about the mutual love between men and women who are potential marriage partners brings to mind the similar inability of a very different Russian playwright, Gogol. As a teenager, Gogol played Creon in a school production of *Oedipus in Athens*. At the beginning of Act II, the blind Oedipus enumerates in a series of anaphorae the beautiful sights he will miss:

> Нет, никогда мой не увидит взор,
> Ни красоты долин, ни возвышённых гор,
> Ни в вешний день лесов зеленые одежды,
> Ни с жатвою полей, оратаев надежды,
> Ни мужа кроткого, приятного чела,
> Которого богов рука произвела;
> Сокрылись от меня все прелести природы.

> No, my gaze shall never behold
> The beauty of valleys, nor lofty mountains,
> Nor the raiment of woods on a springtime day,
> Nor the fields with the harvest, the hope of the ploughmen,
> Nor a modest man with a pleasant countenance,
> Which has been fashioned by the hand of the gods;
> All the charms of nature are concealed from me.

The young Gogol must have found it striking that Ozerov had listed "a modest man with a pleasant countenance" among the wonders of nature that Oedipus misses instead of the face of a beautiful woman, far more expected and canonical in such enumerations. The passage apparently stayed in Gogol's mind, for he repeated it almost *verbatim* ("we admire the modest, fair countenance of a man, but it is not the image of the gods that we behold in him") in his parable "Woman" (1831). In this curiously self-revealing work, Gogol had intended to write a paean to women's beauty, but ended up giving strong intimations of his own homosexuality.[17]

Since Ozerov was one of the most frequently performed playwrights during Gogol's adolescence, Gogol must surely have been aware that in certain portions of *Dimitry of the Don* Ozerov came closer than any other writer of the period to portraying the only form of love that attracted Gogol and that he himself would not dare depict in a play. Despite the public accolades for *Dimitry of the Don*, the central love relationship between Dimitry and Princess Xenia was criticized from the outset as dramatically improbable and historically untenable (the actual Grand Prince Dimitry was married and had children at the time of the play's action). It took all of Ekaterina Semyonova's acting genius and legendary voice to hold her own in the part of Xenia against the patriotic rhetoric of the male characters, which elicited such stormy applause from the audiences. Even so, Semyonova found it necessary to give the public an encore during the initial run of this play by closing the evening with a folk dance she performed in a stylized peasant costume. No such expedient was thought necessary to reinforce her triumphs in *Oedipus in Athens.*

If the scenes between Dimitry and the woman he loves represent Ozerov at his least imaginative, the parallel brief scenes between Dimitry and his young squire Mikhail Brensky contain the most expressive writing of the play. On one level, the relationship between the two men is one of those ardent friendships that were typical for sentimentalist fiction and drama. But on another level, the subplot involving Mikhail forms too striking a contrast with the hackneyed principal plot. The minor role is

17. Cf. lines 5 and 6 of the cited Ozerov passage and the wording in Gogol: "Мы дивимся кроткому, светлому челу мужа; но не подобие богов созерцаем в нем." The repeated words are муж, кроткий, чело, боги. See Simon Karlinsky, *The Sexual Labyrinth of Nikolai Gogol* (Cambridge and London, 1976), pp. 28–30, for a discussion of the significance of this passage in Gogol's "Woman."

written with such intensity that the playwright's heart and imagination must have been more engaged with these portions of the play than with the obligatory patriotism or the love triangle between Dimitry, Xenia, and the Prince of Tver.

Ozerov found Mikhail Brensky in the German history book on which he based the action and characters of his play (except for the character of Xenia, which was not historical). All that his source said was, "Then Dimitry put his princely garments on Mikhail Andreyevich Brenko, who was his favorite and his squire."[18] From this cursory mention, Ozerov derived the young attendant who is Dimitry's closest friend and confidant. At the end of Act I, Mikhail tries to dissuade Dimitry from his infatuation with Xenia, citing political and military reasons. After the arrival of Xenia at the battlefield in Act II (an event Derzhavin ridiculed as a patent impossibility), Mikhail laments: "Чего страшился я, то ныне совершилось!" ("What I had feared, has now come to pass!"). At the end of Act III, Dimitry, who for reasons of state had to yield Xenia to his rival, is resolved to seek an honorable death in battle. In a bid to win him for himself, Mikhail Brensky offers him a suicide pact, which Dimitry seems on the verge of accepting:

Бренский

Стремишься ты на смерть — и я стремлюсь с тобой
И часть мою с твоей не разлучу судьбой.

Димитрий
(вставая)

Приди в объятия, о сердца друг надежный,
Во счастье строгий мне и в злополучьи нежный!
Погибнем вместе мы среди врагов в бою,
Но жизнь в цене драгой им отдадим свою!
Чтобы их тел вкруг нас и взор не мог исчислить:
Погибнем.

Brensky

You are yearning for death and I yearn for it with you,
And I will not separate my lot from your destiny.

18. See the commentary in Ozerov, *Tragedii*, p. 421. This exchange of clothing supplied Ozerov with the denouement of the Mikhail Brensky subplot.

DIMITRY
(as he stands up)

Come into my arms, O my heart's faithful friend,
Severe to me in happiness and affectionate in misfortune!
Let us perish together amidst foes in battle,
But let us yield our lives at a high price!
So that the gaze cannot count their bodies around us,
Let us perish. . . .

But Dimitry decides to live so as to go on fighting the Mongol invaders. In Act IV, he hears Xenia declare that she has suppressed her love for him for the good of the country. The stage direction at this point reads: "Dimitri in despair leans his head on Brensky's breast" (Ozerov uses the archaic and poetic word for breast, *persi*, a plural that usually means a woman's breasts). The two men then have another sentimental colloquy, in which Dimitry compares his loss of Xenia to the sensations of a man at the deathbed of his dearest male friend:

Димитрий

Своей печали он мгновенно не измерит,
Друг смертью похищен, и смерти он не верит.
О рок, какой удар сулил мне испытать!

Бренский

Уклонимся в шатер, чтоб вместе там стенать!
Здесь любопытный взор быть может привлекаем
Сей грустью, коей ты жестоко так терзаем.

DIMITRY

He cannot at the moment measure his sadness;
His friend was abducted by death and he cannot believe this
death.
O fate, what a blow you promised that I would endure!

BRENSKY

Let us withdraw into a tent, so as to groan there together!
Here, we might attract the gazes of the curious
With this sadness that torments you so cruelly.

Just before the battle of Kulikovo, Dimitry insists that Mikhail impersonate him and wear his garments and his battle regalia. Dimitry intends to fight the battle dressed as a common soldier. He routs the foe and wins Xenia. Mikhail, in his disguise, is mistaken for the grand prince by the Mongols, who throw their main forces at him, leaving Dimitry free to lead the Russians to victory. Mikhail is killed. Judging by his actions and his earlier statements, it was a death he chose voluntarily.

Ozerov's biographers, Prince Viazemsky and Rafail Zotov, have searched desperately for a romantic involvement in his life. The most they could come up with was a platonic relationship with a happily married woman, possibly French, whom Ozerov visited and with whom he read French novels. Although the friendship with this woman is said to have been platonic, both Viazemsky and Zotov conjecture that it might have been the key to Ozerov's gloomy view of life and to his later insanity.[19] But in Ozerov's writings, the love for an unattainable woman does not occur, as it does, for example, so often in Zhukovsky's. What his most eloquent characters do express is a love for an unattainable *man*. This is the situation of Heloise, Polyxena, and, if carefully read, of Mikhail Brensky.[20] All three are also clearly in love with death.

Many forms of love that had not previously dared speak their names acquired voices during the age in which Ozerov lived. Tsar Alexander I loved his sister, the Queen of Würtemberg, more passionately than he loved his wife or his various mistresses. Karamzin's most characteristically romantic novella,

19. Zotov, "Biografiia Ozerova," pp. 11–12; P. A. Viazemskii, "O zhizni i sochineniiakh V. A. Ozerova," *Polnoe sobranie sochinenii* (St. Petersburg, 1878), vol. 1, p. 28. Medvedeva, "Vladislav Ozerov," p. 15, repeats Viazemsky's conjectures and speculates that the relationship must have been over by 1794. This would leave Ozerov with no emotional involvements throughout his entire period of activity as a playwright. The semifictionalized treatment of Ozerov's biography in M. F. Gillel'son, *Molodoi Pushkin i Arzamaskoe bratsvo* (Leningrad, 1974), pp. 9 ff. and 31 ff, follows the same tradition.

20. The young Pushkin seems to have sensed that the relationship between Dimitry and Mikhail Brensky was portrayed by Ozerov as an amorous one. According to the recollections of Viazemsky, Pushkin nicknamed a young woman he used to see in a public park and with whom he had become infatuated his "Brensky." On the days she failed to show up at the park, Pushkin would plaintively address to his friend Dimitry's line from Ozerov's play: "Where is Brensky? I do not see Brensky." Quoted from *Pushkin-kritik*, ed. N. V. Bogoslovsky (Moscow, 1950), p. 566.

and one which, unlike "Poor Liza" and "Natalia, the Boyar's Daughter," no one ever thought of adapting for the stage, is "The Isle of Bornholm." It is a gothic tale of two lovers, exiled and imprisoned because they were brother and sister. Byron, the keynote figure of that age, loved his sister, various young men, and death more deeply than he could love Lady Byron. Incest was a central theme in the life and writings of Chateaubriand.

Ozerov's Pyrrhus, in love with the ghost of his father; his Antigone, who loves Oedipus more than she could love a young man her own age; his Heloise, with her sexual fantasies about a mutilated, distant lover; his Polyxena; and his Mikhail Brensky—all fit into that age far better than subsequent criticism realized. It is in this entire complex that the causes for Ozerov's fall from grace, his deep melancholy, and his ultimate madness are to be sought, rather than in Derzhavin's (real) and Shakhovskoy's (imaginary) enmity or in Ozerov's literary friendship with the mysterious married Frenchwoman.

Ozerov's tragic death was commemorated by Semyonova with a revival of the supposedly failed *Polyxena*. This performance led to the realization that the play was Ozerov's masterpiece. Semyonova kept playing Polyxena into her late thirties and then switched to the role of Hecuba, in which she received new acclaim. But by about 1830, with the new recognition of Schiller and of Shakespeare in their unabridged form, there came a general reaction against all forms of neoclassical tragedy in Russia, against Sumarokov as well as Ozerov (the same reaction is observable in the West in Stendhal's celebrated essay on Racine and Shakespeare). Pushkin, who at seventeen had regarded Ozerov as his literary ally and who mentioned his name with approval in *Eugene Onegin*, had come to look on him with disdain by the time he wrote *Boris Godunov*.

For the rest of the nineteenth century, Ozerov was an antiquated relic. In Alexander Ostrovsky's satirical comedy *Enough Simplicity in Every Wise Man (Na vsiakogo mudretsa dovol'no prostoty*, 1868), a crusty old conservative reveals his political backwardness by proposing in the reform decade of the 1860s that theaters revive Ozerov's tragedies. A biographical dictionary published in St. Petersburg in 1905 cites a long string of contemptuous or dismissive nineteenth-century critical judgments on Ozerov, all of them descending from Vissarion Belinsky, and then concludes with this surprising statement: "True, neither Ozerov's biography nor his writings have been to this day studied in detail, but the view of him and of his historical and literary significance is quite firmly established, and subsequent studies are hardly likely to change it."[21] Only the first part of this statement turned out to be true.

Tragedy in verse on subjects from classical mythology returned to Russian literature in the work of symbolist and postsymbolist poets. Some of them, such as Viacheslav Ivanov, went directly to the ancient Greeks for their model, but others, such as Innokenty Annensky, Fyodor Sologub, Valery Briusov, and especially Marina Tsvetaeva in her tragedies of the 1920s, *Ariadne* and *Phaedra*, assimilated both the ancient and neoclassical variants into their twentieth-century reinterpretations. For them, apart from Lomonosov and Trediakovsky, there was only one other viable native neoclassical model—the sentimentalist tragedy of Ozerov.

At this writing, there are still no full-scale biographical or critical studies of Ozerov. Unless some secret documents are found in Soviet archives, there may never be a full reconstruction of his life and times. Twentieth-century informed critical opinions are so rare that one can think of a total of only two: the brief paragraph in Mirsky and Irina Medvedeva's fine essay. Fortunately, there is the poem about Ozerov by one of the greatest Russian poets of all time, Osip Mandelshtam, which says what needs to be said better than volumes of literary criticism could:

> Есть ценностей незыблемая скáла
> Над скучными ошибками веков.
> Неправильно наложена опала
> На автора возвышенных стихов.

21. *Russkii biograficheskii slovar'*, ed. A. A. Polovtsov (St. Petersburg, 1905), vol. 12, p. 190.

И вслед за тем, как жалкий Сумароков
Пролепетал заученную роль,
Как царский посох в скинии пророков,
У нас цвела торжественная боль.

Что делать вам в театре полуслова
И полумаск, герои и цари?
И для меня явление Озерова —
Последний луч трагической зари.[22]

There exists an unshakable scale of values
[That looms] over the boring mistakes of centuries.
It was wrong to impose disfavor
On [this] author of sublime verses.

For, right after the pitiful Sumarokov
Mumbled the role he had learned by rote,
There blossomed forth in our country a solemn pain
Like the royal staff in the prophets' ark of covenant.

What are you to do in [our] theater of indirect suggestion
And of half-masks, O heroes and kings?
But for me the appearance of Ozerov
Was the last ray of tragedy's sunset.

Ozerov's Successors

The opening of Ozerov's *Oedipus in Athens* in 1804 gave neoclassical tragedy in Russia a new lease on life that lasted for another two decades. The other major stimulus for the genre's continued popularity was the presence of a galaxy of renowned performers who specialized in tragic roles: Semyonova, Iakovlev, Shusherin, and, from the 1820s on, Vasily Karatygin. The famed French tragedienne Mlle George came to Russia in 1808 and played in tragedies by Voltaire and Racine and in Ozerov's *Dimitry of the Don* in French translation. In 1811 she entered into an acting competition with Ekaterina Semyonova, each actress performing on alternate nights and in her own language the same tragedies by Voltaire. The stationing of

22. O. E. Mandel'shtam, *Sobranie sochinenii* (Washington, D. C., 1964), vol. 1, pp. 39–40.

Russian troops in Paris after the defeat of Napoleon in 1812 enabled a large number of literate officers to see François Joseph Talma, Mlle Mars, and other French celebrities on their home ground in seventeenth- and eighteenth-century French classics.

All these reinforcements of neoclassical heritage influenced Russian writers to go on producing plays of this genre. No one was able to duplicate Ozerov's emotional tonality or verbal melodiousness. For a brief moment it seemed that Ozerov had acquired a successor in Matvei Kriukovsky (1781–1811), whose patriotic and bombastic *Pozharsky*, as mentioned earlier, received considerable acclaim owing to its timely theme. There is an interesting portrait of Kriukovsky in the memoirs of his friend and neighbor, the journalist Nikolai Grech, who depicts him as an impractical dreamer, bewildered by a notoriety he never sought or expected.[23] Nothing he wrote after that one play was deemed worthy of being published or performed. Kriukovsky died in dejection at age thirty.

Apart from the works of the sentimentalists Ozerov and Kriukovsky, neoclassical tragedy of the first quarter of the nineteenth century was written by authors of Archaist orientation, who disliked sentimentalism and romanticism. They wanted drama to stay with the eighteenth-century models, and they rejected the Karamzinian reform of syntax and lexicon, preferring to saturate their language with Church Slavic words and turns of phrase. This was the case with the previously discussed stillborn tragedies by Derzhavin, and it also applies to Shakhovskoy's biblical tragedy *Deborah* (1809). Influenced by Racine's *Esther*, *Deborah* was produced by the same team (sets by Gonzaga, music by Kozlovsky, with Alexei Iakovlev and Maria Valberg in the principal roles) that was involved in the productions of Ozerov's plays. But it is a pallid, derivative work, lacking the theatrical flair we associate with Shakhovskoy's best comedies.

Alexander Gruzintsev (1779–ca. 1840s) was an early nineteenth-century version of Mikhail Kheraskov, whom he had known as a child and whom he considered his benefactor. In

23. N. I. Grech, *Zapiski o moei zhizni* (Moscow-Leningrad, 1930), pp. 279–86.

imitation of Kheraskov's *The Rossiad*, Gruzintsev wrote two un-readable epic poems, *The Petriad*, for which Alexander I sent him two thousand rubles and a diamond ring, and *Russia Saved and Victorious in the Nineteenth Century*. He also wrote neo-classical tragedies on themes from Greek mythology (*Electra and Orestes* and *The Heraclids* [*Iraklidy*], performed in St. Petersburg in 1809 and 1814, respectively) and Russian history (*Kazan Subdued* [*Pokorennaia Kazan'*, 1811]). *Kazan Subdued* was based (like Sergei Glinka's *Sumbeka*) on an episode in Kher-askov's *The Rossiad*. Gruzintsev's *Radamist and Zenobia* was adapted from Crébillon. Gruzintsev's only noteworthy play is *Oedipus Rex*, published in 1811 and performed in both capitals. It provides a rare instance of a Russian playwright of this period going all the way back to the original Greek source of his tragedy, in this case to Sophocles. But Gruzintsev also turned to the example of Voltaire's early play on the same subject, so that the resultant tragedy has the canonical eighteenth-century five-act structure and the alexandrine couplets that ill accord with the form and the action of the ancient classic. Gruzint-sev's language betrays the impact of Ozerov, which contributes further to the work's stylistic disharmony.[24]

The Younger Archaists

Other neoclassical tragedies worth mentioning that date from this period were written by the literary opponents of Ozerov and Zhukovsky, the younger Archaist poets, most of whom were members of the secret political societies that fo-mented the Decembrist rebellion of 1825. The entire phenome-non of Archaist opposition to romanticism in literature during the first quarter of the nineteenth century had long baffled literary historians. Advocacy of antiquated language and of outmoded dramatic forms could be understood in conjunction with old age and reactionary politics. It could be expected from

24. Gruzintsev's tragedies have been studied in exhaustive detail in Lothar Klemisch's published dissertation *Die antikisierenden Tragödien A. N. Gruzin-cevs. Studien zur spätklassizistichen Tragödie in Russland* (Munich, 1979).

relics of the eighteenth century who had lived into the nineteenth—Derzhavin and Krylov, for instance. But among the Archaists there also were younger men who admired Schiller and Sir Walter Scott, who were often engaged in active opposition to the tsar's government, and who nevertheless espoused Archaist positions in matters of language and literature. It took Iury Tynianov's epochal 1924 study "The Archaists and Pushkin"[25] to unravel the intellectual history of the period, to show the actual motives of the Archaist writers, and, above all, to demonstrate conclusively how it was possible for Pushkin and some of his contemporaries to have one foot in both the Archaist and romantic camps.

Much of the junior Archaists' rhetoric came from the ideas of the French and American revolutions. Within this rhetoric, a heroic ode was preferable to a romantic ballad on folklore themes; and a heroic political tragedy in the manner of Corneille's *Horace* or Voltaire's *Mahomet* was more congenial than a sentimentalist melodrama or Ozerov's brooding *Polyxena*. As Pushkin put it, in trying to formulate the viewpoint of his classmate, the junior Archaist Wilhelm Küchelbecker: "Serving the muses does not tolerate bustle; / What is beautiful ought to be majestic."[26] This sums up the basic premise of the neoclassical tragedies by Fyodor Glinka, Katenin, and Küchelbecker.

Fyodor Glinka (1786–1880), the younger brother of the playwright Sergei Glinka, was one of nineteenth-century Russia's finest mystical poets. He made his literary debut one year after Gogol was born; when he died, Chekhov had already published his earliest stories. Among Glinka's vast output are two impressive historical novellas in verse set in the northern forests of Karelia and several lyrics that ended up as folk songs popular to this day. The tune of one of them is played on the barrel organ in Stravinsky's *Petrushka*, and another one was

---

25. Iu. N. Tynianov, "Arkhaisty i Pushkin," in his book *Arkhaisty i novatory* (Leningrad, 1929; reissued, Munich, 1967). For an updated view of the Archaists and an examination of their roles as the precursors of the Slavophiles, see Mark Altshuller's fine book, *Predtechi slavianofil'stva v russkoi literature (Obshchestvo "Beseda liubitelei russkogo slova")* (Ann Arbor, 1984).

26. A. S. Pushkin, "19 oktiabria," *Polnoe sobranie sochinenii* (Moscow, 1956), vol. 2, p. 276.

parodied by Vladimir Nabokov in his translation of Lewis Carroll's *Alice in Wonderland*.

In 1810, Fyodor Glinka made his first appearance in print with a neoclassical tragedy called *Velzen, or The Liberated Holland* (*Vel'zen, ili Osvobozhdennaia Gollandiia*), written around 1808. It is said to take place "in ancient Amsterdam," though the events depicted were not a part of Dutch history and the names of the characters, except for the title character, are likewise not Dutch. The action concerns the efforts of a group of Dutch princes to rid the country of a low-born invader who has usurped the throne and to effect the return of the legitimate, hereditary monarch. The opening scene contains some ringing tirades, reminiscent of Patrick Henry, such as "Liberty or Death! A country deprived of laws and liberty / Is a mournful tomb and its people are captives" or "Ah, who would not prefer a glorious death to the fate of slaves?" At the time of the play's publication, it was clear to everyone that it was a transparent allegory of Napoleon's usurpation of various European states.[27] Therefore the libertarian passages had no trouble with the censors. As a mature poet, Glinka considered this tragedy a forgettable juvenile work. Its neoclassical format is certainly untypical of his later manner.

In the 1920s, D. S. Mirsky expressed the hope that Fyodor Glinka's metaphysical poetry might be rediscovered and valued as it deserves.[28] What has happened instead is that his peripheral involvement in the Decembrist movement has caused Soviet scholars to concentrate their reevaluation of his work and significance on *Velzen*, which they claim is a revolutionary play aimed at Alexander I rather than Napoleon.[29] Ahistorical as

27. S. S. Landa, "Vmesto predisloviia" ("Instead of a Preface"), in Nina Koroleva, *Dekabristy i teatr* (Leningrad, 1975), pp. 6–9. Against the background of the habitual simplistic falsification of the Decembrists' significance and views in Soviet historiography, Koroleva's book and Landa's introduction are the first reasonably scholarly and factual treatments of the subject published in the Soviet Union since Tynianov's studies of the 1920s.

28. Mirsky, *History of Russian Literature*, p. 106.

29. For example, V. G. Bazanov, introductory essay to F. I. Glinka, *Izbrannye proizvedeniia* (Leningrad, 1957), p. 11 ("The setting of the action in Holland was allegorical, and Glinka obviously had in mind primarily Russia"); and V. A. Bochkarev, the introductory essay to *Stikhotvornaia tragediia*, pp. 37–38 ("*Velzen*

such a view obviously is, it made it possible for a large body of Glinka's mystical poetry to appear in print in the Soviet Union in 1957, something that could not have happened without this kind of "progressive" passport accompanying it.

Two other Russian neoclassical tragedies appeared in the 1820s and were received with respect in literary circles: Pavel Katenin's *Andromache* and Wilhelm Küchelbecker's *The Argives*. They were the last ones of their kind. *Andromache*, begun in 1809 and completed in 1818, was published and performed in St. Petersburg in 1827. Ekaterina Semyonova was scheduled to play the title role, but she dropped out during the rehearsals, leaving the part to another actress. Pushkin read this play with pleasure and approval, even though he had otherwise parted ways with neoclassical tragedy by the mid-1820s and had come to look upon Ozerov with disdain.

Pavel Katenin (1792–1853), one-time adversary and later friend and correspondent of Pushkin, was a singular case of an antiromantic romantic and an unpoetic poet. He sought to counter Zhukovsky's way of russifying ballads by Bürger and Schiller by doing his own, supposedly cruder and more down-to-earth versions of the same ballads. But he could not compete with the magic of Zhukovsky's poetry. A confirmed Archaist in his views of the theater, Katenin did Russian translations of Thomas Corneille's *Ariane*, Racine's *Esther* (which was justly ridiculed by the ultra-romantic Alexander Bestuzhev-Marlinsky for its ludicrous archaisms), and a heavily abridged and "corrected" version of Pierre Corneille's *Le Cid*, which was extravagantly overpraised by Pushkin in *Eugene Onegin* (" . . . our Katenin has resurrected / Corneille's majestic genius").

Katenin's *Andromache* is sometimes mentioned as a trans-

---

by Fyodor Glinka is a characteristic example of allusions as practiced in pre-Decembrist tragedy. . . . Developing the tyrannomachous ideas of *Vadim of Novgorod*, Glinka has created a thematic scheme for the embodiment of Decembrist ideas in tragedy").

As Landa, "Vmesto predisloviia," has pointed out, there were no Decembrist ideas to embody in 1808, because those ideas took shape only in the middle of the following decade. Landa also makes it abundantly clear that the allusions to Napoleon in Glinka's play could in no way be made to apply to Alexander I of Russia.

lation or adaptation of Racine's *Andromaque*. It is, however, a wholly original play, though it does show a knowledge of the plays on the same subject by Euripides and Racine. By the time it was written, Russian verse had had the benefit of the purification of language achieved not only in the tragedies by Ozerov and comedies by Shakhovskoy and Khmelnitsky, but also in the poetry of Zhukovsky and Konstantin Batiushkov. It is thus understandable that in its verbal texture, *Andromache* is far ahead of the tragedies of Kheraskov or Kniazhnin. But in its dramatic essence it is an eighteenth-century play of the kind they wrote. When it saw the stage in 1827, it must have struck its audiences as coming from the period before Ozerov. Katenin himself sensed even earlier that the day of this kind of dogged neoclassicism was over, for his next work for the stage, the dramatic prologue *The Feast of John Lackland*, was a dramatization in rhymed iambic pentameter of several episodes from Scott's novel *Ivanhoe*. It served as a curtain raiser for Alexander Shakhovskoy's dramatic adaptation of this popular novel and was staged in 1821.

The poet and dramatist Wilhelm Küchelbecker (1797–1846) was another romantic with strong neoclassical sympathies in the initial stages of his writing career. A close friend of both Pushkin and Griboedov, he shared with the latter his distaste for sentimentalist elegiac poetry and his belief in the viability of the dramatic genres inherited from the eighteenth century. Küchelbecker made his debut as a playwright with the satirical comedy *Shakespeare's Spirits* (*Shekspirovy dukhi*). Following the earlier example of Shakhovskoy's *The Lipetsk Spa* (discussed in the next chapter), it satirized the excesses of romanticism. Relatives of a mooning young poet who believes himself in touch with higher realities disguise themselves as supernatural characters from *A Midsummer Night's Dream* and *The Tempest* to teach him the folly of confusing real life with poetic fiction. The play was performed in 1825 by a group of amateur players, but the attempts of the famed tragedian Vasily Karatygin to secure a professional production for it came to nought.

Küchelbecker's detestation of tyranny and his ardent commitment to democratic forms of government found their expression in his neoclassical tragedy *The Argives* (*Argiviane*). Based on Plutarch's story of the conflict between the Corinthian tyrant Timophanes and his republican-minded older brother Timoleon, and possibly influenced by various eighteenth-century plays that treated the same subject (especially Joseph-Marie Chénier's passionately Jacobin tragedy *Timoléon*, 1794), *The Argives* was not published or performed in its author's lifetime. But it was known to and appreciated by his literary associates, most notably by Pushkin, who inquired about the progress of *The Argives* in his correspondence and cited a passage from it as an epigraph to the third chapter of his unfinished novel *The Blackamoor of Peter the Great*. Two manuscript versions of *The Argives* survive, one dating from about 1822 and the other completed in 1825, shortly before Küchelbecker's arrest for his participation in the Decembrist rebellion.

In essence a French-style tragedy of love versus duty (the tyrant's brother, wife, and father-in-law are all placed in this traditional predicament), *The Argives* also featured some interesting technical innovations. Instead of the couplets of rhymed iambic hexameter, mandatory for tragedies since the time of Sumarokov, it was written in iambic pentameter, mostly unrhymed, but with some passages containing cross-rhymes. Both versions, but especially the second one, contain spoken choruses that are couched in strophes, antistrophes and epodes, in imitation of Greek classical tragedies. Its innovative aspects and its political message (which is that autocratic tyrants who usurp the power they previously shared with others are to be disposed of by violent means, if need be) have generated a considerable body of critical writing about *The Argives* in Soviet times, beginning with Iury Tynianov's fine study of 1924, included in his book *The Archaists and the Innovators*. But read as either drama or poetry this play—the last of the neoclassical Mohicans—is a dull, plodding piece of writing, its language (except in a few choruses) clumsily archaic and its characters totally lacking psychological verisimilitude.

Küchelbecker's other works in dramatic form were all written in prisons or in the remote regions of Siberia where he was exiled for the rest of his life. In those later plays, he resigned himself to being the genuine romantic poet he had been all along. His finest achievement as playwright is his trilogy of dramatic poems bearing the title *Izhorsky*, the name of the protagonist of all three. Inspired by the example of Goethe's *Faust* and the fantastic comedies of Ludwig Tieck, such as his *Puss-in-Boots* (*Der gestiefelte Kater*, 1797), *Izhorsky* is a sophisticated and poetic instance of the romantic revival of the dramatic modes and structures of the medieval mystery play. It is the Russian counterpart of the period's other dramatic poems on fantastic themes, such as Byron's *Manfred* and Adam Mickiewicz's *Forefathers' Eve*. Barring the special cases of Pushkin and Lermontov, it is assuredly the finest example of romantic drama that Russian literature has produced.

Lev Izhorsky, the central character of the trilogy (his name is derived from a river in the far north of Russia, as were the names of Onegin in Pushkin and Pechorin in Lermontov), is a recognizable, if special, instance of the philosophically disillusioned, emotionally paralyzed romantic hero. He is, however, neither Byronic nor a Russian variant of Faust, as some of Küchelbecker's contemporary critics assumed. Among the possible Western models, the character of Izhorsky seems closest to *Adolphe* of Benjamin Constant (Küchelbecker had associated with Constant during an earlier visit to Paris and was invited by him to lecture at Club Athénée, which Constant headed). But there are also aspects of Izhorsky's character that make him a precursor of Stavrogin from Dostoevsky's *The Possessed*, the novel whose original Russian title is *The Demons*. While the demons with whom the hero of Dostoevsky's realistic novel is involved are metaphorical, the ones in Küchelbecker's romantic fantasy are concretely personified and play major parts in the drama.

In a highly original departure, Küchelbecker drew his principal demons not from Christian or medieval tradition, but from Russian peasant and nursery folklore of his own day. These demons—Kikimora, Shishimora, and Búka (i.e., the Bogeyman, traditionally evoked by nursemaids to frighten little children)—lead Izhorsky to play cruel games with other people's lives, to murder his best friend, and to betray the woman who loves him. In the third play of the trilogy, the penitent Izhorsky escapes from the demonic powers and wins his redemption by joining the Greek fight against Turkish domination. On the canvas of his protagonist's fall and repentance, Küchelbecker deployed a vast panorama, comprising realistic scenes in aristocratic salons and peasant hovels, poetic visions of elemental spirits, Shakespearian and autobiographical reminiscences (Küchelbecker himself appears in one of the scenes), and even an overlay of literary polemics in which the poet rejects both the rigidities of neoclassical rules and the chaotic freedom of overheated romanticism.

The major characters—Izhorsky, his best friend Vesnin, and the three principal demons—are memorably and convincingly delineated. So is the heroine of the first two parts, Princess Lydia, initially a giddy high-society beauty, who in the course of the suffering and humiliation to which her lover subjects her, develops into a mature and compassionate woman. Izhorsky and Lydia are shown against a wide variety of settings, both realistic and fantastic. Subordinate characters include historical persons (such as the Greek-Russian statesman Count Capo d'Istria and the English writer Edward Trelawney), werewolves, and talking animals, as well as representatives of almost every social stratum of the Russian empire. Most important of all is the level of poetic inspiration Küchelbecker attained in this work and the frequently supple and elegant language (immeasurably superior to his clumsy style in *The Argives*) with which he fused together its variegated components.

Izhorsky is a unique and beautiful work that never got much recognition. When the poet's youngest sister (with the aid of Alexander Pushkin) managed to publish its first two parts in 1835, it was violently denounced by the powerful radical critic Belinsky for its romanticism, mysticism, and supposed dependence on Byron, qualities that were for Belinsky incompatible with the realistic trend he was then promoting. Belinsky's authority during the rest of the nineteenth century was such that Küchelbecker ceased being regarded as a poet and became a literary nonperson until the revival of his reputation by Tynianov in the 1920s. Küchelbecker's fate is one of the more striking of several instances in nineteenth-century Russia of a gifted and independent writer being persecuted by both the tsarist government and its radical opponents. Only with the acceptance in the 1930s of the Decembrists as authentic revolutionaries and direct precursors of the present-day Soviet regime (prior to the 1930s, Russian Marxists regarded the Decembrist rebels as mere aristocratic liberals, which they indeed were), does one see academic and critical recognition accorded to Küchelbecker. But even so, the originality and worth of his most important work in dramatic form, the *Izhorsky* trilogy, are yet to be recognized in his native country.[30]

30. See my essay "Trilogiia Kiukhel'bekera *Izhorskii* kak primer romanticheskogo vozrozhdeniia srednevekovoi misterii," *American Contributions to the Seventh International Congress of Slavists, Warsaw, August 21–27, 1973*, ed. Victor Terras (The Hague, 1973), vol. 2, pp. 307–20.

※VIII※

Verse Comedy's Sunburst

The concept of technological progress is not usually applicable to the arts: How could any future progress ever improve on a Dante or a Bach? Evolution in the Darwinian sense does have an application to the development of various artistic genres, though its workings are not as easy to trace as they are in biology or botany. One genre, however, that offers a striking instance of uninterrupted evolution and progress within a given stretch of time is Russian verse comedy at the end of the eighteenth century and the beginning of the nineteenth. From its first viable specimen, Kniazhnin's *The Braggart* in the mid-1780s to Griboedov's *The Misfortune of Being Clever* forty years later, there is a continuous growth in quality; greater technical mastery, more elegant stagecraft, increased fluency of dialogue. The principal landmarks in this advance after *The Braggart* are Kniazhnin's second verse comedy *Odd Fellows* (performed in 1793), followed two years later by Kapnist's *Chicane*. Nikolai Sudovshchikov's verse comedy *An Unheard-of Marvel, or An Honest Secretary*[1] (*Neslykhannoe divo, ili*

---

1. Text most recently reprinted in *Russkaia stikhotvornaia komediia kontsa XVIII–nachala XIX v.* (Moscow-Leningrad, 1964). Edited *con amore* by Moisei Iankovsky, who also provided an excellent introductory essay, this volume contains some of the comedies by Khmelnitsky, Pisarev, Zagoskin, and Kokoshkin that are discussed in the present chapter.

Chestnyi sekretar', published in 1802, first performed in 1809), a melange of themes and characters from comedies by Fonvizin, Kniazhnin, and Kapnist, sums up, in its derivative way, the genre's achievements up to the turn of the century.

A new period in Russian verse comedy was inaugurated with the opening of Alexander Shakhovskoy's *A Lesson to Coquettes, or The Lipetsk Spa (Urok koketkam, ili Lipetskie vody)* in 1815. The worldly tone and the colloquial diction that this comedy attained led a whole pleiad of Shakhovskoy's younger contemporaries to develop and improve on his discoveries, just as two decades earlier Kniazhnin's success with *The Braggart* had stimulated Kapnist to write *Chicane*. Within two years after *The Lipetsk Spa*, Nikolai Khmelnitsky came up with the first of his frothy one-acters in verse, in which, building upon Shakhovskoy's play, he formulated and consolidated the light, aerated style that later generations came to associate with the Pushkin period of Russian literature. Khmelnitsky's and Griboedov's collaboration with Shakhovskoy in the writing of the second-finest verse comedy of the Russian neoclassical tradition, *Within the Family, or The Married Fiancée (Svoia sem'ia, ili Zamuzhniaia nevesta,* 1817), testified to the stylistic and conceptual unity of this entire school of playwrights. During the decade 1815–25, verse comedies and vaudevilles by Shakhovskoy, Khmelnitsky, the short-lived Alexander Pisarev, Fyodor Kokoshkin, and Mikhail Zagoskin loomed large in the repertoire of Moscow and St. Petersburg theatres. Griboedov's great masterpiece both crowned this school of comedy and spelled its natural end. Pushkin's neo-Shakespearian *Boris Godunov* (1825) signaled the turning of Russian drama away from neoclassicism. The victory of romanticism and then of realism led to the critical and historiographic neglect of the verse drama of the first quarter of the nineteenth century, a neglect that began in the 1840s and which, apart from some notable exceptions, is operative to this day. The result has been a gaping hole in the history of the Russian drama of the nineteenth century and, more important, in the history of the Russian literary language.

Alexander Shakhovskoy

Prince Alexander Shakhovskoy (1777–1846) came from a noble family of ancient lineage, though the branch into which he was born was neither important nor wealthy. After serving briefly in the army, he found his life's true calling, which was the theater, to which he devoted his talents and energies for the rest of his days. A prolific playwright and adapter of foreign plays, Shakhovskoy was also an able theater administrator (he devised the organization of the Imperial Theaters, which remained operative until the Revolution), the first notable Russian stage director, an indefatigable discoverer and developer of new acting talent (including such luminaries as Ekaterina Semyonova, Pavel Mochalov, and just about every other important actor and actress from the 1820s through the 1840s), and a historian and theoretician of Russian theater. His was a momentous presence in the theatrical world of his time. More than any other person one can think of, Shakhovskoy charted and directed the path Russian drama and theater took in the first quarter of the nineteenth century.[2]

A concatenation of unfortunate circumstances he could not control or foresee conspired to earn Shakhovskoy a widespread dislike among his contemporaries and to deny him the recognition due him in posterity. Some of these circumstances were personal, such as his grotesque physical appearance—a small head on top of an almost spherically obese body—combined with a squeaky, high-pitched voice and a marked lisp. His durable liaison with the character actress Ekaterina Ezhova, a

2. Realization of Shakhovskoy's significance is so rare among scholars that one can cite a total of three commentators who have done him full justice. They are Bertha Malnick in her essay "A. A. Shakhovskoy," *Slavonic and East European Review* (London) 32(78) (1953): 29–51; Abram Gozenpud in his introduction to A. A. Shakhovskoy, *Komedii, stikhotvoreniia* (Leningrad, 1961), pp. 5–72; and Tadeusz Kołakowski in his extensive review of Gozenpud's edition of Shakhovskoy's comedies and poems in *Slavia Orientalis* (Warsaw) 9(3) (1962): 400–7. One should also mention Leonid Grossman, who in his chapter on "Comedy and Vaudeville" in *Pushkin v teatral'nykh kreslakh* (*Pushkin in the Theater Stalls*) (Leningrad, 1926), makes a strong case for the pivotal importance of Shakhovskoy's *The Lipetsk Spa* for the development of Russian comedy.

battle-ax given to scolding and humiliating Shakhovskoy in public (except when he was directing her in plays, at which times she would bow to his authority), made him a laughing-stock. From the literary point of view, Shakhovskoy's habit of lampooning in some of his best plays the new trends that were to gain general acceptance soon afterwards made him influential enemies and gained him the reputation of a literary reactionary. His ultraconservative personal politics, expressed in two of his most successful plays (*The Lipetsk Spa* and, especially, *The Prodigal Landowners* [*Pustodomy*]) made his name anathema to the utilitarian radicals who controlled much of Russian criticism between the 1840s and the end of the nineteenth century. The very fact of Shakhovskoy's success as both administrator and playwright gave rise to much envious gossip, uncritically accepted and repeated by numerous commentators from his day to ours. The two most striking instances of invidious rumors entering literary history and acquiring the status of facts concern Shakhovskoy's relationships with the actress Semyonova and the playwright Ozerov. The man who discovered, encouraged, and supported their talents and promoted their careers, Shakhovskoy was often said to have persecuted Semyonova and destroyed Ozerov.[3]

Shakhovskoy made his debut as a playwright when Catherine the Great was still alive. His one-act comedy in verse, *A Woman's*

3. In his memoirs, Aksakov tells of how as a young man he resisted the efforts of his Moscow friends to bring him together with Shakhovskoy: "He had numerous enemies in St. Petersburg who created for him a very bad reputation in our society. From my early youth I was accustomed to regard Shakhovskoy as Shusherin's oppressor, intriguer, persecutor of Semyonova's great talent, flatterer, sycophant of the aristocrats in power, and, finally, Ozerov's sworn enemy, who supposedly had harassed him out of envy and even, as many claimed, was the cause of his death." (S. T. Aksakov, *Sobranie sochinenii* [Moscow, 1956], vol. 3, p. 69.) Aksakov eventually got to know Shakhovskoy and became convinced that this reputation was due to a combination of ignorance, envy, and deliberate slander.

In his 1854 review of Zhikharev's memoir "Recollections of an Old Theater-goer," Aksakov especially praised Zhikharev for exonerating Shakhovskoy and documenting the lack of factual basis for his continuing ugly reputation (*ibid.*, p. 608). But Zhikharev was taken to task by other surviving contemporaries, such as Arapov and Viazemsky, who insisted that rumors about Shakhovskoy were so widespread and accepted that he must have indeed been guilty as charged.

Jest (*Zhenskaia shutka*), was presented at the Hermitage Theater in St. Petersburg in October of 1795. The production came about through the intercession of Ivan Dmitrevsky, with whom Shakhovskoy formed a friendship at an early age. The play was apparently well received. But Shakhovskoy later came to see it as an embarrassment and destroyed its text. He waited nine years before writing for the stage again. In 1802, he was sent by the management of the Imperial Theaters to Paris to study French methods of acting and stage production. He spent more than a year there, associating with the theatrical notables of the time. Upon returning to St. Petersburg, he made another stab at playwriting with an adaptation of Gresset's full-length prose comedy *Le Méchant*, which was produced in December 1804 and was a failure. But in May of the next year, Shakhovskoy staged a play that was the beginning both of his success and of his troubles with his fellow-writers.

This was the one-act satirical comedy in prose *The New Sterne* (*Novyi Stern*). Laurence Sterne, mentioned in the title, was only a remote target of Shakhovskoy's satire of sentimentalist affectations, the immediate butt being the followers of Karamzin in the popular drama and prose of the time.[4] A posturing young nobleman, Count Pronsky, after reading Sterne and Karamzin, styles himself "a sentimental voyager" and departs for the countryside to admire nature and consort with the peasants. He is accompanied by his serf valet, Ipat, who apes the count's fashionable sentimentalist jargon and believes that his master is "growing day by day ever more sentimental, more touching, more interesting." To achieve communion with the peasants, whom he visualizes as a race of Arcadian shepherds, the count resolves to marry the country wench Malania (whom he calls Mélanie), a daughter of the woman who runs the local water mill. Malania for her part has no interest in the nobleman's idealistic moonings and prefers the company of her peas-

4. Abram Gozenpud's introduction to Shakhovskoy, *Komedii, stikhotvoreniia*, cites passages from books and poems by several Karamzinian writers of the time that Shakhovskoy parodied in Count Pronsky's and Ipat's speeches. Gerhard Giesemann's attempt to represent *The New Sterne* as an adaptation of a comedy by Kotzebue (*Kotzebue in Russland*, Frankfurter Abhandlungen zur Slawistik, vol. 15 [Frankfurt am Main, 1971], pp. 221 ff.) seems unfounded and unconvincing.

ant boy friend, Phocas, to whom she is engaged. The count's decision to marry Malania is abandoned when the ever-imitative Ipat declares his intention to marry Malania's younger sister and to settle with her "in a hut even humbler than yours" next door. The "sentimental voyager" is willing for philosophic motives to marry a peasant woman, but having his own serf and servant as a brother-in-law is more than his class pride can bear.

For all its brevity, *The New Sterne* is a marvelously amusing play. Shakhovskoy draws fine comic effects from the contrast between the literary conceits that the count believes to be the natural language of the common people and the perception of these conceits by real Russian peasants. The figurative terms introduced into various European languages, including Russian, by the New Sensibility, such as *interesting, touching* (French *touchant*, German *rührend*, Russian *trogatel'nyi*), and *engaging*, still retained their original nonfigurative meanings for the people who had not been exposed to sentimentalist literature. Hence this conversation between the count, Ipat, Malania's mother Kuzminishna, and Phocas:

> KUZMINISHNA: I love my children. They are my only wealth, my one treasure!
> THE COUNT: Good woman, how you do touch me!
> KUZMINISHNA: What are you saying, sir? Heaven help us, I never laid a finger on you.
> PHOCAS: Isn't it a shame to slander an old lady like that?
> IPAT: Those ignoramuses take it all so directly. This "to touch" does not mean "to touch." But what *does* it mean?
> THE COUNT: How pitiful that their senses are not refined. You all live in an unenlightened circle.
> PHOCAS: We don't live in a circle, we live at the water mill.

When the count calls Malania an interesting shepherdess, she is offended: she has her mother to support her, she says, and she has no financial interest in herding other people's cattle.

The New Sterne played all over Russia and made its author's literary name. But many important writers and poets resented the play's mockery of Karamzin's reform of Russian syntax and his introduction of neologisms patterned on Western languages, because they considered these innovations beneficial for Russian culture. During the next ten years, Shakhovskoy did numerous adaptations of foreign playwrights, ranging from Voltaire to Kotzebue. He authored the fourth part of the popular *Water Sprite*, wrote the previously mentioned failed tragedy *Deborah*, and, with his one-act musical play *The Cossack Poet* (*Kazak-stikhotvorets*, 1812) he inaugurated the genre of vaudeville, which was to enjoy much popularity in the next few decades. His biggest single success during that period was the five-act comedy in prose *The Semi-Gentlemanly Projects, or Theater at Home* (*Polubarskie zatei, ili Domashnii teatr*, 1808). It had as its protagonist an uncouth *nouveau riche* named Tranzhirin (something like Mr. Squanderbug) who tries to start a serf theater at his estate and doesn't quite know how to go about it. Tranzhirin became a favorite role with many comic actors of the time, most notably Mikhail Shchepkin. The popularity of the play and of the central role induced Shakhovskoy to provide it with two sequels that featured the same protagonist, in 1822 and 1833, respectively. Still, for all this activity, the best play he wrote during his first twenty years as a playwright remains *The New Sterne*.

Then, in 1815, came *A Lesson to Coquettes, or The Lipetsk Spa*, a play that without fear of exaggeration can be said to have opened a new chapter in Russian drama and in Russian literature. It is a five-act comedy in verse, written with careful observance of the classical unities of action, time (it begins in the morning and ends late in the evening of the same day), and place (all the action takes place in a space between two cottages at a mineral-water resort). If the structure and the unities of the play are traditional, its setting and characters are less so. In depicting a group of transient visitors at a spa, Shakhovskoy was anticipating, whether he knew it or not, a setting that was to be favored by fiction writers of the near future, beginning with Scott's *St. Ronan's Well* (1823), through Bestuzhev-Marlinsky's novellas of the 1820s, "An Evening on the Bivouac" and "An evening at a Spa in the Caucasus," and all the way to Lermontov's novel *A Hero of Our Time* (1840).

The people Shakhovskoy brings together in the small town of Lipetsk in the province of Tambov, famous since the reign of Peter the Great for the curative powers of its mineral springs, are a group of army officers who had fought against Napoleon at the time of Waterloo and were sent to the spa for recuperation, joined by several women who are related to them or are involved with them romantically. Among the good and, as often happens in comedies, less interesting characters are the upstanding and patriotic Prince Kholmsky, his virtuous and modest younger sister Olenka, and his closest friend Colonel Pronsky (apparently no relation to the sentimentalist ninny of the same name who was the protagonist of *The New Sterne*). Pronsky and Olenka are attracted to each other, but as the play opens, Pronsky is drawn to Olenka's cousin, the young widow Countess Leleva, who is the play's central and most memorable character. Leleva is lovely and intelligent, but she is also a hypocrite, who amasses admirers by feigning an interest in their pursuits and hobbies. Out of a mixture of coquetry and malice, she is resolved to break up the relationship between Olenka and Pronsky, while at the same time stringing along her other three suitors: a dapper military man (who turns out to be a coward), an addled romantic poet, and a senile gallant barely able to move.

Leleva's designs on Pronsky are revealed in her Act III soliloquy:

Графиня
(одна)

... Оленька изволит томны взгляды
Кидать на Пронского, и храбрый наш Тезей
Уже готов отплыть с сестрицею моей,
Чему и тетушка и братец очень рады;
Да ошибутся все. —Я здесь его дождусь,
В любви его ко мне признания добьюсь,
Когда же надобно—и замуж выйду.
Ах, муж — и муж педант!—несносен; но обиду
Сноснее ль вытерпеть от девочки пустой?
Притом же Пронский добр, доверчив, тих—и точно
Безгласым мужем быть на свет рожден нарочно,
Так буду я над ним и в доме госпожой.

Моё имение расстроено долгами,
Но вырвет он его из рук ростовщиков.
От сплетен, от клевет, комер и болтунов
Я порассорилась со многими домами;
Но с мужем в Петербург как только появлюсь,
Открою пышный дом и с светом помирюсь.
Все будут ездить к нам! . . .

THE COUNTESS
(alone)

. . . Olenka deigns to cast languid glances
At Pronsky, and our brave Theseus
Is all ready to sail forth with my cousin [*lit.* sister][5]
Which would make her dear aunt and dear brother most
happy.
But they will all be proven wrong. I'll wait for him here
To obtain from him a confession of his love.
Should it be necessary, I'll even marry him.
Ah, a husband—and a pedant husband!—is unbearable.
But to be bested
By that empty-headed slip of a girl, is that more bearable?
Besides, Pronsky is kind, trusting, quiet—and indeed,
He was born into the world just to be a voiceless husband,
So I'll be fully in control of him and of our home.
My estate is encumbered with debts,
But he shall extricate it from the moneylenders' hands.
Because of gossip, slander, *commères,* and prattlers
I have quarreled with many families;
But as soon as I appear in Petersburg with a husband,
I shall furnish an opulent home and make peace with high
society.

Everyone will come to see us! . . .

---

5. By evoking "Theseus ready to sail forth with my sister," Leleva casts Pronsky in the part of the mythological Theseus; Olenka in the part of Ariadne, whom Theseus abandoned on the isle of Naxos after taking her away from Crete as his bride; and herself as Ariadne's sister Phaedra, whom Theseus took home and married.

The lines "Ia zdes' ego dozhdus' / V liubvi ego ko mne priznaniia dob'ius'" anticipate Chatsky's first line in Act III of Griboedov's *The Misfortune of Being Clever*: "Dozhdus' ee, i vynuzhu priznan'e" ("I'll wait for her and compel from her a confession").

234

The plot of *The Lipetsk Spa* (the title under which the play is most usually mentioned) outlines a contest of wills between Prince Kholmsky and Countess Leleva over the outcome of the relationship between Olenka and Pronsky. The experienced warrior is no match for the resourceful and manipulative coquette. But Leleva gets her comeuppance from an unexpected source: Olenka's lady's-maid, the saucy and strong-minded Sasha. With the aid of her lover, Semyon, the son of Kholmsky's peasant orderly and now the manager of the mineral water baths, Sasha mobilizes Leleva's other admirers and lures her into a compromising situation that makes the true motives of the countess known not only to the other characters but to the entire population of Lipetsk. An unwitting agent of Leleva's unmasking is Pronsky's prissy, gossipy, and somewhat effeminate cousin Count Olgin, whose malicious backbiting impels her to speak her mind where Pronsky and others can overhear.

Superimposed upon the plot that deals with personal relationships is the simplistic ideological plot of the play. As Abram Gozenpud has pointed out, *The Lipetsk Spa* contains in a pure form Shakhovskoy's three basic oppositions, found in various forms in many of his other plays as well.[6] His good characters are often level-headed, rabidly patriotic, and sincere. The opposite traits, assigned to unattractive characters, are sentimentalism, love of things foreign, and insincerity. To attract Pronsky, Leleva pretends to be studying Russian history, but in reality she and Olgin are bored by everything Russian and are interested only in whatever comes from abroad. Since the time of the action of the play is shortly after Napoleon's invasion of Russia, Leleva's and Olgin's attitudes contrast most unfavorably with the solid patriotism of the good characters—Pronsky, Olenka, Kholmsky, Sasha, and Semyon. But the play's chauvinistic patriotism must have made it sound dated a decade or so later, when importation of foreign fashions and ideas no longer seemed subversive.

6. Gozenpud, introduction to Shakhovskoy, *Komedii, stikhotvoreniia*. Gozenpud indicates that Shakhovskoy's "favorite triad: groveling before foreign fashions, sentimentalism, and hypocrisy" was first attacked in his 1804 adaptation of Gresset's *Le méchant* (ibid., p. 9).

During the critical storm occasioned by the opening of *The Lipetsk Spa*, Shakhovskoy's opponents sought to impugn the play's originality by claiming that Leleva was really Célimène from Molière's *The Misanthrope* and by citing various other French plays that featured unmasked coquettes.[7] The reason they overlooked the clear-cut similarities between *The Lipetsk Spa* and Bogdan Elchaninov's 1767 comedy *The Giddypate Undone* (see Chapter 5, p. 102) is that by the end of the eighteenth century the playwrights of the Elagin group were forgotten, except for Fonvizin, who had become a national classic. Shakhovskoy, in his diligent research into the past of Russian theater, must have found the text of this play.

It is surely from the character of Elchaninov's dissembling Pulcheria that he developed Leleva. Other points of similarity between the two plays are Pulcheria's confrontation with her disapproving aunt (Leleva has a like one with Olenka's aunt), the character of the aged gallant who courts a young beauty and is constantly humiliated, and, most important of all, the idea that patriotism and love of one's native culture are to be equated with honesty and decency, which is so prominent in both plays. But whatever ingredients Shakhovskoy may have found in Elchaninov's one-act play, he integrated them into his own far broader dramatic conception, vastly different from any eighteenth-century play in its plotting, characterization, and, especially, its language.

The story of the Russian literary language in the second half of the eighteenth century and the first two decades of the nineteenth is the story of its gradual liberation from artificial and archaic slavonicisms in lexicon, grammar, and syntax, from the vestiges of the chancery language of the Muscovite scribes (later to be revived for special effects by twentieth-century poets), and from convoluted word order, never used in ordinary speech. Karamzin had cleared away much of this cumbersome heritage,

7. Gozenpud (ibid, pp. 772–73) rightly disputes the assertion of several nineteenth- and twentieth-century commentators that *The Lipetsk Spa* is an adaptation of de la Noue's *La coquette corrigée*. The cause for such claims, which has escaped both Gozenpud and those he debunks, is that de la Noue's play served as a point of departure for Elchaninov's *The Giddypate Undone*, which in its turn inspired *The Lipetsk Spa*.

but he also gallicized his syntax and vocabulary, adding a new layer of artificiality. Ozerov in his tragedies and Vasily Zhukovsky and Konstantin Batiushkov in their lyric poetry did much to facilitate the transition of the literary language to the much more natural and colloquial stylistic norms of the nineteenth and twentieth centuries.

Like other writers of the time, Shakhovskoy was aware of the new developments in prose and lyric poetry. But the two most decisive examples for him were probably the tragedies of Ozerov, in whose productions he was involved as director, and the publication in 1809 and 1811 of the first two books of fables by his literary ally Ivan Krylov. His association with these two writers showed Shakhovskoy how to abandon for good the literary usages of Russian eighteenth-century comedy and verse narrative. *The Lipetsk Spa* is the work in which this transition is fully accomplished for the first time. The conversational diction of this play's dialogue served as an inspiration for a whole array of verse comedies that appeared on the Russian stage in the next decade. This entire corpus, in its turn, made possible the literary language in which *Eugene Onegin* and *The Inspector General* were written.

The Lipetsk Spa opened in St. Petersburg on September 23, 1815, with a remarkable cast. Alexei Iakovlev played Prince Kholmsky. Another noted tragedian of the period, Iakov Briansky, took the part of Pronsky. Maria Valberg, who had earlier tried to vie with Semyonova in the tragic repertoire, but was so unsuccessful she left the stage voluntarily for a while, made her comeback as Leleva at Shakhovskoy's invitation. The role was associated with her for many years and was her stepping-stone to a new career as a comedienne. Olenka's cantankerous aunt, the Princess, was a part that Shakhovskoy had tailored for the special talents of his redoubtable paramour, Ekaterina Ezhova. The play's success with audiences was genuine. Very soon, there were productions in Moscow and in provincial cities.

The critical response, however, made scant mention of the play's stylistic breakthrough or its dramatic effectiveness. Much of the commentary that followed the premiere of *The Lipetsk Spa* concentrated on an episodic character who appears in a few brief scenes: Leleva's admirer, the romantic poet Fialkin (Mr. Violette). In the worst misjudgment of his entire career, Shakhovskoy used this figure to ridicule the German romantic ballads by Schiller and Bürger and their much-acclaimed Russian adaptations by Vasily Zhukovsky. The pathetic Fialkin bears no resemblance to Zhukovsky or any other romantic poet one can think of, but of the two ballads he recites in the hope of impressing the flirtatious countess, one pokes fun at the gothic poetry of ghosts and graveyards, popularized by Zhukhovsky's adaptations from Bürger, and the other satirizes the sentimentalization of themes from ancient Greek classics, another of Zhukovsky's specialties.

Zhukovsky was the teacher and the inspiration for the entire generation to which Pushkin, Evgeny Baratynsky, and so many other fine poets belonged. To make public fun of him was something they found unforgivable. It was after *The Lipetsk Spa* that rumors about Shakhovskoy having ruined Ozerov's life came to be alluded to in print: a man capable of attacking Karamzin and Zhukovsky, the two best hopes of Russian literature, could well do in a successful colleague out of envy. The battle lines were drawn between the Archaists, to whom Shakhovskoy belonged, and the Innovators (the older sentimentalist writers, who were offended by *The New Sterne*, plus the younger writers of the incipient romantic movement). Zhukovsky himself stayed out of the fray. But numerous others penned poisonous epigrams against Shakhovskoy or denounced him in critical articles. Yet, *The Lipetsk Spa* also brought him some notable allies among the younger generation, such men as Katenin, Griboedov, and Küchelbecker, who valued the play for its clever use of neoclassical structure and unities and who had no patience with the excesses of sentimentalism or romanticism.

No other work of literature can demonstrate the complex and tenuous nature of the disagreement between the Archaists and their opponents as well as *The Lipetsk Spa*. The salient features of the Archaists that had made them so odious to Russian nineteenth-century criticism were political conservatism, adherence to genres and formal structures inherited from the eighteenth century, and a preference for a bookish literary language replete with slavonicisms in its lexicon and grammar. *The Lipetsk Spa* may be a conservative play in its politics and its structure, but its use of language, in rejecting both eighteenth-century and Karamzinian usages, is enormously innovative.

It is indeed paradoxical that while some of the younger Archaists, such as Katenin and Küchelbecker, would go on clinging to stylized eighteenth-century usages for another decade, it was the senior Archaist Shakhovskoy, and after him Griboedov, who launched the modern literary language that was to become standard for the rest of the nineteenth century. None of this was noticed or appreciated at the time. For decades afterward, literary historians wrote of *The Lipetsk Spa* as if Fialkin and his parodistic ballads were the only thing worth mentioning about the play. Actually, Fialkin's few scenes are of so little importance that when Nicholas I wanted the play performed at his court theater in the late 1820s, while Zhukovsky was the tutor of the tsar's son, the character of Fialkin and his scenes were omitted from the performance out of consideration for the poet's feelings, without the play suffering much damage.

Shakhovskoy was so pleased and touched by Maria Valberg's spirited interpretation of Countess Leleva that he resolved to write a verse comedy that could serve as a display case for her acting versatility. This was *Within the Family, or The Married Fiancée*, premiered in January 1818, at a special performance that honored Valberg. As the playwright wrote in the introductory note to the first edition of this play:

> Wishing to compose a new comedy for the benefit performance of Miss Valberg (who had adorned *The Lipetsk Spa* with her enchanting talent), I selected a subject in which she could show the different varieties of her acting and I strove to connect the episodic scenes with a simple plot as best I could. There was a short time left before the day set for the benefit performance, and for fear of not keeping my promise, I asked Alexander Griboedov and Nikolai Khmelnitsky to help me out. Out of the friendship which they bore me, they agreed; the first wrote the entire beginning of the second

act up to the exit of Fyokla Savvishna, and the second wrote the third act scene in which Biriulkin gives Natasha an examination. Both gratitude and justice require that I make this known, so as not to usurp other people's property.

Griboedov was at the time known in theatrical circles only for his one-act verse comedy *The Young Couple*, performed in 1815, while Khmelnitsky had scored a great hit in 1817 with the first of his numerous one-acters in verse adapted from the French, *The Chatterbox*. Shakhovskoy may well have told the truth when he wrote that the collaboration was necessitated by the shortness of time. But, as several commentators have pointed out, the enlisting of Griboedov's and Khmelnitsky's aid may have also been motivated by his desire to dispel his image as an envious persecutor of competing playwrights.

Whatever the motives may have been, the collaboration resulted in a sparkling, well-nigh irresistible play. Other successful Russian comedies may be more significant socially or artistically, but it is hard to think of one with this kind of effervescence and polish. Instead of the more familiar one- or five-act format, *The Married Fiancée* is in three acts. The plot, the overall stylistic conception, and about three-quarters of the text belong to Shakhovskoy. But the contributions of the other two playwrights (Shakhovskoy is known to have edited their texts) fit seamlessly into the whole, so that had we not known the history of the writing of this play, we could not have imagined that it had more than one author.

The somewhat artificial central conceit of the play is as follows: an orphaned young man, Liubim, has secretly married Natasha, a penniless ward brought up by an aristocratic family. Liubim's parents have left a will specifying that he is to lose his inheritance if his prospective bride is not unanimously approved by a committee of relatives. Each of the relatives involved has his or her own preconceived idea of the kind of wife Liubim needs. A penny-pinching aunt, interested in home management to the exclusion of anything else, wants a frugal and practical wife for her nephew. Her sister, a sentimentalist old maid, can relate only to people who live in a world of tears, sighs, sweet sorrows, and moonlit glades. An uncle was once happily married to a simple-minded woman, and he feels that women of this type make the best wives, while a brother-in-law, who also has a say in the matter, is a believer in higher education for women and wants Liubim to marry a bluestocking. Finally, a semiparalyzed ancient grandmother, remembering her own party-going days in the eighteenth century, envisions a fun-loving wife who is adept at giving parties and knows all the latest dances.

With the help of still another of Liubim's aunts (the only one in the family to approach her with no preconceptions and to like her as she is), Natasha uses her vivid imagination and modest doses of hypocrisy to convince the relatives that she is indeed the type of woman that each of them had hoped Liubim would marry. She plays a meek simpleton in her interview with the uncle. She becomes an economical housekeeper for the benefit of the stingy aunt, whom she captivates with a recipe for a carrot cake that uses almost no sugar (their scene, written by Griboedov, represents his best writing for the stage prior to *The Misfortune of Being Clever*). She impersonates a heroine of a tearful melodrama and a nature lover for the benefit of the sentimentalist aunt. She discourses learnedly on philosophical systems and constellations to impress the brother-in-law (Khmelnitsky's contribution), and with the fun-loving grandmother, she becomes a party-loving, giggly madcap. Asked by the grandmother whether she can do a dance of earlier days, called the firecracker (*khlopushka*), Natasha eagerly asks to be shown the steps. The two women, two generations apart, start the dance, which other members of the family gradually join. At the height of the merriment, the miserly aunt threatens to withdraw her approval of the match because she has seen through Natasha's dissembling:

Она комедию играет так прекрасно,
Что бы не замуж ей, а на театр идти.
Ей нынче удалось вас за нос провести,
А кто порука мне, чтоб завтра шутку ту же
От скуки повторить не вздумала на муже?

She plays a comedy so beautifully
That instead of getting married, she ought to go on the stage.

She managed to dupe you all today,
But who will guarantee to me that tomorrow she will not
Take it into her head to play out of boredom the same trick
                                on her husband?

But Natasha explains that she had to dissemble to save her
marriage and that she did not really lie, but only exaggerated
tastes and qualities that she actually has:

                    Наташа

                    . . . И это всё не ложь.
По воле тетушки, кто я, от вас скрывала,
Но в прочем ничего неправды не сказала.
Хотя воспитана была в большом дому,
Но цену знаю я, сударыня, всему.
Как вам, противна мне пустая денег трата,
И я не меньше вас желаю быть богата.
Любезной тетушке приятны ручейки,
Луга зеленые, душистые цветки, —
Так что ж? и я сама природою пленяюсь
И даже иногда луною восхищаюсь.
Наш добрый дядюшка не любит остряков,
Надутых умников, высокопарных слов, —
И я согласна с ним.

. . . .

Что ж занималась я с успехами наукой,
Максим Меркурьич сам вам может быть порукой.
Он мне экзамент дал—и был доволен мной.
А рождена ли я с веселою душой,
Люблю ли резвости, так в этом нет сомненья.

                    NATASHA

                    . . . And it all is not lies.
According to my aunt's wishes, I concealed from you who
                                I am,
But otherwise I said nothing that is not true.
Although I was brought up in an aristocratic house,
I still know, madam, the price of everything.
Just like you, I find wasting money distasteful,
And I desire to be wealthy no less than you do.
Our dear aunt here finds pleasure in brooks,

Green meadows, fragrant flowers.
Well, what of it? I, too, find nature captivating
And sometimes even go into raptures over the moon.
Our dear, kind uncle does not care for smarties,
Pompous know-it-alls, high-flown words,
And I agree with him.

. . . .

Maxim Merkurievich himself can vouch to you
That I have studied science with success.
He gave me an examination and was satisfied with me.
And as to whether I was born with a merry heart,
Whether I love to frolic, why, of that there is no doubt.

The Married Fiancée was Shakhovskoy's most successful
comedy. Widely performed in his own time, it went on being
played after his other plays had been discredited owing to chang-
ing cultural attitudes. Occasional revivals are recorded even in
Soviet times. The casting, which calls for a versatile young comedienne, capable of assuming many contrasting identities, and
for four older character actresses, each of whom has a well-de-
lineated, hilariously funny part, is such that it has continued to
attract acting companies, despite the hostility of the critics of
later times to neoclassicism in general and to Shakhovskoy personally. One notable later production was at the Empress Alexandra Theater in 1896, in commemoration of the fiftieth anni-
versary of the playwright's death. The celebrated Maria Savina
played Natasha on this occasion; Vladimir Davydov, the first
interpreter of Chekhov's *Ivanov*, was the pedantic brother-in-
law; and Antonina Abarinova, who in that same year of 1896
appeared as Polina in the disastrous first production of *The
Seagull* in the same theater, took the part of the kindly aunt
who sponsors Natasha. Another interesting casting of Natasha's
part came in a production put on by an émigré Russian company
in German-occupied Paris during World War II and directed by
Nikolai Evreinov. On this occasion, the heroine of *The Married
Fiancée* was played by a young actress who was later to make a
big name for herself on the French stage and in French and
American films: Lila Kedrova. It is a measure of the disrepute

and/or oblivion into which Shakhovskoy's name had fallen that Evreinov chose to bill *The Married Fiancée* as "a little-known play by Alexander Griboedov."[8]

The Lipetsk Spa and *The Married Fiancée* were to remain Shakhovskoy's most significant and influential contributions as a playwright. Having inaugurated in these plays a new colloquial variety of neoclassical comedy, he seemed content to let his younger contemporaries Khmelnitsky, Zagoskin, and Griboedov develop it further, turning his attention to other, more fashionable forms of drama, such as dramatizations of novels and verse tales by Scott and Pushkin, and writing numerous vaudevilles. Not that he abandoned writing high comedies in verse. But the literary and dramatic level he attained in his two best comedies seemed to elude him after 1818, possibly because of the haste with which much of his work for the stage was written.

He did strike a real dramatic spark in 1820 with the one-act comedy in verse *The Cockatoo, or The Consequences of the Lesson to Coquettes* (*Kakadu, ili Posledstviia uroka koketkam*). This sequel to *The Lipetsk Spa* enabled Maria Valberg to repeat her much-acclaimed characterization of Countess Leleva and to deepen it by showing the crafty coquette's subsequent reaction to her defeat at the end of the earlier play. The cast of *The Cockatoo* is restricted to four characters from *The Lipetsk Spa*. They were shown five years later, the actual time that had elapsed between the productions of these two plays, and were impersonated by the same four actors who had played them earlier. After her disgrace at Lipetsk, Leleva has resolved to give up her selfish games and settle in elegant semiseclusion in her St. Petersburg town house. To show to herself and everyone that she has learned her lesson and bears no grudges, she has hired her one-time nemesis, Sasha, as her lady's-maid. When she is visited by the foppish Count Olgin, we learn from their dialogue and Sasha's acid comments on it that Leleva has not changed her flirtatious and manipulative nature, only repressed it to regain

8. N. Evreinov, *Pamiatnik mimoletnomu* (Paris, 1953), pp. 45–48. A photograph of Lila Kedrova, surrounded by the Paris cast of *The Married Fiancée*, is reproduced facing p. 46.

her position in society. Her new form of dissembling is so successful that she even fools herself.

Leleva and Olgin are caught by Kholmsky's and Olenka's cranky and gossipy aunt, the Princess (another tailor-made part for Ezhova), in an innocent situation that she interprets as compromising. To avoid losing her hard-won social acceptance, Leleva is forced to marry Olgin, a man she finds neither suitable nor desirable. At the end of *The Lipetsk Spa*, Leleva was punished for misleading other people, but here her punishment comes from misleading herself. With its remarkable insight into how the social masks people don for others can end up hiding their own motives from themselves, *The Cockatoo* is Shakhovskoy's most subtle play psychologically. It exhibits precisely the quality that is sadly lacking in the remaining corpus of his verse comedies.

The one-act comedy in verse whose title is a popular Russian proverb, *Don't Listen If You Don't Like It, but Don't Stop Me from Lying (Ne liubo—ne slushai, a lgat' ne meshai*, 1818), is a portrait of a pathological liar. Its literary prototype is clearly Khmelnitsky's successful debut comedy *The Chatterbox* of one year earlier and its real-life prototype was supposedly the publisher Pavel Svin'in, widely known for his prevarications. Compared to *The Chatterbox* and to Shakhovskoy's own better comedies, *Don't Listen* . . . seems on the primitive side, its satire not broadly comic, as in the earlier *The New Sterne*, but schematic and simplistic. One interesting thing about this play is its versification, iambic lines of varying lengths, later to be used by Griboedov in *The Misfortune of Being Clever*, though it had been already introduced into Russian drama in the eighteenth century by Kniazhnin's tragedy *The Clemency of Titus*. Another is the possibility that its central character may have served as a model for Griboedov's Repetilov and Gogol's Khlestakov in *The Inspector General*.

In *The Prodigal Landowners*, a five-act comedy in verse written between 1817 and 1819 and staged in 1819, Shakhovskoy launched a satirical attack on replacing the traditional Russian methods of agriculture with imported foreign ones, mostly English. While his wife is depleting their fortune with her compulsive spending, the pedantic and stupidly ambitious Prince Radugin (Rainbow) is wrecking the economy of their estates by forcing unfamiliar foreign crops and ways of cultivation on his serfs. The couple is surrounded by household retainers who steal them blind and by a few disapproving relatives who vainly try to save them from ruin. The theme of Russian nobles losing their estates through impracticality has been treated by playwrights ranging from Catherine II to Chekhov, but Shakhovskoy's self-destructive Radugins are so unbelievable that one cannot imagine an audience sustaining an interest in their plight for five whole acts, even though some of the subordinate characters are well realized. The chauvinistic central idea that Russian ways of raising crops are always preferable to foreign ones, regardless of results, was later echoed by Pushkin in "Mistress into Maid," by Gogol in the unfinished second part of *Dead Souls,* and by Tolstoy in the description of Vronsky's country estate in *Anna Karenina.*

Shakhovskoy's most carefully written verse comedy, one on which he worked over a period of several years (in contrast to most of his output, written and staged within a matter of weeks), was *Aristophanes, or The Performance of the Comedy "The Knights"* (*Aristofan, ili Predstavlenie komedii "Vsadniki"*). Published in excerpts in various journals from 1824 on, staged in St. Petersburg in 1825 and in Moscow one year later, it appeared as a separate book in 1828. It was styled on the title page as "a historical comedy in the ancient mode, in verse that utilizes the various Greek meters, in three acts, with a prologue, interludes, songs, and choruses. By Prince A. Shakhovskoy, with insertion of many thoughts and maxims from the theater of Aristophanes." The initial impulse for this play must have come to Shakhovskoy during the controversy over *The Lipetsk Spa,* when hostile epigrams alluding to Shakhovskoy's supposed role in Ozerov's demise mentioned Aristophanes' ruining his rivals out of envy. This comparison prompted the playwright to embark on a study of Aristophanes and his times, with the hope of turning his accusers' weapons on themselves.

He found the theme of his play in an apocryphal anecdote about how, when Aristophanes had satirized the tyrant Cleon in his comedy *The Knights* and actors refused to impersonate Cleon out of fear, Aristophanes himself took the part, scoring a triumph over a conspiracy by his enemies to discredit his play. Shakhovskoy turned this plot into a typical nineteenth-century comedy of love and intrigue that bears not the slightest resemblance to Aristophanic theater. He invented the play's most important character, the historically nonexistent Alcinoe, the beautiful and emancipated pupil of Aspasia. She loves Aristophanes (depicted as an impetuous romantic lead out of an operetta), and she enables the threatened performance of *The Knights* to take place by getting Cleon drunk and detaining him at her house until the play is safely over and Aristophanes is acclaimed by the populace.

The confrontations between the heroic Aristophanes and the corrupt and stupid Cleon are obviously patterned upon the similar exchanges between the irreverent Chatsky and the archconservative Famusov in Griboedov's *The Misfortune of Being Clever* (completed at about the time Shakhovskoy was beginning *Aristophanes*). But where Griboedov offered genuine debates between two opposing viewpoints, in Shakhovskoy's play Aristophanes and Cleon engage in scolding matches couched in resonant verse. The profusion of simplistic scolding in the play is further increased by several temperamental scenes, unrelated to the main action, for that noted scold of ancient times, Xantippe, the wife of Socrates, impersonated on the opening night by the almost equally noted scold in Shakhovskoy's life, Ekaterina Ezhova. Considered Shakhovskoy's finest achievement in the field of verse comedy by some commentators,[9] *Aristophanes* can be with greater justice qualified as an embarrassing trivialization of a subject that was beyond its author's scope. Apart from the sketches for the unfinished comedy *The Gamblers* (which has certain parallels with Gogol's *Gamblers*), it was Shakhovskoy's last stab at comedy in verse.

Most of the accusations that his contemporaries flung at Shakhovskoy were unfair. But the accusation of eclecticism may

9. For example, Sergei Aksakov and, in our time, the Polish expert on Shakhovskoy, Tadeusz Kołakowski (see note 2, above).

be conceded as just. A consummate man of the theater for whom his activities as stage director and theatrical administrator were every bit as important as writing plays, he was above all concerned with obtaining success by giving the public whatever it wanted. Three years after indicting sentimentalism in *The New Sterne*, he translated and staged a sentimentalist drama by Kotzebue. Having declared himself an opponent of romanticism, he proceeded to convert Sir Walter Scott's *Ivanhoe, The Fortunes of Nigel*, and *The Black Dwarf* into opulent romantic melodramas. Shakhovskoy worshipped the genius of Alexander Pushkin, but this did not prevent him from converting "Ruslan and Liudmila," "The Fountain of Bakhchisarai," and "The Queen of Spades" (as *Chrysomania*) into lavish pageants with fireworks, ballets, and children's choruses, whose descriptions make one think of Radio City Music Hall, if not of a Las Vegas revue. Shakhovskoy's vaudevilles about the lives of Molière, Voltaire, and Lomonosov and about the founding of Russian theater by Fyodor Volkov and also his adaptations of Shakespeare (*Storm and Shipwreck*, after *The Tempest* in 1821; *Falstaff: A Comedy in One Act with Songs and Dances*, after several scenes in *Henry IV*, Parts 1 and 2, in 1825; and *Daddy's Girl* [*Batiushkina dochka*], a comedy-ballet after *The Taming of the Shrew* in 1827) trivialized their subjects as mindlessly and pointlessly as did *Aristophanes*.

But this flashy showman and theatrical opportunist was also the author of four or five comedies that are the work of a major playwright. Without Shakhovskoy at his best, Russian drama of the nineteenth century would have been very different. The period between *The New Sterne* in 1805 and *The Cockatoo* in 1820 encompasses his still viable work, such as *The Lipetsk Spa, The Married Fiancée*, and perhaps *Semi-Gentlemanly Projects*. Although he went on composing plays until 1841 (Abram Gozenpud's register of Shakhovskoy's original plays, adaptations, and translations encompasses 111 titles),[10] one would be tempted to write off everything after *The Cockatoo* as being of historical interest only, were it not for the 1832 melodrama *The Bigamous Wife, or What You Seek, You Shall Find (Dvu-*

10. *Komedii, stikhotvoreniia*, pp. 816–25.

muzhnitsa, ili Za chem poidesh', to i naidesh'). With its anthro-
pologically reconstructed details of the life of the merchant
class and its depiction of folk customs and rituals, this play, together with the earlier example of Plavilshchikov's *The Salesclerk*, is the obvious point of departure for Alexander Ostrovsky's widely popular melodramas of mid-nineteenth century
about the life of Russian merchants. *The Bigamous Wife* also
had the distinction of inspiring Mikhail Glinka with the plan
of his third opera, which was to follow *A Life for the Tsar* and
Ruslan and Liudmila, but which he did not live to complete.

Nikolai Khmelnitsky

The first proof that the stylistic breakthrough of *The Lipetsk
Spa* was to have a durable impact on the development of Russian
drama came while the controversy occasioned by that play was
still in full swing. This was Mikhail Zagoskin's polemical *Comedy Against Comedy*, written and staged during the first run of
Shakhovskoy's play and devoted to defending it. Though written in prose, Zagoskin's work reflected the new cadences and
nuances that *The Lipetsk Spa* introduced to the Russian stage.
But it took about two years for Shakhovskoy's lessons to sink in
fully and to be absorbed by other writers of comedy in verse. In
May of 1817 came the opening of *The Chatterbox* (*Govorun*),
the first play by Nikolai Khmelnitsky, a playwright who was to
take Russian comedy to new levels of fluency, expressivity, and
sophistication.

Nikolai Khmelnitsky (1789–1845) was the last direct descendant of the Hetman Bohdan Khmelnyts'kyi, the famous
Ukrainian seventeenth-century leader. In government service
from the age of 17, Khmelnitsky served as a diplomatic courier
during Napoleon's invasion of Russia. After the defeat of the
French, Khmelnitsky found himself in Paris, where he fre-
quented the theaters and became partial to the newly popular
form of French musical comedy known as the vaudeville. Successor to the eighteenth-century comic opera of Favart and
Sedaine, the early nineteenth-century vaudeville (not to be confused with the American variety shows that took over this name

in the early twentieth century) had a far more primitive musical texture than its predecessor. Where the eighteenth-century comic opera had scores by able and resourceful composers, such as Philidor or Grétry, and comprised arias, duets, and vocal ensembles, vaudeville comedies often reduced their musical component to witty or topical patter songs called *couplets* (*kuplety*), sung, as often as not, to the tune of some currently popular ditty.

Returning from Paris to St. Petersburg, Khmelnitsky continued his civil service career while simultaneously forming contacts and friendships in the worlds of literature and the theater, first with Shakhovskoy and Griboedov and eventually with Pushkin. At the age of twenty-eight he made his debut as a playwright with *The Chatterbox,* an adaptation of *Le babillard* (earlier translated into Russian by Lukin), a play by an obscure French eighteenth-century author, Louis de Boissy.

From 1817 to 1829 Khmelnitsky produced an even dozen one-act comedies in verse and vaudevilles, all of them invariably well received, premiered by the best acting talent of the time in St. Petersburg and Moscow, and then taken up by provincial theaters and amateur groups throughout the country. All but one or two of these plays were adaptations of eighteenth-century French originals by such figures as Regnard, Destouches, Favart, and Collin d'Harleville.

Khmelnitsky was a miniaturist. Even when his original was a five-act play, he would adroitly compress it into the one-act format he favored. His detractors in the later part of the nineteenth century were right when they accused him of lacking all interest in social problems or philosophical ideas. His plays are usually set in an aristocratic milieu. Almost all them have the same basic plot mechanism: a successful (or, occasionally, unsuccessful) courtship, leading (or not leading) to marriage. But it should be pointed out that Khmelnitsky was able to vary this familiar plot with a great deal of ingenuity and that though his debt to French playwrights is in each case obvious, the plays he derived from their work have a form, a diction, and a style that are unmistakably Russian and unmistakably Khmelnitsky's.

This style is immediately evident in *The Chatterbox.* Count

Zvonov (Bellringing) courts the young widow Prelestina (Mrs. Charming) but loses her to the modest young officer named Modestov, because the count can't resist his urge to dominate every conversation, to brag, and to prevaricate. The comic element is enhanced by Zvonov's noisy bouts of gossiping with Prelestina's aunt Chvanova (Mrs. Pompous) and her five elderly and argumentative friends with such names as Sporkina (Mrs. Arguer) and Vzdorkina (Mrs. Nonsensical). The central figure of the garrulous count (in Boissy's original play, the part was written to demonstrate the power of the leading actor's voice and to show that he could outshout seven clamorous women) not only served as the point of departure for Shakhovskoy's *Don't Listen,* but combined with the hero of that play to provide the obvious model for the two creative, disinterested liars of later Russian comedy, Griboedov's Repetilov and Gogol's Khlestakov.

A person familiar with the major masterpieces of Russian literature of the first half of the nineteenth century has a disturbing sense of *déjà vu* when reading *The Chatterbox* for the first time. There are constant echoes of Griboedov and faint whiffs of Gogol: of the older women spreading gossip about Chatsky in *The Misfortune of Being Clever,* of Dobchinsky and Bobchinsky vying to tell the news and Khlestakov's hyperbolic exaggerations in *The Inspector General,* of the two ladies conspiring to ruin Chichikov's reputation in *Dead Souls.*

Here, for example, is Count Zvonov gushing about his wholly imaginary military distinctions and prefiguring both Colonel Skalozub and Repetilov in *The Misfortune of Being Clever*:

> Я всюду поспевал: был в тысяче сраженьях,
> В траншеях, в приступах, в победах, в пораженьях,
> Везде торжествовал—и в мире, и в войне;
> Спросите всякого: все знают обо мне!
> . . . .
> Граф Знатов в этот штурм чуть жизни не лишился!
> Вы знаете его? Он выгодно женился;
> Жена его мила, в больших теперь связях,
> А лучше что всего—богата так, что страх!
> Но грех завидовать такой его удаче:

Я был вчера у них, они живут на даче,
Представьте...

I managed to be everywhere: I was in a thousand battles,
In trenches, in assaults, in victories, in defeats;
I triumphed everywhere—both in peace and in war.
You may ask anyone, everyone knows about me!

. . . .

Count Znatov almost lost his life in that attack!
Do you know him? He married quite advantageously.
His wife is sweet, has all the important connections,
But what is best of all, she is fearfully rich!
But it is wrong to envy him his success.
I went to visit them yesterday, they are living at their summer
villa,
Can you imagine . . .

The resemblances to Griboedov and Gogol lie not only in
the choice of subjects mentioned or specific words used, but
more significantly in the rhythm and cut of Khmelnitsky's sen-
tences. This is the area where Khmelnitsky is superior to Shakhovskoy and other playwrights of his school and in which his
contribution to the language of later writers cannot be sufficiently stressed. As Moisei Iankovsky, the editor of the most recent
publication of his selected plays, put it, "As we reread these long
forgotten plays, we are astounded to overhear in them the intona-
tions that will be sounded again, more weightily and significantly, in *Eugene Onegin* and *The Misfortune of Being Clever.*"[11] Griboedov was a close friend of Khmelnitsky's at the time
The Chatterbox was written. Pushkin's great enthusiasm for
Khmelnitsky's comedies is well attested and Gogol, at the age
of fifteen or so, played Count Zvonov in a school production of
The Chatterbox. So the impact of Khmelnitsky's tone and style
on their work is not surprising.

Because Khmelnitsky is usually mentioned (when he is at
all) as an unoriginal playwright whose contribution was limited
to translating forgettable French vaudevilles, it should be made
clear that all he derived from his models were the basic situa-

11. Iankovsky, introduction to *Russkaia stikhotvornaia komediia*, p. 22.

tions. Apart from that, he would modernize the action by moving it from eighteenth-century France to nineteenth-century Russia, invent and develop his own sparkling dialogue, all of which added up to raising the often undistinguished French originals to a much higher literary and dramatic plane. His adaptational method may be illustrated by examining what he did with Jean-François Collin d'Harleville's 1789 five-act comedy in verse, *Les châteaux en Espagne,* widely played in France in the first two decades of the nineteenth century.

The French play is a stylish comedy of misunderstandings, wherein a young woman, living at a secluded château, learns that the man her relatives are arranging for her to marry and whom she has never met is planning to visit her under an assumed name to make sure he really wants her. When a chance traveler blunders into the château, the heroine, who has decided to go along with the charade, assumes he is her intended. Complications mount when the real fiancé arrives incognito. Khmelnitsky based not one but *two* plays on this situation. In his comedy *Castles in the Air* (*Vozdushnye zamki,* 1818), the landowning widow Aglaeva is informed by a letter from her aunt that a wealthy nobleman interested in meeting her is to call on her under an assumed name with the pretext that his carriage has broken down in front of her house. A poor and shy retired naval officer, whose carriage has actually broken down, is mistaken for the suitor, is given a warm welcome and encouragement, but is then asked to leave when his true identity is revealed.

The situation is replayed with a different set of characters, in another tonality, and with the opposite outcome in Khmelnitsky's vaudeville *There's No Escaping Your Fated Mate, or There's Nothing Bad That Doesn't Bring Some Good* (*Suzhenogo konem ne ob"edesh', ili Net khuda bez dobra,* 1821). Although two popular Russian proverbs make up its title and subtitle, this play is set in France. Here, the man whose carriage suffers an accident is a rough, brawling hussar who is mistaken for the fiancé of the castle owner's daughter Laure. By the time the misunderstanding is cleared up, his rude manners and unconventional behavior have captured Laure's heart. The characters in these two plays bear no resemblance to the three well-behaved, sentimental young people who form the love triangle in Collin d'Harleville's *Les châteaux en Espagne*. The whimsical Laure and the manipulative Aglaeva, the impractical midshipman and the pushy hussar are wholly Khmelnitsky's creations, and so is the action and the denouement of the two comedies. Except for the borrowed mechanism of the plot, these two works and the rest of Khmelnitsky's output are thus actually his original plays. His reputation as a mere adapter is as undeserved as the concommitant image of this playwright as a mindless entertainer.

Another Khmelnitsky play that deserves mention is *The Irresolute Man* (*Nereshitel'nyi*, 1819), because he had the benefit of Alexander Pushkin's advice while working on it[12] and because of its importance as the possible source of Gogol's *Marriage*. *L'irrésolu* by Destouches and *L'inconstant* by Collin d'Harleville have been cited as its possible models. A portrait of a man unable to make up his mind or to make a choice between two careers, two clothing styles, or two women to love and marry, the amusing comedy is set in a roadside inn halfway between St. Petersburg and Moscow (the protagonist can't decide to which of them to travel) and features the comical figure of Madame Werther, the Russian widow of a German innkeeper.

Khmelnitsky's one comedy in verse whose plot does not seem to have a foreign model is *A Worldly Incident* (*Svetskii sluchai*, 1826). Just the same, it begins with a scene obviously suggested by the *récit* of Agnès in Act II of Molière's *L'école des femmes*. A young woman comes to sit by the window because a mysterious man has been passing by, bowing to her and trying to catch her eye. She eventually responds to his glances and bows and eagerly awaits a chance to meet him. They finally meet when they are introduced by a mutual acquaintance. This Molière-inspired situation was later to turn up in Antony Pogorelsky's popular Hoffmannesque tale of horror, "The Poppy-Seed–Cake Woman

12. As described in Pushkin's letter to Nikolai Gnedich, May 13, 1832.

of Lafertovo" (1825) and in Pushkin's "The Queen of Spades" (1834).

The flirtatious girl by the window is Eugenia, who is already engaged to a self-important young man, Stolitsyn, even though they are not really compatible. The attractive stranger is Stolitysn's old friend Ramirskoy. The comedic device is that Stolitsyn helps Ramirskoy court and win Eugenia, acting under the impression that he is advising him on how to break up someone else's engagement. Trying to be practical and cynical, Stolitsyn brings together two romantic souls made for each other and wrecks his own chance of marrying Eugenia. The clever working out of the plot and the considerable psychological subtlety achieved in this play indicate that Khmelnitsky could write well for the stage even without borrowing his dramatic scaffoldings from foreign sources.

Somewhat apart from his other plays is the pseudohistorical vaudeville in prose, *Actors Among Themselves, or The First Debut of the Actress Troepolskaya (Aktery mezhdu soboi, ili Pervyi debiut aktrisy Troepol'skoi*, 1820), written in collaboration with the amateur author Nikita Vsevolozhsky. The protagonist bears the name of Tatiana Troepolskaya, one of the earliest Russian actresses. Other characters are the actors of Volkov's original company, Iakov Shumsky and Alexei Popov. But the plot and the action have nothing to do with the lives or personalities of these people. Popov and Shumsky are shown courting the married Troepolskaya, who rebuffs them while assuming a variety of different disguises and identities, thus convincing them of her acting talent and inducing them to sponsor her career in the theater.

It was an unfortunate custom of the time, in both France and Russia, to depict the theatrical celebrities of the past in utterly unhistorical ways. Thus, in 1807 Shakhovskoy had staged the Russian translation of Alexandre Duval's preposterous *Shakespeare Amoureux*, in which Semyonova portrayed an aspiring young actress Clarence (a name often assumed to be a woman's in France and Germany to this day) with whom the Bard was supposedly madly in love and whom he won away from a wealthy noble. *Plautus* by Népomucène Lemercier and Shakhovskoy's *Aristophanes* and *Volkov, or The Birthday of Russian Theater* are other instances from that period of reducing theatrical history to conventional superficiality, of which Khmelnitsky's vaudeville about Troepolskaya is a further example.

When his close friend Egor Alad'in published Khmelnitsky's collected plays in two volumes in 1829, the playwright had been working on a new comedy that seemed to be a fresh departure for him. *The Geese of Arzamas (Arzamasskie gusi)*, a fragment of which was published in a literary journal, was to be a satire on the corruption in the administrative system, a play that reached for its precedent all the way back to Kapnist's *Chicane*. The excerpt depicts a bribe-taking judge named Likhvin (the name comes from *likhva*, "excessive profit" or "high rate of interest") and his wife, who reminisce about how poor they were until Likhvin learned to be corrupt. In the meantime, a group of government-owned serfs is waiting outside in the blizzard for a chance to lodge a complaint with the judge. Rather than let them in, the Likhvins discuss the future of their daughter Liubushka, who had just completed her studies at a boarding school in St. Petersburg and returned to her parents' home in the provincial city of Arzamas. Liubushka's mother had always been opposed to higher education for her daughter, but her father had insisted on it, believing in equal education for women and thinking it would improve Liubushka's chances of finding a husband.

The Likhvins are visited by a local gossip monger named Pobrodiazhkin (something like Mr. Straypup) who announces that an inspector general (*revizor*) might soon visit Arzamas. The news alarms the judge. Then Liubushka and Pobrodiazhkin discuss the St. Petersburg flood of November 7, 1824. Liubushka, who had witnessed the flood, describes the casualties and praises the philanthropic behavior of Tsar Alexander I during the calamity. Pobrodiazhkin blames the loss of life on the founder of the city, Peter the Great:

> А кто несчастию причина?
> Блаженной памяти покойный государь

Петр Алексеевич! был умный царь,
Да к морю чересчур подъехал близко.
Как в яме строиться, когда есть материк?
Вот то-то, матушка, и был велик,
А выстроился низко.

And who caused this misfortune?
The late sovereign Peter Alekseyevich
Of blessed memory! He was an intelligent tsar,
But he came much too close to the sea.
Why build in a hole when you have the continent?
So there you are, madam, even though he was great,
He built much too low.

Likhvin tells Pobrodiazhkin that his remarks are disrespectful and the fragment ends with Pobrodiazhkin terrified that he might be punished for having blasphemed Peter the Great.

Written some time after 1825 and published in 1829, *The Geese of Arzamas* contains the kernels of two great works of Russian literature that appeared in the 1830s, Pushkin's "The Bronze Horseman" (1833) and Gogol's *The Inspector General* (1836). Peter's responsibility for St. Petersburg floods may have been a common enough topic of conversations at the time. But the specific contrast between the roles of Peter the Great and Alexander I in the flood of 1824 and the terror of the little, insignificant man who dares to protest against the location of St. Petersburg are far too close to the central conception of Pushkin's poetic masterpiece to be entirely fortuitous. Embryonic though the character of Pobrodiazhkin might be, he combines in a paradoxical way the makings of Pushkin's defiantly protesting Evgeny and of Gogol's ridiculous gossips, Bobchinsky and Dobchinsky. The grim satirical theme of *The Geese of Arzamas* clashes somewhat with its remarkably melodious verse, which Khmelnitsky achieved by ingenious placement of polysyllabic words in iambic lines of various lengths.

Khmelnitsky never finished this promising fragment because the year it was published he was appointed the governor of the Smolensk province. His removal from St. Petersburg terminated his playwriting career. During his tenure as governor, Khmelnitsky initiated and carried out the rebuilding of the ancient citadel in Smolensk. Careless accounting of the government funds allocated for this project led to complaints and an official investigation, during which the authorities learned that Khmelnitsky had refused to cooperate with ecclesiastic efforts to persecute Old Believer splinter sects, the *raskol'niki* (the object of the planned persecutions was to force the "schismatics" to return to the bosom of the Orthodox Church). The investigation resulted in Khmelnitsky's arrest and incarceration in the St. Peter and Paul Fortress in 1837. He remained there for six years, after which he was amnestied by Nicholas I. He tried returning to playwriting in the last two years of his life. But it was a different age. His plays and the dramatic tradition they represented were receding from the stage. Khmelnitsky attempted several romantic historical plays in the manner of the then popular Nestor Kukolnik, but they failed to arouse any interest. He died a broken man, in 1845.

Fifty years after his death there appeared a biographical and critical study of him by a scholar with a Gogolian name, Nikolai Korobka, whose other specialty was denouncing the nascent symbolist movement of the 1890s. This essay sums up to perfection the prevailing literary attitudes of the preceding half century. As Korobka tells the story of Nikolai Khmelnitsky's life and describes his plays, he is constantly lecturing his subject about his lack of social awareness or constructive ideology, "without which one cannot be a major literary figure." "Possessing an indubitable talent, he could not introduce a single idea or even a single literary device; he could not take a single step forward because he lacked a well-considered world view,"[13] Korobka concluded.

One may contrast this with an informed twentieth-century opinion, as expressed by Sergei Danilov: "A dazzling master of versified dialogue, Khmelnitsky perfected the formal aspects of Russian comedy, exerting at the same time a considerable

---

13. N. I. Korobka, "Nikolai Ivanovich Khmel'nitsky (1789–1845)," *Ezhegodnik Imperatorskikh teatrov, Prilozheniia* (St. Petersburg, 1896), vol. 1, pp. 89–118. The quoted passages are on p. 118.

influence on the development of Russian versification as a whole."[14]

Zagoskin and Others

Most literate Russians are likely to have heard of Mikhail Zagoskin (1789–1852) as a historical novelist who successfully applied the formula of Scott's Waverley novels to subjects from Russian history. His novel *Iury Miloslavsky, or Russians in 1612* (1829) enjoyed an enormous popularity and was the subject of a highly complimentary review by Pushkin. In Gogol's *The Inspector General*, the bragging Khlestakov seeks to impress the provincials by claiming that *he* is the author of *Iury Miloslavsky* but is exposed by the mayor's daughter, who happens to know that it was written by "a Mr. Zagoskin." *Roslavlev* (1830), Zagoskin's ultrapatriotic novel about the Napoleonic invasion of Russia, brought forth two impressive creative responses. One was from Pushkin, who in his elegant Jane Austen-like prose fragment, also called "Roslavlev," reinterpreted some of the events described by Zagoskin from a woman's point of view. The other was from Lev Tolstoy, who reread this novel just before setting to work on *War and Peace* and rightly concluded that he could do its theme greater justice. Finally, Zagoskin's third novel, *Askold's Grave* (1833), set in pre-Christian Kievan Russia, was reworked by him into an opera libretto for his closest friend, the composer Alexei Verstovsky. Premiered in 1835, the Zagoskin–Verstovsky *Askold's Grave* was to remain one of the best-loved Russian operas for the rest of the nineteenth century.

Zagoskin's acclaim as novelist and librettist obscured his earlier career as playwright. It began in 1814, when he submitted to Shakhovskoy his first comedy *The Mischief Maker* (*Prokaznik*). The play was eventually produced by Shakhovskoy in December 1815. It had only one performance and was pronounced a failure, but by then Zagoskin's second play had had

14. S. S. Danilov, *Ocherki po istorii russkogo dramaticheskogo teatra* (Moscow-Leningrad, 1948), p. 196.

its successful production in November of the same year. This was his polemical three-act comedy in prose *Comedy Against Comedy* (*Komediia protiv komedii*), an exercise in dramatized literary criticism that followed the precedent of Molière's *La critique de l'École des femmes* and in its turn furnished the model for Gogol's similar work *After the Play* (*Teatral'nyi raz"ezd*, 1842).

A minor official in the administration of St. Petersburg theaters when he began writing plays, Zagoskin was present at the triumphant opening night of *The Lipetsk Spa* and was convinced that it was the most significant new Russian play in decades. He was outraged that the critical response concentrated on the minor detail of Fialkin's ballads and that the stylistic originality of Shakhovskoy's dialogue went unperceived or, when it was perceived, was berated for bringing to verse drama the sort of diction that was supposedly more suitable for prose. *Comedy Against Comedy* was Zagoskin's defense of the literary and dramatic quality of Shakhovskoy's play. Although Zagoskin created his own plot and characters, his text is permeated with deliberate references to *The Lipetsk Spa*.

One way Zagoskin achieves this is by having the characters, most of whom had recently seen Shakhovskoy's play, discuss it and debate its merits. This is where the play most clearly imitates Molière. A silly and snobbish aristocrat, Count Folgin (his name is a variation of Shakhovskoy's Count Olgin; *fol'ga* means tin foil), proclaims the play worthless "from the beginning to its last scene." Asked by the idealistic young man named Izborsky whether he can substantiate this view, the count retorts: "What a funny question! As if I were obliged to substantiate! It is enough that I tell you it is worthless—what else can you want?" The argument between Count Folgin and Izborsky follows the format of the similar one in Molière between the Marquis and Dorante. The count simply keeps reiterating his negative view, while Izborsky takes up and refutes the various charges leveled against Shakhovskoy during the *Lipetsk Spa* controversy.

To the accusation that the play's dialogue just does not sound like verse and must therefore be some kind of prose, Izborsky retorts that writing verse dialogue of such lightness and fluency that the metrical pattern is barely perceptible is a difficult art, not carelessness. He refuses to agree that satirizing romantic ballads represents an *ad hominem* attack against any particular person: "Why is it personal? Is a ballad a person? The author of *The Lipetsk Spa* does not care for this type of compositions, and no wonder. . . . Should this genre find imitators who, not possessing the admirable talents of their model, will undertake to write of nothing but corpses and ghosts, you'll have to admit that it will be small gain for our literature."

In addition to direct discussions, various characters of *Comedy Against Comedy* represent in themselves Zagoskin's commentary on Shakhovskoy's play. A cranky elderly woman enamored of card games and an aged man still trying to court young women claim that they were caricatured in two of Shakhovskoy's lesser characters and they resent it. The witty lady's-maid, Dasha, defends the verisimilitude of Shakhovskoy's portrayal of her colleague Sasha in his play. The hypocritical and manipulative lady killer Count Folgin, the principal opponent of *The Lipetsk Spa* in *Comedy Against Comedy*, is Zagoskin's counterpart not only to Count Olgin, but to Countess Leleva as well. The male coquette is outraged by Shakhovskoy's portrayal of a female one because he recognizes in her some of his own traits.

In a device reminiscent of Pirandello, Zagoskin introduced into his play the character of a playwright, Erastov, who is writing a comedy intended to refute and replace *The Lipetsk Spa* (hence the title of Zagoskin's play). Throughout the action, Erastov is advised by various characters on how to put people similar to themselves into his play in progress and how to develop its action. At the end, it seems that the play Erastov has been writing is actually the play the audience has just seen, "his" *Comedy Against Comedy*. This may appear a twentieth-century procedure—showing the audience characters in the process of being created—but it was known and used in Zagoskin's time and earlier; for instance, Ludwig Tieck's *Puss-in-Boots* (1797) and Gioacchino Rossini's opera *Il turco in Italia* (1814), both of which use the device of bringing their putative authors onstage.

Comedy Against Comedy is not Zagoskin's best play, but it is surely his most original one. It inaugurates the basic formulaic plot on which he was to build almost all of his subsequent comedies. In play after play, he varied the same situation: a daughter or a niece is either forced to or agrees to become engaged to a man who is wrong for her. The action of the play is then devoted to matching her with a Mr. Right and to demonstrating to her or to her misguided parent or guardian why her first engagement was all wrong. In repeating this obsessive formula, Zagoskin did not show anything approaching the flair and ingenuity that Khmelnitsky could achieve in varying his often equally predictable material. Nor did Zagoskin have the verbal felicity of Khmelnitsky or even of Shakhovskoy at his best.

Nevertheless, with the aid of Shakhovskoy, understandably grateful for his defense of *The Lipetsk Spa*, Zagoskin's career as a dramatist was launched. He kept writing comedies in prose and occasionally in verse until the end of his life. He scored one of his greatest successes in 1817 with *Mr. Moneybags, or A Provincial in the Capital (G–n Bogatonov, ili Provintsial v stolitse)*. This is a highly derivative play, whose central character is patterned on Tranzhirin from Shakhovskoy's *Semi-Gentlemanly Projects*, and the rest of the characters and the action are lifted bodily from Molière's *Le bourgeois gentilhomme*. It must have owed its popularity to the much-acclaimed performances of the title role by Elisei Bobrov in St. Petersburg and by Mikhail Shchepkin in Moscow. At the actors' request, Zagoskin brought the character back in the 1820 sequel, *Moneybags in the Country, or A Surprise to Himself (Bogatonov v derevne, ili Siurpriz samomu sebe)*, which was far less successful.

Among more than a dozen plays Zagoskin wrote after *Comedy Against Comedy* only two rise above mediocrity and can still be read with interest. These are the full-length verse comedies *Amateur Theatricals (Blagorodnyi teatr, 1827)* and *The Malcontents (Nedovol'nye, 1835)*. The latter, written when no one else bothered to write Russian comedies in verse any longer, may well be, apart from historical costume drama, the last verse play of note in Russian literature prior to the advent of symbolism in the early twentieth century (Alexander Ostrovsky's anomalous *Snowmaiden* of 1873 is best passed over in silence in this context). That Zagoskin's two best plays should be in verse is odd, since memoirists tell us that he had a poor ear for meter and had to count syllables and feet laboriously when composing his verse dialogue.

Be that as it may, *Amateur Theatricals* was his biggest single success as a playwright, and deservedly so. It is a lively comedy, full of verve, bustle, and mistaken identities, about a constantly endangered performance by a group of amateur players. The basic plot is Zagoskin's usual one about the young woman be-trothed against her will to the wrong man and her efforts to get out of that engagement. But in this case, Zagoskin saves it from banality by contrasting two versions of his stock situation, one among his characters and a parallel one in the play they are rehearsing. The wrong man is an older amateur playwright named Pososhkov who has written what seems to be a Russian adaptation of Molière's *L'École des Femmes*. Pososhkov has cast himself in the role of the jealous guardian, his reluctant fiancée, Olenka, as the guardian's ward, and the young man Olenka loves as the ward's secret lover. The humor of the rehearsal scenes revolves around the failure of Pososhkov and of Olenka's uncle and aunt (in whose home the play is to be performed) to see the parallels between the situation in the play and the lives of the people who are rehearsing it. In a series of *quiproquos*, the prep-arations for the performance are repeatedly sabotaged by the defection of subordinate players and by meddling relatives or friends of the hosts or actors. The most formidable of the med-dlers is a wealthy lady named Kutermina (Mrs. Commotion) who barges in uninvited, demands seats for a whole crowd of her children and retainers, and threatens to wreck the production if not satisfied.

In this one play, Zagoskin caught some of the theatrical and verbal flair that the audiences of the time came to expect from Shakhovskoy and Khmelnitsky at their best. *Amateur Theatri-cals* became a repertoire staple in the 1830s and 1840s and was occasionally revived in later decades. *The Malcontents*, on the other hand, had a brief run in Moscow and St. Petersburg in the season 1835–36 and then lapsed into oblivion. At the time of its premiere, it was condemned, with remarkable unanimity, by Pushkin, Gogol, and Belinsky. But neither Pushkin's and Gogol's brief notices[15] nor Belinsky's detailed review[16] told the readers what *The Malcontents* actually was.

The play is, among other things, an early manifesto of Moscow Slavophilism, proclaimed in its most extreme form. It is a thinly veiled denunciation of those Russians who admired Western historical developments, such as the political thinker Peter Chaadaev, and of Russian converts to Roman Catholicism, such as Princess Zinaida Volkonskaya (there are clear references in the text to these two prominent personalities of the period). But first and foremost, *The Malcontents* is a headlong attack on Alexander Griboedov and his play *The Misfortune of Being Clever*, which by 1835 had acquired the status of a national classic.

Zagoskin's feud with Griboedov went back to 1817, the year he published a review of Griboedov's first play, *The Young Couple*. The review was eulogistic in tone, but Zagoskin found a few of the verses awkward. The touchy Griboedov was outraged. He circulated a nasty lampoon on Zagoskin, a poem called "Bargain-Basement Theater" ("Lubochnyi teatr"). Not satisfied, he caricatured Zagoskin in the protagonist of his comedy *The Student* (1817). Written in collaboration with Pavel Katenin, the comedy ridiculed Zagoskin's humble provincial origins and his desire for a career in the administrative hierarchy.

Described by memoirists as a kindly man, unable to hold a grudge, Zagoskin must have been deeply hurt by Griboedov's cruel and unprovoked attacks. After moving to Moscow in 1820

15. "O komedii Zagoskina 'Nedovol'nye.'" ("On Zagoskin's Comedy 'The Malcontents'"), a manuscript note that Pushkin intended for his journal *The Contemporary*. It was not published in his lifetime but subsequently came to be included in editions of his collected works.

Gogol's four-line notice was likewise intended for *The Contemporary*, but it too did not appear in print. See N. V. Gogol, *Polnoe sobranie sochinenii* (Leningrad, 1952), vol. 8, p. 200.

16. The review originally appeared in the journal *Molva*, no. 48–49 (1835). It has since been reprinted in numerous pre- and postrevolutionary editions of Belinsky's criticism.

and assuming an important post in the theatrical administration there, Zagoskin became closely associated with the literary group that included Aksakov, Kokoshkin, and the young Alexander Pisarev. At the time Griboedov's masterpiece burst on the literary scene in 1824, this Moscow group took exception to the play's denunciation of their city's society and cultural life.[17] Zagoskin did not participate in the literary sniping at Griboedov as his colleague Pisarev did, but he must have still been simmering inwardly about the mistreatment he had suffered earlier from this now-famous fellow playwright. Griboedov's tragic death in 1829 (see page 285) made him something of a national hero. He was by then also regarded as the author of the greatest Russian play ever written. By the time *The Malcontents* appeared, few people could have still remembered the poem and the play in which Griboedov had once ridiculed Zagoskin. To write a play in 1835 aimed at denouncing *The Misfortune of Being Clever* must have seemed so tactless that audiences and reviewers, including Pushkin and Belinsky, chose to ignore the play's principal thrust.

The Malcontents is a satirical and political comedy with no love interest. The satire is aimed at members of the upper stratum of Moscow society who dislike their native country and refuse to acknowledge that it can make progress in any area. Up to a certain point, the author's spokesman, Glinsky, who corresponds to Chatsky in Griboedov's play, goes along with the views expressed in Chatsky's "Little Frenchman from Bordeaux" monologue: he, too, denounces automatic admiration for everything foreign and the concomitant disdain for Russian traditions and institutions. But Glinsky's disagreement with the other characters is actually the reverse of Chatsky's clash with the Moscow conservatives in Griboedov. Where Chatsky lashes out at his opponents for their traditional ways, Glinsky indicts his for failing to notice that beneficial changes are possible and are happening. Glinsky's adversaries are as hidebound as Chatsky's, but the hides that bind them are vastly different.

17. It is surely significant that Aksakov's memoirs about Moscow theatrical life, which cover the period of the first appearance of *The Misfortune of Being Clever*, have nothing to say of its reception in his circle.

The principal malcontents out of the many in the play are representatives of three generations of an aristocratic Moscow family. Prince Radugin is an inept would-be statesman in retirement who regards the Russian government structure as hopeless and gets pleasure from searching in foreign newspapers for denunciations of Russian policies. His aged mother-in-law dislikes present-day Russia because it is unlike that of the past. She runs a spy network among her neighbors' servants that supplies her with the latest gossip, which she hopes to use to control other people's lives and morals. The prince's son Vladimir, a semi-literate good-for-nothing, a wastrel and a cynic, keeps complaining of the backwardness and corruption of Russian life and expressing admiration for Western freedoms and democratic procedures.

The simple plot of the play serves to expose the hypocrisy of these malcontents and of their numerous friends of the same ilk. Through a misunderstanding, Prince Radugin believes he has been offered a cabinet-level post in the government, an offer that was actually meant for the patriotic Glinsky. It turns out that the prince is quite willing to serve the system that he earlier despised and to avail himself of the power and privileges he professed to disdain. When the misunderstanding is cleared up, the prince reverts to denouncing Russia and makes plans to emigrate to Vienna or to Paris, where he thinks his and his son's abilities will be better appreciated. His speech about leaving Moscow is clearly patterned after a similar speech in Griboedov, but it has an exactly opposite meaning. Other strategically placed allusions to *The Misfortune of Being Clever* in the text of *The Malcontents* keep reminding us that much of this play is meant to be a mirror image of Griboedov's. Such characters from *The Misfortune of Being Clever* as Famusov, Molchalin, and Skalozub, who do serve the status quo, have been compressed into Zagoskin's Glinsky, a positive character, while the protesting Chatsky has been subdivided into the Radugins and their friends and given a negative significance.

Glinsky replies to Vladimir's plea for civil rights and political freedoms with an impassioned speech that equates democratic systems with anarchy, mob rule, and license to indulge in vices.

This sentiment was to be echoed in the nineteenth century by Dostoevsky and Tolstoy and in our own time by Alexander Solzhenitsyn—a persistent Russian view that deserves attention, if not necessarily agreement. *The Malcontents* did not have a ghost of a chance to debunk *The Misfortune of Being Clever*, to say nothing of competing with it. It was deservedly forgotten. But its existence does testify to the variety of ideological approaches that Russian neoclassical comedy in verse could accommodate.

Two other neoclassical verse comedies by respected literary figures were published and briefly performed in the early 1820s. Pavel Katenin's *Gossip* (*Spletni*, 1820) owed its existence to his and Griboedov's feud with Zagoskin. In 1819, Zagoskin had written a comedy called *A Fine Fellow* (*Dobryi malyi*), which was a free adaptation of *Le méchant* by Gresset (already adapted earlier by Shakhovskoy). Feeling that he could do better by Gresset than Zagoskin did, Katenin wrote *Gossip*, which was indeed more faithful to the original than Zagoskin's version. To make sure that his play was perceived as a corrective to *A Fine Fellow*, Katenin named the central character Zelsky, where in Zagoskin he was called Velsky. Zagoskin's play may have been conventional and far removed from the original, but what Katenin produced was a comedy couched in a style of stultifying monotony. If in his translations of French tragedies Katenin's diction is heavy, in comedy it attains a viscosity that makes one think of Trediakovsky, except that Katenin lacks Trediakovsky's occasional poetic flashes.

Because of Katenin's high reputation with poets and actors—he was much respected as a teacher of elocution and for his knowledge of literary theory—*Gossip* was staged in St. Petersburg with a cast of such notables as Elisei Bobrov, Iakov Briansky, Ivan Sosnitsky, and Maria Valberg and was received with respect by the literary community. The protagonist's jeremiads against society and the heroine's learning of her loved one's perfidy while she is hidden in a closet at the end of the play may have found their echoes in the great comedy by Katenin's friend Griboedov. Reading *Gossip* today one is left to wonder how anything so inept verbally and dramatically could ever have been taken seriously by Griboedov and Pushkin.

Far more attractive and accessible is Fyodor Kokoshkin's *Upbringing, or Here's Your Dowry* (*Vospitanie, ili Vot prida- noe*), published in 1824 and staged in Moscow the same year. Kokoshkin (1773–1838) was a wealthy amateur of the theater who in the 1820s tried occupying in the theater world of Moscow the same niche that Shakhovskoy had established for himself in St. Petersburg. A kindly, hospitable man (if one believes the mem- oirs of Sergei Aksakov) or a pretentious pedant (if one believes those of Peter Karatygin), Kokoshkin directed plays, taught act- ing, and turned his Moscow home into a theatrical salon, a fa- vorite gathering place for actors and playwrights. Apart from his single original play, his other works for the stage were translations.

Upbringing was a rather old-fashioned play for its time. Its theme is similar to the eighteenth-century plays about right and wrong kinds of education. Like such typical examples of that genre as Goldsmith's *She Stoops to Conquer* and Fonvizin's *The Minor*, Kokoshkin's play shows how a young person can turn out to be a decent human being or a heartless one, depending on the upbringing. Rather than contrast a well brought-up young woman with a poorly brought-up, loutish young man, as was customary in such plays, Kokoshkin made both members of the contrasting pair young women. A flighty maiden lady named Fliugerova (Miss Weathervane) found herself in charge of edu- cating her two orphaned nieces. She placed the older of the girls, Sophia, in a traditional Russian boarding school for young ladies and sent the younger one, Lia, to a *pension* run by a for- mer Parisian *figurante*, Mlle Légère.

As the play opens, the frivolous Lia is the apple of her ap- proving aunt's eye, while the sensible and dutiful Sophia has been reduced to the status of Cinderella before the ball. Fliuge- rova prevents Sophia from marrying the nice young man she loves and is trying, for selfish reasons, to sell her in marriage to an uncouth tax-farmer (*otkupshchik*), a man named Vederkin (Mr. Bucketfull), who made his fortune from a string of lowly saloons he owns. Sophia stoically submits to her aunt's tyranny, but draws the line at marrying the unpleasant Vederkin. Lia repays the aunt's kindness by intriguing against her and eloping with the mercenary young man with whom Fliugerova was foolish enough to get infatuated. After a series of disappointments and humiliations, Fliugerova comes to appreciate the value of the traditional upbringing her elder niece received.

Conventional eighteenth-century fare in many ways, *Upbringing* has the advantage of the light and natural verbal texture that Kokoshkin must have learned from the comedies of Shakhovskoy and especially of Khmelnitsky and that no eighteenth-century comedy could have achieved. Some of the characters are quite well realized, such as the comical villain Vederkin, with his refrain "А мне-то что за дело?" ("And what business is it of mine?"), used to respond to any situation to which he cannot relate. The part of Vederkin was written for the great Mikhail Shchepkin, who must have put that refrain to good use. The soubrette role of Fliugerova's maid, Dasha, is quite a departure from the usual Sashas, Dashas, and Lizas of neoclassical verse comedy, for this Dasha is a manipulator and a blackmailer who betrays the trusting Sophia. The character hardest to take is the positive heroine, Sophia, whose uncomplaining submissiveness is intended to be exemplary but ends up looking either spineless or masochistic.

Evolution of the Vaudeville

> И дельный разговор зашел про водевиль.
> Да! Водевиль есть вещь, а прочее всё гиль.
>
> Our useful talk then touched on vaudeville.
> Yes! Vaudeville's the thing and all the rest is nil.
>
> Repetilov in *The Misfortune of Being Clever*

Alexander Shakhovskoy, who was the first to introduce vaudeville comedy in Russia, once described it as a bastard child of comedy and comic opera. His first work in this form, *The Cossack Poet* (1812), still retained some similarities with Russian comic opera of the eighteenth century. It was set in a peasant milieu (in the Ukraine, rather than in Central Russia), and its plot involved a peasant couple whose plans to marry were endangered by an envious bailiff. But Shakhovskoy's subsequent vaudevilles turned to other plots and settings and depicted a variety of social groups. With the vaudevilles of Nikolai Khmelnitsky, plays of this genre moved to upper social strata, a French château or a Russian drawing room. But Khmelnitsky was able to deal with less exalted settings as well. In the previously mentioned vaudeville about Tatiana Troepolskaya (*Actors Among Themselves*), his characters are theater folk. In his *Quarantine* (1820), the action takes place at a roadside quarantine station during a cholera epidemic and the cast includes middle-class types: a Ukrainian medical inspector and his daughter, a German medical orderly, and a Polish Jew, in addition to a Russian general's wife and her nephew, an army lieutenant.

The third originator of Russian vaudeville, Alexander Pisarev (1803–28), devoted most of his brief playwriting career to works of this genre, every one of them adapted from some more or less ephemeral French original. A son of a provincial landowner, Pisarev made his literary name at the age of twenty, not with a vaudeville but with the verse comedy *Lukavin* (*Mr. Sly*), a reworking of Sheridan's *The School for Scandal*. A well-known Russian translation of this play by Ivan Muravyov-Apostol was first performed in 1793 and regularly played in both capitals in the first two decades of the nineteenth century. This translation retained the prose format and the English setting of the original. Pisarev's treatment of Sheridan typifies the procedure he applied to other foreign plays he transposed into Russian. With the utmost freedom, he not only put the play into verse and moved the action to Moscow, but he also eliminated many scenes and characters and changed the sequence of the scenes he did keep.

In this version, Sir Peter and Lady Teazle have become Russians named Dosazhaev and Dosazhaeva (Mr. and Mrs. Vexing). Sir Oliver Surface and his two nephews have three different family names, so as to accommodate Pisarev's *noms parlants* derived from Russian eighteenth-century comedy. Sir Oliver is called Zdravosudov (Mr. Goodsense), Joseph Surface is Mr. Sly of the title, and his brother Charles is Vetron (Mr.

Flighty). Lady Sneerwell is mentioned by other characters as Nasmeshkina (Mrs. Mocker), but all the scenes that involve her, her coterie, and Mrs. Candour have been eliminated. The entire tone of *Lukavin* is far closer to a comedy by Kniazhnin than to one by Sheridan, though Pisarev's language is unmistakably post-*Lipetsk Spa* in its colloquial fluency. Although his dialogue "reads smoothly," as people sometimes say about translations from languages they cannot read, neither in *Lukavin* nor in his later vaudevilles does Pisarev achieve the polish of Khmelnitsky. One area where Pisarev was truly inferior to other poets and playwrights of his time is in his careless rhymes, at times almost as inept as those in Gogol's juvenile poem *Ganz Küchelgarten*.

The talent of the young Pisarev brought him to the attention of Zagoskin and Kokoshkin, both of whom occupied influential positions in Moscow's theatrical world. He became their protégé, sharing their literary views and their prejudices. During the next five years (1823–28), he wrote a total of twenty-three plays, of which twenty were produced on the stage and twelve published in his lifetime. Sergei Aksakov, who belonged to the same literary group as Pisarev and was a close friend, left a sympathetic portrait of this playwright in his memoirs. As described by Aksakov, Pisarev's was a mind totally immersed in theater and in literary politics. A furiously combative young man, Pisarev included in the *kuplety* of his vaudevilles personal attacks on Viazemsky, Griboedov, the journalist and future playwright Nikolai Polevoy, and other targets, some of whom later commentators have found hard to identify. At the same time, Pisarev would be deeply traumatized when any criticism or adverse commentary was directed *at him*. His death at the age of twenty-five seems to have been caused by a combination of overwork and sheer vulnerability.

Pisarev's vaudevilles, which brought him considerable fame in his day, were done in collaboration with such composers as Alexander Alabiev and Alexei Verstovsky (who had also provided music for vaudevilles by Khmelnitsky). The composers' contributions could include setting the patter songs (which the actors could either sing or recite to music in a manner made familiar in our day by Rex Harrison in the Lerner and Loewe *My Fair Lady*) and supplying the overture, occasional dances, and musical accompaniment for spoken lines. A typical Pisarev vaudeville and one of his most successful was *Mr. Bustle* (*Khlopotun*), first performed in 1824, with a rather elaborate musical score by Alabiev and Verstovsky.

The title character is a fussy, meddling old bachelor Repeikin (Little Bur), on a visit to the landed estate of the friend of his youth, Radimov, whose daughter he hopes to marry. With his manic energy, Repeikin cannot resist interfering with his host's household dispositions, be they disciplining a saucy maid or choosing the recipe for preparing ducks for dinner. "Your cook is asking how to prepare them? *Whom* is he asking? Does he have the slightest notion of preparing ducks? He hasn't the slightest notion!" Repeikin shrieks, rushing off to instruct the cook he immediately assumes to be incompetent. Repeikin sends out his Great Dane to join Radimov's hounds during a wolf hunt, ruining the sport. (Alabiev provided this scene with a parodistic hunters' chorus, complete with howling horns and squealing flutes to imitate the baying of the disappointed hounds.) He undertakes to reconcile Radimov with a neighbor with whom Radimov had a land dispute. Repeikin does not realize that this neighbor and Radimov's daughter love each other. In a device familiar from other plays by Khmelnitsky and Zagoskin, Repeikin becomes his rival's confidant and, through helping him, sabotages his own marriage plans.

Pisarev's *Mr. Bustle* is a good example of the Russian vaudeville of the second and third decades of the nineteenth century. Its characters and action are those of the neoclassical comedy of the time, though a bit more exaggerated than they would appear in high comedy. The musical elements include an overture, the aforementioned hunters' chorus, and a lilting waltz sung by the impertinent maid Sasha. But the main musical ingredient is the usual *kuplety*, which in the finale bring up current topical allusions, such as the political situation between France and Russia and the recent failure of the vaudeville *Which Is the Brother and Which Is the Sister* with a text by Griboedov and Viazemsky. This topicality was a feature of Pisarev's vaudeville that was much relished by his contemporaries and that he managed to introduce into all of his vaudevilles, whether they were set in Russia, France, or the fairy-tale world of the Arabian nights.

Because of Pisarev's great facility, the haste with which he wrote, and his early death, neither *Lukavin* nor his vaudevilles can give a picture of his full potential. We get a better glimpse of the scope of his talent in the surviving fragments of the comedy in verse on which he was working when he died, *Christopher Columbus*. A prologue and a first act were all that he managed to write. They show us the Alexander Pisarev that could have been. The prologue in particular, subtitled "Several Scenes in a Pastry Shop," is remarkable for the sustained wit and grace of its dialogue and verbal texture, not otherwise typical of Pisarev. Its subject is a literary discussion between several writers and critics, briefly joined by an aristocratic lady and an oafish provincial landowner, which in its themes and preoccupations reminds one of both Gogol's *After the Play* and of the ideas on drama expressed in the letters of the young Chekhov. The sensibility is romantic rather than neoclassical, which suggests that had Pisarev lived to complete *Christopher Columbus*, he might have become a major romantic dramatist, something that Russian literature never did produce.

Sergei Danilov rightly dates the emergence of a new phase in Russian vaudeville from the 1830s and attributes it to the impact of the French "bourgeois vaudeville that developed after the July Revolution of 1830, especially the vaudeville of Scribe."[18] This is basically true, except that the long reign of Eugène Scribe on the French stage had already begun having its impact on the Russian theater by 1818, when Shakhovskoy did an adaptation of a Scribe vaudeville. The authors who wrote Russian vaudevilles between the 1830s and the 1870s were mostly professional actors or men otherwise involved in the theater business. Unlike Shakhovskoy or Khmelnitsky, they did not write high comedy or comedy in verse, specializing entirely in prose vaudeville. Topical *kuplety* remained

18. Danilov, *Ocherki*, p. 266.

the central feature of this new form of vaudeville, but instead of special scores composed by Cavos or Verstovsky, their *kuplety* were likely to be sung to melodies from operas by Donizetti or François Boieldieu or to Russian folk songs.

The most interesting and prolific of these actor-playwrights were Peter Karatygin (1805–79), the brother of the celebrated tragedian Vasily Karatygin and later the author of important memoirs; Dimitry Lensky (1805–60); and Fyodor Koni (1809–79), a theatrical journalist and the husband of the character actress Irina Koni (the famed jurist Anatoly Koni, who was a friend of Tolstoy and Chekhov, was their son). The vaudevilles of these authors and of a host of their contemporaries and imitators reflected the age of Balzac and Dickens in which they lived. Instead of the elegant salons and the landed estates of the earlier vaudeville, the genre now dealt with merchants; poor clerks of the type found in Gogol's "The Overcoat" and Dostoevsky's first novel, *Poor Folk*; provincial actors; and other urban middle- and lower-class types. Instead of the one-act format favored by Khmelnitsky and Pisarev, this new vaudeville of the age of realism was often expanded into four or five acts.

The wider social purview of Russian vaudeville from the late 1830s on can be illustrated by Karatygin's one-act *A House in the Petersburg District* (*Dom na Peterburgskoi storone*, 1838). An adaptation of a French original, which was set in Paris, the play depicts a greedy, rent-gouging St. Petersburg landlord, his exploited tenants, and a clever young man who by impersonating a master criminal protects a damsel in distress and forces the landlord to mend his ways. The atmosphere is closer to Dostoevsky's *Crime and Punishment* than to any musical comedy, happy ending or not. Fyodor Koni's *St. Petersburg Apartments* (*Peterburgskie kvartiry*, 1840), adapted from an obscure German play, is not quite so grim. Subtitled "A Vaudeville Comedy in 5 Apartments" (*v 5 kvartirakh*; a humorless Soviet editor changed this to *v 5 kartinakh*, i.e., "in 5 tableaux" [19]) the play takes the audience on a

---

19. *Russkii vodevil'*, ed. V. V. Uspensky (Leningrad-Moscow, 1959), p. 231. This collection offers a representative cross section of both good and mediocre

tour of an interesting cross section of the St. Petersburg populace by using the plot device of a recently promoted government
clerk and his wife looking for a new apartment.

Together with the apartment-hunting couple, we visit the
residences of the following characters: an operatic prima donna, who plans to give up her career in order to marry a wealthy
Englishman named Sir Johndog and who has to hide her im-
pecunious ex-lover in a cupboard from the prospective new
tenants; a plebeian *nouveau riche* couple who hope to buy for
their daughter a noble husband with their money (the intended
groom is locked up in the singer's cupboard); a mendacious
journalist, who blackmails people for goods and services by
threats of adverse publicity; and finally, the prima donna's ex-
lover, who, it turns out, did not want the rich bride and is in
love with the apartment hunters' own nubile daughter. The
complex intrigue and unexpected developments are adroitly
handled by Koni in a manner clearly derived from Scribe. The
play must have been enormously entertaining.

But for all its gains in realism, this later form of vaudeville
seldom attained the quality of the two plays just discussed.
Most of it was jerry-built and obvious. We could dismiss it as
inferior to the earlier variety, as exemplified by Shakhovskoy
and Khmelnitsky, were it not for the fact that it was the
realistic variety of vaudeville that produced the masterpiece
of this genre, which is also one of the best-loved Russian plays
of all time: Dimitry Lensky's five-act vaudeville *Lev Gurych
Sinichkin*. Premiered in Moscow in the fall of 1839, it has
never left the stages of Russian theaters since. In 1956 it was
made into a film with a screenplay by the Soviet playwrights
Nikolai Erdman (the author of *Mandate* and *Suicide*) and Mikhail Volpin. Derived from the vaudeville *Le père de la débu-
tante* by Téaulon and Bayard, which made no splash in its native France and was promptly forgotten there, Lensky's play is
a suspenseful, fast-paced comedy about the efforts of an aged
provincial actor to secure a stage debut for his talented young
daughter.

Russian nineteenth-century vaudevilles. A more recent volume, *Russkii vodevil'*,
ed. N. Shantarenkov (Moscow, 1970), provides a far less interesting selection.

Lev Gurych Sinichkin has been involved with provincial theaters for thirty-seven years. His days of glory are long in the past, when he and his late wife used to ravish provincial audiences in Kniazhnin's *Dido* and Ozerov's *Oedipus in Athens.* In his old age, he still hangs around provincial theaters in any capacity he can—as a kettle drummer in the orchestra or as a ticket taker, if need be. But he has trained his stagestruck daughter Liza and taught her everything he knows about the art they both love. When an ill-tempered leading lady of the local theater, with whom Liza has been friendly, blocks her chances of entering the municipal acting company, Sinichkin cooks up a complicated intrigue to get Liza to step into this actress's part in an opening of a new play.

This plot is familiar enough—a stock situation of backstage drama of the nineteenth century, popularized again in the Busby Berkeley musicals of the 1930s (except that Lensky omits any love interest). But the father and daughter are surrounded by a marvelous gallery of vividly depicted provincial theatrical types of the period. Among them are a resourceful backwoods impresario, willing to present any play or performer as long as they sell tickets; a self-enamored playwright whose new play, *Pizarro in Peru with His Spaniards*, described as "a drama with songs and dances," is all too clearly a plagiarism of Kotzebue's *The Sun Virgin*, very popular at the time in the Russian provinces; a wealthy young landowner who is determined to prevent Liza's debut so that he can make her his concubine; an aged aristocratic roué, who keeps young actresses in chocolates and pin money and hopes to add Liza to his platonic harem; and prompters, carpenters, chorus girls, and other backstage folk, including a waiter from a nearby cafe who doubles as a ticket scalper. The hilarious fifth-act climax occurs when both the leading lady and Liza appear backstage in their Peruvian sun priestess costumes, ready to go on as the play's heroine. The desperate Sinichkin has to resort to physical violence (e.g., he causes people to fall through trapdoors) to make sure that his daughter's debut takes place.

Dated in some of its allusions (such as when the characters refer to the actors and actresses who were actually playing their parts on the original opening night) and a bit frayed around the edges, *Lev Gurych Sinichkin* is still a delightful, bouncy play, written with tremendous verve and theatrical know-how. Its vaudeville format and its apparently dated score (the work of a little-known composer, N. I. Poliakov) have prevented it from becoming exportable. Still, a good idiomatic translation might yet make it performable in a foreign country, a claim that one cannot make for many other Russian plays of the first half of the nineteenth century except for those of Gogol.[20]

In its best examples, vaudeville is the genre that forms a bridge between Russian neoclassical and realist drama. Situations and characters from it keep turning up in Russian plays of the second half of the nineteenth and the early twentieth century. Turgenev's *It Breaks Where It Is Thinnest* and *A Provincial Lady* may have had Musset's proverb plays as their inspiration, but they owe both their inner strength and their seeming fragility to the comedies and vaudevilles of Nikolai Khmelnitsky. The maid Tanya, who is the protagonist of Tolstoy's play *The Fruits of Enlightenment*, is a typical Shakhovskoy or Khmelnitsky soubrette. The matchmaking scene in Koni's *St. Petersburg Apartments* was later reflected in Chekhov's *The Wedding*, which in turn provided the precedent for the matchmaking and wedding scenes of Mayakovsky's *The Bedbug*. Chekhov's old actor in *The Swan Song* may well be a later edition of Lev Gurych Sinichkin, one who didn't happen to have a daughter. Chekhov's *The Bear* is in essence a Khmelnitsky or Pisarev vaudeville, deprived of music and removed to a later part of the same century.

20. Just as the success of Fonvizin's *The Minor* sprouted a host of sequels by other playwrights, the popularity of *Lev Gurych Sinichkin* led several forgettable authors of vaudevilles to appropriate the title character for their own plays. In the 1840s, we find in the repertoire of the Moscow and St. Petersburg theaters such titles as *Gury Lvovich Sinichkin* (who must be Sinichkin's son, though none was mentioned in Lensky's play); *Lev Gurych and Uliana Osipovna Sinichkin* (she must have been Sinichkin's wife, with whom he formed an acting team in his youth); and *Lev Gurych Sinichkin and Makar Alexeyevich Gubkin, Provincial Actors*.

❦ IX ❦

Griboedov,
or The Fortune
of Being Clever

Author of a play that the Russians place among the supreme
masterpieces of their literature, Alexander Griboedov (1794–
1829) remains almost totally unknown outside Russian culture.
The play is *Gore ot uma*, a title so idiomatic that generations
of Russian children have needed to have it explained before
grasping the meaning. The first translator of the play into
English, one Nicholas Bernardaky (his version was published
in London in 1857), in what must have been a fit of despair,
simply transcribed the Russian title into Latin letters. The
usual English title, *The Misfortune of Being Clever*, was devised by the author of one of the best translations, W. S. Pring
(London, 1914). Although possibly patterned on Oscar Wilde's
The Importance of Being Earnest, this title is preferable to
such later tries as *Woe from Wit* and *Brains Hurt*. In the discussion that follows, it will be compressed into *TMoBC*, to save
space.

Defying all translators, the text of the play is as idiomatic
as the title. A blend of uproarious humor and hauntingly subtle verbal music in the original Russian, *TMoBC* is the ultimate proof that the art of literature is on its basic level the art
of words. Griboedov's art is addressed to those who can understand his words instantly in all their finest shadings and ambi-

guities. *Some* knowledge of Russian is no help at all: students at Western universities who know enough of the language to read Turgenev or Akhmatova in the original shrug their shoulders at lines and passages in Griboedov that make native speakers gasp in awed wonder or slap their thighs in mirth. Nor has there yet been a translation into any language that can convey to people in other countries why this play is such a miracle of wit and verbal precision, though the Polish one by Julian Tuwim came close.

Griboedov was born in Moscow into the family of a retired army officer. Home life during his childhood was dominated by his mother, a matriarch with a will of iron who lorded it equally over her husband, children, and serfs. It was a childhood remarkably similar to those of two other outstanding nineteenth-century Russian writers, the novelist and playwright Ivan Turgenev and the novelist and satirist Mikhail Saltykov-Shchedrin. All three were scarred emotionally by maternal tyranny experienced at an early age, and all three, simplistic though it may sound, depicted in their writings situations where strong, energetic women subjugate and oppress the men in their lives. Moreover, all three writers remained outwardly dutiful, loving sons, expressing their filial rebellion only in their literary work.

Griboedov partly escaped from his mother's tutelage when he passed the entrance examinations and enrolled at Moscow University at the age of twelve. He thus beat the record set among Russian playwrights by Denis Fonvizin, who had entered the same university at fourteen. By the time he was fourteen, Griboedov obtained his degree in literary studies, whereupon he promptly enrolled in the law school of the same institution and at sixteen added a law degree to his laurels. Rather than return home, he stayed at the university for further studies in science and mathematics. The Napoleonic invasion of 1812 enabled him to put a distance between himself and his mother. He joined the army and stayed in it until 1816. A visit to St. Petersburg in 1814 brought him the acquaintance and eventually the friendship of Khmelnitsky, Katenin, and Shakhovskoy. Among the literary camps of the time, he chose the Archaist one.

After leaving the army, Griboedov settled in St. Petersburg, where he had obtained a position with the Ministry of Foreign Affairs. This was the beginning of a diplomatic career, which he was to pursue to the end of his life. At Shakhovskoy's instigation, Griboedov did a Russian adaptation of a brief French comedy *Le secret du ménage* by Creuzé de Lesser. Called *The Young Couple* (*Molodye suprugi*), it was performed in St. Petersburg in September 1815 as a curtain raiser for a play that starred Ekaterina Semyonova's younger sister Nymphodora, an actress who specialized in musical comedy and light opera. Because it was a benefit performance in honor of Nymphodora, who was to receive the proceeds, the reigning star of the Russian stage agreed to help her sister out by appearing in *The Young Couple*. She was partnered by the two most popular young leading men of the day, Ivan Sosnitsky and Iakov Briansky.

It is highly instructive to compare the language and verse of *The Young Couple*, written before Griboedov was exposed to either *The Lipetsk Spa* or Khmelnitsky's *The Chatterbox*, with the scenes Griboedov wrote two years later for *Within the Family, or The Married Fiancée*, his very successful collaboration with Shakhovskoy and Khmelnitsky. The dialogue of *The Young Couple* is lively, but it is also a faceless compendium of eighteenth-century speech mannerisms. In his few scenes of *The Married Fiancée*, Griboedov displays a new verve and fluency that he could have learned only from the comedies his two collaborators had produced during the two preceding seasons.

The contribution to *The Married Fiancée* is the only item in Griboedov's early dramatic output that points toward the future author of *TMoBC* and deserves to be mentioned with it. The rest of the early plays are amateurish and would never have been remembered or reprinted had Griboedov not been involved in their authorship. All are collaborations with others. The prose comedy *The Student*, written with Pavel Katenin in 1817 (but not published or performed until the end of the nineteenth century) is, as already mentioned, a merciless lampoon of Mikhail Zagoskin. In typical Archaist fashion, the play also ridicules the sentimentalists and romantics, incorporating into its dialogue burlesqued citations from Karamzin, Zhukovsky, and Batiushkov. The humor is crude and cruel and the satire jejune. The translation of *Les fausses infidélités* by Nicolas Thomas Barthe was done in 1818 together with Griboedov's friend Andrei Zhandr (or Jandre or Gendre) and was called *Pretended Infidelity (Pritvornaia nevernost')*. Literary scholars in search for antecedents of *TMoBC* have on occasion tried comparing characters from this play with those of Griboedov's masterpiece, with results that are, at best, unconvincing.

Griboedov's collaboration with Prince Peter Viazemsky in 1823 on the libretto of the vaudeville opera *Which Is the Brother and Which Is the Sister; or, Deception After Deception (Kto brat, kto sestra, ili Obman za obmanom)* is indicative of how tenuous the battle lines between the Archaists and their one-time opponents had become by the 1820s. Viazemsky had been the main instigator of the press campaign against *The Lipetsk Spa* in 1815. By the end of the decade, he had emerged as the leading theoretician of Russian romanticism, a movement that Griboedov had denounced in *The Student* and had mocked in the first act of *TMoBC* (much of which was already completed by 1823). Yet, neither Viazemsky nor Griboedov thought it odd that, during the latter's visit to Moscow, Fyodor Kokoshkin proposed that they collaborate on a vaudeville. As Viazemsky tells it in his memoirs, he took care of the sung portions, while Griboedov was responsible for most of the prose dialogue.

Which Is the Brother . . . is a *vaudeville en travesti*, a form popular at the time in France, in which the main point was to provide a shapely young actress with a chance to appear in male attire and show off her legs. Shakhovskoy had introduced it to Russia in 1821, with his vaudeville adapted from Scribe, *The Woman Colonel (Zhenshchina-polkovnik)*. In the late 1830s the short-lived Varvara Asenkova had a meteoric career, appearing *en travesti* in roles especially written for her, which her colleague and admirer Shchepkin termed "hermaphroditic." In line with Viazemsky's well-attested Polonophilia, the action was set at a postal relay station in Poland. A young Polish noblewoman, Julia, married to a Russian officer, dons a uniform and pretends to be her own brother in order to cure her husband's brother of his prejudices against women and Poles. Other principal characters are an appealing Polish stationmaster and his two seductive daughters. The composer Verstovsky took advantage of the locale to introduce Polish dance rhythms, such as the polonaise and the mazurka, into his score, which is couched in an *opéra comique* rather than a vaudeville format.

Despite lively situations and attractive music, the Moscow premiere of *Which Is the Brother* . . . was a resounding failure. It was dropped from the repertoire after four performances and never revived. In St. Petersburg it lasted for two performances only. Among the reasons advanced for the poor reception are the inability of the actress who played Julia to sing and the backstage intrigues of Griboedov's Moscow enemies, Zagoskin and especially Alexander Pisarev, who, as mentioned, crowed over the flop in the *kuplety* of his own *Mr. Bustle*, premiered the same year. But we should note that, as Viazemsky wrote, "on the opening night, the play was slowed down and so to speak congealed by the sluggish performances of the actors, many of whom appeared in it unwillingly. And then it should be understood that the audience listened unwillingly."[1] This comment gives us reason to suspect that the play's plea for Russo-Polish amity and its implicit sermon against nationalistic prejudices were not congenial to either the actors or the audience. The stereotypical depiction of Poles as ridiculous, pretentious, or haughty that remained standard in Russian literature and drama from Pushkin's *Boris Godunov*, Gogol's "Taras Bulba," and Zagoskin's *Iury Miloslavsky* all the way to Dostoevsky and the young Chekhov would have been far closer to their expectations. In the twentieth century, Soviet musicologists have rediscovered Verstovsky's score for *Which Is the Brother* . . . and have asserted its artistic importance.[2]

The status of a literary celebrity that Griboedov gradually acquired between 1815 and around 1823 could not have been due to the value of his early plays, since they do not come up to

1. *A. S. Griboedov v vospominaniiakh sovremennikov*, ed. S. A. Fomichev, (Moscow, 1980), p. 82.

2. See A. Gozenpud, *Muzykal'nyi teatr v Rossii* (Leningrad, 1959), pp. 583–86. Verstovsky's score was first published in a piano arrangement by the State Music Publishing House (Moscow-Leningrad, 1949).

the level of Khmelnitsky's or even Zagoskin's. But he was known for his brilliance in many fields: a dazzling conversationalist, a pianist and composer (several of his waltzes for piano were published), a distinguished diplomat (he was appointed the first secretary of the Russian diplomatic mission to Persia and spent the years 1818–22 in Teheran and in the Caucasus), and a participant in a celebrated four-party duel (*partie carrée*) over the famed dancer Istomina that began in St. Petersburg and ended one year later in Tbilisi in Georgia. There was also in Griboedov a mean, bilious streak that many knew, as expressed in his unprovoked literary vendetta against Zagoskin and the equally unprovoked bedevilment of the playwright Vasily Fyodorov, author of the once popular dramatization of Karamzin's "Poor Liza," on an atrocious occasion remembered and recorded by Peter Karatygin and Ivan Sosnitsky.[3]

Though he may have had an idea for a full-length satirical comedy about a young man's conflict with Moscow society as early as 1812, Griboedov began actual work on what later became *TMoBC* only after he saw the performances of *The Lipetsk Spa* and Khmelnitsky's *The Chatterbox*. His collaboration with Shakhovskoy and Khmelnitsky on *The Married Fiancée* helped Griboedov discover the language and the style for his play. The appearance of Shakhovskoy's *Don't Listen* . . . in 1818 taught him the comedic use of iambic lines of varied length, a meter previously reserved for fables and opera libretti.[4] There was an earlier version, subsequently discarded, called *Gore umu* (roughly, *Woe to Wit*). The first two acts of the final version were completed in the Caucasus early in 1823; the entire play was ready by the fall of the next year, though the author kept making last minute changes as late as 1828.

3. P. A. Karatygin, *Zapiski* (Leningrad, 1929), vol. 1, pp. 222–24 (reprinted in *A. S. Griboedov v vospominaniiakh*, pp. 108–9). Sosnitsky's recollection of the same incident, which took place during Griboedov's reading of his play at the home of Nikolai Khmelnitsky, was recorded by Dimitry Smirnov in "K biografii Griboedova," *Istoricheskii vestnik* (St. Petersburg) 116 (1909): 157–58 (reprinted in *A. S. Griboedov v vospominaniiakh*, pp. 251–53).

4. There is a fine study of the versification of *TMoBC* and its antecedents: Boris Tomashevsky, "Stikh 'Goria ot uma,'" in *Russkie klassiki i teatr* (Moscow-Leningrad, 1947).

By that time it had already excited an unprecedented interest in literary and theatrical circles because portions of it were making the rounds in manuscript.

TMoBC is a unique instance of a play that was acclaimed as a masterpiece even before it was completed. Surveying the literary scene of 1824, Alexander Bestuzhev-Marlinsky declared this "manuscript comedy" a phenomenon not seen since Fonvizin's *The Minor*, up to that time by general accord regarded as the greatest Russian play. With admirable prescience, Bestuzhev predicted that many would find the new play offensive for its disregard of dramatic rules but that eventually "prejudices shall melt and posterity will value this comedy as it deserves and place it among the foremost achievements of our nation."[5]

Before the arrangements for the publication and the performance of the play could be completed, there came the death of Alexander I, followed by the events of December 14, 1824, which went down in history as the Decembrist Rebellion. Griboedov must have been aware of the secret political societies that fomented the rebellion, since he satirized them in the Repetilov scene of Act IV of *TMoBC*. He knew some of the ringleaders and had good friends among the rank-and-file participants such as Bestuzhev-Marlinsky and Küchelbecker. He may even have sympathized with some of the rebellion's demands, such as replacing the tsarist autocracy with a constitutional monarchy, achieving a greater freedom of the press, and, possibly, abolishing serfdom. But he was never recruited into any of the Decembrist societies, nor did he know anything about their plans to rebel.[6] He was nevertheless implicated by

5. *Poliarnaia zvezda* facsimile ed. (Moscow, 1960), p. 496.

6. Literature on Griboedov's possible involvement in the Decembrist conspiracy may well exceed in volume the literature devoted to the study of his great play. The record of the government's investigation of the matter and the report of the head of the secret political police, which fully exonerates Griboedov of all complicity, are reprinted in *A. S. Griboedov v vospominaniiakh*, pp. 272–91. But because the current official view is that Griboedov must have been a Decembrist, annotations to this volume persistently cast doubt on the actual historical evidence and give credence to third-hand testimony and rumors that support Griboedov's involvement.

one of the participants, arrested in the Caucasus, and brought back to St. Petersburg for investigation. After several months of confinement and interrogation (during which, however, he was allowed to visit friends, stroll alone in public gardens, and dine at good restaurants),[7] Griboedov was cleared of all charges. He was paid an indemnity for his arrest, was given a promotion in the diplomatic service, and was introduced to the new tsar, Nicholas I.

The rest of Griboedov's biography belongs to diplomatic rather than literary history. *TMoBC* was the last work he completed. He left sketches for several tragedies he intended to write, such as *Georgian Night*, which combines features of Crébillon with the nineteenth-century romantic melodrama of revenge in the manner of Verdi's *Il trovatore*. These sketches indicate that like his fellow junior Archaists, Katenin and Küchelbecker, Griboedov was moving toward a more romantic concept of drama. But his last years were primarily absorbed by his diplomatic career, which was advancing rapidly and, as it turned out, tragically. A few months after marrying the sixteen-year-old Georgian princess Nina Chavchavadze, Griboedov departed for Teheran to negotiate the peace terms for the recently concluded Russo-Persian war.

One of the most contentious issues during the negotiations was the fate of women (Georgians, Armenians, and one or two Germans) who claimed Russian citizenship and who were captured during the war and placed against their will in Persian harems. Griboedov's firm insistence that these women be released and allowed to return to their families was perceived by the clergy as an outrage against Moslem religion and customs. In a series of events eerily reminiscent of the scenes that were telecast from Teheran at the end of the 1970s, mobs incited by the mullahs first demonstrated outside the Russian embassy, then stormed it and massacred Griboedov and his bodyguards. On hearing the news, his pregnant wife suffered a miscarriage.[8]

7. Recollections of Andrei Zhandr, as recorded by Dimitry Smirnov in *Istoricheskii vestnik* 115 (1909):1053–55 (reprinted in *A. S. Griboedov v vospominaniiakh*, pp. 221–22.

8. The last years of Griboedov's life are the subject of Iury Tynianov's

Griboedov's body was brought back to Georgia in an ox-cart. Alexander Pushkin, who was there visiting his brother in the army, encountered the cart on a mountain road. He later described his feelings on that unforeseen occasion in his travelogue *Journey to Erzerum*. Pushkin thought Griboedov's death was "instantaneous and beautiful"—beautiful because it came when he was at the height of his diplomatic career, had just met and married the woman who was the one love of his life, and had already given his country a comedy that "had produced an indescribable effect and in one stroke placed him among our foremost poets." And indeed, although the play had not yet been published or performed at the time of its author's death, his countrymen knew that in Griboedov they had lost a playwright of genius.

The Misfortune of Being Clever

> Mozart was a traditionalist; it did not occur to him to do something new at all costs. He wanted to do it not differently, but better.
>
> Alfred Einstein

In January of 1825, Alexander Pushkin first read *TMoBC* in a manuscript copy. In his letters of the same month to Alexander Bestuzhev and Viazemsky he offered the most valid critique this play ever received (of which more later). One thing he felt safe to predict was that "one half of the play's lines will become proverbs" (letter to Bestuzhev dating from the end of January 1825). Pushkin went on to make this a self-fulfilling prophecy by incorporating lines from *TMoBC* into a later chapter of *Eugene Onegin* and the novella "The Snow-storm." In this, he was one of the first in a never-ending line. References to *TMoBC* permeate Russian language and literature. *Winged Words*, a highly useful compilation by Nikolai and Maria Ashukin of literary quotations that have become

---

thoroughly researched *biographie romancée, Smert' Vazir Mukhtara*. It is available in English under the title *Death and Diplomacy in Persia*, translated by Alec Brown (London, 1938).

standard Russian expressions,[9] lists sixty such instances from *TMoBC*. With this one four-act comedy, Griboedov contributed as many popular sayings to the language as Gogol did with the fourteen volumes of his complete collected works. He is behind Pushkin (ninety-nine entries culled from ten volumes of writing). But, line for line, Griboedov appears to be the champion.

Quotations from *TMoBC* are ubiquitous. One finds them in Dostoevsky's novels and in the stories and personal letters of Chekhov. Tsvetaeva and Pasternak incorporated them into their poems. Nabokov played variations on themes by Griboedov in *Ada*. The futurist poet Velimir Khlebnikov's play *Marquise Desaix* (1909) is a cubistic deformation of *TMoBC*. Lenin cited *TMoBC* ceaselessly in his essays and speeches, and various Soviet delegates at the United Nations do the same, often stumping their interpreters. Just as speakers of English may cite Shakespeare without realizing it, Russians mistake Griboedov's lines for popular clichés. An early translator of *Nicholas Nickleby* introduced a line or two from *TMoBC* into Dickens, leading a critic to object that those Londoners were not likely to have read Griboedov. Igor Stravinsky, who knew the play well and loved it, cited a line in his dialogues with Robert Craft, identifying it only as a popular Russian saying.

Looking again at this text, familiar since the age of ten, after having taught it in classes for two decades and having recently reread pertinent nineteenth- and twentieth-century criticism, I feel stumped. How to see it with a fresh eye, how to disregard the accretions of all the well-meaning misreadings, the misguided denunciations, the short-sighted eulogies? How to avoid repeating the harsh exegeses of Pushkin and Chekhov and also not take the eclectic path of Jean Bonamour, the author of the most detailed, honest, and perceptive study of Griboedov's life and work so far done in any language, vitiated only by the author's willingness to accept *all* viewpoints?[10] One

9. N. S. Ashukin and M. G. Ashukina, *Krylatye slova* (Moscow, 1966). Griboedov entries are tabulated in the index, p. 772.

10. Jean Bonamour, *A. S. Griboedov et la vie littéraire de son temps* (Paris, 1965).

possibility would be to examine *TMoBC* against the background of other Russian verse comedies of its time, which is surely how its contemporaries must have viewed it.

Let us consider a verse comedy written in the first quarter of the nineteenth century. It begins with a Russian nobleman of great moral integrity and uncompromising principles arriving at dawn, after a period of traveling, to a place where there are some people to whom he had felt close earlier. Among them there is a young woman with an independent turn of mind, in whom the traveler had expected to find a friend and ally. But their intentions turn out to be at cross-purposes, and much of the play is taken up with a developing moral duel between these two characters. After some group scenes that feature an array of satirically depicted minor characters, there is a nocturnal confrontation, in which the young woman is shown the error of her ways.

No, this is not an outline of *TMoBC*, though it could have been. It is a summary of the action of Shakhovskoy's *The Lipetsk Spa*, a play without which we would not have had *TMoBC*, a summary that seeks to point out the structural similarities of these two plays, which one might not notice at first glance. The characters involved in the situations mentioned are admittedly quite dissimilar in the two plays. The traveler who barges in at dawn into the home in which the action of *TMoBC* is set is the central character, Alexander Chatsky. The name, spelled Chadsky in early drafts, is derived from *chad*, "fumes," and suggests both that the man fumes a lot and that his head is in a daze. He is a young nobleman who has been absent from Moscow for three years, during which time, as we later learn, he has been a protégé of some cabinet ministers in St. Petersburg who then dropped him; has served in the army; has taken a cure at a spa; and has traveled extensively in the West (the sequence of all these events is never made clear). The home he enters is the Moscow residence of Pavel Famusov, a friend of Chatsky's late father. Famusov (the name is usually derived from the Latin *fama*, though Iury Tynianov has suggested that it comes from the English word "famous" pronounced as if it were French) is a socially prominent widower, an official in charge of the bureau of archives and the father of a strong-willed and beautiful daughter, Sophia.

During Chatsky's previous stay in Moscow, he and Sophia were attracted to each other, though even then she felt uncomfortable with his satirical and caustic turn of mind. Since Chatsky's departure, Sophia has started a platonic and sentimentalist relationship with her father's live-in secretary Molchalin (Mr. Silent), expressed in nocturnal trysts, during which they sigh, hold hands, and play duets on the flute and piano. Famusov, unaware of Sophia's relationship with Molchalin, hopes to marry her off to a wealthy army officer, Colonel Skalozub (Toothygrin). Such is the *Vorgeschichte*, about which the audience learns only gradually.

At the first curtain, we find Sophia's maid Liza sleepily guarding Sophia's door during one of the nocturnal flute and piano duets. When Sophia and Molchalin are almost caught by her father, she fobs him off by making up a dream she supposedly had—a satire on romantic ballads, complete with flowery meadows, ghosts, and monsters. All these features—beginning the play at dawn so as to accommodate the unity of time; a heroine named Sophia (just as in Fonvizin, Kapnist, and Kokoshkin, among many others); her maid named Liza (common in Khmelnitsky, but going back to the innumerable saucy Lisettes in Marivaux, Gresset, and Piron); the satire of sentimentalism in the depiction of Sophia's rendezvous with Molchalin, where sentimentalist attitudes are equated with insincerity, just as they were in *The Lipetsk Spa*; and the parody of a romantic ballad in Sophia's recital of her dream—are the very stuff of Russian neoclassical comedies of the second decade of the nineteenth century. What places this play above all these precedents is Griboedov's magnificent verbal music, the likes of which were to be heard only two more times in Russian verse drama—in 1830 with Pushkin's *The Stone Guest* and *Mozart and Salieri* and in 1906–7 with Blok's *The Fairgrounds Booth* and *The Incognita*. In the richness of his verbal melody, Griboedov is an equal of Pushkin and Blok. In the pithy precision of his epigrammatic wit, he has never been equaled, not even by Pushkin.

Alexander Chatsky rushes in at the end of Act I to throw himself at Sophia's feet (he had not communicated with her or her father for three years) and offers his love. The years of absence have enhanced the quality he most admires in her, her beauty, and the quality she least admires in him, his causticity. In Act II, we are treated to Chatsky's political debate with the old Famusov. Recalling his youth in the reign of Catherine the Great, Famusov eulogizes servility and kowtowing to those in authority for the sake of one's career. Chatsky bursts out into a ringing denunciation of the bad old days and praises the current reign of Alexander I in which courtiers and civil servants no longer need to grovel. This strikes Famusov as revolutionary propaganda. He works himself into such an hysterical state that he mistakes the appearance of a servant announcing a visitor for the beginning of a serf rebellion.

Chatsky's confrontations with Sophia at the end of Act I and with her father at the beginning of Act II unleash the two parallel conflicts of the play—the amorous and the political. The love relationships in the play are hopelessly at cross-purposes from the very beginning, and they stay so to the end. With an astounding lack of perception, Chatsky keeps offering his love to Sophia, who after an initial cordial welcome, treats him with hostility and scorn. After she replies to his Act I offer to go through fire to prove his love with "Yes, it will be good if you burn up, but what if not?" and tells him in Act II that she can't bear the sight of him, he still opens Act III with a paraphrase of Countess Leleva's line from *The Lipetsk Spa*: "I'll wait for her and compel from her a confession: whom does she, finally, love?" When she tells him explicitly that she loves Molchalin, Chatsky refuses to believe her. He still clings to his hope until just before the final denouement.

Sophia's love for Molchalin is equally misguided. A poor and undistinguished young man from the provinces, Molchalin is interested only in his career. Outwardly meek and submissive, inwardly ambitious, he will do anything to curry favor, from playing cards with influential old ladies to joining his boss's daughter in her sentimentalist emotional games in the hope that this will aid his advancement. Bored with Sophia,

Molchalin is attracted to her maid Liza, who resists his over-
tures. Most of Sophia's actions during the first three acts are
motivated by her urge to protect her relationship with Molchalin from Chatsky's scoffing.

Chatsky's political conflict with Famusov and his other
Moscow friends is developed in Acts II and III. Famusov likes
Moscow and its society just as they are. Chatsky denounces
careerism, servility, and respect for rank and uniform, championing the right of young men to travel and to devote themselves to the arts and sciences rather than to civil service. These
themes are broadened in Act III, in which a xenophobic theme
is added: the folly of uncritical importation of fashions from
France and Germany, the ruinous effect of the Westernizing reforms of Peter the Great, and the desirability of cultural isola-
tion as practiced by the Chinese. Chatsky's denunciations are
as torrential as they are often inconsistent: after berating the
military, he advises his friend Platon Gorich to reenlist in the
army; and after attacking Moscow for its backwardness and iso-
lation, he wants it to be cut off from all new or foreign trends.

Act III shows an evening party at Famusov's home and
brings on a whole gallery of unforgettable minor characters.
Among them are the aforementioned Platon Gorich (*gorech'*
means bitterness), once Chatsky's comrade-in-arms, now married to Sophia's friend Natalia, who has subjugated and emascu-
lated him with her smothering care and who drags him to
parties against his will; the acid-tongued spinster Countess Khryumina, Jr. (the name suggests the grunting of a pig), who has
failed to land a husband and drags her deaf and decrepit grandmother to parties by way of substitute; the aged Prince Tugoukhovsky (Hard-of-Hearing), reduced by his domineering
spouse to near silence (his spoken lines consist of a series of
throat clearings), but still accompanying her and their six
daughters to social functions in the hope of finding some husbands for them; and the card sharp and swindler Zagoretsky
(Mr. Catch-Fire), universally despised but received everywhere
because he supplies the women with hard-to-get tickets, puppies,
blackamoor slaves, and other such favors.

It is in Act III that the two cardinal themes of *TMoBC*

are fully sounded, themes that Russian criticism, in its compulsive search for familiar denunciations of autocracy or serfdom, has so far overlooked: gerontophobia and misogyny. Granted that foolish old men (and women) have been the mainstay of satiric comedy since ancient times, is there any other play that shows them as the group that causes most of society's problems? A careful reading of the text leaves no doubt that for Chatsky (and, clearly, for Griboedov) what is really wrong with Moscow is that it is run by corrupt old men ("the older the worse") and by domineering women of all ages. Moreover, there is no indication in *TMoBC* that this situation obtains in St. Petersburg or the rest of Russia. All of Chatsky's speeches that identify old age with corruption—beginning with his famous Act II monologue "And who are the judges?"—are quite specifically aimed at the situation in Moscow (which accounts for the hostility to *TMoBC* by Moscow writers, such as Pisarev and Aksakov).

The trouble with the aged in *TMoBC* is that they shut out the modern world and still see things in eighteenth-century terms. They are physically deaf, as in the funny but hideously cruel scene between Countess Khryumina, Sr., who speaks but cannot hear, and Prince Tugoukhovsky, who tries to communicate with her though he can neither speak nor hear. Or, if they retain their hearing, they cover their ears so as not to hear the truth, as Famusov does in Act II when Chatsky tries to explain his viewpoint. The aged are also obscurantist and hypocritical: Famusov brags about his monastic behavior a few minutes after making a pass at his daughter's maid. In Act II, we learn that he had managed to get a doctor's widow pregnant. In Act III, Famusov and a chorus of elderly women proclaim their hostility to all advances in education and higher learning.

Misogyny in *TMoBC* is so pervasive and so authentically Strindbergian, that one can only wonder why, except for Jean Bonamour, who gingerly touched upon this theme in his book, it has been so totally overlooked in Griboedov criticism. In Famusov's Act II eulogy to the city of Moscow and its society, we hear that women are the real power in the city:

А дамы? — сунься кто, попробуй овладей
Судьи всему, везде, над ними нет судей;
. . . .
Скомандовать велите перед фрунтом!
Присутствовать пошлите их в Сенат!

And the ladies? Let anyone just try and control them.
They judge everything, everywhere; there are no judges over
them.

. . . .

Let them command the military drills!
Send them to legislate in the Senate!

Throughout the rest of the play we get repeated intimations
that this is a society where women are in charge. Molchalin
discusses with Chatsky a certain Tatiana Iurievna, a wealthy
lady who can make or break anyone's career. In the play's last
line, Famusov expresses his fear of the opinion of the hitherto
unmentioned Princess Maria Alexevna. After hearing of all
those female opinion makers and power brokers, we get to meet
one of them in person in Acts III and IV. This is Sophia's
maternal aunt Anfisa Khlyostova (something like Mrs. Spank-
ing), a gossipy, superstitious woman who demands and gets the
highest respect from everyone.

Readers and audiences would better appreciate Khlyostova's majestic first entrance if they remembered (they rarely
do) the story Liza told about her early in Act I: When a young
Frenchman she was keeping escaped from her home, Khlyostova forgot in her chagrin to touch up her hair and from this
point on became officially grey. This incident turns out to be
indicative of the only form of relationship between the sexes
that we ever get to see in *TMoBC*. Platon Gorich and the old
Prince Tugoukhovsky are their wives' slaves. "My husband is a
darling husband," coos Natalia Gorich, and a few scenes later
her words are echoed by Molchalin's praise of Khlyostova's
lapdog: "Your spitz is a darling spitz!" There are significant
parallels between Natalia's methods of subjugating Platon—
expressing excessive concern for his health, ordering him about,
keeping him away from physical exercise—and Sophia's treat-

ment of Molchalin after his fall from a horse in Act II. And indeed, opportunistic and despicable though Molchalin may be, he is a victim in his relationship with Sophia. As Jean Bonamour has pointed out, she has clearly forced him into it and he continues it for fear of reprisals that would hurt his livelihood. Platon Gorich confesses to Chatsky that the only thing he is left free to do is to practice a flute duet, something that Molchalin is already doing when the play opens. Should the embittered Countess Khryumina, Jr., ever find a husband, his only imaginable fate would be enslavement.

The political clash, the love theme, the misogyny, and gerontophobia all converge into one focus in Act III, when Sophia, fed up with Chatsky's endless sneers at Molchalin and the rest of her friends, starts a rumor that Chatsky is insane. In a series of quick, flashing scenes, the rumor spreads. When Chatsky ends the act with his famous "Little Frenchman from Bordeaux" speech about the harm of foreign influences, the crowd takes his opinions for the ravings of a madman and he is ostracized from society. The elderly characters unanimously blame his condition on newfangled education and on institutions of higher learning.

Act IV shows the departure of the guests from Famusov's party. In a succession of vignettes, the already familiar characterizations of the lesser participants are deepened. The shunned Chatsky is unable to leave because his coachman cannot be found. Then, just before the final denouement, Griboedov suddenly brings on one more major character: the unforgettable clown, windbag, and hanger-on to political movements—Repetilov (from the Latin *repeto*; the man has no views or opinions of his own but repeats those of others). Repetilov, being a self-declared enemy of conventions, arrives at Famusov's party just as everyone is leaving. He forces his friendship on people he barely knows. Like the protagonists of Shakhovskoy's *Don't Listen* . . . and Khmelnitsky's *The Chatterbox*, Repetilov is a selfless, inspired liar. Insecure, self-deprecating, compulsively drawn to those who are more intellectual or more independent than he, Repetilov would be just one more—admittedly superior—variation on the standard prevaricator of neoclassical comedy, were it not for his political involvement. Had Griboedov been able to foresee the tragic fate of his good friend Wilhelm Küchelbecker and of the other participants of the Decembrist Rebellion, which took place about a year after Act IV of *TMoBC* was written, he might not have depicted the secret political societies of the Decembrists with so much sarcasm. But the "most secret union," of which Repetilov is a member and into which he tries to recruit the contemptuous Chatsky (and later, quite absurdly, the martinet Colonel Skalozub), with its combination of literary and political interests, its debates "on chambers of deputies, on trials by jury, on Byron and, well, on other important matters," and its call for "radical remedies" to right the social system, is all too recognizably a portrait of typical Decembrist interests and aspirations. Griboedov's familiarity with the inner workings of the Decembrist societies extends even to having Repetilov cite a phrase from Baldassare Galuppi's opera *Didone abbandonata*, "A! non lasciarmi, no, no, no," which was used by the Decembrists as a password.[11]

But the prospect of joining this bunch of idealistic hotheads, described by Repetilov in a series of thumbnail sketches, appeals as little to Chatsky as the company of the conservative elders he has just fled. After failing to drag off either Chatsky or Skalozub to join his political cronies, the ever-irresponsible Repetilov seems on the point of recruiting the shyster Zagoretsky, potentially a police informer, who obligingly pretends to be "a terrible liberal, just like you" and claims to have suffered through being "direct and speaking [his] mind bravely." Significantly, the aristocratic society that had proclaimed Chatsky a Jacobin and therefore certifiably mad, tolerates Repetilov as a tiresome but harmless crackpot.

The denouement of *TMoBC*, which follows the departure of the last guests, has been compared by Jean Bonamour to that of *Oedipus Rex*, where the hero finally discovers the painful truth that has been known to the audience all along. This may apply to Chatsky, but it applies even more to Sophia, who,

11. See V. Filippov's note to this effect in the annotated edition of A. S. Griboedov, *Gore ot uma*, ed. N. Piksanov (Moscow, 1946), p. 238.

by overhearing the nocturnal conversation between Molchalin and Liza, learns the true feelings of the man whom she has been protecting and for whose sake she has been fighting Chatsky throughout the play. Chatsky is surely unfair to call Sophia a dissembler (*pritvorshchitsa*) and to accuse her of luring him with false hopes, since she has been frank and honest with him all along. But his perception of why Sophia has preferred Molchalin to him is absolutely on target:

Подумайте, всегда вы можете его
Беречь, и пеленать, и спосылать за делом.
Муж-мальчик, муж-слуга, из жениных пажей,
Высокий идеал московских всех мужей.

Just think, you can always protect him,
Swaddle him and send him on errands.
A boy-husband, a servant-husband, one of his wife's pages,
The high ideal of all Moscow husbands.

Full of contempt for Sophia and her world dominated by "sinister old women [and] old men who grow ever more decrepit, with their fabrications and nonsense," and having turned down the revolutionary alternative proffered by Repetilov, Chatsky exits, intending "to search through the world for a nook in which to nurse [his] offended feelings." His final desperate cry is for a carriage to take him away, the carriage that Vladimir Nabokov has connected to other carriages "that took Russians to duels, foreign countries, exile, and the Ekaterininsky Kanal" (i.e., the canal in St. Petersburg on the quai of which Sophia Perovskaya and her accomplices assassinated Alexander II in 1881).[12] The gerontophobic and misogynous themes are sounded in the last speech of Famusov. Having understood nothing of the scenes he has just witnessed, he jumps to the conclusion that his daughter and Chatsky are secret lovers and at the final curtain is cringing in fear of the possible reaction to this by the omnipotent matriarchal deity of gossip, the ominous Princess Maria Alexevna.

12. *The Nabokov–Wilson Letters*, ed. Simon Karlinsky (New York, 1979), p. 103.

Russian critics of the nineteenth and twentieth centuries have occasionally compared *TMoBC* to Shakespeare's *Hamlet* and *Timon of Athens*. Specialists in comparative literature were likely to cite the comedies of Beaumarchais and Molière's *The Misanthrope* as the play's immediate predecessors. By the second half of the nineteenth century, when serious study of Griboedov first began, the plays of his senior contemporaries, Shakhovskoy and Khmelnitsky, were out of print and either forgotten or regarded with contempt by the few critics who did remember them.[13] Only in 1926 did Leonid Grossman in his book *Pushkin in the Theater Stalls* point out several passages in Shakhovskoy's *Don't Listen . . .* that are echoed in some lines and situations of *TMoBC*.[14] Grossman's discovery has been occasionally cited by other Soviet scholars.[15] But *Don't Listen . . .* is by no means the only link between *TMoBC* and Russian verse comedies of the preceding decade.

The overall design of Griboedov's play is, as noted at the beginning of this chapter, patterned on that of Shakhovskoy's *The Lipetsk Spa*. Going through *The Lipetsk Spa* scene by scene, one realizes that Pronsky's discussion of his military career in Act I, scene 3, was caricatured by Griboedov in Ska-lozub's account of his war experiences; that Prince Kholmsky's credo in the same scene about respecting other people but not trying to please everyone is the mirror image of Molchalin's cynical Act IV credo about pleasing everyone regardless of cost (Molchalin was taught his credo by his father and Kholm-

13. At some point in the 1850s, Griboedov's relative Dimitry Smirnov, interviewing the actor Ivan Sosnitsky (who was in the first cast of *The Lipetsk Spa*), asked him how such a miserably bad play could ever have been successful and then refused to credit the embarrassed actor's explanations (*Istoricheskii vestnik* 115 [1909]:160).

A. I. Vol'f, the compiler of the *Khronika peterburgskikh teatrov s kontsa 1826 do nachala 1855 goda (Chronicle of St. Petersburg Theaters from the End of 1826 to the Beginning of 1855* [St. Petersburg, 1877], part 1), found it necessary to sneer at or denounce all plays that antedated *TMoBC* and *The Inspector General* in his commentary.

Numerous other examples of such Belinsky-inspired attitudes could be cited.

14. Leonid Grossman, *Pushkin v teatral'nykh kreslakh* (Leningrad, 1926), pp. 142–43.

15. For example, Tomashevsky, "Stikh 'Goria ot uma.' "

sky by his uncle); and that the four-line denunciation of Lipetsk society by the old Princess in Act II, scene 2, of *The Lipetsk Spa* is closely echoed in Countess Khryumina, Jr.'s exit lines in Act IV of *TMoBC*. The maid Sasha's praises of Pronsky to the unresponsive Olenka (II, 3) is the model for Liza's similar eulogy of Chatsky in *TMoBC* (II, 5).

In the character of Chatsky Griboedov combined, in a most unexpected way, certain features of the moralizing *raisonneur* of *The Lipetsk Spa*, Prince Kholmsky—his moral indignation, his dislike of the servile imitation of foreign ways—with some traits of that play's coquette villainess, Countess Leleva. The first grand entrance of the Countess in Act II, in which she berates to her admirers the hypocrisy and artificiality of life in St. Petersburg, emphasizing in particular the dishonesty and stupidity of elderly and aristocratic women, must surely have been the point of departure for a whole swarm of Chatsky's speeches, beginning with his malicious gossiping during his first reunion with Sophia. The idea that the elderly of both sexes are petty and stupid is, in fact, also voiced in *The Lipetsk Spa*, though not with the vehemence of *TMoBC*. Developing the remarkable insight of the Soviet scholar Alexander Slonimsky, Jean Bonamour pointed out that Griboedov's Chatsky traces his descent not only (or not so much) to Molière's Alceste, but to the malicious and gossipy heroine of *The Misanthrope*, Célimène. Chatsky "unites the heart of Alceste with the wit of Célimène," Bonamour wrote.[16] Molière's characters may have been Chatsky's great-grandparents; his actual parents were Prince Kholmsky and Countess Leleva.

Besides similar speeches and situations, one finds a few verbatim quotations from *The Lipetsk Spa* in *TMoBC*, such as the previously mentioned line of Countess Leleva with which Chatsky opens Act III and Count Olgin's "Tak ia u vashikh nog" ("So I am at your feet") at the end of the last act, which Chatsky will repeat at his first entrance as "I ia u vashikh nog" ("And I am at your feet"). The textual parallels between *TMoBC* and Shakovskoy's *Don't Listen . . .* , on which the meter of *TMoBC* was patterned, were, as stated, documented by

16. Bonamour, *A. S. Griboedov*, p. 283.

Leonid Grossman. A whole separate study could be written about the similarities between *TMoBC* and Nikolai Khmelnitsky's first comedy, *The Chatterbox*. They begin with the opening discussion between the heroine and her maid Liza of the merits of her two suitors, which is very much like Sophia's and Liza's Act I comparison of Chatsky with Molchalin. They continue through the chorus of six gossiping women on which the two choruses of the six Tugoukhovsky daughters were patterned, and they go on all the way to the scene where Count Zvonov continues his monologue, not aware that the other characters have left the stage, just as Chatsky is left alone at the end of Act III of *TMoBC*.

These similarities are apparent to a person familiar with the text of *TMoBC* even on a cursory reading of *The Lipetsk Spa* and *The Chatterbox*. A close textual study, perhaps even a computerized one, should reveal a wealth of other phraseological and lexical connections. None of this can affect the artistic status of Griboedov's comedy or impugn its originality. But it should establish beyond doubt the following truths that, with very few exceptions such as Leonid Grossman or Tadeusz Kołakowski,[17] Griboedov criticism has been stubbornly avoiding: (1) *TMoBC* is not a unique phenomenon, but a product of a definite school of playwriting, the neoclassical; (2) Griboedov learned his language and his craft not from Molière or Shakespeare, but from two of his senior contemporaries, Shakhovskoy and Khmelnitsky; and (3) the artistic distance between Griboedov and these two playwrights is not the one that divides genius from mediocrity, but the one that separates the lyrics of Pushkin from those of Zhukovsky and Batiushkov.

In some aspects *TMoBC* is even more akin to Russian eighteenth-century neoclassical comedy than is the nineteenth-century variant initiated by *The Lipetsk Spa*. The obvious *noms parlants*, such as Repetilov, Gorich, and Tugoukhovsky recall Fonvizin and Kapnist or eighteenth-century sentimental

---

17. In his review of the translation of *TMoBC* into Polish by Julian Tuwim (*Slavia Orientalis* [Warsaw] 11[2] [1962]: 227–32), Kołakowski points out the inadequacy of all historical comment on *TMoBC* that ignores the significance of Shakhovskoy for its genesis.

drama rather than Shakhovskoy, who abandoned the use of such names (Khmelnitsky used them in his very first comedy, *The Chatterbox*, but gave them up after that). The satire on aristocratic disdain for the sciences, education, and institutions of higher learning at the end of Act III is a belated echo of a widespread and popular eighteenth-century theme familiar in Russian literature since the satires of Antioch Kantemir. It was, of course, also present in numerous foreign eighteenth-century works, for example, Sheridan's *The Rivals*. Griboedov's modeling of several of his characters on actual people well known in Moscow at the time (this was the case with Famusov, Khlyostova, and Repetilov) was also a popular practice at the time of Sumarokov and Nikolev, but one that Russian playwrights had abandoned by the end of the eighteenth century. In his oft-cited letter to Katenin on the play, Griboedov defended his right as a comedy writer to draw portraits of real people in plays, provided the portraits did not deteriorate into caricatures.[18]

Besides modeling his characters on real people, Griboedov relied on stock types of the neoclassical comedy of his time. Praised throughout the nineteenth century for having broken with the traditions of neoclassicism, Griboedov on the contrary built on them and developed them. Following the example of Shakhovskoy, he tailored certain parts for the abilities of actors and actresses of Shakhovskoy's St. Petersburg company. Liza was surely intended for the beautiful Alexandra Asenkova (the mother of the more famous Varvara Asenkova), who created the important role of the maid Sasha in *The Lipetsk Spa* and for the next fifteen years specialized in the soubrette parts of the neoclassical repertoire. Late nineteenth- and early twentieth-century actresses, such as Maria Lilina , the wife of Stanislavsky, who were unfamiliar with the soubrette tradition of neoclassical comedy (which in Russia went back to comedies by Lukin and Kniazhnin) did not know what to make of Liza: How could Griboedov have made an enserfed peasant maid so uninhibited and witty?

Alexandra Asenkova did not get to play Liza, but Shakhov-

18. Letter to Katenin in A. S. Griboedov, *Sochineniia* (Moscow-Leningrad, 1959), pp. 557–58.

skoy's paramour Ekaterina Ezhova was still around to play
Khlyostova in the earliest productions of *TMoBC* in the 1830s,
just as she had played her predecessor, the old Princess in *The
Lipetsk Spa* two decades earlier. Nor would any actor who had
played Count Zvonov in *The Chatterbox* or Zarnitskin in
Don't Listen . . . have the slightest difficulty with Repetilov.'
Only Famusov gave the first interpreters trouble because there
were no precedents in earlier verse comedy for an old man who
had to be both aristocratic and comical (but not ridiculous,
like Baron Volmar in *The Lipetsk Spa*). This combination
posed problems even for Mikhail Shchepkin.

The two most prominent and developed characters in
TMoBC are of course Alexander Chatsky and Sophia Famu-
sova. At first encounter, Chatsky makes a better impression. On
the stage, he is usually played by the handsomest actor in the
company, who tries to convert him into a Romeo or a Hamlet.
But Sophia wears better in the long run. Chatsky's literary
genealogy, though highly irregular, is decipherable without
much trouble. From his ultimate ancestor, Alceste, Chatsky has
inherited the central quality that André Gide has described
as "his frankness, which more often than not takes an unen-
durably brutal form."[19] Other strains that went into the making
of Chatsky come, as already indicated, from characters who
were originally negative: Cléon, the hypercritical hero of Gresset's *Le méchant* and of its Russian adaptations by Shakhovskoy, Zagoskin, and Katenin, all of which antedated *TMoBC*
(the filiation from Cléon was instantly perceived by Pushkin
when he first read Griboedov's play); and the wickedly witty
médisances of such female characters as Célimène and her remote descendant (via Elchaninov's Pulcheria), Countess Leleva.

It was Griboedov's particular feat in creating Chatsky to
add a plus sign to the previously negative characters such as
Cléon and Célimène and to combine their wit and humor with
the brutal honesty of Alceste. It was Griboedov's intention, as
stated in his letter to Katenin, to write a play in which twenty-
five fools are confronted by one intelligent man (though ear-

19. Quoted by Robert Jouanny in his edition of *Théâtre complet de Molière*,
Classiques Garnier (Paris, n.d.), vol. 1, p. 936.

lier in the same sentence he described Sophia as "by no means stupid"). Here the author touched on the most vulnerable aspect of his play. Is Chatsky the only intelligent person in *TMoBC*? Is he intelligent at all? "Who is the intelligent person in the comedy [*TMoBC*]?" asked Pushkin in the letter he wrote to Bestuzhev after the play was read to him by his friend Ivan Pushchin. Pushkin answered:

> Griboedov. And do you know who Chatsky is? An ardent and noble young man who spent some time with a very intelligent man (namely, with Griboedov) and absorbed his thoughts, witticisms and satirical remarks. Everything he says is very clever. But to whom does he say it all? To Famusov? To Skalozub? To the Moscow grandmothers at the ball? To Molchalin? This is unforgivable. The first sign of an intelligent person is to know from the first glance with whom you are dealing and not to cast pearls before the Repetilovs and their ilk.

A footnote Pushkin added to this passage reads: "Gresset's Cléon does not try to be clever with either Géronte or Chloé."

Belinsky, who valued the social criticism of *TMoBC* but denied that the play contained a valid "central idea," saw in Chatsky the work's greatest liability:

> And then: What sort of a profound person is Chatsky? He is simply a bellower, a phrasemonger, an idealistic buffoon who at every step debases everything sacred that he mentions. Does it really make one a profound person to go out into society and to tell people to their faces that they are imbeciles and brutes?[20]

The protagonist of Chekhov's novella "A Dreary Story" (1889), a wise and experienced professor of medicine, expresses a similar view when he complains of actors "trying to convince me at all costs that Chatsky, who spends much time talking to fools and who loves a foolish woman, is a very intelligent man."[21]

20. V. G. Belinsky, *Sobranie sochinenii* (St. Petersburg, 1911), vol. 1, p. 658.
21. A. P. Chekhov, *Sochineniia* (Moscow, 1977), vol. 7, p. 270.

Belinsky misread many of the characters and relationships in *TMoBC*. He interpreted the opening scenes to mean that Sophia was Molchalin's mistress and that Liza spoke to her with such familiarity because she knew of their liaison and thus held Sophia in her power. But Belinsky did have a valid point when he asked the twofold question also raised by Pushkin and by Chekhov's professor, namely: Why does Chatsky force his views on people who couldn't possibly share them? Why doesn't he seek out more congenial company? Platon Gorich is a close friend, but it is not him that Chatsky takes into his confidence, but Famusov. Among the numerous offstage characters mentioned in the play, all those little *homunculi* who take on momentary life owing to Griboedov's precise descriptions of them, there is Skalozub's cousin, who retreated to the country after a distinguished military career in order to read and improve his mind, and Princess Tugoukhovskaya's nephew Prince Fyodor, who has studied chemistry and botany, shuns women, and has no regard for rank. Silly and obnoxious as Repetilov might be, couldn't Chatsky have found some likeminded men in his club, men similar to Skalozub's cousin or Prince Fyodor, who might be more interested in what he has to say than the man-devouring females and the "decrepit old men" whom he finally flees in despair? Real as these objections may be, they are easily dispelled in reading or hearing the potent poetry with which Griboedov managed to invest his hero's diatribes and ravings.

The other principal character, Sophia, raises different problems. "Sophia is not clearly drawn," wrote Pushkin in the previously cited letter to Bestuzhev, "she is something halfway between a slut and a provincial miss [московская кузина]." Commentators, ranging from Belinsky to Alexei Suvorin at the turn of the century, misread her involvement with Molchalin as a sordid liaison and recoiled from her in revulsion. But within the conventions of the neoclassical comedy of Griboedov's time, attraction for a person of lower social standing (as in *The New Sterne*) is a part of the general sentimentalization of the emotional life of the period, something that Griboedov regarded with as jaundiced an eye as Shakhovskoy. It is not only of her misguided love for Molchalin that Sophia is cured at the end of the play, but of the distorting sentimentalist perspective that made this love possible.[22] Unlike Chatsky, with his multitude of literary antecedents, Sophia is Griboedov's own creation and a highly original one at that.

Beyond the sighing sentimentalist, beyond the embryonic female praying mantis, there looms an admirably intelligent, quick-witted, and self-reliant young woman. "Sophia is not a type, but she is a person," wrote D. S. Mirsky.

> She is a rare phenomenon in classical comedy: a heroine that is neither idealized nor caricatured. There is a strange, drily romantic flavor in her, with her fixity of purpose, her ready wit, and her deep but reticent passionateness. She is the principal *active* force in the play, and the plot is advanced mainly by her actions.[23]

That a critic as discerning as Mirsky could find Sophia so attractive is a triumph of the character over her creator's profound misogyny. By convincing the audience of Sophia's intelligence and spirit, Griboedov brought to this play a genuinely tragic note. She is Chatsky's enemy and nemesis, and yet the audience, despite all the handicaps, sympathizes with her and understands her plight. This situation leaves us with an impossible choice between Sophia's truth and Chatsky's, something that gives *TMoBC* a place among such other comedies with a tragic central kernel as *Measure for Measure, The Misanthrope* and *The Cherry Orchard*.

22. The importance of the antisentimentalist polemics of the Archaists for understanding Sophia's character and its historical dimensions is stressed in Jurij Striedter's fine essay "Griboedovs Sophie als historischer Typus," *L'annuaire de l'Institut de Philologie et d'Histoire Orientales et Slaves*, vol. 18, (*1966–1967*) (Brussels, 1968), pp. 357–69. Griboedov criticism has often treated Sophia in negative terms, but it is her few defenders that have produced some of the more stimulating writing on the subject. At the turn of the century, Izabella Grinevskaya brought a mildly feminist perspective to the topic in her two essays "Oklevetannaia devushka ("The Slandered Girl") and "Kogo liubit Sof'ia Pavlovna?" ("Whom does Sophia Pavlovna Love?"), *Ezhemesiachnyia sochineniia*, no. 10 (1901): 129–39, and no. 11 (1901):209–21. See also Gerald Janacek. "A Defense of Sof'ja in *Woe from Wit*," *Slavic and East European Journal* 21(3) (1977): 318–31.

23. D. S. Mirsky, *A History of Russian Literature* (New York, 1960), p. 112.

Nineteenth- and Twentieth-Century
Views of Griboedov

Unlike the fictitious history of censoring Fonvizin's *The Minor* that one finds in Soviet textbooks, the censorship history of *TMoBC* is real. The reign of Nicholas I, which was inaugurated with the Decembrist Rebellion, saw the installation of censorship controls that were among the most stringent ones in Russian history and were outdone only in Soviet times. In the wake of the rebellion's suppression, the political debates between Famusov and Chatsky and Repetilov's prattlings about secret political societies did not seem suitable for presentation on the stage. During the few years he had left to live after completing his comedy, Griboedov got to see it performed only once—by a group of amateurs in Georgia. His tragic death opened the way to performances of the play in theaters, at first piecemeal, one act at a time. The first complete performance took place in 1831 in a version disfigured by a number of cuts that suppressed not only the political allusions but the indications that Molchalin had spent the night in Sophia's room. Deferring to the nascent Victorian era were abridgments of the scenes where Famusov and then Molchalin make passes at Liza.

It should have seemed a folly to attempt censoring a play that by the end of the 1820s was universally known from numerous handwritten copies (*TMoBC* is one of the earliest cases of Russian *samizdat,* a phenomenon far more familiar in the twentieth century than in the nineteenth). Yet, Griboedov's play was not performed or published in its entirety until after the reforms of the early 1860s. Even so, it became within a few years the most beloved and most widely performed play of the Russian repertoire. In the early stages of its success, interestingly enough, the play was most warmly championed by the more conservative critics. Osip Senkovsky and Faddei Bulgarin (the latter a close personal friend of Griboedov's, who entrusted him with the manuscript of *TMoBC* and assigned to him the right of its publication[24]), both of whom were to attack Gogol's

24. Griboedov's well-documented friendship with Faddei Bulgarin, the

The Inspector General as subversive, wrote of *TMoBC* with glowing admiration. Gogol praised the play's civic consciousness in his most reactionary book, *Selected Passages from Correspondence with Friends.* At the end of the nineteenth century, Chatsky was seen as their ideological ally by such ultraconservative writers as Chekhov's publisher friend Alexei Suvorin and Vasily Rozanov.

And indeed, stripped of its gerontophobia, xenophobia, and antifeminism, Chatsky's political outlook may be reducible to an individualistic defense of the exceptional and the talented against the dull-witted herd. This was sensed by Belinsky when he pointed out that Chatsky's main characteristic is setting himself above society. Disagreeing with Griboedov, Belinsky affirmed that: "Society is always more right and higher than any one man, and one person's individuality is a reality and not a phantom only inasmuch as it expresses society."[25] Even Chatsky's oft-extolled opposition to serfdom is based on the two examples he cites of *old men* who mistreat their serfs outrageously, the "Nestor of distinguished scoundrels" and the owner of the bankrupt serf ballet. Both of these examples come from the "And who are the judges?" speech that denounces the corrupt old men who run Moscow. To imagine that Chatsky, the proprietor of 300 to 400 "souls," who has his serf valet and serf coachman wait for him outside while he attends Famusov's party and who communicates with them by snarls, is a proponent of the abolition of serfdom is to indulge in wishful thinking.

But Chatsky's passion and vehemence, his volcanic rhetoric, and the poetic flights of his denunciatory speeches were too

---

ultraconservative journalist and novelist, a spy in the service of the tsar's secret police, and a bitter enemy of Pushkin, is a source of perpetual embarrassment for Griboedov's biographers. The previously cited 1980 collection of documents and memoirs about Griboedov, *A. S. Griboedov v vospominaniiakh*, includes several memoirs of people whose contacts with him were brief and casual, but omits Bulgarin's detailed memoirs about his encounters with Griboedov. But because Bulgarin's memoirs are factually indispensable, they are frequently drawn upon in the editor's annotations.

25. Belinsky, *Sobranie sochinenii*, p. 657.

big a prize not to be coveted by the antigovernment and radical camps of mid-nineteenth-century Russia. In his essays of the 1860s, Alexander Herzen several times put forth the idea that Chatsky's irony and indignation had to express the ideals of the best men of that age and that he was therefore a Decembrist in the depth of his heart. As long as Herzen speaks of the *Zeitgeist* of the pre-Decembrist period, one can go along with him, even though Chatsky *praises* the reign of Alexander I in the first act of the play and scornfully rejects the Decembrist societies in Act IV. Besides, Herzen was honest enough to note in his 1868 essay "Bazarov Once More" that Chatsky's protest was equally likely to find further expression in joining the Decembrists, converting to Roman Catholicism, hating everything Slavic, or becoming a Slavophile.[26] While Herzen at least left Chatsky several options for his future development, Dostoevsky, in his notebooks and in drafts for *The Possessed*, simply took it for granted that Griboedov's hero was a Decembrist revolutionary and condemned him for his lack of all contact with the Russian common people and also condemned him for his final flight abroad, which Dostoevsky interpreted as permanent emigration.[27]

In the second half of the nineteenth century, *TMoBC* was often claimed by the liberal camp, which was wont to see Chatsky as a fighter for the kind of reforms that Alexander II had implemented in the 1860s.[28] This approach came gradually to influence the interpretations of the play on the stage. A tradition was formed that Vladimir Nemirovich-Danchenko sought to overcome with his 1906 production of *TMoBC* at the Moscow Art Theater. Nemirovich wanted the play to be centered on the intimate drama of Sophia, Chatsky, and Molchalin. As he pointed out,

26. For a summary of Herzen's views on Chatsky and the Decembrists, see M. V. Nechkina, *Griboedov i dekabristy* (Moscow, 1951), pp. 12–15.

27. For Dostoevsky's views, see ibid., pp. 20–21.

28. The novelist Ivan Goncharov expressed this liberal-reformist view of *TMoBC* in his 1871 essay "Mil'on terzanii" ("A Million Torments"), included in most editions of his collected writings. It was also published as a separate brochure (Moscow, 1956).

Most actors play Chatsky as, at best, an ardent *raisonneur*. They overload his image with the significance of Chatsky as a fighter for civil rights. They seem to perform not the play, but those political essays that it has engendered, which is the most antiartistic approach imaginable to this role.[29]

Fighting for civil rights was understandably more appealing to audiences than preaching hatred of the elderly and fear of female power, which is what Chatsky actually does much of the time.

Unlike the liberals, the radical factions of the late nineteenth and the early twentieth century felt no particular kinship to Chatsky. Marxist commentators, whether before the October Revolution (Mikhail Olminsky) or after (Peter Kogan and Anatoly Lunacharsky) regarded the Decembrists as aristocratic liberals. They knew that Griboedov was not a participant in the Decembrist uprising and they saw the question of whether Chatsky embodied the Decembrist ideas or not as irrelevant to socialism and proletarian revolution.[30] This outlook helped shape Vsevolod Meyerhold's brilliantly perverse staging of *TMoBC* in 1928. Where the same director's previous production, Gogol's *Inspector General*, was an imaginative revelation and enhancement of the surrealistic essence of Gogol's comedy, his approach to Griboedov seemed motivated by a desire to stand the play on its head and to negate its very text, to which Meyerhold returned its work-in-progress title, *Gore umu*. With a frail, timid Chatsky, who spent much of his time on the stage playing Beethoven and Schubert on the piano, with a sensuous, promiscuous Sophia, found at the beginning of the

29. Quoted by N. Piksanov, "Stsenicheskaia istoriia 'Goria ot uma,'" in A. S. Griboedov, *Gore ot uma* (Moscow, 1946), p. 190. Nemirovich-Danchenko's evolving views of the play are described in the collection of essays *Gore ot uma. Postanovka Moskovskogo khudozhestvennogo teatra* (Petrograd, 1923). See also Iu. A. Golovashenko, "Problemy stsenicheskogo istolkovaniia 'Goria ot uma,'" in *A. S. Griboedov. Tvorchestvo. Biografiia. Traditsii*, ed. S. A. Fomichev, (Leningrad, 1977).

30. For a hostile, but factually informative summary of the views of Olminsky, Kogan, and Lunacharsky, see Nechkina, *Griboedov i dekabristy*, pp. 36–39. Their views are stated in passages aimed primarily at debunking the writings of the dean of twentieth-century Marxist specialists on Griboedov, Nikolai Piksanov.

play not performing a flute and piano duet but visiting a gypsy nightclub, with a youthful, jovial Famusov and an athletic, insolent Molchalin, Meyerhold's interpretation was not only ahistorical, but it did not contain a single character as Griboedov wrote it.[31]

Any kind of historical or factual approach to Griboedov and to *TMoBC*, whether Marxist or not, came to an end in the Soviet Union with the publication of the monumental, 600-page study *Griboedov and the Decembrists* by the arch-Stalinist historian Militsa Nechkina.[32] After the appearance of its second edition in 1951, the book came to be seen as the embodiment of the official party line on the play and its creator. Soviet critics and scholars may disagree with it only at their peril. With considerable erudition and subtle casuistry, Nechkina forces logic to perform a double somersault. The aim of her book is to convince the reader that, whatever the historical record may show, Griboedov was a Decembrist revolutionary and wrote his play as a piece of revolutionary propaganda; and that the Decembrists, despite their plans for a constitutional monarchy and a democratically elected parliament, were the direct predecessors of the Bolsheviks and that therefore the present-day Soviet Union represents the fulfillment of their dreams.

Today, all published commentary on *TMoBC* and all stage productions in the Soviet Union have to accommodate themselves to this view of the play and of its meaning. The fundamental, thoroughly Marxist study of the play's origins by Nikolai Piksanov, first published in 1928, had to be rewritten for its 1971 edition to bring it into line with Nechkina's conception.[33] The introduction to a recent collection of Griboedov

---

31. On Meyerhold's production of *TMoBC*, see K. Rudnitsky, *Rezhisser Meierkhol'd* (Moscow, 1969), pp. 380–93, and Iu. A. Golovashenko, "Problemy stsenicheskogo istolkovaniia."

32. *Griboedov i dekabristy*. Even the very best Soviet literary monographs seldom go through more than one edition. Nechkina's book is a very rare instance of a literary study that has by now appeared in three editions (between 1948 and 1971). The first edition was awarded a Stalin Prize.

33. Cf. N. K. Piksanov *Tvorcheskaia istoriia "Goria ot uma"* (Moscow, 1928), with the same book's 1971 edition.

studies attacks Tynianov's biographical novel *The Death of Vazir Mukhtar*, until now considered a classic of Soviet literature, because its portrayal of Griboedov's last years is divergent from his character as decreed by Nechkina.[34] Yet, as Anna Akhmatova has pointed out, Griboedov's brilliant diplomatic career after 1825 is incontrovertible proof that he could not have possibly taken part in any of the Decembrist societies. Akhmatova agrees with her friend Tamara Gabbe that Nechkina's book contains no real Griboedov and no real Decembrists and that all its hundreds of pages are devoted to justifying the middle part of its title, that is, the word "and."[35]

Like the genuine classic that it is, *TMoBC* resists being tied to any one ideology or epoch. In the 1960s, an angry editorial in the official party journal *Kommunist* charged that one of Leningrad's theaters had the outrageous notion of staging *TMoBC* as if it took place today. The idea seems eminently workable: different as the Soviet society is from Russia under Alexander I, it contains recognizable speciments of the types Griboedov described. There are entrenched old party officials who, just like Famusov, fear new intellectual and political trends; powerful old women like Khlyostova, who had been influential under an earlier regime (Stalin's, not Catherine's) and do not like those who endanger their eminence; military types like Skalozub, who can make sense of the world only in terms of army ranks; careerists like Molchalin; and shady dealers in hard-to-get goods like Zagoretsky. And there are dissident young men like Chatsky, who rock the boat and, yes, are declared insane by those whose ideology or interests they threaten. Griboedov's Moscow is more alive today than ever, and this is one of the reasons, though not the main one, why Russians love the play so much.

The main reason for the eternal popularity of *TMoBC* has nothing to do with political ideas or social systems. The play is an incomparable feast of the Russian language, just as *Hamlet*

---

34. S. A. Fomichev, "Avtor 'Goria ot uma' i chitateli komedii," in the collection he edited, *A. S. Griboedev* (see note 29, above).

35. Lidiia Chukovskaia, *Zapiski ob Anne Akhmatovoi* (Paris, 1980), p. 12. Also in the collection *Pamiati Akhmatovoi* (Paris, 1974), pp. 67–68.

or *Antony and Cleopatra* are feasts of English and *Faust*[36] is of German. All the parts are marvelously playable, even the least important ones. Stage careers have been launched by good performances of Prince Tugoukhovsky's almost wordless role. Olga Knipper, the widow of Chekhov, while at the height of her renown did not disdain to appear in the supposedly minor part of Countess Khryumina, Jr. From Sophia and Chatsky down to the nameless Mr. D. and Mr. N. at the party, all characters are geniuses at the art of verbal expression.

Khlyostova may be a pompous and gossipy old woman, but just listen to her talk, listen to what she does with her words. What she does is a difficult trapeze act executed without a net and always with faultless precision. Under any imaginable political system, people who are sensitive to poetry, sensitive to nuances of language, will want to see this play, to read it for the tenth, for the fiftieth time. Misogyny? Decembrists? Ah, but listen to that old woman, just listen to the way she puts it!

36. In an amazing feat of literary detection, Irina Medvedeva discovered that at least seven passages in *TMoBC* are paraphrased translations of lines from Goethe's *Faust*. See her commentary in A. S. Griboedov, *Sochineniia v stikhakh* (Leningrad, 1967), p. 494.

Pushkin and Neoclassical Drama

> "Pushkin is our first classicist and romanticist, which makes him a realist." . . . (The latter definition depends upon the epoch, and also the temperament of the commentator.)   Igor Stravinsky[1]

It has been the fate of many a great Russian writer to acquire in Western countries an image that is the very opposite of what he has actually stood for and believed. Ultraconservatives, such as Gogol and the mature Dostoevsky, are venerated as fearless indicters of tsarist tyranny. The humanitarian activist Anton Chekhov, with his wide-ranging program of social betterment and environmental concern, is seen as a gloomy prophet of despair and doom. Vladimir Mayakovsky, who detested anything bucolic and put his hopes for a better future in industrialization and urbanization, was depicted in an American educational film as a poet of farms, herds and open plains.

Most misunderstood of all in popular lore is Alexander Pushkin (1799–1837). A writer whose work represents the culmination of Russian eighteenth-century neoclassicism and is

1. Igor Stravinsky, "Pushkin: Poetry and Music," in Eric Walter White, *Stravinsky: The Composer and His Music* (Berkeley and Los Angeles, 1966), p. 542 (appendix). The quoted portion is Stravinsky's idea of a typical Russian muddle-headed view of Pushkin.

pervaded by it, Pushkin is usually seen as someone who finally and definitively put an end to the neoclassical tradition. More deeply steeped in French language and literature than any other Russian writer, Pushkin is often credited with emancipating Russian literature from French influence. Beneficiary of the advances in the development of literary Russian that were achieved earlier by Karamzin, Zhukovsky, Batiushkov, Krylov, and, eventually, by Shakhovskoy and Khmelnitsky, Pushkin is still often said to have created the modern literary language all by himself, with no outside help.

Pushkin was interested in drama and the theater from his childhood. He reputedly attempted composing comedies while he still lived at his parents' home, even before he was enrolled at the boarding school, the Lyceum of Tsarskoe Selo in the environs of St. Petersburg, at the age of twelve. His classmates at the Lyceum recalled that during his school years he began writing a verse comedy in the French neoclassical manner, a work that was later destroyed. The literary tastes of the teenaged Pushkin are outlined in detail in his poem "Small Town" ("Gorodok"), written when he was sixteen. The longest eulogy in the poem is reserved for Voltaire, "the rival of Euripides, the gentle friend of Erato [i.e., the muse of amorous poetry], and a descendant of Ariosto and Tasso." In a later passage devoted mainly but not totally to his favorite playwrights, Pushkin lists Ozerov, Racine, Molière ("the gigantic Molière"), Fonvizin, and Kniazhnin.

Kniazhnin (as the author of verse comedies) and Fonvizin were to remain Pushkin's lifelong favorites, as evidenced by the epigraphs from their plays and allusions to them in his prose works of the 1830s. Ozerov initially attracted Pushkin through Ekaterina Semyonova's performances in his tragedies and because of the myth that his untimely death was caused by harassment inflicted by his envious literary enemies. But in the essay "My Remarks on the Russian Theater," which dates from January 1820 and usually opens the volume of Pushkin's critical essays in the academic editions of his collected works, we read of "the unfortunate Ozerov's imperfect creations," indicative of Pushkin's later disdain for Ozerov's tragedies, a disdain that led to disagreements with his friend and literary ally, Viazemsky, Ozerov's biographer and champion.

At the time of the opening of Shakhovskoy's *The Lipetsk Spa* Pushkin was the youngest member of the literary club "Arzamas," founded by Zhukovsky and Viazemsky to oppose the Archaists' attacks on sentimentalism and nascent Russian romanticism. With youthful fervor, Pushkin had earlier ridiculed Shakhovskoy in epigrams directed against the conservatism of the Archaists' literary position. Disgusted by Shakhovskoy's mockery of Zhukovsky, whom Pushkin regarded as his poetic teacher, and by the lampooning through the character of Countess Leleva's admirer, the retired hussar Ugarov, of two other people close to him—his uncle (the minor poet Vasily Pushkin) and Sergei Uvarov (later Pushkin's enemy, but at the time a fellow member of "Arzamas")—the teenaged Pushkin recorded in his diary for 1815 "My Thoughts on Shakhovskoy," a murderous denunciation of the playwright, his personality, and his supposed technical deficiencies.[2]

In a few years, however, as Iury Tynianov has shown in his study "The Archaists and Pushkin," Pushkin's friendship and literary alliance with the junior Archaist Katenin put an end to his hostility to the Archaist camp. By 1819, Pushkin was introduced to Shakhovskoy by Katenin and became a regular visitor to Shakhovskoy's "garret," that is, the literary salon presided over by Shakhovskoy's mistress, Ekaterina Ezhova. In his letter to Katenin from his Mikhailovskoye exile, written on September 12, 1825, Pushkin recalled the reading by Katenin of his *Andromache* at the "garret" as one of the happiest evenings of his life. Pushkin's coining of the term "the Lipetsk flood" to describe the resurgent popularity of verse comedy after 1815 shows his awareness of the importance of Shakhovskoy's first verse comedy for this development. Subsequently, Pushkin not only authorized but even encouraged Shakhovskoy's dramatizations of his "Ruslan and Liudmila" in 1824, "The

---

2. See Gozenpud's introductory essay to his edition of A. A. Shakhovskoy, *Komedii, stikhotvoreniia* (Leningrad, 1961), pp. 35–37, for an analysis of allusions to Vasily Pushkin and Sergei Uvarov in *The Lipetsk Spa*.

Fountain of Bakhchisarai" in 1825, and "The Queen of Spades" in 1836.

No initial unpleasantness marred Pushkin's personal and literary contacts with Nikolai Khmelnitsky. The record of their encounters is scant, especially in Pushkin's writings. In his letter to Nikolai Gnedich of May 13, 1823, Pushkin recalls being shown the manuscript of Khmelnitsky's comedy *The Irresolute Man* and offering Khmelnitsky his advice. Pushkin's letter of early May 1825 to his brother Lev mentions that the poet received a copy of the journal *The Russian Thalia* that contained some excerpts from a comedy by Khmelnitsky and adds: "And Khmelnitsky is my old love [Pushkin used the word *liubovnitsa* in the theatrical sense of "the woman with whom a character is in love"]. I have such a weakness for him that I'm prepared to place an entire couplet in his honor in the first chapter of *Onegin* (but what the deuce! They say he gets angry if one mentions him as a playwright)."

A possible cause for this purported anger may have been Khmelnitsky's rapid advancement in the civil service hierarchy, which was soon to lead to his appointment to the governorship of Smolensk. By failing to evoke Khmelnitsky's name in the first chapter of *Eugene Onegin*, Pushkin cheated him of the kind of immortality he had bestowed on Kniazhnin, Ozerov, Shakhovskoy, and Katenin by including theirs in stanza 18 of that chapter. But mentioned or not, Khmelnitsky is, as we shall see, very much present in the first chapter of *Eugene Onegin*. Pushkin's profession of love for Khmelnitsky's plays in the cited letter to his brother helps explain the impact Khmelnitsky had on the two major works that were being written or planned at the time, *Boris Godunov* and "Count Nulin." The last mention of Khmelnitsky in Pushkin's correspondence occurs in the letter addressed to him on March 6, 1831, in his capacity as the governor of Smolensk, in response to a request that Pushkin donate copies of his books to the Smolensk municipal library. After a ceremonious first section of the letter addressed to His Excellency the Governor, Pushkin switches to an informal second section in which he protests that while he respects the governor, he loves Khmelnitsky the man as "my favorite poet."

Pushkin's supremacy in Russian literature was established with the publication in 1820 of "Ruslan and Liudmila," a mock-heroic epic that incorporated what he had learned from the narrative poems of Ariosto and Voltaire, from Russian eighteenth-century humorous poems by Maikov and Bogdanovich, and, as Leonid Grossman has persuasively shown, from the ballets of his contemporary, the French choreographer Charles Dide-lot.[3] His narrative poem "The Gabrieliad" (1821) had its roots in the blasphemous and erotic eighteenth-century poems by Voltaire and Evariste Parny. With his hugely successful verse tales "The Prisoner of the Caucasus" (1820–21) and "The Fountain of Bakhchisarai" (1821–23), Pushkin turned to Byron for the model of his verse narratives and plunged into the typically romantic exoticism of the idealized Near East, made popular in France and England by Chateaubriand and Byron.

Pushkin's trajectory from this point on has been traditionally described by Russian scholars as a gradual overcoming of the romanticism of this period and finding his way to a realistic and socially critical depiction of the iniquities of Russian life of his time. Yet, a detailed examination of his dramatic projects that date from the same period as his "Southern" verse tales and an awareness of Pushkin's continuous fascination with the neoclassical verse comedy as practiced by Shakhovskoy, Khmelnitsky, and, eventually, Griboedov, indicate that Pushkin's neoclassical tastes remained alive and well throughout, despite the veneer of his later romantic and realistic orientation.

Pushkin's earliest surviving attempts to write for the stage date from his time of exile in the south of Russia, where Alexander I had banished him for some youthful revolutionary poems. Parallel with the composition of the ultraromantic "The Fountain of Bakhchisarai," Pushkin made sketches for a comedy in couplets of iambic hexameter and for a neoclassical

3. *Pushkin v teatral'nykh kreslakh* (Leningrad, 1926), pp. 122–31. Despite a few factual errors, Grossman's book is an excellent summary of Pushkin's early theatrical impressions that found wide reflections in his narrative poems of the 1820s.

tragedy in five acts in the manner of Sumarokov and Kniazhnin. The latter project is all the more amazing because by that time Pushkin had made amply evident his disdain for the neoclassical tragedy not only of Sumarokov but even of Ozerov.

The subject he had selected was that of Vadim of Novgorod, the episode from the *Primary Chronicle* that had already been dramatized by the Empress Catherine and Kniazhnin. But where Catherine couched her version in the form of an imitation of Shakespeare and Kniazhnin draped the fragmentary legend of Vadim on a framework borrowed from Corneille and Metastasio, Pushkin was planning his own treatment of the situation, while retaining the usual anachronistic confusion between the pre-Christian Novgorod of the ninth century and the republican city-state that was destroyed by the rulers of Moscow five centuries later. Because Pushkin could not decide whether he wanted to write a tragedy or a narrative poem about Vadim and left sketches for both, we have a reasonably clear idea of his conception. Had the tragedy materialized, it would have been the familiar eighteenth-century love-versus-duty play, with a heroine named Rogneda (the Old Russian equivalent of the Scandinavian name Ragnhild, which was the name of the heroine of Kniazhnin's *Vladimir and Iaropolk*), who is torn between her duty to her father and her love for Vadim, the leader of the republican resistance to the autocratic rule of Riurik the Varangian. Interesting as an indication of the antimonarchist sympathies of the young Pushkin, his play about Vadim had no future, as Pushkin himself must have realized. Had he completed it, it would, for all his genius, most likely have joined such other stillborn, belated exercises in neoclassical tragedy as Katenin's *Andromache* and Küchelbecker's *The Argives*.

Far more promising and giving greater cause for regret that it was not completed is the fragmentary comedy about gambling fever that Pushkin began sketching in his Kishinyov exile in 1821. Printed in academic editions of his writings under the title derived from its first words, "Say, by What Chance" (*Skazhi, kakoi sud'boi*), the fragment has been dubbed *The Gambler* by some scholars. There is only one completed scene, couched in the kind of iambic hexameter in which Kniazhnin and Kapnist wrote their comedies. But in tone and diction it is far more reminiscent of Khmelnitsky. There also exists a disjointed but detailed outline of the other scenes, which has enabled Alexander Slonimsky, among others, to postulate the plot and the action of this unwritten comedy.[4] The milieu is of the kind that was more usually associated in the eighteenth century with melodrama than with high comedy: the world of addicted gamblers and of the cardsharps who prey on them. The characters bear the names of the actors of Shakhovskoy's St. Petersburg company, for whom Pushkin clearly intended this play.

The completed scene shows a young widow Valberkhova (i.e,. the actress Maria Valberg, who had played young widows in *The Lipetsk Spa*, Khmelnitsky's *Castles in the Air* and, for that matter, in Molière's *The Misanthrope*), bickering with her gambler brother Sosnitsky (i.e., the part was intended for the actor Ivan Sosnitsky). In the unwritten portion, a young man in love with Valberkhova (he was to be played by the tragedian Iakov Briansky) plots to cure her brother of gambling in order to win Valberkhova's heart. His strategy is to induce a professional gambler (the character actor Alexander Ramazanov) to fleece Sosnitsky until he stakes on a card his old serf tutor (Mikhail Velichkin, who specialized in playing comical old

4. In his commentary to this fragment in A. S. Pushkin, *Polnoe sobranie sochinenii* (Leningrad, 1935), vol. 7, pp. 673–77. The seventh volume of the edition of Pushkin's complete collected works, issued to commemorate the centenary of his death in 1937, was the first one of the series to be published. It contained both his completed and uncompleted dramatic works and included some 350 pages of detailed scholarly commentary by the finest Pushkin specialists of the period, among them Boris Tomashevsky, Mikhail Alexeyev, and Sergei Bondi. The scope and the scrupulously honest scholarship of this commentary make this volume the best single source of information on Pushkin the dramatist that has ever been published. But the objectivity of the commentators and the absence in their work of mandatory ideological and nationalistic biases angered the Soviet government. The commentary was dropped from subsequent printings of the volume (reportedly, on the personal order of Stalin), and the rest of the centenary edition was published without scholarly annotations.

The intellectual integrity of the editors of the 1935 volume contrasts heartbreakingly with the compulsory clichés that pervade some of their later publications on Pushkin (e.g., Sergei Bondi's book *O Pushkine* [Moscow, 1978]). In the notes that follow, this volume will be referred to as Pushkin, 1935.

men, such as Baron Volmar in *The Lipetsk Spa*). Horrified that he has gambled away the freedom of a trusted old servant who has looked after him since childhood, Sosnitsky renounces cards forever. Then the ruse is explained to him and everything ends happily. Similar in many ways to the worldly comedies of Shakhovskoy, Pushkin's projected *The Gambler* was also meant to sound a serious note about the abuses of serfowners' privileges, the theme of Pushkin's own impassioned poem, "The Village" (1819). In the 1920s, the Symbolist poet Valery Briusov did a reconstruction of this play, calling it *Urok igroku* (*A Lesson to a Gambler*), which in the opinion of Slonimsky missed the point of the relationship between Valberkhova and her suitor.[5]

In his book *On Pushkin*, Sergei Bondi has proposed a four-step periodization for Pushkin's activity as playwright. Step one comprises his "Decembrist" projects, the unfinished tragedy and comedy of 1821–22; step two is the "realistic" *Boris Godunov*; step three is the plays of 1830, that is, the "little tragedies" and *Rusalka*; and step four is the unfinished drafts for "social dramas" set in medieval Western Europe that date from the mid–1830s.[6] Up to a certain point this periodization works, even though its transparent aim is to sustain the official Soviet conception of Pushkin moving toward ever greater realism, nationalism, and social awareness. Yet, it is unsatisfactory in the long run, not only because it distorts the progression of Pushkin's ideas, but because it ignores several other drafts that do not fit Bondi's scheme and fails to notice the mutual interpenetration of the dramatic and narrative genres that is so important in Pushkin's output in the 1820s.

While working on the drafts for his neoclassical tragedy about Vadim, Pushkin was at the same time introducing elements of romantic drama into his narrative poems. The center of "The Fountain of Bakhchisarai" is an impassioned melodramatic monologue by Zarema, one of the two heroines of the poem. This monologue later became the showpiece for Ekaterina Semyonova in Shakhovskoy's adaptation of this poem for the stage. Another narrative poem, "The Gypsies" (1824), is written

5. See Pushkin, 1935, p. 668.
6. Bondi, *O Pushkine*, p. 179.

319

for much of its length in the form of dramatic dialogues that read like a romantic play in verse. The diction of these dramatized poems owes nothing to any conceivable neoclassical model. But the case is very different with two other verse narratives dating from the first half of the 1820s, the opening chapters of *Eugene Onegin* and, especially, "Count Nulin" (1825).

The novel in verse *Eugene Onegin* is, of course, Pushkin's greatest achievement, an ever-fascinating poem that is also one of the central, most influential works of Russian literature. Volumes have been written about its style, so amazingly precise and so relaxed at the same time. Every possible source and influence have been analyzed by commentators. However, Pushkin himself acknowledged his debt to the two most important stylistic predecessors who helped shape the tone of *Eugene Onegin*. He encoded quotations from them in the first four lines of his novel:

> Мой дядя самых честных правил,
> Когда не в шутку занемог,
> Он уважать себя заставил
> И лучше выдумать не мог.

> My uncle, a man of most honest principles,
> When he became so ill it was no joke,
> Forced me to respect him
> And could invent nothing better.

These somewhat opaque opening lines of *Eugene Onegin* can be recited by heart by most Russians. Numerous commentators have pointed out that the words *samykh chestnykh pravil* (of most honest principles) are a quotation from Ivan Krylov's fable "The Donkey and the Peasant," which Pushkin heard Krylov recite at a party in 1819, the year the fable was published.[7] The citation is usually interpreted as an act of homage to Krylov, whose fables Pushkin valued above La Fontaine's.

---

7. In his annotated translation of *Eugene Onegin* (New York, 1964), Vladimir Nabokov devotes almost two pages to detailed explication of this three-word quotation from Krylov (vol. 2, pp. 29–31). For some reason, Nabokov chose to render "The Donkey and the Peasant" ("Osel i muzhik") as "The Ass and the Boor."

But the fourth line of this quatrain is also a paraphrased quotation, in this case from the third scene of Khmelnitsky's *Castles in the Air*, which Pushkin must have seen when it premiered in St. Petersburg in July of 1818. The maid Sasha, in praising her employer Aglaeva's late husband for having willed all his property to his widow, says: "Umnee nichego on vydumat' ne mog" ("He could invent nothing more intelligent"). In incorporating this Khmelnitsky phrase into the opening of his masterpiece, Pushkin both got around the obstacle of not being able to mention Khmelnitsky the playwright (about which he wrote to his brother) and paid Khmelnitsky as handsome an homage as he did to Krylov in the first line. Since Onegin's uncle and Aglaeva's husband are both characters whose main significance lies in their dying and leaving an inheritance to the protagonists, Pushkin connected the beginning of *Eugene Onegin* to Khmelnitsky's comedy on a deeper level than a mere citation of words.

It was after he had completed the opening chapters of *Eugene Onegin* in 1824–25 that Pushkin became interested in Shakespeare and began a serious study of his plays. As Mikhail Alexeyev has shown in his excellent study of the relationship of Pushkin to Shakespeare, it was a question of relinquishing the eighteenth-century prejudices against Shakespeare that Pushkin had inherited from La Harpe and Voltaire in favor of the more up-to-date French view of Shakespeare brought about by the critical writings of Mme de Staël and the commentary of François Guizot and Amedée Pichot in their revised 1821 edition of Pierre Letourneur's old translations, originally published in the 1770s.[8] "Mais quel homme que ce Schakespeare! [*sic*] Je n'en reviens pas. Comme Byron le tragique est mesquin devant lui!" Pushkin wrote to his friend Nikolai Raevsky in July of 1825. The full realization of Shakespeare's magnitude led Pushkin, as it did so many other writers of his generation, to lose his former high regard for both Molière and Byron.

Boris Godunov (1825, published 1830), Pushkin's only completed full-length play, was the result of his study of the man he came to call "our father Shakespeare." In honor of Shakespeare, Pushkin dispensed with the unities of time, place, and (though he denied it) action, something that only the Empress Catherine had had the audacity to do before in Russia. The violation of the unity of style, a unity previously taken for granted in Russian drama, is flaunted by mixing scenes in blank verse, rhymed verse, and prose. The central conception, however, is a profoundly eighteenth-century one, because *Boris Godunov* is an instance of "adaptation to our customs" of Shakespeare's historical plays just as Kniazhnin's *Vladimir and Iaropolk* was of Racine's *Andromaque.*

The overthrow of Tsar Boris in 1605 by the low-born pretender known as the False Dimitry became a subject for dramatic works within a few years after it occurred. From Lope de Vega's *El gran Duque di Moscovia,* published in 1617 but apparently written earlier, to Kotzebue's melodrama and Friedrich Schiller's unfinished last tragedy about the False Dimitry, both at the very end of the eighteenth century, there appeared in the West more than one hundred tragedies, novels, and even harlequinades about this series of events.[9] In Russia, there were at least two plays called *Dimitry the Impostor,* one by Sumarokov (1771) and one by Narezhny (1800). Studying Shakespeare's *Richard II, Richard III,* and both parts of *Henry IV,* Pushkin must have noticed that all these plays deal with the toppling of an incumbent monarch whose claims to the throne are uncertain or tainted, by a self-appointed pretender whose claims are even less secure. Reading the story of Boris Godunov's fall in *The History of the Russian State* by Nikolai Karamzin (whose version of the events has been disproven by later historians), Pushkin realized its similarity to Shakespeare's histories and its suitability for a Shakespearean dramatization. He dedicated the play to Karamzin's memory.

Because it is a play about Russian history, written by Russia's national poet, there is general agreement among Russian

---

9. For a survey of Western treatments, see M. P. Alexeyev, "Boris Gudunov i Dimitry Samozvanets v zapadno-evropeiskoi drame," in *"Boris Gudonov" A. S. Pushkina,* ed. K. N. Derzhavin (Leningrad, 1936), pp. 79–124.

commentators that *Boris Godunov* is one of the great master-pieces of Russian drama. Some critics, confusing Pushkin's play with the choral sections of Modest Musorgsky's opera, have described it as a folk tragedy, as a depiction of a people's revolution, or as a profound analysis of the dialectics of history.[10] But patriotic homilies aside, *Boris Godunov* is on many levels an unsatisfactory play. Both Mirsky and Nabokov saw it as something of a failure. No director has ever been able to make it work on the stage. Although Pushkin copied many of Shakespeare's techniques, he somehow failed to notice that in each of the historic plays he imitated there is a dramatic arch that unites the activities of the antagonists and allows for the development of their characters and for a satisfactory final resolution of the play's action.

But in *Boris Godunov*, as John Bayley has aptly pointed out, "between Boris and the pretended Dimitry there is no dramatic relation at all. Not only do they never meet but each is absorbed in his own affairs, and their historical antagonism is not transposed into psychological terms but left in the realm of the accidental or the historically determined."[11] Individual scenes may contain wonderful poetry or function as effective self-contained dramatic units (e.g., the scene at the fountain between Dimitry and Marina or the scene at the inn on the Lithuanian frontier), but they do not add up to a viable continuum. The addition of Musorgsky's tense and haunting music does make Pushkin's tragedy work in a theater, but it is a music light years removed from the tone and the atmosphere of the original play. John Bayley was quite right when he wrote that Pushkin made a far better application of the dramatic principles of Shakespeare's stagecraft in his historical narrative poem "Poltava" (1828–29) than in his tragedy.[12]

10. A rare instance of cogent argument for the originality of Pushkin's historical insights in *Boris Godunov* is Ilya Serman's fine essay "Paradoksy narodnogo soznaniia v tragedii A. S. Pushkina 'Boris Godunov'" ("Paradoxes of Popular Consciousness in Pushkin's *Boris Godunov*"), *Russian Language Journal* 35 (Winter 1981): 83–88.

11. John Bayley, *Pushkin: A Comparative Commentary* (Cambridge, 1971), p. 166.

12. Ibid.

In the midst of his work on *Boris Godunov*, Pushkin became acquainted with Griboedov's *The Misfortune of Being Clever*. Charmed by the new possibilities of rhymed iambic lines of varying lengths that Griboedov so effectively exploited for dramatic purposes in his comedy, Pushkin added to *Boris Godunov* the beautifully wrought scene in Marina Mniszech's dressing room. In the lilting dialogue between Marina and her maid Rózia (the Polish diminutive of Rose), Pushkin abandons Shakespeare's manner for Griboedov's and Shakespeare's and Karamzin's matter for that of the same third scene of Khmelnitsky's *Castles in the Air* already quoted in the first quatrain of *Eugene Onegin*. Marina's dreams of being a tsarina in Moscow, and Rózia's lively advice and comments closely follow Aglaeva's dreams of marrying a count and moving to St. Petersburg and her conversation with her maid. Despite having strayed into the beginning of the seventeenth century and having acquired a Polish name, Rózia is an unmistakable soubrette of early-nineteenth-century Russian verse comedy in general and a near-twin of Sasha from *Castles in the Air* in particular. Pushkin must have understood that for all its charm, this scene did not belong in his Shakespearean tragedy. He removed it from the main text and relegated it to an appendix, where it now regularly appears.

The combination of Shakespeare and Khmelnitsky, ludicrous as such a conjunction may sound to most people, was also responsible for "Count Nulin," a lively and witty narrative poem Pushkin wrote one month after completing *Boris Godunov*. As Pushkin put it in a later explanatory note on "Count Nulin," the idea for this poem came to him as he was rereading "The Rape of Lucrece," which he qualified as "a rather feeble poem by Shakespeare." It set him wondering what would have happened if, instead of submitting to Tarquin, Lucrece had routed the man by slapping his face. Tarquin might have desisted and, Pushkin says, "the world and its history would have been different."

The beginning of "Count Nulin," with its description of a lusty country squire's departure for the hunt with a pack of hounds and the boredom and loneliness of the wife he leaves behind, has no connection to either Shakespeare or Khmelnitsky. But then a carriage bell is heard, the carriage overturns, an unknown but attractive male traveler and his servant are invited into the house to recuperate, and we are suddenly in Pushkin's favorite Khmelnitsky comedy, *Castles in the Air*. The strategem of having the male protagonist's carriage break down in front of the heroine's home in order to get them acquainted was in fact a trademark of Khmelnitsky's, to which he resorted, as Moisei Iankovsky has pointed out,[13] in no less than three of his twelve plays. It was Khmelnitsky's own invention, because in Collin d'Harleville's *Les châteaux en Espagne*, on which two of these three plays were based, there are no carriage accidents. There, the young man blunders into the chateau by mistake, after having lost his way. That Pushkin borrowed the patented device of his "favorite poet" so openly to start the action of "Count Nulin" should leave no doubt that he wanted the connection of this poem to Khmelnitsky to be obvious. It may well be that "Count Nulin" is the equivalent of that couplet in honor of Khmelnitsky of which Pushkin had written to his brother a few months earlier.

Pushkin's treatment of *Castles in the Air* in "Count Nulin" is similar to the procedure Khmelnitsky applied to the full-length French comedies on which he based his brief Russian plays. Only the general situation and a few concrete details are retained. The characters placed in this situation are each writer's own. The bored wife in Pushkin is quite unlike Khmelnitsky's ambitious widow Aglaeva, and the serious, modest midshipman of *Castles in the Air* is nothing like the feather-brained fop Count Nulin. But the experiences that these two couples have during their encounter are, up to a point, remarkably alike. In both cases, the lady of the house hears a carriage bell, hopes it is a visitor, witnesses a carriage breakdown through the window, and invites the accident victim and his manservant into the house. In both cases, the man is pleasantly surprised to find himself hospitably received by an attractive and seeming available young woman, is encouraged by her to

13. In *Russkaia stikhotvornaia komediia kontsa XVIII–nachala XIX v.* ed. Moisei Iankovsky (Moscow-Leningrad, 1964), pp. 24–25.

press his suit, and then, to his consternation, rejected and encouraged to leave.

The main difference is that Aglaeva dismisses the unlucky midshipman on the day of his arrival, after realizing that he is not the wealthy count for whom she took him. Count Nulin is invited to spend the night, and it is during his nocturnal visit to the bedroom of his hostess that the poem turns into a comical parody of the analogous scenes in "The Rape of Lucrece." The repulsed seduction is the dramatic high point of "Count Nulin" and because of it this poem is generally described as Pushkin's parody of Shakespeare.[14] But the allusions to Khmelnitsky's comedy (which also include the character of the heroine's soubrette confidante Parasha, not needed for the action of the poem except to serve as the counterpart of Sasha in *Castles in the Air*; and the discussion of the news and newspapers by the two protagonists), take up far more space and contribute more to the poem's narrative plot than do the elements drawn from Shakespeare.

Pushkin was to succumb to the temptation of the demon of neoclassical verse comedy on two more occasions, in a sketch for a play that dates from approximately 1827 and in a novella written in 1830. The sketch is an expository dialogue between a gentleman and the maid of the lady to whom he is engaged. It begins:

— Насилу выехать решились из Москвы.
— Здорова ль, душенька? — Здоровы ль, сударь, вы?

"It has taken you a long time to resolve yourself to leave
Moscow."
"Have you been well, my dear?" "And you, sir, are you
well?"

The maid works for two sisters. The older, Olga Pavlovna, is a widow engaged to the traveler just arrived from Moscow. The younger, Sophia Pavlovna (the name and patronymic of the heroine of *The Misfortune of Being Clever*), has a suitor

14. George Gibian, "Pushkin's Parody On 'The Rape of Lucrece,'" *The Shakespeare Quarterly* 1 (October 1950): 264–66.

named Èlmirov. Finding an unsigned amorous note from Èl-mirov to Sophia, the nameless protagonist tries to bribe the maid with a gift of jewelry so that she will pass the note to Olga. His apparent aim is to test Olga's fidelity.

Brief as it is, the fragment makes mincemeat of all the standard schemes of dividing Pushkin's work into classical, ro-mantic, and realist stages, schemes that were mocked by the epigraph from Stravinsky's essay on Pushkin at the head of the present chapter. If it really dates from 1827 (the dating is ap-proximate), it is contemporary with the seventh chapter of *Eugene Onegin*. This is the chapter in which the impact of Griboedov's comedy on Pushkin is most evident, both in its epigraph from that comedy and in the satirical description of Tatiana's Moscow relatives, which echoes Chatsky's and Famu-sov's speeches about the elderly women and men who run Mos-cow society. (Tatiana's romantically surrealistic dream in the fifth chapter also owes something to the dream of Griboedov's Sophia.) The verse of the 1827 fragment is likewise derived from Griboedov.

The opening scene of *The Lipetsk Spa*, which shows Prince Kholmsky's conversation with Olenka's maid Sasha, was the probable model for the opening scene of this projected comedy. Bribing a maid with a gift of jewelry occurs in both Shakhov-skoy's *Don't Listen . . .* and Griboedov's *The Misfortune of Being Clever*. A plot that involves an act of entrapment in order to test a woman's fidelity was already old in 1789 when Lorenzo da Ponte based his libretto for Mozart's *Così fan tutte* on it. In Russian neoclassical comedy of the nineteenth century it is central to Khmelnitsky's *Mutual Tests (Vzaimnye ispy-taniia,* 1819) and Griboedov and Zhandr's *Pretended Infidelity.*

The itch to write a verse comedy in the Shakhovskoy-Khmelnitsky manner is also evident in the 1828 sketches for Pushkin's translation of *Le mari à bonnes fortunes* by Casimir Bonjour. This was to be an abridgment of a light French com-edy that was a hit in Paris in 1824, rendered in couplets of rhymed iambic pentameter and with the action transposed to Moscow from Paris. But Pushkin must have realized that the day of this type of comedy was over in Russia. Shakhovskoy had not written in this form for almost a decade, Khmelnitsky was about to retire from playwriting, Alexander Pisarev (for whose vaudevilles and comedies Pushkin had a low regard) died in 1828. Though Pushkin had already written a masterful verse comedy with preservation of the classical unities in "Count Nulin," his love affair with the genre did not find its final resolution until the 1830 prose novella "Mistress into Maid" ("Baryshnia krest'ianka").

The cycle of five novellas Pushkin wrote in Boldino in the fall of 1830 is united by the framework of a fictitious narrator Ivan Belkin who has supposedly collected these stories. The cycle is therefore called *The Tales of Belkin*. As Vasily Gippius has shown in a masterful essay, these tales operate on two levels: as entertaining narratives and as witty parodies of literary and dramatic conventions.[15] Thus "The Coffinmaker" is a gentle debunking of Hoffmannesque tales of the supernatural. "The Station Master," which Gippius says cannot be understood without knowing the sentimental dramas of Beaumarchais, Lessing, and Schiller, reverses the familiar plot of the seduction of a daughter of a lower-class family by a dissolute aristocrat, a plot that was also familiar in Russia from the dramatizations of Karamzin's "Poor Liza" by Ilyin and Fyodorov.

"The Snowstorm" plays with the improbable coincidences of sentimentalist drama, while "The Shot," despite outward trappings that point to adventure tales by Bestuzhev-Marlinsky, is a parodistic retelling of Victor Hugo's *Hernani*.[16] "Mistress into Maid" is a neoclassical comedy turned into a prose narrative. Belinsky, who took a strong dislike to this story, discerned

15. V. V. Gippius, "Povesti Belkina," in his book *Ot Pushkina do Bloka* (Moscow-Leningrad, 1966), pp. 7–45.

16. See David M. Bethea and Sergei Davydov, "Pushkin's Saturnine Cupid: The Poetics of Parody in *The Tales of Belkin*," *PMLA* 96(1) (1981): 18–19 (note 11). This is an excellent study of the literary models and parodistic content of *The Tales of Belkin*. Its survey of earlier commentators shows that every possible source and resemblance has been explored, except for the Karamzinian drama and neoclassical comedy of Pushkin's time. "Mistress into Maid" ("The Lady Peasant" in this study) has been traced to sources as remote as *Romeo and Juliet* and Scott's *The Bride of Lammermoor* (note 24 on p. 20). Proximate sources, such as the plays about "Poor Liza" and Shakhovskoy's comedies remained outside the commentators' purview.

its origins when he described it as "improbable, vaudevillelike, showing the life of landowners from its idyllic side."[17] Pavel Katenin saw "Mistress into Maid" as a reworking of *Le jeu de l'amour et du hasard* by Marivaux into a short story in a manner analogous to Pushkin's later reworking of Shakespeare's *Measure for Measure* into his narrative poem "Angelo."[18] And yet, apart from the young noblewoman Silvia disguising herself as a servant—a widespread ploy in eighteenth-century opera and comedy, including *The Marriage of Figaro* and *She Stoops to Conquer*—there is little in common between Pushkin's novella and the comedy of Marivaux. The comedies that were on Pushkin's mind while he was writing "Mistress into Maid" were not by Marivaux but by Katenin's good friend Shakhovskoy.

The presence of Shakhovskoy is initially signaled by a quoted line from his First Satire (addressed to Molière) that appears on the first page of "Mistress into Maid." The passage from which this line comes ridicules Russian landowners who seek to improve the crop yields of their estates by introducing new-fangled agricultural methods imported from England and go broke as a result. The thesis about the wastefulness and absurdity of imitating English-style farming, expressed in the 1807 satire, was developed by Shakhovskoy in 1819 into a full-length comedy *The Prodigal Landowners*, which contrasted the silly Anglomaniac Prince Radugin with his uncle General Radimov, who prospers by staying with the traditional Russian farming methods.

'This is precisely the theme of the opening pages of Pushkin's "Mistress into Maid," which describe the feud between two neighboring landowners, the sensible traditionalist Berestov and the Anglomaniac Muromsky, who slowly ruins himself by forcing his serfs to farm à l'anglaise. The Shakhovskoy connection is further driven home by the information that Muromsky is a close relative of Count Pronsky, a distinguished and powerful statesman. This must be the one-time sentimentalist of *The New Sterne*, who has come to his senses and made an important career in the quarter century that separates Push-

17. V. G. Belinsky, *Sobranie sochinenii* (St. Petersburg, 1911), vol. 3, p. 489.
18. Cited in Gippius, "Povesti Belkina," p. 26.

kin's novella from the play, rather than Colonel Pronsky of *The Lipetsk Spa*, who was not a count. The appearance of Berestov's son Alexei, a healthy and lusty young fellow who affects a Byronic pose of disappointment and dejection, is Pushkin's mocking of emotional stances that imitate literary fads, just as *The New Sterne* was Shakhovskoy's mockery of an earlier variant of the same phenomenon.

Muromsky's daughter Liza disguises herself as a peasant wench in order to meet the son of her father's enemy. The description of the two young people's romance moves away from Shakhovskoy and becomes a parody of all those Karamzinian plays where a young aristocrat woos a peasant maiden named Liza who later turns out to be a nobleman's daughter, a connection that is emphasized when Pushkin makes Alexei and Liza read Karamzin's "Natalia, the Boyar's Daughter." Pushkin's Liza is a mistress of numerous disguises, just as Shakhovskoy's Natasha was in *The Married Fiancée*. She has to impersonate not only a peasant but also an affected, bejeweled, and heavily made-up society lady. For each of these impersonations, Liza develops a new personality and a set of appropriate speech mannerisms. Despite her lack of any theatrical training, she is an accomplished comedienne, as inexplicably as Shakhovskoy's Natasha.

The resolution of "Mistress into Maid," which involves the reconciliation of the feuding fathers, Alexei's plans to marry the young woman he thinks is a peasant, and the lucky chance that reveals her true identity to him, is worked out with the sure hand of a writer of eighteenth-century comedies of intrigue and disguise. Especially typical of that whole genre is the character of Liza's serf confidante and abettor in her disguises, the soubrette Nastya. Pushkin was capable of depicting believable, realistically observed Russian serfs and servants: Tatiana's nurse in *Eugene Onegin*, Masha's maid Palasha in *The Captain's Daughter*, and the hero's serf tutor in the same novel. But whenever he writes something inspired by the tradition of the neoclassical verse comedy of the Shakhovskoy-Khmelnitsky-Griboedov type, we invariably get lively and witty soubrettes of the French and Russian comedic traditions who could not possibly have existed in actual Russian life. Nastya in "Mistress into Maid" is the last of this line, which also includes Rózia in the dressing-room scene of *Boris Godunov*, Parasha in "Count Nulin," and the nameless maid in the 1827 draft for a comedy.

Writing "Mistress into Maid" must have exorcised Pushkin's fascination with the spirit of neoclassical comedy, for it is absent from his plays, verse tales, and prose narratives written from that point on. Within weeks after completing the last of *The Tales of Belkin*, Pushkin set to work on his cycle of "little tragedies" (this was during the miraculously productive Boldino autumn of 1830, when in a period of three months he produced, besides the cycle of stories and the cycle of plays, a large number of lyric poems and essays, in addition to writing "The Little House in Kolomna" and completing *Eugene Onegin*).

Inspired by a genre devised by Barry Cornwall (pen name of Bryan Waller Proctor, a rather pallid poet admired in his day by Byron and Keats) of brief dialogues in verse that combined features of drama and narrative poetry, Pushkin had been planning since 1826 to write a series of what he called "dramatic investigations" or "dramatic studies," each one concentrating on an analysis of one particular passion. In 1827, he listed the subjects he intended to use in these investigations: The Miser, Romulus and Remus (in which the she-wolf that raised them was to be a character), Mozart and Salieri, Don Juan, Jesus, Berald of Savoy, Tsar Paul I, A Devil in Love, Dimitry and Marina (whose relationship was left dangling in *Boris Godunov*), and Prince Kurbsky (the one-time adviser of Ivan the Terrible who later went over to the Poles and wrote the tsar famous vituperative letters; Kurbsky's son, invented by Pushkin, appeared in *Boris Godunov*).

Only three of these projects were realized in 1830. "The Miser" became *Skupoi rytsar'*, the brief play Pushkin preferred for personal reasons to palm off as a translation of a nonexistent English play *The Covetous Knight* by William Shenstone.[19] The ruse was necessitated by the similarity between the disagree-

19. On the possible connection between Pushkin and Shenstone, see Richard A. Gregg, "Pushkin and Shenstone: The Case Reopened," *Comparative Literature* 17(2) (1965): 109–16.

ments on money matters between the old Baron and his rebellious son in the play and the actual situation between Pushkin and his father; "covetous" is not the right word to convey the Russian title, "avaricious" being much closer. *Mozart and Salieri*, converted in recent times into a London and New York hit play *Amadeus* by Peter Schaffer and stemming from newspaper reports about Antonio Salieri's deathbed confession that he had poisoned Mozart,[20] is a study of envy.

The Stone Guest, the longest and most dramatic of the "little tragedies," derived, very remotely, from Molière's play about Don Juan and da Ponte's libretto for Mozart, investigates various kinds of amorous involvement between men and women. The three female characters are Inez (in an earlier draft she was a miller's daughter) whom Don Juan seduced and abandoned and who died because of it; the actress Laura, whose relationship with him is that of a friend and equal, despite their sexual involvement; and Donna Anna, who in this version is not the daughter, but the widow of the Comendador, a man Don Juan had killed in a duel. Donna Anna's particular attraction is her virtue and unavailability, which compel the famous seducer to love rather than merely desire her. In a provocative study of *The Stone Guest*, Anna Akhmatova has argued persuasively that this play, written just when Pushkin was to give up the sexual freedom of his earlier life in order to marry, contained elements of self-portraiture in both Don Juan and the Comendador.[21]

In addition to being studies of particular passions—avarice, envy, sexual drive—the three "little tragedies" are also united by the theme that was central to *Boris Godunov*: the incumbent defending his status from an aggressive usurper. Just as

20. On the origins of the legend about Salieri's murder of Mozart and Pushkin's sources for the play, see Mikhail Alexeyev's detailed study in Pushkin, 1935, especially pp. 525 ff. It is curious that Pushkin's poetic genius unjustly convicted two people who had actually lived, Boris Godunov and Antonio Salieri, of murders they did not commit. On affinities between Pushkin and Mozart, see Vladimir Markov, "Mozart: Theme and Variations," in *The Bitter Air of Exile*, ed. Simon Karlinsky and Alfred Appel, Jr. (Berkeley and Los Angeles, 1977), pp. 455–57.

21. Anna Akhmatova, " 'Kamennyi gost' Pushkina," in her book *O Pushkine* (Leningrad, 1977), pp. 89–109, and also note 7 on p. 168.

Boris had to defend his throne from the False Dimitry, the Baron in *The Covetous Knight* has to defend his hoard from his son Albert, Salieri has to defend his position in the musical world from Mozart, and the statue of the Comendador has to stop his murderer from possessing his wife. The outcome of this situation, common to all four plays, is variable. In *Boris Godunov* and *The Covetous Knight*, the usurpers triumph, while in *Mozart and Salieri* and *The Stone Guest* they are destroyed by the defending incumbents.

Usually grouped with the three "little tragedies," but only because it was written at the same time with them, is *Feast During the Plague*, Pushkin's compressed adaptation of several scenes from John Wilson's romantic drama *The City of the Plague*.[22] A dramatic poem rather than a play, it is a disturbing and beautiful meditation about our perpetual fascination with death. It treats in romantic terms what Ozerov had expressed in sentimentalist and neoclassical terms in *Polyxena*. It is also utterly unstageable (though its production has been tried). *Feast During the Plague* and the three "little tragedies" are philosophically complex works, they contain magnificent poetry, but none of them is very effective dramatically. Because they are by Pushkin, Russian theaters keep staging them. But like all of Pushkin's plays, the "little tragedies" function far better on the operatic stage than as spoken drama. The operatic setting of *The Stone Guest* is by Alexander Dargomyzhsky, of *Mozart and Salieri* by Rimsky-Korsakov (with the utilization of much of Mozart's own music), and of *The Covetous Knight* by Sergei Rakhmaninov.

Both Anna Akhmatova and Naum Berkovsky have connected the figure of the gentle Inez, the miller's daughter in the draft for the first scene of *The Stone Guest*, with the genesis of Pushkin's most effective play, dramatically and poetically: the regrettably unfinished folk drama *Rusalka*.[23] Like Shakespeare and Molière before him, Pushkin did not disdain borrowing

22. See Henry Gifford, "Pushkin's *Feast in the Time of Plague* and Its Original," *American Slavic and East European Review* 8 (February 1949): 37–46.

23. Akhmatova, *O Pushkine*, pp. 165 and 169. N. Berkovsky, " 'Rusalka,' liricheskaia tragediia Pushkina," in his book *Stat'i o literature* (Moscow-Leningrad, 1962), pp. 357–403.

themes from unimpressive sources. The magic operas about the water sprites of the Dnieper, based on *Das Donauweibchen* (see pp. 186ff.), took up residence on the stages of Russia when Pushkin was four years old and they remained there for at least a decade after he died. It was the plot of the first of the *Water Sprites* that Pushkin decided to convert into a drama couched in an idiom derived from his detailed studies of Russian folklore.[24]

In *Das Donauweibchen* and its four Russian avatars, the heroine is an elemental spirit who has had an affair with a mortal man, has a daughter by him, and objects to his plans to marry a mortal woman. In an early draft for *Rusalka* that dates from 1826, it can be seen that Pushkin intended to keep this situation. In the final version written in part in 1829 and in part in 1832, he chose to follow the widespread Slavic folk legend, which also served as the source for Adolphe Adam's ballet *Giselle*, about a peasant maiden who is seduced and abandoned by a nobleman and who then returns to haunt him as a supernatural creature.[25] Instead of having to choose between a woman and a mythological being, Pushkin's Prince is initially involved with a poor miller's daughter whom he abandons when dynastic reasons force him to take a bride of his own social standing.

24. For a thorough analysis of *Rusalka's* connection to *The Water Sprite* comic operas, see Sergei Bondi's commentary in Pushkin, 1935, pp. 623–36.

25. The manuscript of this play contained no title. The editors, recognizing the similarity of Pushkin's play to *The Water Sprite*, gave it the same title, *Rusalka*. The word *rusalka* refers in the Russian poetic and dramatic tradition to three different kinds of beings. In *The Water Sprite* operas, as in Zhukovsky's romance in verse *Undina*, it is an undine, a water sprite in female form. In Russian translations of Western fairy tales, such as Hans Christian Andersen's "The Little Mermaid," the word *rusalka* is used to denote a mermaid, a creature half-woman half-fish, who lives in the ocean. Neither an undine nor a mermaid was originally a human being.

But in Pushkin's play, just as in Gogol's story "May Night," *rusalka* is a young woman who is driven to drown herself because of her misfortunes and is only then reincarnated as a supernatural, water-dwelling being, whose aim is to punish those who have caused her suffering—a very different being from either an undine or a mermaid. Despite the similarity of the plot of Pushkin's play to *Water Sprite*, the heroine has a totally different nature and this is why I prefer to use the word *rusalka* for her, rather than water sprite or mermaid.

The language of *Rusalka* is an expressive blend of high romantic poetry and of diction derived from traditional Russian songs and laments. Dramatically, it is enormously effective. *Rusalka* is the only play by Pushkin in which the principal characters really interact with one another. As in a folk legend, there are no proper names, yet the characters are individualized and their emotional predicaments are convincingly drawn. The miller's daughter, who drowns herself in the Dnieper after she is betrayed by her lover and is then reincarnated as a *"rusalka, cold and powerful"*; her scheming father, who is driven insane by the realization of what he had done to his daughter; her initially faithless and then penitent lover, the Prince; the Prince's neglected, anxious wife; the *rusalka's* young daughter, born into a supernatural world, but curious about her human origins—all these are splendid creations, believable on the psychological level, hauntingly poetic, and dramatically absorbing.

Rusalka was potentially the great and original folk drama that Pushkin's countrymen have credited him with having written in *Boris Godunov*. Its lack of an ending is so self-evidently deplorable that numerous hands have tried supplying it with one. Three amateurish attempts were made in the second half of nineteenth century, and one of them was temporarily accepted by critics as the discovery of Pushkin's own manuscript for the conclusion of his play. In the twentieth century, final scenes for *Rusalka* were written by Valery Briusov and Vladimir Nabokov, but matching Pushkin's language proved beyond even their considerable talents. The ending Dargomyzhsky devised for his 1856 opera is at best a makeshift solution. Only Pushkin himself could have provided an appropriate finale, but in the last five years of his life he seems to have lost interest in writing drama in verse.

Pushkin's involvement with Shakespeare, which began in 1824, was crowned in 1833 by "Angelo," his reworking of *Measure for Measure* into a narrative poem.[26] Pushkin himself considered it the finest of his narrative poems, but it remains to this day undeservedly neglected by both critics and general

26. See Alexeyev, *Pushkin*, pp. 276 ff.

readers.[27] After abandoning *Rusalka*, Pushkin made sketches for three historical dramas in prose, set in Western Europe in medieval times. All three were to show persons of humble origins rising to great social prominence and then coming into conflict with the ruling elite of their time. In 1835 Pushkin wrote several scenes for the first of these projects, which had no title in his manuscript and was called by later editors *Scenes from the Time of Knighthood*. Like the majority of Pushkin's dramatic projects, it has literary sources, in this case *La Jacquerie* by Prosper Mérimée, the story "Tournament in Revel" by Alexander Bestuzhev-Marlinsky (1825), and one of the same author's critical essays.[28]

Set in Germany, the play was to include among its characters Berthold Schwartz, the semilegendary inventor of gunpowder, and to be centered on a revolt against the local feudal hierarchy led by a merchant's son who has become a minnesinger. The sketches are so pallid and undramatic that it is hard to believe they are the work of the mature Pushkin. The other two of this group of projects exist only as outlines. One is about the son of a hangman in France who ends up as a feudal lord. The other is based on the medieval legend of Pope Joan, an artisan's daughter whose love of learning led her to study theology in male attire and who was elected pope and then exposed as a woman when she gave birth to a child (by the Spanish ambassador to the Vatican) in a public place.[29] This was to be a Faustian drama, with devils and other supernatural beings participating in the action. Pushkin was not sure whether the

27. See George Gibian, *"Measure for Measure* and Pushkin's 'Angelo,' " *PMLA* 66 (June 1951): 426–31.

28. See Bondi's commentary in Pushkin, 1935, pp. 652 ff. The excommunication of Alexander Bestuzhev (1797–1837; Marlinsky was his pen name) from Russian literature by Belinsky in 1840 prevents critics to this day from examining the impact on Pushkin of this important romantic critic and innovative prose writer, who was Pushkin's close friend and correspondent. The vast field of *Eugene Onegin* studies has still to discover the affinities between Bestuzhev's travelogue in verse and prose, *A Journey to Revel*, published in 1821, and Pushkin's celebrated novel in verse, begun in 1823.

29. On the legend of Pope Joan and an account of Pushkin's interest in it, see Iulian Oksman's commentary in Pushkin, 1935, pp. 695–700.

subject was more suitable for a drama or a poem in the manner of Coleridge's "Christabel."[30]

"The twentieth century began in the fall of 1914 together with the war, just as the nineteenth century began with the Congress of Vienna. Calendar dates mean nothing," wrote Anna Akhmatova in her "Fragments of Memoirs."[31] For the study of Russian literature, a far clearer picture emerges if we assume that the eighteenth century began in 1730 (Trediakovsky's proposal to use contemporary vernacular in imaginative literature) and ended in 1830, the date of publication of *Boris Godunov*. Poet-playwrights of Pushkin's generation may have been exposed to sentimentalist and romantic currents from the time of their adolescence, but they were all born in the eighteenth century and came to literary maturity when neoclassicism was still the norm. Some of them, such as Khmelnitsky and Alexander Pisarev, never quite emerged from it. Others were converted to romanticism, first Pushkin and after him, one by one, Katenin, Griboedov, and Küchelbecker. For these men, such a conversion was still a matter of choice.

But by 1830, the literary compass needle of Russian drama had permanently shifted from the pole of Molière to that of Shakespeare and Schiller (and, on a lower level, from Metastasio to Kotzebue and from there to Scribe). Playwrights born in the second and third decades of the nineteenth century turned their backs on neoclassical drama. The last to learn his craft from Russian neoclassical comedy was one of Russia's greatest play-

30. To demonstrate Pushkin's ties to the verse comedy of the Shakhovskoy-Khmelnitsky school, the present chapter has had to encompass discussions of the poet's nondramatic writings. The points could best be made through examining his literary practices and ignoring his theories about drama, which, though highly important, do not always reflect his true stylistic orientation. The reader will find valuable discussions of the relationship between Pushkin's theories on drama (as stated in his essays and personal correspondence) and his plays in the chapter "The Drama" in John Bayley's *Pushkin* and in the other critical sources mentioned in the annotations to the present chapter. See also two of Pushkin's essays on drama theory in *Russian Dramatic Theory from Pushkin to the Symbolists, An Anthology*, ed. Laurence Senelick (Austin, 1981).

31. Anna Akhmatova, *Sochineniia* (Paris, 1983) vol. 3, p. 146.

wrights, Nikolai Gogol. His *Inspector General* (1836) casts a long, lingering look of farewell at the theater of Fonvizin, Kapnist, and Shakhovskoy and then sets off, full sail, for the new shores of nineteenth- and twentieth-century drama, where Russian playwrights would become an integral part of the international theatrical world.

Index of Names

Page numbers in bold type indicate detailed identification or discussion in the text.

Beethoven, Ludwig van, 199, 308
Belinsky, Vissarion, vii–viii, x, xii,
125, 214, 224, 264–65, 297n, 302–3,
306, 328–29, 336n
Belkin, Anatoly, 3n
Bely, Andrei, ix
Bergner, Elisabeth, 83
Berkov, Pavel, 72, 96n, 101n, 122n,
125n, 130n–31n, 169n, 171n, 177n,
179n
Berkovsky, Naum, 333
Bernardaky, Nicholas, 278
Berner, Paul, 38
Bertati, Giovanni, 117, 121
Bestuzhev-Marlinsky, Alexander,
220, 232, 284, 286, 302–303, 328, 336
Bethea, David M., 328n
Betsky, Ivan, 134
Bianchi, Francesco, 117, 121
Bidloo, Nikolaas, 31
Blok, Alexander, xx, 289
Bobrov, Elisei, 262, 267
Boccaccio, Giovanni, 51
Bochkarev, V. A., 191n, 219n
Bogdanovich, Ippolit, 130, 316
Bogoiavlensky, S. K., 44n–45n
Bogoslovsky, N. V., 212n
Boieldieu, François, 274
Boileau, viii, 60–61, 65, 72, 79
Boissy, Louis de, 250–51
Bonamour, Jean, 287, 292, 294–95,
298
Bondi, Sergei, 318n, 319, 334n, 336n
Bonjour, Casimir, 327
Borodin, Alexander, 80
Boucher, François, 117
Brahms, Johannes, 58
Brauneck, Manfred, 9n
Brecht, Bertolt, 9n, 123
Briansky, Iakov, 237, 267, 280, 318
Britten, Benjamin, 5
Briusov, Valery, 214, 319, 335
Brown, Alec, 286n
Bruce, Count Iakov, 81
Bulgarin, Faddei, 305–6n
Bullandt, Anton, 144
Bürger, Gottfried August, 202, 220,
238
Burns, Robert, xx
Busch, Wolfgang, 27n

Byron, Lord George Gordon, 213,
223–24, 295, 316, 321, 331

Cagliostro, Alessandro di, 87
Calderón de la Barca, Pedro, 47
Campbell, Oscar James, Jr., 155n
Campistron, Jean Galbert de, 97
Canaletto, Bernardo Bellotto, xx
Capo d'Istria, Count Ioann, 224
Carroll, Lewis, 219
Catherine I, 24, 31
Catherine II (the Great), xvi, 63,
70–71, 80–81, 83–92, 93, 110, 116,
119, 121, 123–24, 126, 130, 133–37,
139–40, 142, 144, 146, 147n, 153n,
157, 159, 162, 165–69, 175, 182,
188, 190, 192, 196, 229, 246, 290,
310, 317, 322
Caussin, Nicholas, 12
Cavos, Catterino, 182, 188, 274
Cervantes, Miguel de, 49
Chaadaev, Peter, 143, 264
Charles XII (King of Sweden), 27
Chateaubriand, François-René de,
193, 213, 316
Chavchavadze, Nina, 285
Chebotarev, Khariton, 135, 168
Chekhov, Anton, ix, xix–xx, 90,
130, 158, 179, 218, 243, 246, 274,
277, 282, 287, 302–3, 306, 311–12
Chénier, André, xx
Chénier, Joseph-Marie, 222
Cherniavsky, Evgeny, 155n
Chukovskaya, Lidiia, 310n
Cicognini, Giacinto Andrea, 47
Cimarosa, Domenico, 84
Claudel, Paul, 17n
Cocron, Frédéric, 39n
Colardeau, Charles, 196
Coleridge, Samuel Taylor, 337
Collin d'Harleville, Jean-François,
250, 253–54, 325
Constant, Benjamin, 223
Constantine, Porphyrogenitos, Em-
peror, 1
Corneille, Pierre, viii, xv, 33, 60–61,
66–69, 72, 73n, 76, 80–81, 114,
133, 137–38, 141, 145, 194–95,
200, 218, 220, 317
Corneille, Thomas, 47, 220

Index of Plays

Page numbers in bold type
indicate discussion in detail.

349